050802

SERIES
IN
HUMAN
RELATIONS
TRAINING

The Annual handbook for
group facilitators.

THE
1974 ANNUAL
HANDBOOK
FOR GROUP
FACILITATORS

(Third in a Series)

Edited by

J. WILLIAM PFEIFFER, Ph.D.
Human Relations Consultant
La Jolla, California

JOHN E. JONES, Ph.D.
Human Relations Consultant
La Jolla, California

UNIVERSITY ASSOCIATES PUBLISHERS, INC.
7596 Eads Avenue
La Jolla, California 92037

PREFACE

In the human relations training field, a peculiar problem exists concerning authorship of materials. A facilitator may use a structured experience or an instrument for years, making it a part of his training repertoire, and forget where he originally obtained it. If he later finds another facilitator using a version of "his" material, he may feel he has not been acknowledged for something he "owns." As one consultant said, "I have been using my own instrument for so long that I simply assumed it was the only version in the world."

The attempt to attribute authorship to the proper person has become a difficult and time-consuming search. Despite the fact that we have made considerable efforts to locate originators, authors, and developers of particular materials, we acknowledge that the accuracy of our research may not be unassailable.

As our intent—indeed, our publishing "mission"—is to make human relations training materials widely available, we impose few restrictions on their reproduction.

This *Annual* is copyrighted, but for education and training purposes, users should feel free to duplicate and modify all materials: forms, charts, structured experiences, descriptions, instruments, work sheets, lecturettes, resources.

We wish that more publishers would adopt a similar policy. Copyrighted materials *are* being duplicated for use in learning designs; we think it is unnecessary that those who duplicate such materials should be made to feel guilty.

If, however, materials are to be reproduced in publications or are intended for large-scale distribution, prior permission of the editors is required.

Although one of our aims is to provide wide dissemination of the materials we publish, we have had some concern about their use by untrained group leaders. If the facilitator's own adjustment is precarious, and if his motives are based on his own needs rather than the needs of his participants, it is possible that he will be harmful instead of helpful.

On the other hand, if the facilitator is a healthy personality, psychologically mature and well integrated, it is very unlikely that he will cause harm by using the materials available in human relations training.

The materials and exercises themselves are neither helpful nor harmful. How they are used and by whom, we have come to believe, are the critical variables determining their effects on participants.

Since this *Annual* is intended for group facilitators, it is written and compiled with the human relations practitioner in mind. It is a record of structured experiences, instruments, theoretical positions, and ideas for applications as they develop in the field. We encourage facilitators to submit structured experiences, instruments, and papers which they feel would be of interest to other practitioners. In this way, we intend that our Series in Human Relations Training will continue to serve as a clearinghouse for original and adapted ideas developed by group facilitators.

One final comment: In addition to our abiding belief in the wide distribution of human relations training materials, we also experience a constant undercurrent of excitement and challenge as we create, collect, collate, use, and disseminate this emerging technology.

La Jolla, California J. William Pfeiffer
February, 1974 John E. Jones

UNIVERSITY ASSOCIATES
Publishers and Consultants

 University Associates is an educational organization engaged in human relations training, research, consulting, publication, and both pre-service and in-service education. The organization consists of educational consultants and experienced facilitators in human relations, leadership training, and organization development.

In addition to offering general laboratory experiences, University Associates designs and carries out programs on a contractual basis for various organizations. These programs fall under the following areas of specialization: Human Relations Training, Leadership Development, Organization Development, and Community Development.

TABLE OF CONTENTS

°See the Introduction to the Structured Experiences section, pp. 4-5, for explanation of numbering.

GENERAL INTRODUCTION TO THE 1974 ANNUAL

The *1974 Annual Handbook for Group Facilitators*, like its predecessors, the 1972 and 1973 *Annuals*, is designed to be a convenient, practical, flexible, and current collection of materials for human relations training. Group facilitators typically have bulky files of loose papers picked up at conventions, workshops, and laboratories. The *Annual* is intended as a vehicle for sharing such materials.

This *Annual* continues the basic format and divisions of previous *Annuals*: Structured Experiences, Instrumentation, Lecturettes, Theory and Practice, and Resources. Its content, however, is entirely new. No *Annual* overlaps in content with any other.

The Structured Experiences section follows the format developed in *A Handbook of Structured Experiences for Human Relations Training*, Vols. I, II, III, and IV. These items are useful in personal growth designs, in leadership/management training, and in organization development efforts.

Instrumentation is an outlet for a variety of instruments that can be used by group facilitators.

The Lecturettes section offers ideas and background in a readily usable, brief, simplified lecture form that can be coordinated with structured experiences.

Although more complex and lengthy than lecturettes, Theory and Practice papers address themselves to the practitioner rather than to the scholar. Most of these contributions are prepared especially for the *Annual*. Combined with the shorter pieces in the Lecturettes section, they provide highly relevant background reading for facilitators in the field.

The Resources section offers access to tools—books, research, information, addresses, reviews—that can guide, support, and enrich the facilitator's work.

Contributors to the *1974 Annual* are listed alphabetically at the end of the book. Titles, mailing addresses, and telephone numbers have been included so that users of the *Annual* can direct their comments and communications to individual authors.

The materials in the *Annual* are, as we indicated, a collection. Their quality, complexity, length, depth, and dimensions vary. In some cases they are adaptations stemming from "old" ideas; in others, they represent "in progress" reports. Our intention is to offer a stimulating source of ideas and a wealth of practical and varied materials for the use of the group facilitator.

INTRODUCTION TO THE STRUCTURED EXPERIENCES SECTION

Structured experiences—designed to focus on individual behavior, constructive feedback, processing, and psychological integration—are infinitely varied and variable. They can easily be adapted to the particular needs of the group, the aim of a training design, or the special competencies of the facilitator. In publishing these structured experiences, we assume that facilitators are, by their nature, innovators. As one friend remarked, "I use your materials all the time, but I almost never do things the way you guys describe them."

The "Variations" section of each experience is intended as a suggestive extension. We hope it will trigger other ideas, adaptations, developments, expansions, and transformations.

Adaptation is also the purpose of cross-referencing similar structured experiences that supplement or complement each other. Additionally, references to appropriate lecturettes and other materials in *Annuals* are included for the facilitator's convenience.

Since the expertise of individual facilitators varies, we have arranged the structured experiences in the *1974 Annual* as we have done in previous *Annuals* and in Vols. I, II, III, and IV of our *Handbooks*: in order of the degree of understanding, skill, and experience required by the facilitator. The first structured experiences generate less affect and data than do later ones, thus demanding much less background of the facilitator to use them effectively and responsibly.

We are concerned that all human relations training experiences have adequate processing so that the participants are able to integrate their learning without the stress generated by unresolved feelings or a lack of understanding. It is here that the expertise of the facilitator becomes crucial. If the structured experience is to be responsive to the needs of the participants, the facilitator must be capable of assisting participants in successfully processing the data that emerge from that experience. Thus, he should select an activity on the basis of two criteria—his own competence and the participants' needs.

The publication of these structured experiences is aimed at sharing. We are pleased that facilitators around the world are using these materials and that they agree with our philosophy of sharing rather than "owning" ideas as being in the true spirit of human relations theory.

CONSIDERATIONS IN DEVELOPING A STRUCTURED EXPERIENCE

To further the creation and availability of these valuable materials, we are including some points and questions to be considered when developing a structured experience.

Goals. These should be limited in number and stated in language that participants can understand. A good goal is *specific*, not general; it is *performance oriented*, to guide the person toward what he is going to *do*; it *involves* the individual in his goal objective; it is *observable*, so that other people can see the result; and, most important, it is *realistic*. For maximum effectiveness, a goal must be attainable.

Group Size. The minimum and maximum numbers of participants, the optimum size of the group, and the number and size of subgroups should be noted where relevant. If there are extra participants, how should they be utilized? (They could, for example, be designated as observers or be added to subgroups.)

Time Required. This should be a realistic expectation, based on actual trials of the experience. If the experience requires a long period of time, can it be divided into more than one session?

Materials. The criteria here are easy availability, utility, and uncomplicated preparation. The specific forms, sheets of information, or worksheets needed and the quantities of each should be listed. If appropriate, an observer sheet should be devised for the activity. Audio-visual aids (such as felt-tipped pens, newsprint, sound or film equipment, etc.), pencils and paper, and any other special materials should be indicated if applicable.

Physical Setting. What are the participants' needs: Must groups be private, quiet, isolated? Do participants sit around tables or lie on the floor? Do they need writing surfaces? Can the experience take place outdoors? Do rooms need to be specially designated or arranged for certain groups or subgroups? Easily moveable furniture is usually desirable to aid in the flexibility of the group.

Process. This is a step-by-step procedure which should indicate what the facilitator *does* and *says* and what the participants *do* in the appropriate sequence. The beginning and end of each step should be specified. A time estimate may be useful for each step or phase.

Variations. Adaptations may be noted to vary the activity's content, sequence, use of observers, time for each step, materials, size of groups, complexity of the process, and use with intact groups.

References. If and when relevant, similar structured experiences, lecturette sources, or background reading should be indicated.

Credit Line. Ideas and designs of others should be acknowledged; if there is more than one author to be credited, authors' names should be given in the order of the significance of their contributions, the senior author or contributor listed first.

Worksheets. These should be designed and written so that they have sufficient room in which the participants may write; are simple and easy to reproduce; have clear instructions; and are necessary and meaningful to the activity. Wherever possible, each worksheet should be on one page, with type large enough to read easily. It is practical to have the worksheet contain its own instructions. If it does not, it should tell the participant that the facilitator will give oral instructions. Sources for worksheets should be acknowledged.

Handouts. This format is especially useful for a discussion of the theory underlying new behavior suggested by the structured experience. Unless necessary, participants should not be allowed to read handout materials while the process is running. However, if handouts are to be provided, participants should be told at the beginning of the experience so that they will not have to take notes.

CATEGORIES OF STRUCTURED EXPERIENCES

All structured experiences published in our *Annuals* and *Handbooks* are numbered consecutively. In the *1974 Annual*, structured experiences begin with number 125, following the last structured experience in Vol. IV of the *Handbooks*, Structured Experience 124.

Categorizing structured experiences is somewhat arbitrary, since they can be adapted for a variety of training purposes. The following page lists each structured experience in Vols. I, II, III, and IV and in the 1972, 1973, and 1974 *Annuals*, classified according to its category of use. Each item is included only once, even though any given experience could conceivably be used for several different purposes. The numbers refer to structured experiences, *not* to pages.

The longer we work in human relations, the more we become aware of the infinite variety and adaptability of structured experiences. We hope that facilitators and practitioners in the field will find some useful ideas, variations, and materials in this section of the *Annual*.

STRUCTURED EXPERIENCE CATEGORIES

125. HUM-DINGER: A GETTING-ACQUAINTED ACTIVITY

Goals

I. To break a large group into smaller groups in a nonthreatening manner.

II. To facilitate contact between all members of a large group in a related climate of fun and humor.

III. To explore a novel way of generating movement and activity.

Group Size

Unlimited. There should be a minimum of eight participants.

Time Required

Approximately thirty minutes.

Physical Setting

A room large enough for all participants to circulate and converse in smaller groups.

Materials

A folded strip of paper with the title of a common, popular song for each member of the group (one set of song title strips for each subgroup desired).

Process

I. The facilitator begins by stating that "There is a great deal of talent and skill in this room. We are here to explore some of this talent. Each of you will be given a piece of paper on which is written the title of a common song. Please look at the title, but don't share it with anyone else. When I say go, please mill around the room humming your tune until you find all of the other members of your group with the same song."

Suggested Songs:

"Three Blind Mice," "Jingle Bells," "Home on the Range," "Auld Lang Syne," "Happy Birthday," "Deep in the Heart of Texas," "Today," "Kum Bah Yah," "For He's a Jolly Good Fellow."

II. When the groups have been formed, the facilitator asks each group to sit in a circle. Groups are instructed to discuss how they felt beginning and during the exercise, how they felt when they found the first group member, and how they felt when their subgroup was completely identified.

III. The total group is reassembled to share its feelings and expectations.

Variations

I. When the facilitator has prior knowledge of the participants, the songs can be pre-arranged to form desired groupings.

II. The facilitator can tell the participants how many others have the same song. This will accelerate the activity.

III. Instead of one song per strip, several songs can be listed. For example: (1) "Mary Had a Little Lamb," (2) "Jingle Bells," (3) "Home on the Range." The first song is used to form dyads, the second song quartets, and the third a task group of any number for some later activity.

IV. Group members can be assigned the task of coming up with a group name or a song title to express their feeling as a group.

Similar Structured Experiences: *Vol. I:* Structured Experience 1, 5; *Vol. II:* 42, 47; *Vol. III:* 49; *'73 Annual:* 87, 88; *Vol. IV:* 101; *'74 Annual:* 129.

Submitted by A. Donald Duncan.

126. COG'S LADDER: A PROCESS-OBSERVATION ACTIVITY

Goals

  I. To enhance awareness of factors which distinguish process from content in group interaction.

  II. To explore a model of group development.

Group Size

  A minimum of seventeen participants.

Time Required

  One hour.

Materials

  I. A set of the eleven Cog's Ladder Observation Sheets (one sheet for each of the eleven observers).

  II. Pencils and paper for all participants.

Physical Setting

  I. A room large enough to accommodate the group comfortably.

  II. A round table in the center of the room where the six "active" participants are to be seated.

  III. Desk chairs for the eleven observers, seated in a circle around the six at the table in group-on-group fashion.

Process

  I. The facilitator gives a lecturette on the Cog's Ladder model of group development. (See the Lecturettes section of this *Annual*.) Then he asks for six volunteers to help demonstrate usual behavior in groups. He asks that volunteers not be hypersensitive to criticism and that they not volunteer if they are tempted to sabotage the experience by behaving in nontypical ways. (The six volunteers are not to sit at the round table until they are directed to do so by the facilitator.)

  II. The facilitator distributes one of the Cog's Ladder Observation Sheets and a pencil to each of the remaining participants. While these sheets are being studied, volunteers are instructed to reflect quietly on their "usual" behavior in groups.

  III. Participants are instructed to arrange themselves in a group-on-group design.

  IV. The facilitator tells the volunteer group members that he will present them with a problem that they must solve in twenty minutes. He tells them that they are to rank the five characters in a story in the order in which they appeal to the group. (These instructions are *not* repeated after the story is read.)

  V. The facilitator reads the following story aloud.

The Girl and the Sailor

A ship sank in a storm. Five survivors scrambled aboard two life boats: a sailor, a girl, and an old man in one boat; the girl's fiancé and his best friend in the second.

During the storm, the two boats separated. The first boat washed ashore on an island and was wrecked. The girl searched all day in vain for the other boat or any sign of her fiancé.

The next day, the weather cleared, and still she could not locate her fiancé. In the distance she saw another island. Hoping to find her fiancé, she begged the sailor to repair the boat and row her to the other island. The sailor agreed, on the condition that she sleep with him that night.

Distraught, she went to the old man for advice. "I cannot tell you what is right or wrong for you," he said. "Look into your heart and follow it." Confused but desperate, she agreed to the sailor's condition.

The next morning the sailor fixed the boat and rowed her to the other island. Jumping out of the boat, she ran up the beach into the arms of her fiancé. Then she decided to tell him about the previous night. In a rage, he pushed her away and said, "Get away from me! I don't want to see you again!" Weeping, she started to walk slowly down the beach.

Seeing her, the best friend went to her, put his arm around her, and said, "I can tell that you two have had a fight. I'll try to patch it up, but, in the meantime, I'll take care of you."

VI. After twenty minutes, the facilitator directs observers to make brief reports. Then the volunteers are encouraged to respond to this feedback.

VII. The facilitator leads a discussion of the group-growth processes in terms of the Cog's Ladder Model, relating the various stages to the members' observations.

Variations

I. The group's task may be chosen to fit the particular setting or experience of the participants if the structured experience is used as part of an OD effort.

II. The observer sheets can be typed on reusable 5" by 8" cards.

III. For groups with fewer than seventeen participants, observers can be given more than one observation sheet. For larger groups, several persons can be assigned to observe each dimension of group process.

IV. Copies of the Cog's Ladder Lecturette can be distributed as handouts.

V. Observers can be instructed to provide process feedback twice—in the middle and at the end of the volunteer group's meeting.

VI. A different model of group development can be used.

Similar Structured Experiences: *Vol. I:* Structured Experience 6, 9, 10; *Vol. II:* 37, 39; *Vol. III:* 55; '72 *Annual:* 79; '74 *Annual:* 135.

Lecturette Sources: '73 *Annual:* "A Model of Group Development"; '74 *Annual:* "Cog's Ladder: A Model of Group Development."

Submitted by George O. Charrier.

COG'S LADDER OBSERVATION SHEETS

Polite Phase

Look for the *Polite* phase. This will be going on while people are volunteering to sit in the inner group. It may last less than a minute. Make notes on polite behaviors.

Why We're Here Phase

Note the *Why We're Here* phase. How many times during the twenty-minute discussion does the group revert to this phase by trying to redefine the task? Does one person in the group bring the group back to this phase more often than others?

Bid for Power Phase

During the *Bid for Power* phase people make unsolicited statements and opinions. Note the number of unsolicited comments made during this phase. Also, note how many suggestions or ideas are presented which elicit no response from the other members.

Number of unsolicited comments_____

Number of suggestions_____

Constructive Phase

The *Constructive* phase is characterized by an open mindedness of the group members. It can be measured by the number of "real" questions directed at others in the group for the purpose of bringing out facts. Note the number of such questions.

Number of questions_____

This phase is also evidenced by such comments as:
   "I never thought of that."
   "Yes, that's right."
   "I believe you have a point."

Note the number of times a person shifts his position based on the facts presented.

Number of times_____

Esprit Phase

Note characteristics and individual behavior during the *Esprit* phase, if it develops, although it is very unlikely to occur during this short period of time. This phase is present when you hear such comments as, "I think we did a good job on that." There may be a feeling of good will and comradeship among the members.

Cliques

Spend the first five minutes watching the group to determine which two members agree with each other more than any other pair. During this five-minute period, also note which two people seem to disagree more than any other pair. During the final fifteen minutes record the number of times the positive members agree with each other either verbally or nonverbally. Also record the number of times the negative members disagree with each other either verbally or nonverbally.

	Agrees	Disagrees
Positive Clique	_____	_____
Negative Clique	_____	_____

Hidden Agenda

This task is possibly the most difficult of all. Try to determine, if you can, the real reason that any one person volunteered to be a member of the inner group. Reasons might be a desire to learn more about group dynamics, a desire for self-knowledge, or a need to gain approval. Remember that any conclusion you draw will be your impression, not necessarily the actual reason. However, you may want to check your impression later with other group members.

Need for Approval

Your task is to determine the level of the group's (not necessarily individual members') *Need for Approval*. You can determine this by counting the number of comments of the "motherhood-and-apple-pie" type (ideas which cannot be refuted or criticized). Sometimes a group has a need for approval from the spectators; you can determine this by noticing the reactions of the spectators. Humorous cross-play is one indication of this situation.

Need for Identity

The need for identity appears in the fifth (*Esprit*) phase. Because it is doubtful that the group will reach this phase, you probably will not find evidence of a need for identity. If it is present, however, it will be shown by the desire of the group to call itself by a special name or to wear a special badge, emblem, or insignia.

Variety of Participation

In every group, some people talk more than others. This is called *Variety of Participation*. Your task is to spend the first five minutes determining which member talks the most and which member talks the least. The last fifteen minutes should be used to record the number of comments made by each of these two members.

Greatest Talker_____   Least Talker_____

Number of Comments_____   Number of Comments_____

Structure

Structure is the expressed or unexpressed hierarchy within the group. Note, if you can, the evolution of a leader. Note any comments relating to structure in the work situation. Listen for any evidence of deference, subordination, or attempts to control.

127. LEADERSHIP CHARACTERISTICS: EXAMINING VALUES IN PERSONNEL SELECTION

Goals

I. To compare the results of individual decision-making and group decision-making.

II. To explore values underlying leadership characteristics.

III. To examine effects of value judgments on personnel selection.

Group Size

Between six and twelve participants. Several groups may be directed simultaneously. (Smaller groups tend to be more effective.)

Time Required

Approximately two hours.

Materials

I. A copy of the Leadership Characteristics Worksheet for each participant.

II. A copy of the Leadership Characteristics Situation Description Sheet for each participant.

III. A copy of the Leadership Characteristics Volunteers Description Sheet for each participant.

IV. Pencils for all participants.

Physical Setting

A room large enough for the groups to meet separately.

Process

I. The facilitator distributes a Leadership Characteristics Worksheet to each participant. He tells participants that they have ten minutes to complete their individual rankings.

II. The facilitator collects the worksheets and explains that participants will next become engaged in a personnel selection task. He divides the participants into groups of six each.

III. When the groups have been located comfortably around the room, the facilitator distributes a copy of the Leadership Characteristics Situation Description Sheet and the Leadership Characteristics Volunteers Description Sheet to each participant. He tells participants that they have ten minutes to make their choices independently. Groups then have thirty minutes to choose five chairmen from the volunteers.

IV. Each group shares its choices and rationale with the total group.

V. The facilitator leads a discussion of the experience with the total group, comparing judgments made on the basis of factual information and those made on values.

VI. The facilitator redistributes to each participant his Leadership Characteristics Worksheet. Each group is asked to reach a consensus-ranking.

VII. In a final discussion, the facilitator focuses upon leadership characteristics exhibited during the entire experience.

Variations

I. To determine the relative influence of individuals on group outcomes, two scoring phases can be included. The selection-phase participants can be instructed to count how many of their private choices match the group consensus. After the characteristics consensus-ranking, individuals can sum the differences between their ranks and the group ranks (make them all positive and add them up). In the latter case, high scores would presumably indicate acquiescence and low scores would indicate high influence on the group's decision-making.

II. Instead of collecting and redistributing the ranking sheet, the facilitator can have the consensus-seeking phase precede the personnel-selection activity.

III. The individual-ranking selection steps can be deleted.

IV. New groups can be formed for the consensus-ranking activity.

V. Process observers can be assigned to groups. They can use the Leadership Characteristics Worksheet on ranking as a guide in observing the leadership that emerges in the group.

Similar Structured Experiences: Vol. I: Structured Experiences 3, 9, 11, 12, 15; Vol. II: 30, 34, 41; Vol. III: 64, 69, 73; '72 Annual: 77, 80, 82; '73 Annual: 98; Vol. IV: 115, 117; '74 Annual: 134, 135.

Lecturette Sources: '73 Annual: "Synergy and Consensus-Seeking," "Conditions Which Hinder Effective Communication."

_____

Submitted by Charles Kormanski.

LEADERSHIP CHARACTERISTICS WORKSHEET

NAME _____GROUP _____

Instructions: Under the column marked "Individual Ranking," you are to rank-order the twelve characteristics listed below. Place the number one (1) before the characteristic you feel is most important for a good leader, the number (2) before the second best, etc. The characteristic ranked twelfth will be least important. Later, your group is to arrive at a consensus-ranking that each of you can agree with, at least partially. This ranking is noted under the column marked "Group Ranking."

Individual Ranking	Group Ranking	Characteristics
_____	_____	A. Maintains an orderly meeting most of the time.
_____	_____	B. Is friendly and sociable.
_____	_____	C. Has new and interesting ideas—is creative.
_____	_____	D. Listens and tries to understand others.
_____	_____	E. Is firm and decisive, not hesitant.
_____	_____	F. Admits errors openly and easily.
_____	_____	G. Makes sure everyone understands what is expected.
_____	_____	H. Provides opportunities for group members to aid in decision-making activities.
_____	_____	I. Uses praise frequently and negative criticism sparingly.
_____	_____	J. Is willing to compromise.
_____	_____	K. Follows strictly accepted rules and procedures.
_____	_____	L. Never expresses anger or dissatisfaction with others.

LEADERSHIP CHARACTERISTICS SITUATION
DESCRIPTION SHEET

You are one of six coordinators who will plan a weekend activity program for your organization. The task of the group is to select five committee chairmen for the event. Twelve persons have volunteered.

The five committees and their functions are described below:

1. *Social Activities*—develop activities to bring together participants and guests with an emphasis on fun and enjoyment.

2. *Intellectual Activities*—stimulate an interest in learning and knowledge by having exhibits, demonstrations, discussions, etc., with an emphasis on discovery.

3. *Public Relations*—publicize information regarding the event as well as report on its progress and conclusion via the news media.

4. *Food and Housing*—prepare a menu, including refreshments, and provide for rooms and meals for invited guests.

5. *Finances*—plan a budget and distribute money, sell admission tickets, record expenditures, and prepare a financial report.

You must choose five chairmen from the descriptions of volunteers provided on the Leadership Characteristics Volunteers Description Sheet.

| | Chairmen Selected | |
Committee	Individual Choice	Group Choice
1. Social Activities	_____	_____
2. Intellectual Activities	_____	_____
3. Public Relations	_____	_____
4. Food and Housing	_____	_____
5. Finances	_____	_____

LEADERSHIP CHARACTERISTICS VOLUNTEERS
DESCRIPTION SHEET

Jim is an army veteran with combat experience in Vietnam. Although he is somewhat cold and impersonal, he is excellent at organizing and planning. This past term he was largely responsible for the success of a community "Blood Donor Day."

Bob is an outstanding athlete and popular with females. Baseball has been his only activity the past few years. He is a perfectionist, however, and is easily frustrated when working with people.

Frank is a political activist. He seems to be continually involved in some cause or demonstration. He has proven leadership qualities and organized a successful supermarket boycott in the community.

Mary is a very attractive, popular woman who has participated in a number of beauty pageants. She has not been involved in any "task-oriented" activities except for helping to decorate the country club summer dance after being chosen queen.

Jerry is rather shy and withdrawn; his volunteering was a surprise. It is rumored that Jerry is seeing a psychiatrist on a weekly basis. The leadership position could be very therapeutic.

Marcia is quite outspoken and at times obnoxious. She usually volunteers for many activities, but she is rarely chosen. She is, however, a very diligent and persistent worker.

Joan did an excellent job in a leadership position for one of the political parties during the past elections. Her political views conflict with Frank's, and they have frequent arguments. She is currently experiencing some marital difficulties, and there are rumors of a possible divorce.

Sue is active with a local dramatic club. She was co-chairman of a community art show which was well received but sparsely attended. However, she and Mary are dating the same young man and presently are not speaking to each other.

John is engaged in a few social organizations and does an adequate job. He is somewhat hypersensitive and prefers to do things himself instead of delegating. As a result, lateness is one of his consistent characteristics.

Adam had a major part in the establishment of a local service organization. He is outgoing and enjoys his social life. During the past year, however, he has been arrested twice on charges of disorderly conduct.

Margie is a pert, smiling individual, who is quite popular with men and never lacks a date. She is not very popular with her female co-workers.

Anne is already over-involved in activities, but she volunteered because she felt she was needed. She has done public relations work for past events and can do an excellent job if she can find enough time.

128. RE-OWNING: INCREASING BEHAVIORAL ALTERNATIVES

Goals

I. To assist participants in exploring aspects of themselves that they might not be presently aware of or may be underutilizing.

II. To extend the range of behavioral alternatives open for effective communication.

Group Size

Unlimited number of triads.

Time Required

Approximately one hour.

Materials

I. Newsprint and felt-tipped marker.

II. Paper and pencils for all participants.

Physical Setting

A large enough area for triads to have relative privacy.

Process

I. The facilitator begins with a brief lecturette on Wallen's Triangle, pointing out that the human personality can be viewed as some combination of Tough Battler, Logical Thinker, and/or Friendly Helper. He illustrates this on the chart pad.

II. Participants, as a total group, are then instructed to draw the triangle on their paper and to label the points, as illustrated.

They are then directed to place an "X" somewhere within or on the triangle that best represents how they see themselves. (First impressions are usually the best.)

III. The facilitator then tells the participants to draw a *smaller* triangle within the larger one, having the same centerpoint as the larger. (He illustrates on newsprint.)

IV. The facilitator then suggests that if a participant's "X" does not fall within the smaller triangle, he (the participant) may be underutilizing or disowning a relevant aspect of himself. The facilitator may want to develop this concept here, e.g., pointing out that a Tough Battler who is in the process of disowning his Logical Thinker may be well on his way to overdependence on the other two behavioral modes.

V. The facilitator forms triads for a multiple role-play.

VI. He gives the following instructions:

(A) Each triad is a "family" comprised of a father, an older daughter, and a younger son. (This can vary depending on the male-female ratio of the participants.)

(B) The triad's task is to plan a joint vacation for its "family."

(C) Each member of the triad is to retain his role throughout the role-play. However, every ten minutes the group will

18

rotate through the different personality types until each member of the triad has been Tough Battler, Logical Thinker, and Friendly Helper. (Note: it may help avoid confusion during the role-play by starting with the "father" as Tough Battler, "older daughter" as Logical Thinker, and "younger son" as Friendly Helper and have them rotate clockwise through the personality types.)

(D) Each personality type is to be played to its *fullest* extreme.

VII. When the triads have completed the role-play, the participants discuss the experience and give each other feedback.

VIII. The total group reassembles, and the facilitator leads a general discussion processing the reactions. He may wish to focus on "Which role was the most difficult?"; "What was it like when you were in your 'disowned' role?"; etc.

Variations

I. If the participants are a work group, the roles might switch to Worker, Supervisor, and Executive. The task might be created to represent more closely an organizational problem, *e.g.*, a committee to plan a company recreational activity.

In this mode the facilitator could also introduce probe questions in the general discussion such as: "Was there one style predominately more disowned than the others?" "If so, does this say something about this organization's norms?" "What was it like rotating through the personality roles being in the superior/middle/subordinate position?"

II. Members of triads can have "alter-ego" observers to coach them during the role play.

III. Observers may be briefed (privately) to listen for statements that include the words "just" and "only," which indicate disowning and discounting.

Similar Structured Experiences: *Vol. I:* Structured Experience 13; *Vol. II:* 37, 38; *Vol. IV:* 109, 123; *'74 Annual:* 129.

Lecturette Sources: *'72 Annual:* "Risk-Taking and Error Protection Styles"; *'73 Annual:* "Johari Window."

Submitted by H. B. Karp.

129. FORCED-CHOICE IDENTITY: A SELF-DISCLOSURE ACTIVITY

Goals

I. To gain insight about oneself.

II. To facilitate self-disclosure and feedback.

III. To encourage community-building.

IV. To enhance enjoyment of the group experience through a change-of-pace activity.

Group Size

A minimum of ten participants.

Time Required

Approximately two hours.

Materials

I. A 5" by 8" card and a pencil for each participant.

II. Pins or masking tape.

III. Newsprint and felt-tipped marker.

Physical Setting

A room large enough for the participants to move from place to place.

Process

I. The facilitator explains that the purpose of the experience is to give each participant an opportunity to see himself in new ways, in the process of making difficult and competing choices. Sets of four alternate choices will be offered. (See "Suggested Sets of Alternatives" at the end of this structured experience.) In each set, the participant is to choose the *one* adjective or noun (even if more than one alternative is applicable) that is *most* descriptive of how he sees himself at that moment.

II. The four alternatives in each set are posted at the same time, each one on a sheet of newsprint placed in separated areas of the room. (The facilitator may need the assistance of three participants for this step.)

III. Each participant makes his choice from alternatives and records it on his card in large letters so that others can read it. After all participants have written their choices, they are instructed to walk to the area of the room where their choice is posted.

IV. When all participants have gathered in appropriate parts of the room, the facilitator directs any large groups to divide into subgroups. Participants discuss the basis for their choice with the other people they find in their group. Individuals are told they may wish to re-evaluate their choices after considering which participants share their group. The participants discuss how they feel about being in that particular area of the room. Then the facilitator asks them to survey the locations of other persons around the room and to comment on the appropriateness of others' choices. Participants may change their choices by moving to another location in the room; they may also suggest changes for others.

V. The facilitator then posts the second set of choices and the process is repeated for as many rounds as time permits.

VI. When the series of choices has been completed and each participant has listed his choices on his card, the facilitator asks participants to pin their cards on their chests.

VII. The facilitator forms small groups and asks group members to share and discuss their reactions to one another's choices.

Variations

I. More than four alternatives can be provided for large groups.

II. The design can be abbreviated as a getting-acquainted activity.

III. Other alternatives can be devised to fit a particular group. Choices might represent positions on issues, points on scales of agreement with attitude statements, or words associated with the backgrounds of participants.

IV. The list of alternatives can be reproduced for use as an instrument in self-assessment and feedback.

Similar Structured Experiences: *Vol. I:* Structured Experience 5, 20; *Vol. II:* 38, 42; *Vol. III:* 49; *'72 Annual:* 84; *'73 Annual:* 88, 90; *Vol. IV:* 101, 107, 109.

Lecturette Source: *'73 Annual:* "Johari Window."

Submitted by John J. Sherwood, this structured experience is a modification of a design created by Campbell Crockett.

SUGGESTED SETS OF ALTERNATIVES

active	passive	colorful	optimistic
adult	man	woman	mature
father or mother	husband or wife	brother or sister	son or daughter
White	Black	American	religious
growing	happy	competent	secure
deliberate	impulsive	adventuresome	compulsive
aggressive	creative	conscientious	obedient
warm	restrained	introverted	romantic
brilliant	sparkling	intense	persistent
rigid	determined	flexible	indecisive
aesthetic	practical	intellectual	worldly
in the group, I accept authority	in the group, I fight authority	in the group, I run from authority	in the group, I am authority
in the group, I am an integral member	in the group, I am a marginal member	in the group, I am an alienated member	in the group, I am an angry member

130. CONFLICT FANTASY: A SELF-EXAMINATION

Goals

I. To facilitate awareness of strategies for dealing with conflict situations.

II. To examine methods of responding to conflict.

III. To introduce the strategy of negotiation and to present the skills required for successful negotiation.

Group Size

Eight to forty participants.

Time Required

Approximately forty-five minutes.

Materials

I. Newsprint and felt-tipped marker.

II. Pencils and paper for all participants.

Physical Setting

A quiet room protected from intrusions during private portions of the experience.

Process

I. The participants are asked to join the facilitator in a fantasy designed to help them examine their individual conflict-resolution strategies. For approximately ten minutes, the facilitator guides the group through the following fantasy. (The facilitator should feel free to embellish the fantasy and to change the setting to fit the particular group.)

II. (Getting into the fantasy.) The facilitator asks participants to get comfortable, close their eyes, get in touch with themselves at the present moment (the sounds around them, the feel of their bodies, etc.), and relax.

III. (The fantasy.) The facilitator says, "You are walking down a street (or a hallway or a trail) and begin to see in the distance a familiar person. Suddenly you recognize that it is the person you are most in conflict with at present. You realize that you must decide quickly how to deal with this person. As he/she comes closer, a number of alternatives flash through your mind. . . . Decide right now what you will do and then imagine what will happen."

The facilitator pauses to let the fantasies develop.

"It's over now. The person is gone. How do you feel? What is your level of satisfaction with the way things went?"

IV. (Getting out of the fantasy.) The facilitator asks participants to begin to return to the present, gradually to become aware of the pressures on their bodies, of the chair, of the floor, then to attend to the sounds in the room, and finally to open their eyes when they feel ready.

V. After participants emerge from the fantasy, the facilitator asks them to spend five minutes writing (1) the alternative ways of acting they had considered, (2) the one they chose to act upon, and (3) the level of satisfaction they felt as to the fantasized outcome.

VI. Each participant is asked to share with two others the alternatives considered, the one chosen, and the level of satisfaction attained. (It is not necessary that the particulars of the personal situations be shared.) A volunteer in each triad keeps a list of all types of alternatives mentioned during the discussion.

22

VII. The whole group is reconvened to share all the alternatives generated. These are listed on newsprint.

VIII. The facilitator displays on newsprint A Continuum of Responses to Conflict Situations and explains it with a lecturette. (See the Lecturettes section in this *Annual*.) Then he asks participants to sort the alternatives listed into the appropriate strategy categories.

A Continuum of Responses to Conflict Situations

IX. The facilitator leads a discussion of the levels of satisfaction of persons choosing various strategies on the continuum. He starts with avoidance strategies and ends with the negotiation type of confrontation strategy. Volunteers are asked to give very brief accounts of their fantasy experiences.

X. The facilitator summarizes the outcomes of the experience and presents a brief theory input on negotiation as the strategy with the greatest potential payoff (win-win strategy). He emphasizes the skills necessary for successful negotiation.

Variations

I. A participant can volunteer his fantasies to be role-played in front of the entire group.

Role-players can be coached by subgroups. Several role-plays can be carried out in succession.

II. Role-playing can be done in the triads, with one of the participants as an observer, one as the confronter, and one as the confrontee. Three rounds can take place, with roles switched on each round.

III. The fantasy can be restricted to include only persons present in the group. Participants volunteer to act out their fantasies in front of the group. Afterwards, participants can be encouraged to share their fantasies with the individuals toward whom they felt some conflict.

IV. Members of the triads can be encouraged to assist each other in planning appropriate confrontation strategies.

Similar Structured Experiences: *Vol. I:* Structured Experience 14, 16; *'72 Annual:* 75; *'73 Annual:* 97.

Lecturette Sources: *'72 Annual:* "Transcendence Theory"; *'73 Annual:* "Win/Lose Situations," "Confrontation: Types, Conditions, and Outcomes"; *'74 Annual:* "Figure/Ground," "Conflict-Resolution Strategies."

Submitted by Joan A. Stepsis.

131. ROXBORO ELECTRIC COMPANY: AN OD ROLE-PLAY

Goals

I. To provide an experience in sensing organizational problems.

II. To provide feedback on interviewing effectiveness.

III. To explore organizational diagnosis and action-planning.

Group Size

Eighteen participants (nine company roles and nine OD consultant roles). (Additional roles can be created, and one or more roles can be combined if necessary. Additional participants may be assigned as observers.)

Time Required

Approximately two and one-half hours.

Materials

I. For company role-players:
   Roxboro Electric Company Background Sheet
   Roxboro Electric Company Organization Chart
   Roxboro Electric Company Interview Schedule
   Roxboro Electric Company Interview Feedback Guidelines

II. For consultant role-players:
   Roxboro Electric Company Interview Schedule
   Roxboro Electric Company Interviewing Guidelines
   Roxboro Electric Company Diagnosis and OD Strategy Guidelines
   Pencils and paper

III. Signs to denote "offices" of consultants.

IV. Newsprint and felt-tipped marker.

Physical Setting

I. A room large enough to accommodate the entire group and to allow nine concurrent interviews to be undertaken without distraction.

II. Three small rooms where OD consultant teams can meet.

Process

I. The facilitator briefly introduces the experience to the entire group, explaining that participants will obtain experience in interviewing, in diagnosing organizational problems, in planning OD strategies, and in giving feedback on these processes. The facilitator assigns participants to company roles and OD consultant roles. The company personnel are directed to one briefing room and the consultants to another.

II. (A) Company role-players are briefed on their roles; the Roxboro Electric Company Background Sheet is distributed to them, and the Roxboro Electric Company Organization Chart is studied to clarify the relationships among the various roles. Participants are encouraged to elaborate on their roles if they desire, once they have this information. The facilitator answers any questions and gives participants ten minutes to get into their roles and to discuss their roles with one another. The briefing ends with an explanation of the Roxboro Electric Company Interview Schedule.

(B) Concurrently, consultant role-players are briefed on their roles. They are *not* given the Background Sheet but are simply told that they have been called in from corporate headquarters by the president to identify and help solve problems associated with getting a new TV model designed and produced each year. The Organization Chart is displayed on newsprint, and they are told that as three teams of three consultants each they will interview the nine company members shown on the chart. Their task will be to gather data to enable them to diagnose organizational problems and to develop an OD strategy for responding to these problems. Each consultant is given a copy of the Roxboro Electric Company Interviewing Guidelines. Consultants are allowed ten minutes to meet in teams to discuss their approach to the upcoming interviews. The briefing ends with an explanation of the Interview Schedule.

III. In the main room, nine concurrent interviews are set up, with "offices" consisting of pairs of chairs facing each other, with the title of the company member attached to one chair. The company members go to their offices. Then the consultants are brought into the room and the interviews begin. After ten minutes, the consultants move to another interview, and the process is repeated. (The Interview Schedule should be posted in the main room for reference.) When the third round of interviews has been completed, the company role-players remain in the main room and the consultant team members are directed to three adjacent meeting rooms.

IV. (A) The facilitator briefs the company members on giving feedback to the OD consultants on their interviewing style. Each participant receives a copy of the Roxboro Electric Company Interview Feedback Guidelines. If time permits, the company members may discuss, out-of-role, the organizational problems the company faces and the kind of strategy they would develop for dealing with these problems.

(B) Concurrently, consultant role-players are instructed to pool their interview data with members of their triad, diagnose the organizational problems, and describe the main elements of an action plan for dealing with these problems. Each member is given a copy of the Roxboro Electric Company Diagnosis and OD Strategy Guidelines. Each group selects a spokesman to report its conclusions to the total group in the final session with all participants.

V. The interview schedule is repeated so that the company members can give feedback to the consultants.

VI. The entire group reassembles to discuss the experience. The participants report the feelings they had as role-players.

VII. Each OD interviewing team reports its diagnosis and action planning. The facilitator leads a discussion on the similarities and differences among reports.

VIII. The facilitator offers a brief lecturette on sensing, diagnosis, and action planning or on other topics appropriate to the sophistication of the group.

Variations

I. Observers may be assigned to each of the interview stations to assist in the feedback phase. They may be reassigned to teams during the diagnosis and action-planning phase.

II. Consultants can be encouraged to experiment with different interviewing styles, such as reflective, probing, asking no questions, etc.

III. The company role-players can engage in some preliminary activity in order to generate interpersonal data that may emerge during the interviews.

IV. The content of the "case" can be varied to be relevant to a particular group. The data could reflect an actual situation if the training occurs within an organization.

Similar Structured Experiences: *Vol. II:* Structured Experience 34, 40; *Vol. III:* 66, 67, 68, 73; *'72 Annual:* 80, 82, 83; *Vol. IV:* 110, 111, 116, 117, 118; *'74 Annual:* 133, 134, 135.

Lecturette Sources: *'72 Annual:* "An Introduction to Organization Development," "Seven Pure Strategies of Change," "Notes on Freedom"; *'73 Annual:* "The Sensing Interview," "An Informal Glossary of Terms and Phrases in Organization Development"; *'74 Annual:* "The 'Shouldist' Manager," "Models and Roles of Change Agents."

Submitted by Harvey Thomson. This structured experience was created in a University Associates workshop. Participants assisting in the development of the activity were Bill Bell, Mike Brosseau, Pat Fleck, and Edith Kahn.

ROXBORO ELECTRIC COMPANY BACKGROUND SHEET

We observed the process of designing a new-model TV set in one company. The engineering department is, of course, the one most directly concerned, and it consists of five sections. *Electrical* determines in theoretical terms how the set will be made (technically: what the overall "system" will be). *Mechanical* tries to fit the components together; it often finds that *Electrical's* theoretical plans are impractical or even that one electrical engineer's theoretical suggestions are incompatible with those of another. *Chassis* designs the cabinet; close coordination is required if the components are to fit the cabinet. This is not as easy as it sounds, since *Electrical* and *Mechanical* are constantly designing improvements which give better reception, but which conflict with the company's overall goal of producing an ever-thinner, lighter set.

Automation designs the machinery which makes the printed circuits and attaches the tubes to it; in contrast to *Electrical*, which wants an ever-more "sophisticated" set, *Automation* wants one that is simple enough to be reduced to printed circuitry and put together mechanically. *Industrial Engineering* determines the techniques by which the set will be manufactured (other than the operations that are 100 percent automated). Like *Automation*, it seeks to eliminate what it feels to be unnecessary frills.

Further complicating overall coordination are the pressures brought by outside departments: *Sales* wants an attractive product that will sell easily, and *Manufacturing* wants a set that is easy to put together. And management as a whole is interested in keeping costs low, profits high.

Note that in this case no one section can make modifications without affecting all the others. A change in a cabinet, for instance, may require adjustments by every other section, yet each adjustment may in turn require further compensating adjustments elsewhere. Each section has its own vested interest. *Electrical*, with its goal of technical perfection, conflicts, for example, with *Industrial Engineering's* goal of manufacturing ease.

Since a new model must be designed each year, intergroup conflicts tend to reach a crescendo as the time for a final decision approaches. During the early part of the year there is little pressure to resolve agreements, and each section is free to work on its own pet projects. As the deadline draws near, an increasing number of compromises and adjustments must be made, tempers grow raw, and human-relations problems begin to complicate the technical ones. Each engineer likes to feel that he has *completed* his end of the job and hates to reconsider his position just to please another section. No engineer likes to sacrifice his own brainchild.

Complicating all these problems are the changing status relationships between departments. When TV was new, the major problem was to design a workable set, and *Electrical* was the highest-status section. Today the emphasis is on sales appeal and manufacturing ease. *Electrical* still thinks its function is the most important one, but management seems to favor other sections when it makes critical decisions and hands out promotions.

This extract is taken from George Strauss and Leonard R. Sayles, *Personnel: The Human Problems of Management* © 1960. Reprinted by permission of Prentice-Hall, Inc., Englewood Cliffs, New Jersey.

ROXBORO ELECTRIC COMPANY
ORGANIZATION CHART

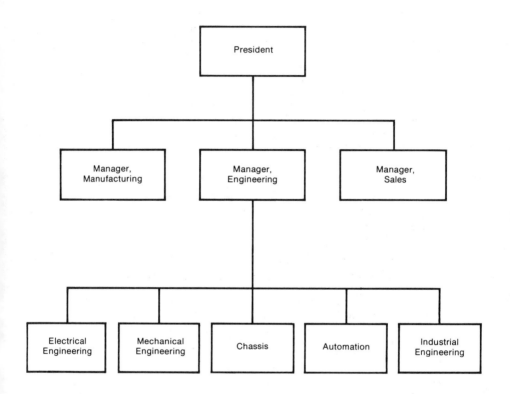

ROXBORO ELECTRIC COMPANY INTERVIEW SCHEDULE

INTERVIEWEE

TEAM	CONSULTANT	Round 1	Round 2	Round 3
Blue	A	President	Chassis Head	Manager, Engineering
	B	Manager, Sales	Automation Head	Electrical Head
	C	Manager, Manufacturing	Industrial Engineering Head	Mechanical Head
Green	D	Manager, Engineering	President	Chassis Head
	E	Electrical Head	Manager, Sales	Automation Head
	F	Mechanical Head	Manager, Manufacturing	Industrial Engineering Head
Brown	G	Chassis Head	Manager, Engineering	President
	H	Automation Head	Electrical Head	Manager, Sales
	I	Industrial Engineering Head	Mechanical Head	Manager, Manufacturing

ROXBORO ELECTRIC COMPANY
INTERVIEW FEEDBACK GUIDELINES

TASK:

To give meaningful feedback to interviewers, showing them how effective their interviewing seemed to be.

QUESTIONS TO CONSIDER:

1. Did the interviewer introduce himself to you and explain the purpose of the interview?

2. Did the interviewer explain how the data were to be used? (By whom? In what form? Confidentiality?)

3. Was the interviewer at ease? Did he put you at ease? (Verbal cues and/or nonverbal behavior.)

4. How directive was the interviewer?

5. Do you feel the interviewer obtained the essential information?

ROXBORO ELECTRIC COMPANY
INTERVIEWING GUIDELINES

TASK:

To obtain data to use in diagnosing organizational problems and in developing an OD action plan for responding to these problems.

SUGGESTED QUESTIONS:

1. What are some of the things the organization does well?
2. What are some of the problems the organization is experiencing?
3. How can the organization be improved?

ROXBORO ELECTRIC COMPANY
DIAGNOSIS AND OD STRATEGY GUIDELINES

TEAM TASK:

1. To diagnose organizational problems in the light of information gathered in the interviews.
2. To formulate on OD action plan to deal with the problems identified.

GUIDELINES:

A. Diagnosis

1. What are the specific organizational problems you have identified?
2. What systems or subsystems are affected?
3. How ready is the organization for change?
4. What are the driving and restraining forces for change?
5. How do you expect the present managers to cope with change?

B. Action Plan

1. What specific actions might be initiated or undertaken by members of the organization?
2. Over what time spans?
3. What would be the expected outcomes?
4. What evaluation procedures should be used?
5. How should feedback be handled?
6. What should be the role of the OD team?

132. PLANNING RECOMMENDATIONS OR ACTION: A TEAM-DEVELOPMENT GUIDEBOOK

Goals

I. To study the process of group decision-making.

II. To explore action-planning.

Group Size

Any number of groups of six participants each.

Time Required

Approximately three hours.

Materials

I. One Guidebook for Planning Recommendations or Action for each participant. The Guidebook should be presented in such a way that a participant can work on one page at a time. (Copies of preassembled Guidebooks may be ordered from University Associates. The price is 50¢ each, and the minimum order is twelve copies.)

II. Newsprint and felt-tipped markers.

III. Masking tape.

IV. Paper and pencils.

Physical Setting

Tables and chairs for each group.

Process

I. The facilitator forms groups and instructs them to assemble around prearranged tables.

II. He distributes the Guidebooks and tells the groups to proceed, beginning with page 1.

He indicates that he will function as a "roving consultant."

III. At the designated time the total group reassembles to hear each subgroup's spokesman report.

IV. The facilitator leads a discussion of what participants learned about problem-solving and planning processes.

Variations

I. If participants are all from the same organization, several steps can be taken:

(A) They conduct a problem survey among themselves and form groups to work on the identified issues.

(B) After the brainstorming phase, a period of cross-group sharing can be established. Two approaches: (1) Half of each group stays at the table while the other half disperses (each to a different group). The "new" group members add ideas to the brainstorm list. (It is important that this not become an "oh-we-already-thought-of-that" session. (2) Participants have a carnival tour of the room, with one person from each group staying at his display to receive and record suggestions from the others.

(C) An information-retrieval center can be established where pertinent facts can be obtained on call.

(D) Groups can be assigned to work in offices, with telephone numbers of groups made available to all.

II. The Guidebook can be worked through in segments of approximately one hour each.

III. A lecturette on force-field analysis can precede the group problem-solving.

IV. Individual group members can work through a force-field analysis independently before the group problem-solving.

Similar Structured Experiences: *Vol. II:* Structured Experience 40; *Vol. III:* 53; *'73 Annual:* 91; *Vol. IV:* 111.

Lecturette Sources: *'73 Annual:* "Force-Field Analysis"; *'74 Annual:* "Cybernetic Sessions: A New Technique for Gathering Ideas," "Models and Roles of Change Agents."

————

Submitted by Robert P. Crosby.

GUIDEBOOK FOR PLANNING RECOMMENDATIONS OR ACTION

page 1

Suggested Procedure:
1. Read this booklet.
2. Decide details, like length of meeting, etc.
3. Then turn to page 4 and begin.
   Estimated time for first reading of this booklet—fifteen minutes.
   Estimated time for use of booklet in guiding problem-solving—approximately three hours.

page 2

A Basic Assumption about the group using this booklet is that members have agreed to work on a common issue which has been determined prior to using this booklet.

page 3

A Brief Summary of the Problem-Solving Process in This Booklet
1. Making sure you are clear on the issue (see page 7 of this booklet).
2. Analyzing before solution (see page 10).
3. *Brainstorming* action ideas (see page 16).
4. Selecting action ideas (see page 18).
5. Writing out recommendation or action (see page 19).
6. Reporting out (see page 21).

page 4

Organization Suggested for Each Small Group
Choose a secretary—not a chairman. The secretary is asked to turn in to the facilitator the information requested on page 19 or on postscript 4. (Why not a chairman? Because groups often get hung-up on his role. Instead we recommend allowing the leadership to emerge and perhaps shift spontaneously.)

This guidebook was developed and copyrighted by Robert P. Crosby of the Leadership Institute of Spokane, Inc. It is adapted and used here with his permission.

This booklet is intended as a *guide* to your work process. At *no* point does it attempt even slightly to influence your opinion or your group conclusion. It *does* attempt to support problem-solving methods that have been found to be effective and to help you avoid traps.

READ THE ENTIRE BOOKLET BEFORE YOUR GROUP BEGINS

The next page uses the words *issue* and *goal*.

> *Avoid Trap 1*—getting hung up on words like *issue*, *goal*, or *problem*.

Some people prefer to talk about *goals* ("a positive approach," they say); others about *problems* ("everybody has problems, so why not admit it"); others about *issues* ("it's more neutral"); but all goals reflect implicit problems and all problems and issues reflect implicit goals.

Clarification of Issue or Goal

Off the "top of your head" write the issue or goal area that you think this group is working on:

When you have written the issue or goal, compare it with what others have written. If all agree, turn to page 9; if not, turn to the next page and Trap Two.

> *Avoid Trap 2*—arguing about the issue or goal of your group.

Rather, inquire into the understanding of each member and then either

1. agree on a *common issue*, or if you cannot agree soon,

2. split into separate action or recommendation groups.

Write the issue below.

You are ready to begin solving the problem.

Your TASK is to work on your issue and eventually to come up with a recommendation to the appropriate decision-making group (or no recommendation if you so choose), or plans for further work which may result in a recommendation of action on your part.

The product—a recommendation or action—is most likely to be effective if you use the following steps.

1. Make sure you are clear on the issue (see page 7).
2. Analyze before solving (see page 10).
3. *Brainstorm* action ideas (see page 16).
4. Select action ideas (see page 18).
5. Write out recommendation (see page 19).
6. Report out (see page 21).

This booklet guides you in a *problem-solving process* which may help you avoid the common traps groups fall into when trying such a task. If you have trouble, see postscript 1.

This is an analysis of your issue.

> It will help *avoid Trap 3*—the premature suggestion of solutions before a careful analysis.

List forces° preventing you from reaching your goal or preventing you from finding an effective solution.

WORK ALONE . . .

_____

_____

_____

Write your group's issue in this box:

```
┌─────────────────────────────────────┐
│                                      │
│                                      │
│                                      │
│                                      │
└─────────────────────────────────────┘
```

. . . and then turn the page.

°forces may be personal, interpersonal, institutional, societal; they may be values, conflicts, attitudes, a lack of skills or knowledge or time or energy, power conflicts, poor communication. See postscript 2 for a rationale.

Start by writing each individual's forces on newsprint. Now discuss what each has written in an inquiry mode (*i.e.*, paraphrase, try to understand rather than disagree, help each person illustrate his point).

Add additional forces as they occur.

Avoid Trap 4—arguing during this step.

Critical judgment is crucial to problem-solving *but not at this time.* This is a time to *suspend* critical judgment and let your mind expand by understanding the view of others. Create an accepting, inventive mood in your group rather than a fighting, competitive mood.

Put up an INFORMATION NEEDED newsprint sheet at this time. As forces are being clarified, keep asking, "What additional data do we need?" Whenever there is a clear difference of opinion, do not waste time arguing. Rather, clarify what information is needed and check with the resources available for the requested data. You may eventually differ—even turn in counter-recommendations—but get to the facts first.

Assign someone to "bird-dog" that chart by continually asking, "Do we need more facts?"

Now is the time to use CRITICAL JUDGMENT.

1. Go over the forces and agree on the 3, 4, 5, or 6 forces that you think are most important.

2. Rate the forces just chosen for solvability (by you or someone available).

3. Circle the solvable, important forces.

Avoid Trap 5—endlessly discussing or arguing about unsolvable items or opinions without accurate data.

Avoid Trap 6—ranking (*i.e.*, 1st, 2nd, 3rd); rather, choose several forces that rate "most" important, "less" important, and "least" important.

You've been working on a task.

Like a car, a group needs maintenance. While working on a *task* a group needs to be explicit about its problem-solving and interpersonal process.

> *Avoid Trap 7*—working on a task as if you can avoid the maintenance of the group and still have a good product.

(Turn the page immediately after reading this.)

Fill in this sheet individually. Then read page 15 before discussing it. You will be asked to share what you write with the others.

(Circle a number)

What I say is prized and valued here	6	5	4	3	2	1	What I say is being ignored here

Our group is falling into traps	6	5	4	3	2	1	Our group is avoiding traps

When you have completed this form, *but before talking*, turn the page.

Read this page; then talk about your rating.

HELPFUL You will tend to be *helpful* when you are specific (*i.e.*, "I felt prized by you, John, because often you asked me to say more when I spoke," or "An example of when I thought we fell into a trap is . . ." or "I felt put down when you . . .").

NOT HELPFUL You will tend to be judgmental and *not helpful* when you are general and evaluative (*i.e.*, "You're the kind of person who puts people down," or "This group isn't working well").

Now, talk about your ratings using specific illustrations. Pay special attention to different ratings. Invite those whose perceptions differ from yours to describe what they saw. Plan ways to improve your group's effectiveness during your work on the rest of your issue.

Take 10 to 15 minutes for this discussion. When it is completed, turn the page.

> Turn to postscript 3 for a further rationale.

Now, write on newsprint the several important, solvable forces arrived at from the instructions on page 12.

This is another time to suspend critical judgment.

On newsprint, brainstorm ways (action ideas) to reduce the restraining forces.

Brainstorm . . . . nobody says "No."

Brainstorm . . . . nobody says "It will never work."

Brainstorm . . . . nobody says "That's a poor (or good) idea."

Brainstorm . . . . nobody says "That has already been mentioned."

When you run out of brainstorming ideas, turn the page.

Next, using an inquiry mode (see postscript 1 to review the inquiry mode), work for a clear understanding on each of the action ideas. (During this inquiry, you may wish to restate any ideas that are unclear.)

Continue to *suspend critical judgment* until after clarification is completed.

After clarification, turn the page.

This is another time to use critical judgment.

1. Select several action ideas.

2. Decide what group, groups, person, or persons should expedite these.

3. Formulate these into recommendations.°

If your group is developing its own *action* strategy as a part of its recommendation or instead of its recommendation, heed this

WARNING:

If you want action, do not leave this meeting until you know clearly WHO will do WHAT, WHEN, HOW, and HOW you will know it gets done.

°If your group is not turning in a recommendation, use postscript 4 rather than the form on the next page.

This recommendation is addressed to: _____

(Appropriate decision-making body)

RECOMMENDATION:

Names and phone numbers of work group members (asterisk the two who are to be contacted if necessary):

> You may turn in more
> than one recommendation.

Check with your "appropriate decision-making body" to see if that group will make the following commitment. Perhaps they will be even more specific.

**"WE WILL DO OUR BEST TO HAVE ALL
RECOMMENDATIONS RESPONDED TO IN A WAY
THAT YOU CONSIDER RESPONSIBLE."**

If there is to be a report meeting:

1. Check the amount of time you have been given.

2. Choose a spokesman.

3. Let him practice on you.

4. Help him revise or shorten his report.

> In large programs, 30-second reports have been found to be effective—in fact, exciting.

Report the issue, the important and solvable forces, and the recommendation.

If you have trouble:

A disagreement is inevitable. It is neither desirable nor undesirable. Disagreement is important to the health of your group. Each of you is different. You will be likely, therefore, to disagree.

However, a disagreement will be destructive if it is:

1. avoided
2. exclusively argumentative (I disagree and must convince you).

It will be constructive if it is done in an inquiry mode.

Inquiry Mode:

I disagree and want to find out:

1. Do I understand your viewpoint correctly?
2. What assumptions or opinions or facts do you have that cause you to take that point of view?
3. What information can we request from available resources to help our inquiry?

In an Inquiry Mode:

I can paraphrase (repeat to you the meaning—not the exact words—I received) and have you correct my understanding.

I can inquire into your assumptions, opinions, or facts.

I can invite you to do the same to me.

If it seems to a third party that there is a disagreement and no change in point of view, or if persons persist in arguing or avoiding without inquiry, you may:

1. follow the suggestions on page 8.
2. take a personal risk (maybe without group approval) and call in a consultant. Perhaps consultants or resource leaders are on call who will move into your group.

Rationale for looking at restraining forces

You are asked to focus on restraining forces because these are frequently overlooked.

Change will happen when the real restraining forces are reduced. Remember that the forces you have listed are opinions and not necessarily facts. Keep asking, "How can we know whether these forces are really operating?" Use your Information Needed sheet and check with outside resources when needed.

Do not assume that your forces are accurate. Check them out or acknowledge that they are private opinions, perhaps incorrect.

How about a *supporting force* or forces pushing *towards* the goal you want? You may want to list them and (when you get to page 16) suggest ways to use them to achieve your goal or resolve your issue successfully.

A further rationale for looking at process

The deeply personal and human feelings of being prized or ignored, whether they are influential or not, can and must be understood in order to increase the probability of success in a problem-solving situation.

If these feelings are not taken into account, creativity is stifled, and problem-solving is adversely affected.

Look at it this way:

You have a task to complete.

You are working on the task in a certain way or with a certain *process*.

The two questions asked on page 14 are about the process of working. It's like stopping at a service station for maintenance.

Information requested from the secretaries of work groups that do not turn in a recommendation:

A. State the issue:

B. List forces arrived at by directions on page 12, item 3:

C. Why didn't you turn in a recommendation?

D. Further plans of your group to meet, if any.

E. List the members of your group and phone numbers:

Put asterisks by two persons on the list who are to be called if necessary for further information.

Secretary's Name _____ Phone _____

133. FARM E-Z: A MULTIPLE-ROLE-PLAY, PROBLEM-SOLVING EXPERIENCE

Goals

I. To study the sharing of information in task-oriented groups.

II. To learn to distinguish a true problem from those which are only symptomatic.

III. To observe problem-solving strategies within a group.

Group Size

Unlimited number of five-person groups.

Time Required

Approximately two hours.

Materials

I. For each five-person group the following packets are prepared. Each contains the two sheets coded GNL (General) and the sheets specific to the given role:

New Products Coordinator
NPC: 3 sheets

Sales Manager   SM: 12 sheets

Chief Engineer CE: 4 sheets

Manufacturing Superintendent
MFG: 7 sheets

Manager of Accounting
ACCT: 4 sheets

Each package also contains a name tag for that role.

II. A copy of the Farm E-Z Problem Classification Sheet for each participant.

III. A copy of the Farm E-Z Problem Categorization Sheet for each participant.

IV. Pencils for all participants.

Physical Setting

One room large enough so that the five-person groups can work without being disrupted or influenced by other groups. Or, one room large enough to hold all participants for instructions and final discussion, and several smaller rooms where subgroups can work undisturbed during the problem-solving.

Process

I. The facilitator establishes groups of five by any appropriate method.

II. The facilitator distributes the sets of five packets to each group. He explains that, throughout the problem-solving experience, each team member will play the role designated on his name tag. The materials in his packet are designed to assist him in that role. The facilitator announces that the group is to begin its meeting in ten minutes.

III. After the designated study period the groups go to their meeting rooms to begin the problem-solving phase. (A minimum of forty-five minutes is allowed for this step.)

IV. The facilitator distributes the Farm E-Z Problem Classification Sheet and directs the groups to follow its instructions.

V. After all groups have completed the classification task, copies of the Farm E-Z Problem Categorization Sheet are handed out. Groups are instructed to compare their classifications with the "appropriate" one.

VI. Groups are instructed to develop generalizations about the processes that emerged during their original work phase.

VII. The facilitator elicits generalizations from each group about problem-identification strategies.

VIII. The importance of information-sharing and symptoms vs. "real" problems is discussed.

Variations

I. Observers can be assigned to groups to make notes on the problem-solving styles of each. (An example of an appropriate observer sheet can be found in *Vol. IV*, pp. 12-13.)

II. The content can be changed to be more relevant to other groups.

III. The classification of problem areas (step IV in the process) can be done individually or by group consensus.

IV. The group size can be increased to six, with the additional role being the General Manager, who calls the meeting.

Similar Structured Experiences: *Vol. I:* Structured Experience 9, 12; *Vol. II:* 34; *'72 Annual:* 80, 82; *Vol. IV:* 117; *'74 Annual:* 131, 134, 135.

Lecturette Source: *'74 Annual:* "Cybernetic Sessions: A New Technique for Gathering Ideas."

———

Submitted by Jon L. Joyce.

FARM E-Z ITEM GNL-1

For this exercise in problem-solving, you hold the position listed on your packet and name tag.

Background

Farm E-Z has been in operation for fifteen years, serving the East and portions of the Midwest. It has become well established as a producer of a line of on-the-farm, feed grinding and mixing equipment. Annual sales are approximately $4 million. The Farm E-Z production plant in Huntersville employs forty-five men. The following is a partial organization chart of the company:

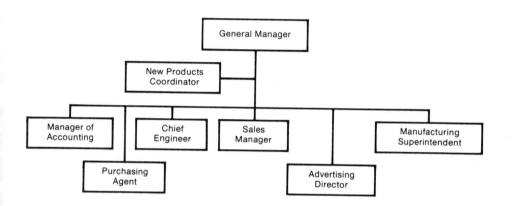

Present Situation

Last year Farm E-Z introduced a new product, a grinder-blower. Priced at about $100 over the market, the new product was designed with some unique and desirable features. One of these, the load-control device, was a special invention of Farm E-Z. The grinder-blower and the grinder-mixer are marketed through thirty-five distributors upon whom Farm E-Z's ten salesmen call.

Although profits at first were as projected, there has been a decided slump during the past six months. The New Products Coordinator, at the urging of the General Manager, has called a meeting to determine why profits on this new product have turned to losses. That meeting is scheduled to begin ten minutes from now. The purpose of the meeting will be to try to identify the problem and search for the best solution to it.

Before the meeting, look over the attached correspondence. It includes correspondence sent *to you* and *by you* to others. The top item of correspondence is an urgent memo from the General Manager to all senior managers. Other items of correspondence will provide you with background information to prepare you for the meeting.

FARM E-Z ITEM GNL-2

URGENT

TO: Senior Managers

FROM: General Manager   SUBJECT: Losses on grinder-blower

Immediate consideration needs to be given to the critical situation
regarding losses on the grinder-blower which we introduced a year ago.

Records of sales, costs, and profit/loss by quarters over the past
year are as follows:

Quarter	Number Sold	Gross Sales	Direct Cost	Profit/Loss
2nd, last year	185	$110,000	$93,000	+ $17,000
3rd, last year	180	108,000	92,400	+ 15,600
4th, last year	90	54,000	76,200	- 22,200
1st, this year	75	45,000	73,500	- 28,500

Obviously, we have not regained the 2nd and 3rd quarter trend towards
profit. Neither were we correct in assuming that the winter months
were "just lagging" in profits. I am asking this group to find out
what the *real* problems are.

FARM E-Z ITEM NPC-1

FARM E-Z MEMORANDUM

TO: New Products Coordinator

FROM: Purchasing Agent   SUBJECT: Grinder-blower

We just received a report that the Switch Company will probably be on
strike within a week, and that it will be a long one!

The Switch Company has been supplying the bearings for the grinder-
blower since we began to produce it last year. We ought to make sure
that we need this high-quality bearing because prices have increased
considerably in the last six months.

If you could convince the Chief Engineer and the Manufacturing Superintendent to make some changes in the bearing specs, the cost
problem--and profit problem--of the grinder-blower would be solved.
I can get a good quality main support bearing for at least $35 less
each ($70 per grinder-blower) and with an assured supply, if they
will only change their specs slightly.

FARM E-Z ITEM NPC-2

New Products Coordinator
Farm E-Z, Inc.
Huntersville

Dear Mr. New Products Coordinator:

I have been a distributor of Farm E-Z's products for nearly all the years that Farm E-Z has been in business, and I have never run into a problem like the one we have been having with the grinder-blower. It has trouble with the load control, mostly. I know your company is working on that and I am sure it will be solved.

Also, your grinder-blower is priced too high. For $100 less, farmers in our area can buy a competitive product that will do the job just as well as yours. And, I can make more, if I wanted to, by selling the Mix-Well line. Their margin is a lot more than the 15% margin we get on yours.

It's not causing me a great deal of trouble, because not many are buying it, and I only keep one or two on hand...but it must be a real headache for you. I understand from the Sales Manager that you are the one responsible for this new machine and I thought I'd drop you a line to suggest that you might want to re-think the problems of cost and margin. Maybe the thing just ought to be dropped. Hope this has helped.

Sincerely,

Bill Dodson, Farm E-Z Distributor

FARM E-Z ITEM NPC-3

General Manager
Farm E-Z, Inc.
Huntersville

Dear General Manager:

I have been a customer of Farm E-Z for ten years and have been highly satisfied with all the products I've bought from you.

And now, you introduce a new grinder-blower, just at the time when I was considering buying one. When I saw the ads, I thought, "Great!" Then I saw the price. Your other products don't seem to be over-priced, but $700 for the grinder-blower is a bit much--especially when I compared prices and discovered that not one well-known brand comes even within $50 of your cost. Most are about $100 less.

I'd surely like to buy Farm E-Z, but a dollar is a dollar. Can something be done about the price?

Sincerely yours,

Harry Gillmore,
Profittown

FARM E-Z ITEM SM-1

TO: Sales Manager

FROM: Advertising Director   SUBJECT: Grinder-blower

I would like to suggest to you that we might increase profits on the grinder-blower by further advertising which would increase sales.

If the advertising budget could be upped just 4% for the next three months, we could increase our advertising as follows:

- Increase direct mail advertising 10%
- Add several radio spots in crucial farm areas
- Increase magazine advertising 3%

That, plus a new tack in the advertising--to suggest that the grinder-blower is better than any other and that's why it costs a bit more-- ought to do the trick!

FARM E-Z ITEM SM-2

General Manager
Farm E-Z, Inc.
Huntersville

Dear Sir:

Last summer I bought one of your new grinder-blowers, having heard about its tremendous value from a neighbor of mine. I had also seen a couple of your ads. However, I am disgusted with the thing. I have had the Distributor service it three times. They keep trying to repair it, but we don't seem to get it working for long. Since I'm not getting anywhere with them, I thought I would write directly to you.

The problem isn't a very big one, I guess. It's the load control that keeps going on the bum. It does cause great inconvenience and loss of valuable time. After all, when you pay as much as $700 for a thing like that, you expect it to work!

Do something about it, please.

Sincerely yours,

Jethro Pearson

FARM E-Z ITEM SM-3

FARM E-Z MEMORANDUM

TO: Sales Manager

FROM: Manufacturing Superintendent   SUBJECT: Returns of Grinder-
blowers

For your information: We have had to take back, from dissatisfied
customers, a good number of grinder-blowers over the past three
quarters.

Returns, since the product was introduced a year ago:

QUARTER	NUMBER RETURNED
2nd quarter, last year	None
3rd quarter, last year	3
4th quarter, last year	6
1st quarter, this year	8

We have been forced to take these back because the salesmen have not
been competent in handling complaints from customers.

FARM E-Z ITEM SM-4

TELEGRAM

GENERAL MANAGER FARM E-Z INC STOP WHAT ARE YOU TRYING TO DO TO US
ANYWAY STOP I AM GETTING FED UP WITH TRYING TO FIND OUT ANYTHING IN
THIS COMPANY STOP ALL I GET OUT OF YOUR SALESMEN IS PRESSURE TO SELL
YOUR NEW PRODUCTS BUT NO HELP STOP IF YOU REALLY WANTED US TO SELL
YOUR NEW GRINDER BLOWER YOU WOULD PROVIDE A DECENT DISTRIBUTOR MARGIN
STOP CANCELLING DISTRIBUTORSHIP CONTRACT IMMEDIATELY STOP
JIM HUTCHINSON FARM E-Z DISTRIBUTOR

FARM E-Z ITEM SM-5

FARM E-Z MEMORANDUM

TO: Sales Manager

FROM: Salesman Petroski

Been thinking about the new grinder-blower.

You know, part of the problem might be that you are not offering enough
incentive to the Farm E-Z salesmen. $20 per unit is not much when you
consider the size of the average purchase. Maybe everyone would get
out and work harder if the personal reward were greater.

You know the old story about the carrot?

FARM E-Z ITEM SM-6

FARM E-Z MEMORANDUM

TO: Sales Manager

FROM: Manufacturing Superintendent   SUBJECT: Production Capability

The production capability of our plant, as presently set up, is 105 of the grinder-blowers per month. We have not been geared to this, although we could handle 105.

Originally, because of sales projections, we produced 90 each of the first six months it was on the market. In December, we reduced production to 80. In February, we cut back to 50.

If we could change our plant set-up, we could possibly produce as many as 175 a month, should the market warrant such production.

It is possible that our present set-up may need revision, anyway, in order to continue present production capabilities. New Union rules as to job descriptions indicate that we may need to hire a few more new men to work on the grinder-blower. (We already know we need three more men to keep up production of other lines.)

Can sales sustain a production of 175 units per month twelve months from now?

FARM E-Z ITEM SM-7

FARM E-Z MEMORANDUM

TO: Sales Manager

FROM: General Manager   SUBJECT: Salesman Turnover

What is happening to our salesmen? My memory has been jogged on the losses we have been having when I studied the payroll list this morning. So, I looked it up and discovered that we lost two good salesmen three years ago, three good salesmen two years ago, and four good salesmen last year. Why? Can't something be done to correct this?

FARM E-Z ITEM SM-8

FARM E-Z MEMORANDUM

TO: Sales Manager

FROM: General Manager   SUBJECT: Grinder-blower

While I think that your advertising of the grinder-blower has just been "all right," I don't think it's been up to the usual good work you and the Advertising Director produce.

Think about ways we can strengthen our advertising on it and bring me some ideas.

A few thoughts that occurred to me:

- Emphasize its economy even more than you have.
- Compare it to our biggest competitor, by name--get details from engineering.
- Develop testimonials from happy customers (users).
- Develop more promotional material for distributor use.

FARM E-Z ITEM SM-9

FARM E-Z MEMORANDUM

TO: Sales Manager

FROM: Harold Dropwatter, Salesman   SUBJECT: Grinder-blower

I need some help. I'll be at the plant office next week, but I thought I'd send this memo in advance so maybe we can get our heads together to come up with some answers for me.

The problem is this: Distributors are reporting customer irritation with the grinder-blower. Apparently, it's nothing terribly serious-- but it is causing a lot of service calls. And--I frankly don't know how to handle the distributors or the customers (I've encountered a few really "hot" ones) on this.

Plus, distributors are not at all interested in emphasizing the grinder-blower to their customers. They say that it's too much trouble to fix the part causing most of the problems. I've told distributors over and over the advantages of selling our grinder-blower, but no dice.

See you next week.

FARM E-Z ITEM SM-10

Sales Manager
Farm E-Z, Inc.
Huntersville

Dear Sales Manager:

I've been a Farm E-Z distributor for over ten years now, and I can't remember a time when I ever wrote the company with a complaint. This one isn't really earth-shaking, but it has been persistent over the past year or so and I thought I'd call it to your attention so you can do something about it. It may help you--and it will certainly help me if something can be done.

The salesmen who have called on me over this past year just plain don't seem to know what they're talking about--especially in terms of that grinder-blower you started sometime last year.

Can you do something about this? I do like the new salesmen--don't get me wrong. I just can't get the proper information out of them. I've told the new man that I was going to write to you, because I've told him the same thing I've just told you.

Sincerely yours,

Carson Treadwile

FARM E-Z ITEM SM-11

FARM E-Z MEMORANDUM

TO: Sales Manager

FROM: Tom Matthison, Salesman   SUBJECT: Groaning About Grinders

Our new grinder-blower isn't doing so well. My distributors just can't seem to move them. And they are also wondering why we took on the line. I keep telling them it's a big new profit opportunity but they don't seem to be interested in expanding their line.

Anyway, sales don't look so good this month. I'd sure like some advice on how to get this thing moving. I'll call you in a few days.

FARM E-Z ITEM SM-12

FARM E-Z MEMORANDUM

TO: Sales Manager

FROM: Bob Johnston, Salesman

Just wanted you to know that this looks like a good month for our
grinder-blower. Distributor Ken Perkins has sold five this month
alone. With only two weeks of the month gone, I am already over
quota.

I think it's a great product.

FARM E-Z ITEM CE-1

FARM E-Z MEMORANDUM

TO: Chief Engineer

FROM: Manufacturing Superintendent   SUBJECT: Grinder-blower

The problem of assembling the grinder-blower seems to get worse, not
better. The process you designed for the final assembly of the
grinder-blower involves way too much backtracking. Machines and men
seem to just run around, back and forth. It is a real problem--and
a waste of time and effort that is undoubtedly causing some of the
profit loss we are experiencing.

Therefore, I suggest that you redesign the process. I'll be glad to
consult with you on it. It is probably the key to the problems we are
having with the machine.

The men in the plant, I am sure, will be able to produce more efficiently with a simpler process--a straight one with no backtracking.
They complain about this a lot--and I can see that it slows them
down, too.

FARM E-Z ITEM CE-2

TO: Chief Engineer

FROM: Staff Engineer   SUBJECT: Production of Grinder-
blower

I have been studying the problem of profit loss on the grinder-blower.
It seems to me that we could cut production costs if we did the
following:

- Combine the stamping processes for stamping shell and top
  cover into one, instead of two, processes. This would
  cut waste by 15%.
- Use another alloy in the gears (I've just found a better,
  cheaper alloy) which would cut costs 10%.
- Rearrange the assembly so that the flailer is assembled
  just prior to installation rather than separately. This
  would save time, and, I estimate, cut costs 5%.

These changes would require only minimal change in the production
line, but would offer these benefits:

- Make the machine more durable.
- Cut production costs by 20%.

FARM E-Z ITEM CE-3

FARM E-Z MEMORANDUM

TO: Chief Engineer

FROM: Project Engineer   SUBJECT: Grinder-blower

I know we have been getting a lot of complaints about the new load-
control device. We have now completed a considerable amount of
rechecking to determine if there were some problems in the device
that we were unaware of. The tests included some 450 hours of
running time using the new load control. We encountered *absolutely
no trouble.*

On *all* of the load controls returned because of customer complaints
we have found faulty adjustment. Admittedly, the new load control
is a more sophisticated piece of equipment than the distributors
have encountered to date, but that is no excuse for the shoddy
service work they have been performing to date.

Anyway, all of the problems seem to be in getting the field service
men to make the proper adjustments on the equipment when it is
installed and at service-call intervals.

FARM E-Z ITEM CE-4

General Manager
Farm E-Z, Inc.
Huntersville

Dear General Manager:

After four service calls to have the load control on my new Farm E-Z grinder-blower fixed, I told your distributor to keep the damn thing and that I was going to write to you to register a complaint. In fact, I've been so mad I have thought of suing you for false advertising. Your distributor encouraged me to write to you.

Anyway, the load control on the thing is just plain faulty. And I just don't have time to fool around with it.

Just when you need it, it quits!

You keep this up and Farm E-Z will be a bad name around here. I've a neighbor who has the same trouble with his, and I've heard from a few others the same thing.

Disgustedly yours,

Tom MacFarland

FARM E-Z ITEM MFG-1

FARM E-Z MEMORANDUM

TO: Sales Manager

FROM: Manufacturing Superintendent   SUBJECT: Returns of Grinder-blowers

For your information: We have had to take back, from dissatisfied customers, a good number of grinder-blowers over the past three quarters.

Returns, since the product was introduced a year ago:

QUARTER	NUMBER RETURNED
2nd quarter, last year	None
3rd quarter, last year	3
4th quarter, last year	6
1st quarter, this year	8

We have been forced to take these back because the salesmen have not been competent in handling complaints from customers.

FARM E-Z ITEM MFG-2

FARM E-Z MEMORANDUM

TO: Sales Manager

FROM: Manufacturing Superintendent   SUBJECT: Production Capability

The production capability of our plant, as presently set up, is 105 of the grinder-blowers per month. We have not been geared to this, although we could handle 105.

Originally, because of sales projections, we produced 90 each of the first six months it was on the market. In December, we reduced production to 80. In February, we cut back to 50.

If we could change our plant set-up, we could possibly produce as many as 175 a month, should the market warrant such production.

It is possible that our present set-up may need revision, anyway, in order to continue present production capabilities. New Union rules as to job descriptions indicate that we may need to hire a few more men to work on the grinder-blower. (We already know we need three more men to keep up production of other lines.)

Can sales sustain a production of 175 units per month 12 months from now?

FARM E-Z ITEM MFG-3

FARM E-Z MEMORANDUM

TO: Manufacturing Superintendent

FROM: General Foreman   SUBJECT: Discontent in Plant

I want to advise you that there has been considerable upset among the men in the plant during the past three months over the change in pre-work coffee time.

When the men were permitted to have a cup of coffee in the lunch room and exchange the morning's news before beginning their day's work, they seemed content.

Now, since that privilege has been removed--along with the coffee pot--they spend a good bit of time grumbling each morning. It appears, from what I hear and see, that they get started working later than they used to. I wonder if this is not reducing efficiency and productivity.

Please advise.

FARM E-Z ITEM MFG-4

FARM E-Z MEMORANDUM

TO: Manufacturing Superintendent

FROM: Purchasing Agent   SUBJECT: Switch Company--
                                             Possible Strike

The other day we had a telephone call from the Shipping Agent of the
Switch Supply Company saying that they are anticipating a shut-down
strike in a week. They expect the strike would last no longer than
six weeks. He wanted to know how many main bearings we can order
now so that they can supply us out of their present inventory.

I checked inventory: we have only 1,000 bearings in stock.

FARM E-Z ITEM MFG-5

FARM E-Z MEMORANDUM

TO: Chief Engineer

FROM: Manufacturing Superintendent   SUBJECT: Grinder-blower

The problem of assembling the grinder-blower seems to get worse,
not better.

The process you designed for the final assembly of the grinder-blower
involves way too much backtracking. Machines and men seem to just
run around, back and forth. It is a real problem--and a waste of
time and effort that is undoubtedly causing some of the profit loss
we are experiencing.

Therefore, I suggest that you redesign the process. I'll be glad to
consult with you on it. It is probably the whole key to the problems
we are having with the machine.

The men in the plant, I am sure, will be able to produce more
efficiently with a simpler process--a straight one with no backtracking. They complain about this a lot--and I can see that it
slows them down, too.

58

FARM E-Z ITEM MFG-6

Manufacturing Superintendent
Farm E-Z, Inc.
Huntersville

Dear Manufacturing Superintendent:

I am calling to your attention--again!--that we of Producers Union
are getting increasingly more upset by the complaints of the men
working in your production plant.

The pitch of the complaining is getting even higher. I do not like
to be a trouble-maker, but rather a trouble-shooter, and I thought
I would write to you, once more, to let you know that I think the
grumbling from the men is about at the explosion point. I like to
think that, together, we can solve this problem.

It seems that the men are quite upset over the changes that keep
coming in the production of the grinder-blower. They have been
trained for their jobs, and these continuing changes in production
and assembly leave them feeling as if they are incompetent.
Really, they are not; but they are entitled, *by contract,* to having
the same, secure job.

I suggest that you look into this immediately. It appears that this
might be reducing efficiency for you. It certainly is causing us
problems. I will investigate further.

Sincerely yours,

Mr. Union Steward

FARM E-Z ITEM MFG-7

FARM E-Z MEMORANDUM

TO: Manufacturing Superintendent

FROM: Manager of Accounting   SUBJECT: Profit loss on
                                              Grinder-blower

Urgently call to your attention the surplus parts inventory we are
carrying for the grinder-blower. At present, we have a $50,000
inventory which we are not using. The interest on that capital
investment amounts to $3,000 a year in profits!

FARM E-Z ITEM ACCT-1

FARM E-Z MEMORANDUM

TO: Manufacturing Superintendent

FROM: Manager of Accounting   SUBJECT: Profit loss on
                                                 Grinder-blower

Urgently call to your attention the surplus parts inventory we are
carrying for the grinder-blower. At present, we have a $50,000
inventory which we are not using. The interest on that capital
investment amounts to $3,000 a year in profits!

FARM E-Z ITEM ACCT-2

FARM E-Z MEMORANDUM

TO: Manager of Accounting

FROM: Purchasing Agent   SUBJECT: .018" Sheet Steel
                                                 for Grinder-blower

We have just been advised by the American Steel Company that the
sheet steel we are using on the grinder-blower will go up, effective
the first of next month--3%.

In reviewing the records on .018" sheet steel, I note that the price
has gone up three times since we began producing the grinder-blower:

- August--1%
- October--an additional 1%
- December--another 2%

And, now, this new rise. I call it to your attention, aware that
profits on the grinder-blower are in serious trouble.

FARM E-Z ITEM ACCT-3

FARM E-Z MEMORANDUM

TO: Manager of Accounting

FROM: Purchasing Agent   SUBJECT: Alloys in Grinder-blower

Not only has the cost of the alloy used in the gears of the grinder-
blower gone up, but we are having a difficult time keeping our
receiving records in agreement with their shipping records and
invoices. The cost of the alloy rose 2% last month.

FARM E-Z ITEM ACCT-4

FARM E-Z MEMORANDUM

TO: Manager of Accounting

FROM: Bookkeeper   SUBJECT: Expense Accounts

You asked me to keep an eye on salesmen expense accounts and report any unusual rises.

Two months ago there was an increase in expense account total of $1\frac{1}{2}$%--but I wasn't concerned because I knew general costs were rising.

However, last month, and again this month, expense account charges have gone up considerably:

- Last month--up 3%
- This past month--up another $3\frac{1}{2}$%.

FARM E-Z PROBLEM CLASSIFICATION SHEET

Instructions: Classify each of the following problem statements into one of the four categories by placing an "x" in the appropriate columns.

Problem Area	Symptom	True Problem	Future Problem	Not Relevant
1. Distributors and salesmen not satisfied with the new line				
2. Insufficient training on servicing the load control				
3. Salesmen who cannot explain how to sell the grinder-blower to the distributor				
4. Rate of service calls for load control				
5. Insufficient salesman training on marketing the product				
6. Distributors not pushing the new line				
7. Insufficient distributor training on marketing the product				
8. Insufficient advertising				
9. Salesman turnover				
10. Production capabilities				
11. Distributor cancellation				
12. Grinder-blower returns				
13. Complaints about over-priced grinder-blower				
14. Union complaint				
15. Grinder-blower assembly				
16. Switch company strike				
17. Bearing quality				
18. Pre-work coffee time				
19. Gear alloy				
20. Salesmen expense accounts				
21. Cost of steel				
22. Surplus stock inventory				
23. Salesman incentive				
24. Distributor margin				

FARM E-Z PROBLEM CATEGORIZATION SHEET

Below are listed the appropriate problem classifications. Compare them with the ones you selected on the Farm E-Z Problem Classification Sheet.

Problem Area	Symptom	True Problem	Future Problem	Not Relevant
1. Distributors and salesmen not satisfied with the new line	X			
2. Insufficient training on servicing the load control		X		
3. Salesmen who cannot explain how to sell the grinder-blower to the distributor	X			
4. Rate of service calls for load control	X			
5. Insufficient salesman training on marketing the product		X		
6. Distributors not pushing the new line	X			
7. Insufficient distributor training on marketing the product		X		
8. Insufficient advertising				X
9. Salesman turnover	X			
10. Production capabilities				X
11. Distributor cancellation	X			
12. Grinder-blower returns	X			
13. Complaints about over-priced grinder-blower	X			
14. Union complaint			X	
15. Grinder-blower assembly			X	
16. Switch company strike			X	
17. Bearing quality				X
18. Pre-work coffee time				X
19. Gear alloy				X
20. Salesmen expense accounts				X
21. Cost of steel				X
22. Surplus stock inventory				X
23. Salesman incentive		X		
24. Distributor margin		X		

134. HUNG JURY:
A DECISION-MAKING SIMULATION

Goal

To study decision-making processes.

Group Size

Groups of five to twelve participants each.

Time Required

Approximately two hours.

Materials

I. Hung Jury Case Packets A and B for each participant: (A) State of California vs. Ralph B. Anderson, and (B) State of California vs. Leonard A. Walsh.

II. Copies of Hung Jury Verdict Sheets (A and B) for each participant.

III. Paper and pencil for each participant.

Physical Setting

A large room where groups can be seated around tables. These tables should be located in such a way that groups cannot overhear each other.

Process

I. The facilitator explains to the participants that they will engage in a decision-making experience that simulates a jury at work on criminal cases.

II. He divides the participants into groups or uses existing groups and seats them at the tables around the room.

III. The facilitator distributes the first Case Packets and a supply of pencils and paper to each group. He explains that group members will function as a jury which will have thirty minutes in which to vote on a final verdict of guilty or not guilty. They

may vote as many times as they wish, but they must come up with a final vote count at the end of the time limit. If they are unable to reach a unanimous decision, they must submit the last vote taken before the session ends. The facilitator adds that they may elect a foreman if they wish, but this must be done by majority vote.

IV. The facilitator tells the juries when to begin and does not interrupt the session once it has begun except to announce the time in ten-minute intervals.

V. When the first session is finished, the facilitator indicates that juries are to discuss the processes that emerged during the decision-making. Afterwards, he distributes the Jury Verdict Sheets for the first case.

VI. He distributes the second Case Packets and begins the timing again.

VII. When the second session is finished, groups discuss the decision-making processes that they experienced during the two cases. Any differences in the two experiences are isolated and discussed.

VIII. The facilitator leads the entire group in a discussion of the various processes which emerged in reaching the verdicts, such as consensus-seeking pressure by group leaders, and the various roles that participants played.

Additional Note

These cases were presented to one of the district attorneys in Pomona, California, in order to determine whether there was enough evidence to support the stated decisions. After reviewing both cases, he decided the decisions would be supported in a court of law.

Variations

I. If time is limited, only one case can be used. The session can also be split in the middle for two one-hour periods.

II. An intergroup competition can be established, with winning based on scoring the final votes as follows:
+ 10 points for each correct vote;
− 15 points for each incorrect vote;
− 15 points for each abstention.
Each group computes its net score.

III. New groups can be formed for the second case materials.

IV. The structured experience can be used as a diagnostic activity for an intact work group such as a committee or team.

Similar Structured Experiences: *Vol. II:* Structured Experience 29, 31; *'72 Annual:* 77, 80; *Vol. IV:* 102, 103, 117; *'74 Annual:* 135.

Lecturette Sources: *'73 Annual:* "Synergy and Consensus-Seeking."

Submitted by Stephen C. Iman, Blake D. Jones, and A. Steven Crown.

HUNG JURY PACKET A
State of California vs. Ralph B. Anderson

Item 1.   Instructions to the Jury

On May 24, 1974, Ralph B. Anderson was brought to court and tried for the murder of
Stanley M. Walker. You are the jury involved in this case and it is your job, based on
the information provided, to determine whether or not Mr. Anderson is guilty or not
guilty. Submit your decision to the bailiff once a decision has been reached. If no
unanimous decision can be reached, submit the results of the last vote taken before
the end of the session.

Item 2.   Coroner's Report: 5/14/74

Deceased: Stanley Martin Walker
            987 East Elm Ave. (Cyprus Apts.)
            Apartment 1B
            Colby, California

Age: 42
Height: 5'11"
Weight: 175
Race: Caucasian
Hair: Black
Eyes: Brown

Occupation: C.P.A. of First United Bank, Colby Branch.
Cause of Death: The deceased was shot by a .32 caliber pistol in the head and in the
                 shoulder.
Time of Death: Between 1:10-1:15 AM.
Location: 987 East Elm Ave., Apt. 1B, Colby, California.
Remarks: Victim was dead on arrival at Imperial Valley Hospital. Autopsy
                 revealed two slugs from a .32 caliber pistol, one lodged in the
                 brain and one lodged below the left clavicle. No other internal or
                 external injuries were noted.

/S/ William H. Stone, Coroner

Item 3. Summary of Testimony by: Mr. John R. Adams
987 East Elm Ave. (Cyprus Apts.)
Apartment 1A
Colby, California

Mr. Adams, 47, manager of the Canfield Department Store, testified that at approximately ten minutes after one in the morning on May 14, while he was getting into bed, he was disturbed by what he thought were firecrackers. He said that the neighborhood kids were constantly setting them off and that it was about time for him to put an end to it. He turned on the light, got out of bed, and went to the window. Looking out of the window, he saw some kids across the street in an alley. He went back to his closet, put on a robe, and went out the door. As he was going out the door of his ground floor apartment, he saw a man dressed in a blue business suit run from his neighbor's apartment down the hall and quickly turn the corner, heading in the direction of the parking lot. Although confused and startled by what had transpired, he noticed that his neighbor's door had been left wide open. Upon entering the room, he found the body of his neighbor, Stanley Walker, on the living room floor, apparently shot in the head. Mr. Adams then stated that he heard the screech of tires and rushed to the window just in time to see a red convertible tear down the street. When asked how he was sure that it was a red convertible, Mr. Adams explained that the street was adequately lit at the time. (This fact was confirmed by subsequent investigation.) Mr. Adams said he returned to the room and called the police, who arrived minutes later. Mr. Adams claimed that he had gotten a good look at the apparent murderer and could identify him if he saw him again.

Item 4. Summary of Testimony by: Mr. Stuart J. Mills
1786 Park Ave.
Newberry, California

Mr. Mills, 68, security guard of Cyprus Apts., stated that while he was patroling the grounds at around 1:15 AM on May 14, he saw a man wearing a business suit run towards the parking lot, jump into a red convertible, and then drive away at an excessive speed. Mr. Mills said that he was unable to catch a glimpse of the man's face or see the license plate of the vehicle. Further questioning provided no additional information.

Item 5. Summary of Testimony by: Officer Albert Mann
6734 College Street
Colby, California

Officer Mann, 38, police officer of the Colby Police Dept., testified that at 1:20 AM on the morning of May 14, while writing out a speeding ticket for Mr. Ralph Anderson, he received an A.P.B. on any man wearing a business suit driving a red convertible in or near the 900 block of Colby. Since Mr. Anderson's car was a red convertible, and he was wearing a dark business suit and found driving in the vicinity, Officer Mann requested Mr. Anderson to accompany him down to the Police Station for some routine questioning. Mr. Anderson agreed to do so.

Item 6. Summary of Testimony by: Mr. Ralph B. Anderson (Defendant)
1933 Hawthorne Lane
Imperial, California

(After arriving at the police station and being informed of his rights, Mr. Anderson waived the right of the presence of an attorney and offered to answer any questions.)

Mr. Anderson, 37, City Councilman of Imperial, stated that he was guilty of speeding when the officer stopped him. When asked what he was doing in that neighborhood at that hour of night, he said that he had just arrived from a meeting in Redwood City at the Baxter Building, 234 Harrington Street, in which he and other town officials were discussing urban problems. (This information was confirmed by a call to some of the individuals who attended this meeting.) He said that the meeting broke up at about 11:30 PM and he decided to visit some friends who lived in San Bristo on his way home. Once he arrived at their residence at 2324 Orange Ave., he found them not at home and therefore decided to continue to his house to work on some important papers.

Mr. Anderson was then informed that a Mr. Walker had been murdered in his (Walker's) residence and that a man of Anderson's description was seen leaving the scene of the crime driving a red convertible. When Mr. Anderson was asked if he had ever had contact with or known the victim, he stated, "I don't know what the hell this is all about. I hope you realize who you're talking to and that I have some very influential friends in the Police Department. This is an outrage! I've never met this Mr. Walker nor have I been anywhere near his apartment. It's too bad that this guy was shot but you can't hang anything on me. All you've got is circumstantial evidence. Hell, there are a lot of red convertibles in this valley; the Department of Motor Vehicles can probably verify this. I refuse to be interrogated like this until I call my attorney."

Item 7. Police Report

Filed by: Sergeant Patterson and Officer Grant
Date: May 14, 1974
Time   2:45 AM

RE: Based on the information supplied by Mr. John R. Adams, 987 East Elm Ave.,
Apt. 1A, Colby, California, the residence of Mr. Stanley M. Walker was then
inspected for possible clues or evidence relating to the murder. After a thorough investigation the following items were found:

(1) Two glasses of Scotch and soda were found on the coffee table in the living
room. One glass had the fingerprints of the deceased, the second glass
showed signs of having been wiped clean.

(2) Three recently burned Camel cigarettes were found in an ashtray on the
coffee table. (Mr. Walker was known not to have smoked.)

(3) The alleged murder weapon, a .32 caliber pistol, was found behind a chair
in the living room with no fingerprints.

(4) The radio was found on when the police arrived.

(5) An envelope was found in the top dresser drawer of the deceased's bed-
room. Contents: $2000.00 in small bills.

(6) Deceased was shot in the head and shoulder—found DOA.

(7) There was no sign of a struggle anywhere in the apartment.

Witnesses: Mr. John R. Adams—neighbor
987 East Elm Ave. (Cyprus Apts.)
Apt. 1A
Colby, California

Mr. Stuart J. Mills—security guard, Cyprus Apts.
1786 Park Ave.
Newberry, California

Item 8. Police Report

Filed by: Lieutenant Masterson
Date: May 14, 1974
Time: 2:30 AM

RE: Mr. John R. Adams and Mr. Stuart J. Mills were brought down to Police Headquarters for possible identification of the alleged murderer. In separate sessions, both witnesses identified Mr. Ralph Anderson from a line-up as the man
they saw run from the crime. Mr. Adams was willing to sign an affidavit to this
effect; however, Mr. Mills was not sure whether Mr. Anderson was the man he
saw. Mills stated that Anderson looked similar to the man in question.

Other: Mr. Ralph Anderson smoked Camel cigarettes.

Item 9.   Description of Defendant

Name:	Anderson, Ralph Benjamin
Address:	1933 Hawthorne Lane
	Imperial, California
Sex:	Male
Eyes:	Brown
Hair:	Brown
Race:	Caucasian
Birthdate:	2/15/37
Height:	6'1"
Weight:	184
Marital Status:	Single
Social Security:	665-34-8573
Occupation:	City Councilman of Imperial

Item 10.   Mileage Distances

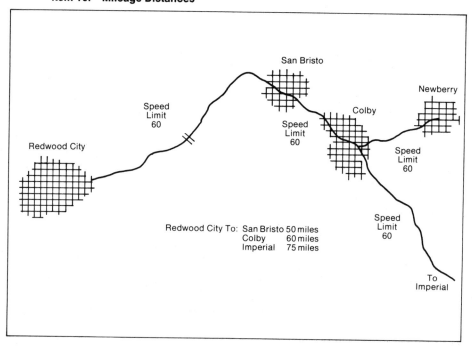

HUNG JURY VERDICT SHEET A

Case: State of California vs. Ralph B. Anderson

Verdict: GUILTY

Reason:
 The defendant, Ralph Anderson, is found guilty because of the following reasons:

(1) The fact that he was wearing a blue business suit and was caught driving a red convertible in the vicinity of the crime shortly after the murder might be considered circumstantial; however, if he is the murderer this fact would not be circumstantial.

(2) There was one eye-witness, Mr. Adams, who was willing to sign an affidavit stating that he saw Mr. Anderson coming out of his neighbor's apartment.

(3) The evidence that makes Anderson truly guilty is that he knew too much about the crime in his testimony. The fact that he denied ever knowing Mr. Walker but knew that he lived in an apartment demonstrates some knowledge of the victim. Finally, Anderson was only informed that Mr. Walker had been murdered, but he knew that the victim had been shot, demonstrating that he knew how the victim had been murdered.

(4) Blackmail is the motive indicated. Mr. Walker was an accountant at a bank and thus had access to the books. Mr. Anderson kept a separate account in Colby where he was unknown, and Walker had knowledge of Mr. Anderson's under-the-table dealings. Since Anderson was a politician, he might have done anything to keep his record clean.

Item 1.   Instructions to the Jury

On June 1, 1974, Leonard Walsh was brought to court and tried for the hit and run death of Susan Moore. You are the jury involved in this case and it is your job, based on the information provided, to determine whether Mr. Walsh is guilty or not guilty. Submit your decision to the bailiff once a decision has been reached. If no unanimous decision can be reached, submit the results of the last vote taken before the end of the session.

Item 2.   Coroner's Report: 5/11/74

Deceased:	Susan D. Moore
	1507 Oak Street
	San Bravura, California

Age:	23
Height:	5'3"
Weight:	112
Race:	Caucasian
Hair:	Blonde
Eyes:	Blue

Cause:	The deceased was struck by an automobile.
Time:	Approximately 6:20-6:30 PM.
Location:	600 Block, 18th Avenue.

Remarks: Victim was dead on arrival at San Bravura Hospital. The victim's body exhibited signs of multiple fractures and abrasions, and severe internal injuries.

/S/ Albert A. Simpson, Coroner

Item 3. Summary of Testimony by: Mrs. Wilma Ferguson
1308 Edwards Street
San Bravura, California

Mrs. Ferguson, 38, housewife, testified that as she came out of the A&P store, 725 18th Avenue, shortly after 6:00 PM that evening, she heard a "screech of tires" and saw the victim, Susan Moore, collapse on impact with the automobile. At this point she dispatched a box boy to summon an ambulance and the police. Mrs. Ferguson then rushed to aid the victim. She remained with the victim until the ambulance arrived, at which point she was questioned by police. Mrs. Ferguson identified the vehicle as a white BMW. As a result of being approximately one-half block away, Mrs. Ferguson said she could not make out the license number of the vehicle. However, she testified that she was sure the vehicle had a blue California license plate. When asked about the nature of the individual operating the alleged white BMW, Mrs. Ferguson stated positively that it was a man. She concluded her testimony by saying the vehicle drove off at a high rate of speed and turned south (right) on Harper Street.

Item 4. Summary of Testimony by: Mr. Barney J. Schaffer
806 Royal Street
San Bravura, California

Mr. Schaffer, co-owner and operator of Barney & Al's Standard Service Station, corner of Royal and 18th, stated he completed the work on Mr. Walsh's vehicle and turned it over to him a little after 6:00 PM on May 11, 1974. Mr. Schaffer testified that he could not recall seeing a dent in the front fender of Mr. Walsh's vehicle. When allowed to see the impounded vehicle, Mr. Schaffer said he was absolutely sure the dent had not been there during the time he worked on the vehicle. Mr. Schaffer was certain that Mr. Walsh proceeded east on 18th Street.

Item 5. Summary of Testimony by: Mr. John L. Richards
1888 Harper Street
San Bravura, California

Mr. Richards, 51, pharmacist, testified that he was walking home from work (Kelley's Drug Store, 1765 King Street), along the 600 block of 18th, when the accident occurred. Although his vision was partially obscured by the parked cars, he was able to see the victim struck. When called on by the police to help identify the vehicle involved, he noted it was a white BMW. He testified that he told police that the license number of the vehicle was 4---IB. Mr. Richards said he could not positively ascertain what the other numbers or letters were. However, he thought that the license was made up of a combination of three numbers followed by three letters. Mr. Richards substantiated the testimony given by Mrs. Ferguson in that it was a man driving; he also added that he believed the man was Caucasian. When asked how he was able to take in all this information from the sidewalk, Mr. Richards revealed that he had dashed into the street upon seeing the victim struck. The defense sought to discredit Mr. Richards' testimony by pointing out that he wears glasses. However, a test of Mr. Richards' vision revealed a 20/20 score with glasses. Mr. Richards concluded his testimony by agreeing with Mrs. Ferguson that the car turned south (right) on Harper Street.

Item 6. Summary of Testimony by: Mr. Leonard A. Walsh (Defendant)
1185 13th Avenue
San Bravura, California

The defendant, 33, Leonard A. Walsh, an architect, testified that he picked up his automobile, a 1969 white BMW, at Barney & Al's Standard Service Station shortly after 6:00 PM, May 11, 1974. It was in for a lube job and oil change. He stated that he had ridden to and from work via RTD. Mr. Walsh testified that he went directly home upon receipt of the keys from Mr. Schaffer, except for a brief stop at McDonald's for dinner. When asked about the dent in the right fender of his car, Mr. Walsh explained that it was due to a bag of fertilizer falling off a shelf, which he had hit while parking in his garage that evening. (Two 50-pound heavy-duty bags of fertilizer were found in Walsh's garage. One bag was open and in the corner of the garage while the other bag was still on a shelf.)

Item 7. Police Report

Filed by: Officers Roarke and Stevens
Date: May 11, 1974
Time: 11:30 PM

RE: Based on information supplied by two witnesses: Mrs. Wilma Ferguson, 1308 Edwards Street; and Mr. John Richards, 1888 Harper Street; and through the use of the computer crime lab, we were able to determine and locate the owner of the alleged hit-and-run vehicle, a Mr. Leonard Walsh, 1185 13th Avenue. The computer was programmed to isolate the number of registered BMWs in the State of California and provide a breakdown as to model, color, year, license number, and owner. Of the 18,567 BMWs in the state, 1271 are white, and only one of them bears the license combination 4---IB. This vehicle belongs to the above mentioned suspect. With this information we were dispatched to locate Mr. Walsh, whom we found in his driveway washing his white BMW. Upon inspection of the exterior of the vehicle, we noted a dent in the front hood and grill. We informed the suspect of the hit-and-run accident and notified him of his rights. He consequently requested the presence of an attorney before he would answer any questions.

Other: A Department of Motor Vehicles check on Mr. Walsh's driving record revealed that he had been issued 3 citations in the past six months. The first one, issued 11/17/73, was for speeding; the subject was cited for doing 40 in a 25-mph zone. The second violation occurred 1/22/74; the subject was cited for doing 65 in a 40-mph zone. The third citation was given to Mr. Walsh on 3/18/74; he was charged with driving while intoxicated. The subject hired a lawyer and succeeded in getting the sentence reduced to negligent driving. The judge, however, saw fit to place Mr. Walsh on probation for a year. Any citation would result in the loss of all driving privileges.

Name: Walsh, Leonard Allan
Address: 1185 13th Avenue
           San Bravura, California
Sex: Male
Eyes: Blue
Hair: Brown
Race: Caucasian
Birthdate: 1/21/41

Height: 5'11"
Weight: 173
Marital Status: Single
Social Security: 534-78-6995
Occupation: Architect

Item 8. Department of Motor Vehicles Report (upon impoundment)

May 11, 1974

Type:	BMW
Year:	1969
Model:	2002, manual transmission
Color:	White
License Number:	416QIB
Registered Owner:	Leonard A. Walsh
	1185 13th Avenue
	San Bravura, California

Condition of Vehicle:

Mileage:	64,874
Body:	dent in right front hood and fender, paint flaking off on doors, dent in left rear fender.
Tires:	worn, bald
Brakes:	worn, in need of repair.
Engine:	good condition, rebuilt at 58,506
Transmission:	good condition
Lubrication:	last oil change, 64,873
Exhaust System:	poor condition, anti-smog device nonfunctional
Other:	Front windshield cracked on driver's side (approximately six inches), two hubcaps missing

Item 9. Map of San Bravura

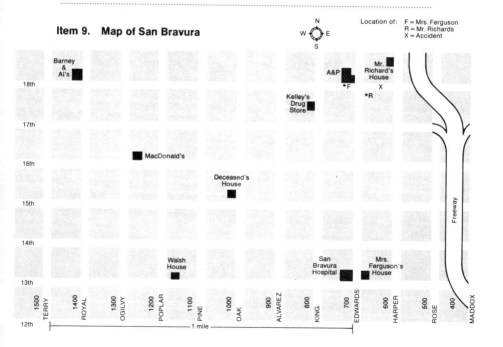

HUNG JURY VERDICT SHEET B

Case: City of San Bravura vs. Leonard A. Walsh

Verdict: NOT GUILTY

Reason:
  The defendant, Leonard A. Walsh, is found not guilty for the following reasons:

(1) The fact that his odometer registered less mileage than was necessary in order to have been involved in the accident and return via the shortest route to his house constitutes reasonable doubt.

(2) The fact that Mr. Walsh's testimony supported the objectivity of his odometer reading further substantiates the claim for reasonable doubt.

(3) The evidence of the license plate number was limited to include only vehicles in the State of California; however, several other states, including New York, also have the blue and gold format.

(4) Finally, the evidence of the positive recognition of the numbers and letters also reinforces the concept of reasonable doubt, for if one looks at the numbers and letters recognized by Mr. Richards, there is a definite possibility that at a quick glance the supposed letters could have been numbers, thus making the license plate from another state.

135. KIDNEY MACHINE: GROUP DECISION-MAKING

Goals

I. To explore choices involving values.

II. To study problem-solving procedures in groups.

III. To examine the impact of individuals' values and attitudes on group decision-making.

Group Size

Any number of groups of five to seven participants each.

Time Required

Approximately one hour.

Materials

I. A copy of the Kidney Machine Description Sheet for each participant.

II. A copy of the Kidney Machine Biographical Sheet for each participant.

III. A copy of the Kidney Machine Psychological Reports Sheet for each participant.

Physical Setting

A circle of chairs for each group, spaced for privacy.

Process

I. The facilitator briefly discusses the goals of the activity. He may wish to begin with a discussion of the role of "values" in group problem-solving, stressing that decision-making is comparatively easy when groups are dealing with factual problems; however, many groups are called upon to deal with problems which are more subjective in nature, for which there is no "correct" answer or "right" solution. Thus, the group must make a reasoned judgment between several possible solutions, perhaps none of which is totally desirable. It is then the task of the group to weigh intangibles and to call upon its sense of values in making the decision.

II. The facilitator forms small groups and distributes copies of the Kidney Machine Description Sheet, the Kidney Machine Biographical Sheet, and the Kidney Machine Psychological Reports Sheet to the participants and allows them a short time to read through the materials. To heighten the realism of the task, he may mention that there really is a Swedish Hospital in Seattle with a kidney machine and that there really are groups of people at that hospital who meet to screen candidates for the machine.

III. The groups are given approximately thirty minutes to arrive at a solution. The facilitator may ask them to specify the criteria they followed in reaching their solution.

IV. When the time is up, the facilitator instructs the groups to evaluate their work in terms of the following:
1. Who their choice was and why.
2. Whether their task would have been easier had they had more information about each candidate.
3. What effect(s) the psychological data had on their decision.
4. To what extent they were motivated to *avoid* making a decision, perhaps by picking a candidate through flipping a coin, drawing straws, or otherwise leaving the matter to chance.
5. To what extent the groups favored novel or unusual solutions, such as proposing that all candidates be attached

to the machine for one-fifth of the time, or proposing that all candidates be allowed to die.

6. To what extent they tried to "objectify" an essentially subjective judgment by working out "formulas," "point systems," etc., for rating the candidates numerically, and whether this was effective.

V. The facilitator may wish to point out that the candidates are actually stereotypes of certain groups of people (*e.g.*, the hard-working scientist, the career woman, the student radical). He may then ask participants to re-evaluate the decision they would have made with different stereotypes (*e.g.*, if Bill were a Black militant).

Variations

I. The candidate biographies can be revised.

II. In an OD workshop, the situation might be changed to determine which employee to retain and which ones to fire during a personnel cutback.

III. To add a "confounding variable" to the problem, the facilitator may wait until the groups are halfway through the task before distributing the Psychological Reports Sheet.

IV. The decision can be made independently by each group member prior to decision-seeking.

V. The consensus task can be changed to make a priority listing of all candidates.

VI. Role-playing can be incorporated into the design in two ways: Patients could appear before the committee, and/or a representative of the committee could inform patients of the results.

Similar Structured Experiences: *'73 Annual:* Structured Experience 94; *Vol. IV:* 115, 124; *'74 Annual:* 134.

Lecturette Sources: *'73 Annual:* "Synergy and Consensus-Seeking," "Some Implications of Value Clarification for Organization Development."

KIDNEY MACHINE DESCRIPTION SHEET

Located at Swedish Hospital in Seattle, Washington, is the famous kidney machine. A marvel of technological ingenuity, it is the only hope of life for people with a rare kidney disease.

In actuality, the machine functions as a kidney for people who have lost the use of their own. By connecting themselves to the machine for twenty-four hours each week, people with renal failure can remain alive indefinitely—or until they are killed by some other ailment not connected with their kidneys.

There are several problems associated with using this machine, for there are many more people who need it than there is time available on the machine. In fact, only about five people can be placed on it at any one time. Doctors examine all potential patients and determine those who could profit most from connection to the machine. They screen out those with other diseases, for whom the machine would be only a temporary expedient, and they turn their list of recommended patients over to the hospital administration. At present, the doctors have submitted the names of five persons for *one* place on the machine.

The committee assembled to make the decision has been given a brief biography of each person appearing on the list. It is assumed that each person has an equal chance of remaining alive if allowed to use the machine. Thus, the committee is asked to decide which *one* of these may have access to the machine.

You are asked to act as if you were a member of this committee. Remember, there is only one vacancy, and you must fill it with one of these five people. You must agree, *unanimously*, on the single person who is to be permitted to remain alive, and you must decide your own criteria for making this choice.

The only medical information you have is that people over forty seem to do poorer on the machine than those under forty (although they do not necessarily find it useless). It is up to you.

© 1974 University Associates Publishers, Inc.

KIDNEY MACHINE BIOGRAPHICAL SHEET

Alfred: White, male, American, age 42. Married for 21 years. Two children (boy 18, girl 15), both high school students. Research physicist at University medical school, working on cancer immunization project. Current publications indicate that he is on the verge of a significant medical discovery.

On the health service staff of local university, member of county medical society, member of Rotary International, and Boy Scout Leader for 10 years.

Bill: Black, male, American, age 27. Married for five years. One child (girl, 3), wife six months pregnant. Currently employed as an auto mechanic in local car dealership.

Attending night school and taking courses in automatic-transmission rebuilding. No community service activities listed. Plans to open auto-transmission repair shop upon completion of trade school course.

Cora: White, female, American, age 30. Married for eleven years. Five children (boy 10, boy 8, girl 7, girl 5, girl 4 months). Husband self-employed (owns and operates tavern and short-order restaurant). High school graduate. Never employed.

Couple has just purchased home in local suburbs, and Cora is planning the interior to determine whether she has the talent to return to school for courses in interior decoration. Member of several religious organizations.

David: White, male, American, age 19. Single, but recently announced engagement and plans to marry this summer. Presently a sophomore at large eastern university, majoring in philosophy and literature. Eventually hopes to earn Ph.D. and become a college professor.

Member of several campus political organizations, an outspoken critic of the college "administration," was once suspended briefly for "agitation." Has had poetry published in various literary magazines around the New York area. Father is self-employed (owns men's haberdashery store), mother is deceased. Has two younger sisters (15, 11).

Edna: White, female, American, age 34. Single, presently employed as an executive secretary in large manufacturing company, where she has worked since graduation from business college. Member of local choral society; was alto soloist in Christmas production of Handel's *Messiah*. Has been very active in several church and charitable groups.

KIDNEY MACHINE PSYCHOLOGICAL REPORTS SHEET

Re: Patients for Kidney Machine
From: Hospital Psychological Staff

In routine preadmission interviews the following patients were examined and evaluated as per the following data:

Re: **Alfred**—He is presently distraught about his physical condition and reports that it interferes with his work. Seems very committed to his work and appears to be legitimately on the verge of an important cancer discovery. It was hard for the staff to get him to talk about his work in terms that they could understand.

Family relations seem strained and have been for some time because of his commitment to his work. The staff feels that he is a first-rate scientist and scholar who has contributed much and could contribute more to medical research. But they also believe him to be a mentally disturbed individual who, in time, will probably need psychiatric help.

Re: **Bill**—He is a well-oriented Negro, who does not appear to be swayed by the blandishments of black extremist groups. He is strongly devoted to his family and appears to be an excellent husband and father.

Bill's capacity for growth in his chosen occupation, however, seems limited. His high school record was poor, although he had no record of delinquency and was always regarded by his teachers as a student who tried hard. Therefore, he will probably not succeed with his business plans and will remain employed at a fixed rate permanently.

His wife is trained as a legal secretary. Her prognosis for employment is good, although Bill has discouraged her from seeking work because of mutual agreement to have her be a full-time mother. Bill seems unaware of the serious implications of his illness.

Re: **Cora**—One of the staff members evaluating Cora described her as a *professional Jew*. She is president of the local Hadassah organization and seems able to talk about nothing but her religion and her children. Although her recently found interest in interior decorating may be a sign of change, it was not clear to the staff whether this interest was real or only generated artificially when she heard of the interview requirement.

She seems resigned to her illness and likely death. Her husband works long hours, is in good health, and enjoys the respect and love of his children. Cora's mother, who also lives with the family, handles most of the child care.

Re: **David**—Typical of young student activists, David is a bright—almost straight "A"—student who enjoys the respect of most of his teachers and friends. But he appears confused about his future and demonstrates a penchant for jeopardizing it by involving himself in various student "causes." Indeed, his college's dean of student affairs regards him as an individual who will "demonstrate for anything."

He is bitter, almost paranoid, about his illness. His father has invested a good deal of money, time, and emotion in him and has always hoped that David would become a lawyer. His relations with his father are presently strained, however, and he seems only mildly concerned about his two sisters, although they still think highly of him. His future father-in-law, who is a highly successful businessman, expects him to enter the family enterprise upon college graduation.

Re: **Edna**—She is a self-contained, inner-directed woman and a model of the "career girl." It was clear to the staff that her natural aggressiveness and combative tendencies militated against any sort of marital attachment, and it is not impossible that she has lesbian tendencies.

Her employers regard her as indispensable. Her work record is superb, and her activities in church and charitable groups have been very effective. She is well regarded by all who know her, although she seems to have few, if any, close friends. She appears resigned to her death. In fact, she indicated that she would prefer to have someone other than herself go on the machine. Her offer did not seem in the least insincere.

136. RELAXATION AND PERCEPTUAL AWARENESS: A WORKSHOP

Goals

I. To learn basic techniques of physical relaxation, breathing processes, and self-awareness.

II. To experience one's physical state of existence and personal perceptions of inner and outer reality and fantasy.

Group Size

Unlimited.

Physical Setting

Preferably outside in a relatively secluded area or a carpeted room large enough to allow for adequate personal space.

Time Required

Three hours.

Materials

I. Blankets or cushions.

II. Record player or tape recorder with mood music recordings.

Process

The workshop is composed of a series of three-step cycles: a breathing exercise, a basic physical relaxation activity, and a short fantasy or Gestalt awareness experience. The breathing and relaxation steps are repeated due to the need for frequent practice if adequate learning is to take place. The alternating fantasy and Gestalt experiences move from simple to complex as the workshop progresses. Each cycle requires approximately fifteen minutes to complete. *It is important to note that after each activity participants should be given time for processing.*[1]

_____

[1]See *Vol. I,* Structured Experience 16, for a brief discussion of considerations concerning the use of fantasy.

I. (A) Breathing exercise: Standing-breathing exercise aids the body in learning to relax and in becoming attuned to its energy flow. It includes using the entire body in learning to breathe from the diaphragm (Brodsky, 1972).

(B) Relaxation: Participants are guided through a complete relaxation of the upper body. This is accomplished by instructing them to sequentially tighten and relax the large muscle groups. Each time they are to note the difference between the tight and relaxed muscle (Jacobsen, 1962).

(C) Fantasy: Participants lie in a comfortable position and get in touch with problems of the day which they have brought with them. They should put these problems, one at a time, into their fantasy closet for future retrieval. The facilitator should attempt to clear their minds of all that is disruptive.

II. (A) Breathing exercise: "Posture of Complete Relaxation" (Savasana). Participants are told to lie flat on the floor, arms extended away from the body, hands open, palms upward, legs apart with feet falling outward, head straight, eyes closed, mouth closed, teeth slightly apart. They are to breathe normally, then change to deep, calm, nasal breathing. Deep breaths should start in the diaphragm and move upward (Zorn, 1968, p. 44, method 2).

(B) In the same reclining position, the participants keep working at total upper-body relaxation by alternating tightening and loosening of the muscle groups.

(C) Still in a reclining position, the participants are instructed to slowly clear their minds of disruptive thoughts.

III. (A) "Abdominal Breathing": The partici-pants lie on the floor, place their fingers on their abdomens, raising their abdomens as they inhale and lowering as they exhale; their fingers rise and fall as they breathe. They should not force their breath. Then participants try the same exercise in sitting and standing positions (Zorn, 1968, p. 46).

(B) Again in a reclining position, members work at relaxing the lower body, using the same method as before.

(C) Remaining in the reclining position, the participants are instructed to become mentally aware of their physical states and clear their minds of disruptive thoughts. They use that awareness to direct their fan-tasies.

IV. (A) The "Victorious Breath": Sitting up-right on their heels in the "Thunderbolt Posture" (Vajrasana), the participants breathe in deeply through both nostrils, hold their breath, and exhale vigorously through the mouth, stretching the entire set of face muscles (Ujjayi).

(B) In a reclining position, the partici-pants continue to work at total relaxation of the entire body. They should notice any tightness and then attempt to let all ten-sion go.

(C) Internal-body Gestalt awareness. Par-ticipants are guided through a mental awareness of their internal body. The facil-itator teaches the specific focusing tech-niques which require an awareness of only one physical aspect at a time, like being aware of just the beating of the heart, or the expansion/contraction of the lungs.

V. (A) "The Compact Breath": Lying on their backs in the Savasana position, par-ticipants are instructed to take deep, calm, abdominal breaths; they should continue to breathe in while fully expanding their chests, raise their shoulders and collar-bones slightly, hold their breath for a few seconds comfortably, and slowly exhale (Zorn, 1968, p. 47).

(B) Total body relaxation. They become more and more relaxed in a shorter and shorter time.

(C) The facilitator instructs participants to enter and explore their own bodies and become aware of the detail and complexity of their physical beings.

VI. (A) "Concentration on the Breath": The participants now repeat "The Compact Breath," concentrating on the air as it en-ters, works its way through, and leaves the body (Zorn, 1968, p. 65).

(B) Again, the participants work at total body relaxation.

(C) External reality Gestalt awareness: Participants are guided through an aware-ness of sight, hearing, smell, and outside pressures on the body. Exercises help par-ticipants to become aware of internal re-sponses to outside influences.

VII. (A) Advanced Savasana: Lying in the Sav-asana position, participants consciously withdraw all tension in the body—begin-ning in the toes, releasing through the top of the head—allowing themselves to get in contact with deep, calm breaths. They should remain motionless for five minutes, stand up, breathe deeply, raise their hands above their heads, and stretch their bodies completely.

(B) Participants return to a prone position and continue to work at total body relaxa-tion. The process of tightening and relax-ing each muscle group should be quite fast by now. More time should be allowed for individual quiet time.

(C) Paired Gestalt Awareness (for the first time the participants are working in pairs): The pairs sit knee to knee and are guided through a contact and withdrawal process in which they first become aware of them-selves and then become aware of their partners.

VIII. (A) Paired Breathing: Still working in pairs, the participants are guided through experiences which will allow each to be aware of the other's breathing. One should lie in the Savasana position while the other lightly places his fingers on the breather's stomach to note the physical qualities of breathing. A variation may be to place fingers close to the nostrils to feel the air moving in and out. After several minutes, pairs reverse positions.

(B) Paired relaxation: Each person in turn is allowed the opportunity to touch basic muscle groups in tight and relaxed states. Awareness of self and one another is stressed.

(C) Paired fantasy: Each participant in turn closes his eyes and shares "My fantasy about you is . . . ."

IX. (A) "Rhythmic Breathing": While sitting in an upright position with back straight, participants inhale deeply and calmly for two seconds, hold their breath for four seconds, and exhale through nostrils for four seconds. When this becomes easy, it can be increased to 3:6:6 (Zorn, 1968, p. 50).

(B) Individual total relaxation: A slow and complete review of the total relaxation of the entire body.

(C) Gestalt perception combined with interpretation: The participants are instructed to guess what their former partners thought of them, to guess about reality, and to interpret as they see fit. They are constantly reminded that what they are doing is speculation and may not be grounded in reality.

X. (A) Alternate Nostril Breathing: Sitting in an upright position, participants block their left nostril with one hand, inhale deeply through their right nostril for five seconds; block both nostrils, holding breath for five seconds; and repeat, beginning this time with left nostril. They should go through the complete exercise several times. Time for breaths can be increased if comfortable for participants (Zorn, 1968, p. 51).

(B) In a reclining position, participants return to a state of complete body relaxation.

(C) Fantasy: Each member should find a mountain meadow that suits him, and should become a child in that meadow . . . . "Slowly grow up as you are in that meadow. Enter the near-by forest . . . . Leave the forest and climb the mountain . . . . Discover that it is becoming impossible . . . . With super-human effort, reach the top and be aware of what you see . . . . Slowly descend the mountain, noting your awareness . . . . Enter the valley where your special, important people are found . . . . Return to the meadow."

XI. The facilitator forms subgroups for processing. Participants are encouraged to reflect on what they have learned about themselves.

XII. The facilitator leads a discussion of the implications of using these techniques for personal development.

Variations

I. Each cycle's timing can be varied.

II. The facilitator may expand or reduce various descriptive comments or instructions.

Similar Structured Experiences: *Vol. I:* Structured Experience 16, 19; *Vol. II:* 47; *Vol. III:* 71; *'72 Annual:* 84, 85; *'73 Annual:* 89; *Vol. IV:* 119.

REFERENCES

Brodsky, G. Shaping up: Take a breather. *Gentlemen's Quarterly,* October, 1972.

Jacobsen, E. *You must relax.* New York: McGraw-Hill, 1962.

Stevens, J. O. *Awareness: Exploring, experimenting, experiencing.* Lafayette, Ca.: Real People Press, 1971.

Zorn, Y. W. *Yoga for the mind.* New York: Coronet Communications, Inc. Paperback Library, 1968.

Submitted by John L. Hipple, Michael Hutchins, and James Barott.

INTRODUCTION TO THE
INSTRUMENTATION SECTION

This section of the *Annual* continues the presentation of instruments begun in *A Handbook of Structured Experiences for Human Relations Training*, Vols. I, II, III, and IV, and the 1972 and 1973 *Annuals*.

These volumes (listed in order of their publication) contain the following instruments:

Volume I
"T-P Leadership Questionnaire" (pp. 10-11)
"Opinionnaire on Assumptions About Human Relations Training" (pp. 110-113)

Volume II
"Force-Field Analysis Inventory" (pp. 82-84)
"Life-Planning Program" (pp. 103-112)

Volume III
"Group-Climate Inventory" (p. 25)
"Group-Growth Evaluation Form" (pp. 26-27)
"Feedback Rating Scales" (pp. 28-29)
"Postmeeting Reactions Form" (p. 30)
"Learning-Climate Analysis Form" (pp. 36-38)
"Group-Behavior Questionnaire" (p. 39)
"Intentions and Choices Inventory" (p. 40)
"Polarization: Opinionnaire on Womanhood" (p. 61)

'72 Annual
"Supervisory Attitudes: The X-Y Scale" (pp. 67-68)
"Interpersonal Relationship Rating Scale" (pp. 73-74)
"Intervention Style Survey" (pp. 79-85)
"Group Leadership Questionnaire (GTQ-C)" (pp. 91-103)

'73 Annual
"Motivation Feedback Opinionnaire" (pp. 44-45)
"Helping Relationship Inventory" (pp. 55-70)
"Scale of Feelings and Behavior of Love" (pp. 73-85)

"Involvement Inventory" (pp. 89-94)
"LEAD (Leadership: Employee-orientation And Differentiation) Questionnaire" (pp. 97-102)

Volume IV
"Risk-Taking Behavior in Groups Questionnaire" (pp. 110-111)

'74 Annual
"Reactions to Group Situations Test" (pp. 91-96)
"Interpersonal Communication Inventory" (pp. 98-101)
"Self-Disclosure Questionnaire" (pp. 104-111)
"S-C Teaching Inventory" (pp. 118-122)

Instruments are included in the *Annual* to make available to group facilitators some scales useful in research on groups, teaching, training, and sensing.

Using an instrument properly, that is, obtaining the best possible value from it, entails seven different phases: (1) administration; (2) theory input; (3) prediction; (4) scoring; (5) interpretation; (6) posting; and (7) processing (Pfeiffer & Heslin, 1973; see the review in the Resources section of this *Annual*).

In the first step, *administration*, a nonthreatening atmosphere should be established and the purposes of the instrument discussed. In larger groups particularly, the administrator may need to tell those individuals who finish first to wait quietly for the others to finish.

Next, the facilitator should take a few minutes to give the participants some *theory input* for the instrument, by explaining the rationale behind its use.

Each participant should be asked to make a *prediction* about his score(s) by estimating whether he will score high, medium, or low and recording his estimate.

Scoring can be done in a number of ways. Some instruments require templates, some are self-scoring, and some require that scores be announced, written on newsprint, or handed out on a mimeographed sheet. The sophistication of the particular group is a gauge to the most appropriate method of scoring. Sometimes it is more efficient for the facilitator or an assistant to do the scoring than to have participants do it. In this way, of course, individuals do not get instant feedback, but often the instrument can be administered before a meal break and the results made available immediately after the break. The essential guideline in scoring is that it should not detract from the data being generated.

The manner in which *interpretation* is handled may vary widely, depending on the group and the style of the facilitator. One suggested way is to use two stages: (1) an interpretation of the administrator's (or another staff member's) scores, and then (2) an interpretation between pairs of participants. Thus, participants can first see how interpretations are made. Also, if staff members are willing to share their scores, participants find it less threatening to share theirs.

The sixth phase is *posting*. Displaying scores on newsprint can dissipate some people's concerns about possible negative values attached to their scores. At the same time, it can generate additional useful data for the group. Posting scores for discussion is particularly effective in subgroups.

The final, and perhaps most crucial, phase of instrumentation is *processing*. Group processing can simultaneously defuse negative affect and promote integration of the data concepts. Six to twelve participants form a group of ideal size for processing.

Authors of instruments in the *Annual* are interested in feedback on the use of the scales. They will welcome any sharing of norms, summary statistics, study results, and adaptations. (Contributors' mailing addresses are provided at the end of the *Annual*.)

REFERENCE

Pfeiffer, J. W., & Heslin, R. *Instrumentation in human relations training.* San Diego: University Associates, 1973.

REACTIONS TO GROUP SITUATIONS TEST

This instrument is a useful introduction to Bion's influential theory of groups (Bion, 1959). Much of the material on which Bion based his theories comes from his work with small groups at the Tavistock Clinic in London. Bion sees every group as being composed of *two* simultaneous groups: a "work group" and a "basic-assumption group." The "work group" aspect of the group concentrates on the group's real task—its purpose for meeting. A planning committee or a staff review committee is an example of the work group.

Basic-assumption groups, on the other hand, operate on certain *basic* or *tacit* assumptions; Bion has identified three distinct "basic assumptions": dependency, fight-flight, and pairing.

The dependency-assumption group assumes that its reason for existence is its own security. Its members look to the leader for authority, decisions, and wisdom. However, since no one individual can meet the exalted demands of the dependency-group members, the leader is bound, eventually, to fall from his position. This group's manifestation of the need for dependency is childlike.

A fight-flight-assumption group is most concerned with its self-preservation; whether by fleeing or by fighting, action is essential in this group. Thus, a leader is even more necessary than in the dependency-assumption group. The fight-flight-assumption group tends to be anti-intellectual and nonintrospective.

In a group based on the pairing assumption, reproduction or creation is the central aim of the group: the creation of a new leader, a new idea, a new approach to life. This group is pervaded by hopeful expectation.

Clearly, all three basic-assumption groups are very different from the work group. Unlike the work group, which is oriented outward toward reality, basic-assumption groups are oriented inward toward fantasy. It seems that the basic-assumption group represents an interference with

the work aspect of the group. However, basic assumptions can be used in a sophisticated manner by the work group. For example, the church and the armed forces are work groups that use, respectively, the dependency assumption and the fight-flight assumption in a positive manner.

In Bion's terms, the value of a group experience is the conscious experience of the possibilities of the work group. This implies the development of each individual's ability and skills to accomplish a common task. In a work group, an individual may be very much on his own; he is not reluctant to act or make decisions. He is less anxious about losing his own identity in that of the group, a common fear of group members.

The "Reactions to Group Situations Test" (RGST) is a useful way to sensitize participants to these important dimensions of group relations. It offers the chance to manipulate group composition; it can function as a diagnostic device or as a discussion starter.

It is pleasant to take, can be administered quickly (in about ten to fifteen minutes), and can be scored easily and quickly (in about twelve to eighteen minutes).

Five scoring scales indicate preferences for certain kinds of behavior in group settings: the *Work* (Inquiry) *Mode*, the *Fight Mode*, the *Pairing Mode*, the *Dependency Mode*, and the *Flight Mode*.

In the *Work Mode*, indicated preferences are for task-oriented behavior; group-oriented responses aimed at helping accomplish group objectives; a problem-solving orientation; the attempt to understand and deal with issues; and the effort to make suggestions for analyzing and for dealing with a problem.

In the *Fight Mode* the indicated preference is an angry response. This may be expressed as attack, subtle resistance, or manipulation to impose one's will on the group.

In the *Pairing Mode*, indicated preferences are supporting another person's idea; expressing intimacy, warmth, and supportiveness to another member; and expressing warmth and commitment to the whole group.

In the *Dependency Mode*, indicated preferences are appeals for support and direction; reliance on rules, regulations, or a definite structure; reliance on the leader or outside authority; and expressions of weakness or inadequacy.

In the *Flight Mode*, indicated preferences are tuning out (withdrawal or lessened involvement); joking, fantasizing, and daydreaming; inappropriate theorizing; overintellectualized, overgeneralized statements; total irrelevancy; changing the subject; leaving the group; and excess activity in busywork.

A scoring key follows the instrument. The responses to the fifty items are arranged in a balanced design. Each emotional modality is paired five times with each other item. Each of the five scores can range from 0 to 20.

It is important to remember that any psychological variable (such as the RGST's Work, Fight, Pairing, Dependency, and Flight modes) is defined both by the instrument *and* by the procedures of interpretation (Thelen, undated). There are two ways of using this instrument. One may assume that every person's performance can be understood in terms of the way certain basic traits or emotional drives combine in any one situation. In this view, effort is directed toward achieving a set of variables that will represent all areas of human functioning. A person can then, for all intents and purposes, be replaced by a set of these variables.

In the second view, little importance is attached to the actual "scores" for the test's five variables. Instead, it is the unique *pattern* of responses that is considered to be significant. The five variables of the RGST are seen as *conceptual* variables; no assumption is made that they represent *real* behavior. The scores may have a weak relation to other variables, but the items themselves may be very informative, especially when seen in the light of a precise knowledge of the test or the behavioral situation. Thus, the value of the test depends on how it is to be interpreted and for what purposes it is to be used.

The RGST in its "objective" form was developed from a sentence-completion test devised by Dorothy Stock (Whitaker) and her associates at the Human Dynamics Laboratory at the University of Chicago. Some evidence of reliability and validity are reported in Thelen, Hawkes, and Strattner (1969).

REFERENCES

Bion, W. R. *Experiences in groups.* New York: Basic Books, 1959.

Rioch, M. J. The work of Wilfred Bion on groups. *Psychiatry: Journal for the Study of Interpersonal Processes*, 1970, 33 (1), 56-66.

Thelen, H. A. To persons inquiring about the "Reactions to Group Situations Test." University of Chicago, Department of Education, mimeographed sheet (no date).

Thelen, H. A., Hawkes, T. H., & Strattner, N. S. *Role perception and task performance of experimentally composed small groups.* Chicago: The University of Chicago, 1969.

REACTIONS TO GROUP SITUATIONS TEST
Herbert A. Thelen

You will be presented with one-sentence descriptions of the kinds of incidents that frequently occur in groups.

Each of these descriptions is given in an incomplete sentence that can be finished in either of two ways, *A* or *B*. *Decide which way you prefer* to finish each sentence. On the separate Answer Sheet, either *A* or *B* (not both) should be marked opposite the number of the sentence, to complete the sentence.

Make your selections quickly. Don't linger over the items—your first impression is good enough.

Please do not leave out any items.

1. When I wanted to work with Frank, I . . .
   A. felt we could do well together.
   B. asked if it would be all right with him.

2. When the group wanted his views about the task, Sam . . .
   A. wondered why they wanted his views.
   B. thought of what he might tell them.

3. When the leader made no comment, I . . .
   A. offered a suggestion of what to do.
   B. wondered what to do next.

4. When Don said he felt closest to me, I . . .
   A. was glad.
   B. was suspicious.

5. When I felt helpless, I . . .
   A. wished that the leader would help me.
   B. found a friend to tell how I felt.

6. When Henry was annoyed, Ray . . .
   A. thought of a way to explain the situation to him.
   B. realized just how he felt.

7. When Ned felt eager to go to work, he . . .
   A. got mad at the late-comers.
   B. wanted to team up with Jim.

8. When Glenn bawled me out, I . . .
   A. lost interest in what we were supposed to be doing.
   B. thought that some of his ideas would be useful.

9. When the leader lost interest, Mort . . .
   A. suggested a way to get everybody working.
   B. started talking with his neighbors.

10. When Phil felt warm and friendly, he . . .
    A. accomplished a lot more.
    B. liked just about everyone.

From H. A. Thelen, *Classroom grouping for teachability.* Copyright © 1967 by John Wiley & Sons, Inc. Reprinted by permission of John Wiley & Sons, Inc.

11. When the leader was unsure of himself, Norm . . .
    A. wanted to leave the group.
    B. didn't know what to do.

12. When the group just couldn't seem to get ahead, I . . .
    A. felt like dozing off.
    B. became annoyed with them.

13. When the group wasn't interested, I . . .
    A. just didn't feel like working.
    B. thought that the leader should do something about it.

14. When the leader said he felt the same way I did, I . . .
    A. was glad that I had his approval.
    B. thought we would probably begin to make progress now.

15. When I became angry at Jack, I . . .
    A. felt like dozing off.
    B. ridiculed his comments.

16. When the leader wanted me to tell the class about my plan, I . . .
    A. wished I could get out of it.
    B. wished that he would introduce it for me.

17. When Art criticized Bert, I . . .
    A. wished that the teacher would help Bert.
    B. felt grateful to Art for really expressing what we both felt.

18. When Henry and Mary enjoyed each other's company so much, I . . .
    A. thought that I'd like to leave the room.
    B. felt angry.

19. When the leader changed the subject, Al . . .
    A. suggested that they stick to the original topic.
    B. felt glad that the leader was finally taking over.

20. When the others became so keen on really working hard, I . . .
    A. made an effort to make really good suggestions.
    B. felt much more warmly toward them.

21. When I felt angry enough to boil, I . . .
    A. wanted to throw something.
    B. wished that the leader would do something about it.

22. When Lee was not paying attention, I . . .
    A. did not know what to do.
    B. wanted to tell him he was wasting our time.

23. When Harry thought that he needed a lot of help, Martin . . .
    A. warmly encouraged him to get it.
    B. helped him analyze the problem.

24. When Jack reported his results so far, I . . .
    A. laughed at him.
    B. was bored.

25. When everyone felt angry, I . . .
    A. suggested that they stop and evaluate the situation.
    B. was glad that the leader stepped in.

26. When no one was sticking to the point, I . . .
    A. got bored with the whole thing.
    B. called for clarification of the topic.

27. When Herb said he felt especially friendly toward me, I . . .
    A. wanted to escape.
    B. wanted to ask his advice.

28. When the group agreed that it needed more information about how members
    felt, I . . .
    A. described my feelings to the group.
    B. wasn't sure I wanted to discuss my feelings.

29. When the leader offered to help Carl, Joe . . .
    A. wanted help too.
    B. resented the leader's offer.

30. When Dave and Lou argued, I . . .
    A. asked Hank how he felt about them.
    B. hoped they would slug it out.

31. When Chuck felt especially close to Steve, he . . .
    A. let him know it.
    B. hoped he could turn to him for assistance.

32. When several members dropped out of the discussion, Henry . . .
    A. thought it was time to find out where the group was going.
    B. got sore at what he thought was their discourtesy.

33. When Stan told me he felt uncertain about what should be done, I . . .
    A. suggested that he wait awhile before making any decisions.
    B. suggested that he get more information.

34. When Jim realized that quite a few people were taking digs at each other he . . .
    A. wanted to call the group to order.
    B. got angry at the stupidity of their behavior.

35. When the group suggested a procedure, I . . .
    A. thought the teacher ought to express his approval or disapproval of it.
    B. thought we ought to decide whether to carry it out.

36. When Ed seemed to be daydreaming, Bill . . .
    A. winked at Joe.
    B. felt freer to doodle.

37. When Tom and Mary arrived twenty minutes late for the meeting, the group . . .
    A. went right on working.
    B. was very annoyed.

38. During the argument, Roy's opposition caused Earl to . . .
    A. withdraw from the discussion.
    B. look to the teacher for support.

39. When Marvin suggested we evaluate how well we were working as a group, I . . .
    A. was glad that the period was almost over.
    B. gladly backed him up.

40. When the group seemed to be losing interest, Pat . . .
    A. became angry with the other members.
    B. thought it might just as well adjourn.

41. Together John and Fred . . .
    A. wasted the group's time.
    B. supported one another's arguments.

42. When Mal offered to help me, I . . .
    A. said I was sorry, but I had something else to do.
    B. was pleased that we would be partners.

43. When the other group became so interested in their work, George . . .
    A. wanted to ask their leader if he could join them.
    B. felt resentful that his group was so dull.

44. When Art left the meeting early, Dick . . .
    A. and Michael told each other what they felt about Art.
    B. was glad that he had gone.

45. When Lou turned to me, I . . .
    A. wished that he would mind his own business.
    B. asked him for help.

46. When Hal felt hostile to the group, he . . .
    A. wished he would not have to come to the meeting.
    B. was glad that Bob felt the same way.

47. While Dan was helping me, I . . .
    A. became annoyed with his superior attitude.
    B. felt good about being with him.

48. When I lost track of what Paul was saying, I . . .
    A. asked the teacher to explain Paul's idea to me.
    B. was pleased that it was Mike who explained Paul's idea to me.

49. While the group was expressing friendly feelings toward Bill, Ken . . .
    A. thought that now Bill would be able to work.
    B. opened a book and started to read.

50. When the leader offered to help him, Pete . . .
    A. said that he did not want any help.
    B. realized that he did need help from someone.

REACTIONS TO GROUP SITUATIONS TEST
ANSWER SHEET

1.	A	B		26.	A	B
2.	A	B		27.	A	B
3.	A	B		28.	A	B
4.	A	B		29.	A	B
5.	A	B		30.	A	B
6.	A	B		31.	A	B
7.	A	B		32.	A	B
8.	A	B		33.	A	B
9.	A	B		34.	A	B
10.	A	B		35.	A	B
11.	A	B		36.	A	B
12.	A	B		37.	A	B
13.	A	B		38.	A	B
14.	A	B		39.	A	B
15.	A	B		40.	A	B
16.	A	B		41.	A	B
17.	A	B		42.	A	B
18.	A	B		43.	A	B
19.	A	B		44.	A	B
20.	A	B		45.	A	B
21.	A	B		46.	A	B
22.	A	B		47.	A	B
23.	A	B		48.	A	B
24.	A	B		49.	A	B
25.	A	B		50.	A	B

REACTIONS TO GROUP SITUATIONS TEST
ANSWER KEY

Instructions: For each item below circle the letter corresponding to the way you marked the item on the RGST Answer Sheet. For example, if you marked A for item 1, circle the letter *P* on this Answer Key for that item. To obtain each of the five scores, count the number of times you circled each letter. (The letters denoted as "Stub" tell what type of item you were responding to.)

Stub	Response A	B		Stub	Response A	B
1. (W)	P	D		26. (Fl)	Fl	W
2. (W)	F	W		27. (P)	Fl	D
3. (D)	W	D		28. (W)	W	Fl
4. (P)	P	F		29. (D)	D	F
5. (D)	D	P		30. (F)	P	F
6. (F)	W	P		31. (P)	P	D
7. (W)	F	P		32. (Fl)	W	F
8. (F)	Fl	W		33. (D)	Fl	W
9. (Fl)	W	P		34. (F)	W	F
10. (P)	W	P		35. (W)	D	W
11. (D)	Fl	D		36. (Fl)	P	Fl
12. (D)	Fl	F		37. (P)	W	F
13. (Fl)	Fl	D		38. (F)	Fl	D
14. (P)	D	W		39. (W)	Fl	P
15. (F)	Fl	F		40. (Fl)	F	Fl
16. (W)	Fl	D		41. (P)	Fl	P
17. (F)	D	P		42. (D)	Fl	P
18. (P)	Fl	F		43. (W)	D	F
19. (Fl)	W	D		44. (Fl)	P	F
20. (W)	W	P		45. (P)	F	D
21. (F)	F	D		46. (F)	Fl	P
22. (Fl)	D	F		47. (D)	F	P
23. (D)	P	W		48. (Fl)	D	P
24. (W)	F	Fl		49. (P)	W	Fl
25. (F)	W	D		50. (D)	F	W

Score

W = Work _____
F = Fight _____
Fl = Flight _____
D = Dependency _____
P = Pairing _____

INTERPERSONAL COMMUNICATION INVENTORY

Being an effective communicator seems to be based on five interpersonal components: (1) an adequate self-concept, the single most important factor affecting people's communication with others; (2) the ability to be a good listener, a skill which has received little attention until recently; (3) the skill of expressing one's thoughts and ideas clearly—which many people find difficult to do; (4) being able to cope with one's emotions, particularly angry feelings, and expressing them in a constructive way; and (5) the willingness to disclose oneself to others truthfully and freely. Such self-disclosure is necessary for satisfactory interpersonal relationships. (See the "Self-Disclosure Questionnaire" by Sidney M. Jourard in this section of the *Annual.*)

In recent years, several research techniques and devices have been developed in a number of areas involving the study of interpersonal communication: marriage counseling, parent-child counseling, group therapy, and small-group communication.

The "Interpersonal Communication Inventory" (ICI) is applicable generally to social interaction in a wide variety of situations. It is an attempt to measure general tendencies in interpersonal communication and it may be used as a counseling tool, as a teaching device, as a supplement to an interview, by management, or for further research.

A 54-item scale measures the process of communication as an element of social interaction; it is not intended to measure content but to identify patterns, characteristics, and styles of communication.

The items included were drawn from a review of the literature in the field and from the author's counseling experience and his work on related communication scales.

The instrument is probably best suited for individuals of high school age or older. It can be adapted to either sex and any marital status.

Items in the ICI are designed to sample the dimensions of self-concept, listening, clarity of expression, difficulties in coping with angry feelings, and self-disclosure.

This instrument is closely linked to Dr. Myron R. Chartier's article, "Five Components Contributing to Effective Interpersonal Communications," which appears in the Lecturettes section of this *Annual.* The lecturette discusses and develops aspects of the "Interpersonal Communication Inventory."

Engaged in on-going research, the author would like to collaborate with others using the ICI. He has also developed a guide to the ICI which may be obtained from him upon request.

REFERENCES

Bienvenu, M. J., Sr. Measurement of parent-adolescent communication. *The Family Coordinator*, 1969, **18**, 117-121.

Bienvenu, M. J., Sr. Measurement of marital communication. *The Family Coordinator*, 1970, **19**, 26-31. (a)

Bienvenu, M. J., Sr. Parent-adolescent communication and self-esteem. *Journal of Home Economics*, 1970, **62**, 344-345. (b)

Bienvenu, M. J., Sr. An interpersonal communication inventory. *The Journal of Communication*, 1971, **21** (4), 381-388.

INTERPERSONAL COMMUNICATION INVENTORY
Millard J. Bienvenu, Sr.

This inventory offers you an opportunity to make an objective study of the degree and patterns of communication in your interpersonal relationships. It will enable you to better understand how you present and use yourself in communicating with persons in your daily contacts and activities. You will find it both interesting and helpful to make this study.

Directions

- The questions refer to persons *other than your family members or relatives.*

- Please answer each question as quickly as you can according to the way you feel *at the moment* (not the way you usually feel or felt last week).

- Please do not consult anyone while completing this inventory. You may discuss it with someone after you have completed it. Remember that the value of this form will be lost if you change *any* answer during or after this discussion.

- Honest answers are very necessary. Please be as frank as possible, since your answers are confidential.

- Use the following examples for practice. Put a check ($\sqrt{}$) in *one* of the three blanks on the right to show how the question applies to your situation.

	Yes (usually)	No (seldom)	Some-times
Is it easy for you to express your views to others?	_____	_____	_____
Do others listen to your point of view?	_____	_____	_____

- The **Yes** column is to be used when the question can be answered as happening *most of the time* or usually. The **No** column is to be used when the question can be answered as *seldom* or *never.*

  The **Sometimes** column should be marked when you definitely cannot answer **Yes** or **No.** *Use this column as little as possible.*

- Read each question carefully. If you cannot give the exact answer to a question, answer the best you can but be sure to answer each one. There are no right or wrong answers. Answer according to the way *you* feel *at the present time.* Remember, do not refer to family members in answering the questions.

	Yes (usually)	No (seldom)	Some-times
1. Do your words come out the way you would like them to in conversation?	_____	_____	_____
2. When you are asked a question that is not clear, do you ask the person to explain what he means?	_____	_____	_____
3. When you are trying to explain something, do other persons have a tendency to put words in your mouth?	_____	_____	_____

	Yes (usually)	No (seldom)	Some-times
4. Do you merely assume the other person knows what you are trying to say without your explaining what you really mean?			
5. Do you ever ask the other person to tell you how he feels about the point you may be trying to make?			
6. Is it difficult for you to talk with other people?			
7. In conversation, do you talk about things which are of interest to both you and the other person?			
8. Do you find it difficult to express your ideas when they differ from those around you?			
9. In conversation, do you try to put yourself in the other person's shoes?			
10. In conversation, do you have a tendency to do more talking than the other person?			
11. Are you aware of how your tone of voice may affect others?			
12. Do you refrain from saying something that you know will only hurt others or make matters worse?			
13. Is it difficult to accept constructive criticism from others?			
14. When someone has hurt your feelings, do you discuss this with him?			
15. Do you later apologize to someone whose feelings *you* may have hurt?			
16. Does it upset you a *great deal* when someone disagrees with you?			
17. Do you find it difficult to think clearly when you are angry with someone?			
18. Do you fail to disagree with others because you are afraid they will get angry?			
19. When a problem arises between you and another person, can you discuss it without getting angry?			
20. Are you satisfied with the way you settle your differences with others?			
21. Do you pout and sulk for a long time when someone upsets you?			
22. Do you become very uneasy when someone pays you a compliment?			

	Yes (usually)	No (seldom)	Some-times
23. Generally, are you able to trust other individuals?			
24. Do you find it difficult to compliment and praise others?			
25. Do you deliberately try to conceal your faults from others?			
26. Do you help others to understand you by saying how you think, feel, and believe?			
27. Is it difficult for you to confide in people?			
28. Do you have a tendency to change the subject when your feelings enter into a discussion?			
29. In conversation, do you let the other person finish talking before reacting to what he says?			
30. Do you find yourself not paying attention while in conversation with others?			
31. Do you ever try to listen for meaning when someone is talking?			
32. Do others seem to be listening when you are talking?			
33. In a discussion is it difficult for you to see things from the other person's point of view?			
34. Do you pretend you are listening to others when actually you are not?			
35. In conversation, can you tell the difference between what a person is saying and what he may be feeling?			
36. While speaking, are you aware of how others are reacting to what you are saying?			
37. Do you feel that other people wish you were a different kind of person?			
38. Do other people understand your feelings?			
39. Do others remark that you always seem to think you are right?			
40. Do you admit that you are wrong when you know that you are wrong about something?			

Total Score [   ]

INTERPERSONAL COMMUNICATION INVENTORY
SCORING KEY AND NORMS

Instructions: Look at how you responded to each item in the ICI. In front of the item write the appropriate weight from the table on this page. For example, if you answered "Yes" to item 1, you would find below that you get three points; write the number 3 in front of item 1 in the inventory and proceed to score item 2. When you have finished scoring each of the forty items, add up your total score. You may wish to compare your score to the norms listed below.

	Yes	No	Sometimes		Yes	No	Sometimes
1.	3	0	2	21.	0	3	1
2.	3	0	2	22.	0	3	1
3.	0	3	1	23.	3	0	2
4.	0	3	1	24.	0	3	1
5.	3	0	2	25.	0	3	1
6.	0	3	1	26.	3	0	2
7.	3	0	2	27.	0	3	1
8.	0	3	1	28.	0	3	1
9.	3	0	2	29.	3	0	2
10.	0	3	1	30.	0	3	1
11.	3	0	2	31.	3	0	2
12.	3	0	2	32.	3	0	2
13.	0	3	1	33.	0	3	1
14.	3	0	2	34.	0	3	1
15.	3	0	2	35.	3	0	2
16.	0	3	1	36.	3	0	2
17.	0	3	1	37.	0	3	1
18.	0	3	1	38.	3	0	2
19.	3	0	2	39.	0	3	1
20.	3	0	2	40.	3	0	2

Means and Standard Deviations for the ICI

Age Groups	Males		Females	
17-21	Mean	81.79	Mean	81.48
	S.D.	21.56	S.D.	20.06
	N.	53	N.	80
22-25	Mean	86.03	Mean	94.46
	S.D.	14.74	S.D.	11.58
	N.	38	N.	26
26 and up	Mean	90.73	Mean	86.93
	S.D.	19.50	S.D.	15.94
	N.	56	N.	45
All Age Groups by Sex	Mean	86.39	Mean	85.34
	S.D.	19.46	S.D.	18.22
	N.	147	N.	151
All Age Groups; Males and Females Combined	Mean	85.93		
	S.D.	19.05		
	N.	298		

SELF-DISCLOSURE QUESTIONNAIRE

Disclosing oneself to others is one of the most important concepts in human relations training. Through the process of feedback and self-revelation one can make himself known to others and learn how others see him.

Self-disclosure may be either verbal or nonverbal. Each person reveals himself not only through what he says, but through what he does, how he acts and reacts, and through such means as mannerisms or personal style.

One human relations goal is to encourage an individual to move toward self-disclosure, allowing new information about himself to become apparent to others. To do so, a person must be able to accept and trust both himself and others.

Different people have different degrees of readiness to confide in others. It has been suggested (Jourard, 1958) that accurately portraying oneself to others is an identifying criterion of a healthy personality. A neurotic individual, on the other hand, may be incapable of knowing his "real" self and of revealing that self to others.

The "Self-Disclosure Questionnaire" raises and deals with certain questions: For example, do subjects disclose themselves differently to different "target" persons, such as mother, father, or friend? Do subjects tend to disclose certain areas of information about themselves more fully than other areas? Do sex differences have any bearing on self-disclosure?

Preliminary findings from the use of this questionnaire show that self-disclosure is measurable and that this method of assessing it has some validity. Many more questions about self-disclosure are open for exploration, based on relevant factors—groups, target-persons, aspects of self, individual differences.

This questionnaire can be useful as a self-inventory in personal growth laboratories or as an outcome measure in research on human relations training.

The sixty items of the questionnaire have been classified into six groups of ten related items each. Each group concerns a general category of information about the self (*aspects*).

REFERENCES

Jourard, S. M. *Personal adjustment: An approach through the study of healthy personality.* New York: Macmillan, 1958. (2nd ed., 1963).

Jourard, S. M. *The transparent self.* (Rev. ed.) New York: D. Van Nostrand, 1971.

SELF-DISCLOSURE QUESTIONNAIRE
Sidney M. Jourard

The Answer Sheet which you have been given has columns with the headings "Mother," "Father," "Male Friend," "Female Friend," and "Spouse." You are to read each item on the questionnaire and then indicate on the Answer Sheet the extent that you have talked about that item to each person; that is, the extent to which you have made yourself known to that person. Use the rating scale that you see on the Answer Sheet to describe the extent that you have talked about each item.

Attitudes and Opinions

1. What I think and feel about religion; my personal religious views.
2. My personal opinions and feelings about other religious groups than my own, *e.g.*, Protestants, Catholics, Jews, atheists.
3. My views on communism.
4. My views on the present government—the president, government, policies, etc.
5. My views on the question of racial integration in schools, transportation, etc.
6. My personal views on drinking.
7. My personal views on sexual morality—how I feel that I and others ought to behave in sexual matters.
8. My personal standards of beauty and attractiveness in women—what I consider to be attractive in a woman.
9. The things that I regard as desirable for a man to be—what I look for in a man.
10. My feeling about how parents ought to deal with children.

Tastes and Interests

1. My favorite foods, the ways I like food prepared, and my food dislikes.
2. My favorite beverages, and the ones I don't like.
3. My likes and dislikes in music.
4. My favorite reading matter.
5. The kinds of movies that I like to see best; the TV shows that are my favorites.
6. My tastes in clothing.
7. The style of house, and the kinds of furnishings that I like best.
8. The kind of party or social gathering that I like best, and the kind that would bore me, or that I wouldn't enjoy.
9. My favorite ways of spending spare time, *e.g.*, hunting, reading, cards, sports events, parties, dancing, etc.
10. What I would appreciate most for a present.

This questionnaire is taken from *The Transparent Self* by Sidney Jourard. Copyright ® 1971. Reprinted by permission of D. Van Nostrand Company.

Work (or Studies)

1. What I find to be the worst pressures and strains in my work.
2. What I find to be the most boring and unenjoyable aspects of my work.
3. What I enjoy most, and get the most satisfaction from in my present work.
4. What I feel are my shortcomings and handicaps that prevent me from working as I'd like to, or that prevent me from getting further ahead in my work.
5. What I feel are my special strong points and qualifications for my work.
6. How I feel that my work is appreciated by others (e.g., boss, fellow-workers, teacher, husband, etc.)
7. My ambitions and goals in my work.
8. My feelings about the salary or rewards that I get for my work.
9. How I feel about the choice of career that I have made—whether or not I'm satisfied with it.
10. How I really feel about the people that I work for, or work with.

Money

1. How much money I make at my work, or get as an allowance.
2. Whether or not I owe money; if so, how much.
3. Whom I owe money to at present; or whom I have borrowed from in the past.
4. Whether or not I have savings, and the amount.
5. Whether or not others owe me money; the amount, and who owes it to me.
6. Whether or not I gamble; if so, the way I gamble, and the extent of it.
7. All of my present sources of income—wages, fees, allowance, dividends, etc.
8. My total financial worth, including property, savings, bonds, insurance, etc.
9. My most pressing need for money right now, e.g., outstanding bills, some major purchase that is desired or needed.
10. How I budget my money—the proportion that goes to necessities, luxuries, etc.

Personality

1. The aspects of my personality that I dislike, worry about, that I regard as a handicap to me.
2. What feelings, if any, that I have trouble expressing or controlling.
3. The facts of my present sex life—including knowledge of how I get sexual gratification; any problems that I might have; with whom I have relations, if anybody.
4. Whether or not I feel that I am attractive to the opposite sex; my problems, if any, about getting favorable attention from the opposite sex.
5. Things in the past or present that I feel ashamed and guilty about.
6. The kinds of things that make me just furious.
7. What it takes to get me feeling real depressed or blue.
8. What it takes to get me real worried, anxious, and afraid.
9. What it takes to hurt my feelings deeply.
10. The kinds of things that make me especially proud of myself, elated, full of self-esteem or self-respect.

Body

1. My feelings about the appearance of my face—things I don't like, and things that I might like about my face and head—nose, eyes, hair, teeth, etc.
2. How I wish I looked: my ideals for overall appearance.
3. My feelings about different parts of my body—legs, hips, waist, weight, chest or bust, etc.
4. Any problems and worries that I had with my appearance in the past.
5. Whether or not I now have any health problems—*e.g.*, trouble with sleep, digestion, female complaints, heart condition, allergies, headaches, piles, etc.
6. Whether or not I have any long-range worries or concerns about my health, *e.g.*, cancer, ulcers, heart trouble.
7. My past record of illness and treatment.
8. Whether or not I now make special efforts to keep fit, healthy, and attractive, *e.g.*, calisthenics, diet.
9. My present physical measurements, *e.g.*, height, weight, waist, etc.
10. My feelings about my adequacy in sexual behavior—whether or not I feel able to perform adequately in sex relationships.

SELF-DISCLOSURE QUESTIONNAIRE
ANSWER SHEET

Use the following rating scale for each item on the "Self-Disclosure Questionnaire":

0: Have told the other person nothing about this aspect of me.

1: Have talked in general terms about this item. The other person has only a general idea about this aspect of me.

2: Have talked in full and complete detail about this item to the other person. He knows me fully in this respect, and could describe me accurately.

X: Have lied or misrepresented myself to the other person so that he has a false picture of me.

| | | | Target Person | | |
Self-Disclosure Aspect	Mother	Father	Male Friend	Female Friend	Spouse
Attitudes and Opinions					
1.					
2.					
3.					
4.					
5.					
6.					
7.					
8.					
9.					
10.					
Tastes and Interests					
1.					
2.					
3.					
4.					
5.					
6.					
7.					
8.					
9.					
10.					

Target Person

Self-Disclosure Aspect	Mother	Father	Male Friend	Female Friend	Spouse
Work (or Studies)					
1.					
2.					
3.					
4.					
5.					
6.					
7.					
8.					
9.					
10.					
Money					
1.					
2.					
3.					
4.					
5.					
6.					
7.					
8.					
9.					
10.					

Target Person

Self-Disclosure Aspect	Mother	Father	Male Friend	Female Friend	Spouse
Personality					
1.					
2.					
3.					
4.					
5.					
5.					
6.					
7.					
8.					
9.					
10.					
Body					
1.					
2.					
3.					
4.					
5.					
6.					
7.					
8.					
9.					
10.					

SELF-DISCLOSURE QUESTIONNAIRE SCORING SHEET

Instructions: On the Answer Sheet compute the sums for each target person in each self-disclosure aspect and copy each sum on the Scoring Sheet.

			Target Person			
Aspect	Mother	Father	Male Friend	Female Friend	Spouse	**Total**
Attitudes and Opinions						
Tastes and Interests						
Work (or Studies)						
Money						
Personality						
Body						
Total						

Plot these scores on the accompanying Profile Sheet.

SELF-DISCLOSURE QUESTIONNAIRE PROFILE SHEET

Instructions: Draw profiles for each of your "target" persons on the chart below. (You may wish to use different colored pencils.) Locate your five scores for Mother, for example, and connect these with straight lines. Do the same for each of the other persons.

On the scale representing your total self-disclosure scores, write the *names* of the target persons at their appropriate level.

Interpretation Suggestions: Studying the chart below, (1) look for similarity/dissimilarity of profiles between target persons, and (2) look for high and low self-disclosure aspects across target persons.

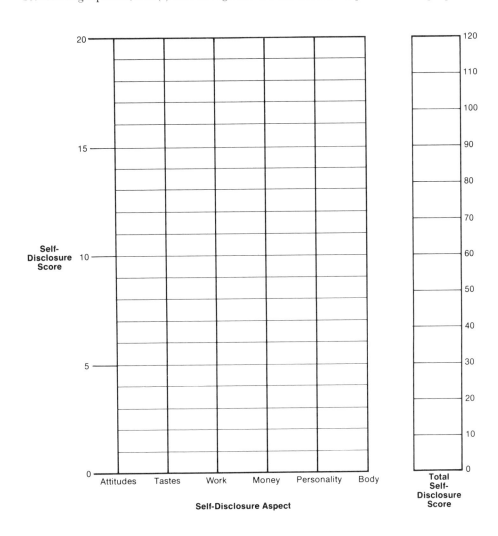

S-C (STUDENT-CONTENT) TEACHING INVENTORY

Morris S. Spier

The "S-C Teaching Inventory" (SCTI) is an "armchair" instrument. There has been no standardization or investigation of its statistical properties. The inventory was not developed to classify behavior or to measure teacher effectiveness. It was not developed to define or monitor "successful" classroom methods or the "right" philosophy of education. It *is* a device designed to help respondents focus on, organize, and understand their own experiences in the teacher-student interaction.

DEVELOPMENT

First, several hundred statements reflecting the kinds of experiences that might be encountered in the real world of teaching were generated. Each statement was typed on a separate 3 x 5 card. Working independently, four of my colleagues and I sorted the statements into the following four categories.

Category I
Statements which reflect a teacher's willingness to share classroom authority and responsibility with students.

Category II
Statements which reflect a teacher's tendency to centralize classroom authority in his or her own hands.

Category III
Statements which reflect a teacher's concern for the content of the job, *i.e.*, the performance of task activities, including planning and scheduling course content and evaluating student progress.

Category IV
Statements which reflect a teacher's concern for the "role attributes" of the job, including

having the respect of students and colleagues, being an expert, or modeling behavior for students to evaluate.

Statements falling into none of the above categories were discarded, and only those items placed in a particular category by all five judges were retained.

The second step involved pairing every statement in Category I above with every statement in Category II, and every statement in Category III with every statement in Category IV. Each resulting pair of statements was typed on a separate 3 x 5 card and sorted into two dimensions by the five judges. Again, only those statement-pairs which all five judges placed in the same dimension were retained. The two resulting dimensions were the following orientations.

Student Orientation (S)
These items allow a teacher to choose between attitudes and behaviors reflecting an emphasis on sharing vs. an emphasis on personally retaining classroom authority.

Content Orientation (C)
These items allow a teacher to choose between attitudes and behaviors reflecting emphasis on job activities vs. emphasis on role attributes.

In its present form, the SCTI contains forty items (*i.e.*, pairs of statements) measuring the dimensions outlined above. Twenty items drawn from the Category I & II statement-pairs comprise the student-orientation (S) scale, and twenty items drawn from the Category III & IV statement-pairs make up the content-orientation (C) scale.

ADMINISTRATION

A nonthreatening climate is important. This is not a "test." There are no "right" or "wrong" answers. The instrument will simply help to make some of the issues covered in this introduction more meaningful and useful.

It is helpful if the facilitator reads the instructions aloud while the participants read them silently to themselves. He should emphasize particularly:

- the repetitiveness of some of the items, noting that this is not an attempt to measure the participant's response consistency;
- that it may sometimes be difficult to choose the "most important" statement of two equally attractive alternatives, but the participant must choose one or the other;
- that participants may find some items in which they feel both alternatives are unattractive, but they should still choose the "most important," i.e., the statement that they feel is least unattractive; and
- that participants should not spend too much time on any single item, since first impressions may be best.

If some participants complete the instrument sooner than others, they should sit quietly until all persons are finished. Most persons complete the inventory in about 15 to 20 minutes.

THEORY INPUT

The way a teacher runs his or her classroom does not "just happen." Instead, a teacher's behavior is determined by his or her *beliefs* about the real world. One set of beliefs centers on aspects of the "psychological contract" between teachers and students. The other set of beliefs centers on aspects of the "psychological contract" between teachers and the educational system.[1]

---

[1]Research has shown two similar dimensions to be important in determining leadership behavior in organizations. Blake and Mouton (1964) built a model to understand leadership styles in organizations (the Managerial Grid) and named the dimensions "concern for people" and "concern for production." The former stresses a manager's concern for the needs of the people who work for the organization. The latter stresses his concern for the needs of the organization.

Basic Assumptions

First, what a teacher does in the classroom reflects some basic assumptions and beliefs about students and learning. Every teacher's behavior reflects his or her personal answer (voiced or unvoiced) to the question "Do you really believe that people *want* to learn and are capable of taking responsibility for their own learning, or that they need to be coerced or seduced into receiving an education?" Thus, a teacher who gives frequent "pop quizzes," reviews students' notebooks to be sure they are taking notes, and checks off homework assignments reflects certain beliefs about students' attitudes toward learning—as does a teacher who is friendly and easy-going in his approach.

Second, a teacher's behavior also reflects voiced or unvoiced answers to questions about a teacher's role in the learning process. Teachers who emphasize planning and organizing course content, meeting with students, and designing new approaches to class material reflect certain beliefs about the expectations of their administrators and the educational system. So do other teachers who emphasize personal expertise, respect, and setting an example for students.

In the SCTI, a teacher's assumptions and beliefs about students' attitudes toward learning and how a teacher should respond to students' needs are measured by the S scale. A teacher's assumptions and beliefs about his or her role in the classroom are measured by the C scale.

Both orientations, of course, exist simultaneously in the behavior of every teacher. A teacher can be highly student oriented and highly content oriented at the same time. It is a teacher's philosophy that determines the emphasis he places on each orientation. Some teachers, who feel that the needs of students and of the system are mutually exclusive and inevitably in conflict, strive to resolve the conflict by concentrating on one or the other set of needs. Other teachers, while also feeling that a conflict between incompatible needs is inevitable, work toward some compromise or balance in which neither orientation is fully emphasized. Still other teachers see the student orientation and content orientation as functionally related. They

114

aim to *integrate* student and system needs by emphasizing both.

FIVE TEACHING STRATEGIES

Five "pure" teaching strategies (or styles) result from (1) the interaction of the student and content orientations, and (2) the differing degrees of emphasis which teachers place on each orientation. The five styles are discussed below and are visually depicted in Figure 1, "Models of Teaching Strategies" (adapted from Blake & Mouton, 1964).

Strategy 1

The strategy at the lower right-hand corner of the diagram defines the style of a teacher whose basic philosophy dictates that student and system needs are mutually exclusive. Thus, this teacher resolves the conflict by placing maximum emphasis on content orientation, and minimum emphasis on student orientation.

For this teacher, the syllabus defines what should be taught; the length of the term governs the time available. Since students naturally resist school and learning, a teacher's primary responsibility is to make sure the material *gets taught*. It is important to set definite standards of classroom performance and to check continually to see that students are meeting the standards. This is accomplished by giving frequent "pop" quizzes, taking attendance at all classes, constructing some test questions from minute points contained in footnotes in the text, and so on.

Strategy 2

This teacher, whose strategy appears at the upper left-hand corner of the diagram, also feels that student and system needs are incompatible and in conflict. Like his Strategy 1 colleague, he feels that students really do resist school and learning. But he disagrees that the basic need-conflict can be overcome by tight classroom control. Instead, this teacher places maximum emphasis on student orientation, and minimum emphasis on content orientation.

Students will be taught by teachers they like—so being liked is both practical and personally gratifying for this teacher. He feels that a teacher's primary responsibility is to be supportive and to win the friendship of his students. This is accomplished by putting on a "good show" in the classroom, ignoring attendance, allowing students to set their own course grades, inviting students to his house, and so on.

Strategy 3

Like his Strategy 1 and 2 colleagues, the teacher whose strategy is defined in the lower left-hand corner of the diagram also believes in the conflict of student and system needs and in students' natural resistance to learning. But, unlike his colleagues, he feels helpless to deal with the situation.

Students will learn what they want to learn, when they want to learn it. A teacher simply cannot change this fact. Thus, his primary responsibility is to present the information and to do what his job description requires. If a teacher gets a "good class," he is lucky; if he gets a "bad class," there is nothing he can do about it. Those students with initiative will learn. For this teacher, his philosophy justifies his dull, mechanical presentations. At the university level he may prefer to teach "advanced seminars" and shun the basic core courses.

Strategy 4

At the middle of the diagram is the strategy of another teacher who believes in the basic incompatibility of student and system needs. But he aims for a compromise, or balance, by fully emphasizing neither the student orientation nor the content orientation.

Both system needs and student needs matter, but this teacher cannot see how to put them together. He ends up with a moderate level of concern for each. Thus, the system requires the teacher to give examinations, but he may specify the exact pages in the text from which questions will be drawn. Similarly, since he is required to give grades, he may "grade on a curve," allow students to omit one or more test scores in computing final grades, give extra points for class attendance, or allow students to write an "extra" paper or book review to improve their grades.

Figure 1. Models of Teaching Strategies

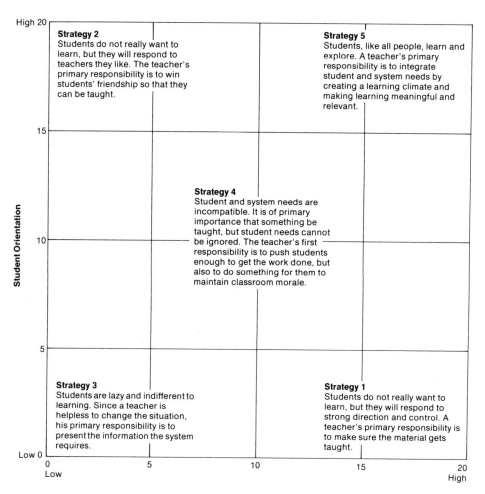

High 20

Strategy 2
Students do not really want to learn, but they will respond to teachers they like. The teacher's primary responsibility is to win students' friendship so that they can be taught.

Strategy 5
Students, like all people, learn and explore. A teacher's primary responsibility is to integrate student and system needs by creating a learning climate and making learning meaningful and relevant.

15

Strategy 4
Student and system needs are incompatible. It is of primary importance that something be taught, but student needs cannot be ignored. The teacher's first responsibility is to push students enough to get the work done, but also to do something for them to maintain classroom morale.

Student Orientation

10

5

Strategy 3
Students are lazy and indifferent to learning. Since a teacher is helpless to change the situation, his primary responsibility is to present the information the system requires.

Strategy 1
Students do not really want to learn, but they will respond to strong direction and control. A teacher's primary responsibility is to make sure the material gets taught.

Low 0

0   5   10   15   20
Low   High

Content Orientation

Strategy 5

At the upper right-hand corner of the diagram is the strategy of a teacher who believes that students are always learning. In his mind, student and system needs are not *inevitably* in conflict. He aims to *integrate* both sets of needs by placing maximum emphasis on both student and content orientations.

This teacher feels that a teacher's primary responsibility is not to see that something is *taught*, but rather to see that something is *learned*. Thus, it is important to create a climate in which learning is involving, meaningful, and relevant. Learning activities are structured to bring maximum benefit to the student, the teacher, and the school system.

The preceding descriptions are clearly caricatures of teacher behavior; they are not intended to be descriptions of real people. Certainly there are as many different classroom strategies as there are teachers. The strategy descriptions exaggerate behaviors that differentiate types of teachers not to simplify behavior, but to make it more understandable. If the strategies are defined, they can be changed. The "S-C Teaching Inventory" is a way of opening this process by providing a vocabulary, a model, and some self-involving experiences to focus on one's own behavior.

REFERENCE

Blake, R., & Mouton, J. S. *The managerial grid*. Houston: Gulf Publishing, 1964.

S-C TEACHING INVENTORY
Morris S. Spier

The following inventory concerns your feelings about some teaching practices. Its purpose is to provide you with meaningful information about yourself as a teacher.

There are no right or wrong answers. The best answer is the one most descriptive of your feelings and opinions. Therefore, answer honestly, because only realistic answers will provide you with useful information.

Each of the forty items consists of two statements, either about what a teacher can do or ways he can act. Circle the letter (A or B) in front of the statement that *you* think is the more important way for a teacher to act. In the case of some items you may think that both alternatives are important, but you still should choose the statement you feel is *more* important. Sometimes you may think that both alternatives are unimportant; still you should choose the statement you think is *more* important.

It is more important for a teacher:

1. (A) To organize his course around the needs and skills of every type of student.
   (B) To maintain definite standards of classroom performance.
2. (A) To let students have a say in course content and objectives.
   (B) To set definite standards of classroom performance.
3. (A) To emphasize completion of the term's course syllabus.
   (B) To let students help set course goals and content.
4. (A) To give examinations to evaluate student progress.
   (B) To allow students a voice in setting course objectives and content.
5. (A) To reward good students.
   (B) To allow students to evaluate the performance of their instructor.
6. (A) To allow students to make their own mistakes and to learn by experience.
   (B) To work to cover the term's subject matter adequately.
7. (A) To make it clear that he is the authority in the classroom.
   (B) To allow students to make their own mistakes and to learn by experience.
8. (A) To be available to confer with students on an "as needed" basis.
   (B) To have scheduled office hours.
9. (A) To give examinations to evaluate student progress.
   (B) To tailor the course content to the needs and skills of each class.
10. (A) To draw a line between himself and the students.
    (B) To let students plan their own course of study according to their interests.
11. (A) To take an interest in the student as a person.
    (B) To make it clear that the teacher is the authority in the classroom.
12. (A) To draw a line between himself and the students.
    (B) To be available for conferences with students on an "as needed" basis.
13. (A) To modify his position if one of his students shows him where he was wrong.
    (B) To maintain definite standards of classroom performance.
14. (A) To allow students to have a say in evaluating teacher performance.
    (B) To draw a line between himself and the students.
15. (A) To see that the class covers the prescribed subject matter for the course.
    (B) To be concerned about the student as a person.
16. (A) To let students learn by experience.
    (B) To maintain definite standards of classroom performance.

17. (A) To allow students a voice in setting course objectives and content.
    (B) To make it clear that he is the authority in the classroom.
18. (A) To discourage talking among students during class time.
    (B) To establish an informal classroom atmosphere.
19. (A) To allow student evaluation of faculty.
    (B) To make it clear that the teacher is the authority in the classroom.
20. (A) To draw a line between himself and the students.
    (B) To let students make mistakes and learn by experience.
21. (A) To be an authority on the class materials covered.
    (B) To keep up to date in the field.
22. (A) To be respected as a person of high technical skill in the field.
    (B) To up-date class and lecture materials constantly.
23. (A) To attend to his own professional growth.
    (B) To be an authority on the class materials covered.
24. (A) To attend to his own professional growth.
    (B) To set an example for his students.
25. (A) To see that each student is working at his full capacity.
    (B) To plan, in considerable detail, all class activities.
26. (A) To construct fair and comprehensive examinations.
    (B) To set an example for his students.
27. (A) To be known as an effective teacher.
    (B) To see that each student is working at his full capacity.
28. (A) To construct fair and comprehensive examinations.
    (B) To see that each student is working at his full capacity.
29. (A) To be an authority on the class materials covered.
    (B) To plan and organize his coursework carefully.
30. (A) To be a model for his students to emulate.
    (B) To try out new ideas and approaches on the class.
31. (A) To see that each student is working at his full capacity.
    (B) To plan and organize course content carefully.
32. (A) To have scheduled office hours to meet with students.
    (B) To be an expert on the course subject matter.
33. (A) To set an example for his students.
    (B) To try out new ideas and approaches on the class.
34. (A) To teach basic courses as well as more advanced courses.
    (B) To be a model for his students to emulate.
35. (A) To plan and organize the class activities carefully.
    (B) To be interested in and concerned with student understanding.
36. (A) To be an authority on the course content.
    (B) To be known as an effective teacher.
37. (A) To give examinations to evaluate student progress.
    (B) To be an authority on the class materials covered.
38. (A) To attend professional meetings.
    (B) To be respected as a person of high technical skill in the field.
39. (A) To be respected for his knowledge of the course subject matter.
    (B) To try out new ideas and approaches on the class.
40. (A) To be an authority on the course content.
    (B) To construct fair and comprehensive examinations.

S-C TEACHING INVENTORY SCORING SHEET

The instrument may be self-scored directly on the questionnaire or it may be scored using a template. To score directly on the questionnaire the following steps should be used.

1. Participants are asked to draw a line across the page under item 20.
2. Items 1 to 20 comprise the S scale. The following "answers" are read to the group, calling out first the item number, then the response. The participants should place an "X" next to each item for which they have chosen the response indicated below.

Item	Response	Item	Response	Item	Response
1	A	8	A	15	B
2	A	9	B	16	A
3	B	10	B	17	A
4	B	11	A	18	B
5	B	12	B	19	A
6	A	13	A	20	B
7	B	14	A		

3. Items 21 to 40, which comprise the C scale, are scored as in Step 2 above. The "answers" follow.

Item	Response	Item	Response	Item	Response
21	B	28	A	35	A
22	B	29	B	36	B
23	A	30	B	37	A
24	A	31	B	38	A
25	B	32	A	39	B
26	A	33	B	40	B
27	A	34	A		

4. The number of X's scored for items 1 through 20 are counted. This number should be written in the top square of the box (next to the S) on the Summary Sheet.
5. The number of X's scored for items 21 through 40 are counted and written in the bottom square of the box (next to the C) on the Summary Sheet.
6. Next, both S and C scores should be plotted on the chart on the Summary Sheet. The score in the S box should be plotted on the left side (vertical scale) of the chart. The score in the C box should be plotted on the bottom (horizontal scale) of the chart. The participants make a mark on the chart where their S and C scores intersect.

If preferred, a scoring template can be made by taking another sheet and punching out holes for the appropriate responses as indicated above. Then the number of X's showing for items 1 through 20 and the number showing for items 21 through 40 are counted. Steps 4 through 6 follow as above.

Since the statistical properties of the inventory are presently being studied, the author would greatly appreciate receiving scores obtained from the use of the instrument and especially, if possible, the actual questionnaires. They should be sent to the address listed in the Contributors section of this *Annual*.

INTERPRETATION OF SCORING

With a score of 20 denoting a "high" or maximal concern and a score of 0 denoting a "low" or minimal concern, teaching *philosophies* may be interpreted in terms of the degree of emphasis placed on each of the respective orientations.

A high score on the S scale of the SCTI means that the participant agrees that students should have a voice in planning, organizing, implementing, and evaluating classroom activities. A low score on this scale means that the participant rejects student involvement in these activities and feels that classroom authority should be centered in the hands of the teacher.

A high score on the C scale means that the participant stresses the performance of the task activities of the teaching job, including the planning and organizing of course content and the evaluation of student progress. In contrast, a low score on this scale means that the participant stresses the role attributes of the teacher's job, including being an expert, being respected, and setting an example for students to emulate.

Similarly, teaching *styles* may be interpreted in terms of the interaction of the S and C scales, that is, in terms of the degree of student orientation vs. content orientation which a given teacher exhibits. The intersect of the S and C scores, when plotted on the graph provided on the Summary Sheet, will place every participant somewhere on the chart. For example, an S-C intersect falling in the lower right-hand quadrant is indicative, as discussed above, of a Strategy 1 teaching style.

Finally, participants may review their responses to the specific items which resulted in their particular S- and C-scale scores. Discussion can then be generated about the specific teaching *behaviors* defined by the individual items. When participants are asked to go back over the questionnaire noting items which caused them particular difficulty or about which they have particularly strong feelings, some lively small-group discussion is likely to result.

S-C TEACHING INVENTORY
SUMMARY SHEET

Name _____ Date _____

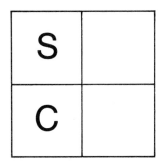

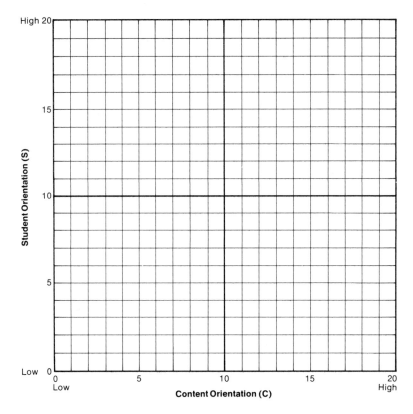

INTRODUCTION TO THE
LECTURETTES SECTION

Learning based on direct experience is not the only kind of learning appropriate to human relations training. Contrary to some criticisms of the field, group facilitators are not exclusively concerned with "gut-involved" experience; "head" learning is just as valuable and useful.

Lecture Method

Although the lecture method can easily be overused, it is one of the simplest ways of providing additional, vicarious learning to participants. Facilitators can use the lecturette materials in this section as short explanations in processing sessions, as handouts, or as introductions to group activities. Each facilitator needs to develop a repertoire of theory and background that he can use in a variety of situations and activities.

The facilitator will usually find that such theoretical material is better received when it is accompanied by visual aids, such as posters, diagrams, charts, etc.

Lecturettes in this section are purposely simple and direct, with an emphasis on clarity and ease of presentation. They are not intended to be comprehensive or technical statements of theoretical positions. Where appropriate, references to sources have been included.

One of Four Components

However valid the use of the lecturette may be, it is only one of four major components utilized in designing human relations laboratories.

The use of intensive small groups is the basic component of laboratory education. An almost endless variety of small groups exists, including the most common, the T-group (training group), the D-group (developmental group), or the N-group (new group).

Structured experiences of several types (e.g., ice-breakers, dyadic designs, or communication activities) help to generate and focus the data of a laboratory. The facilitator will find that a given structured experience can be equally appropriate in a personal-growth design or in a leadership-development laboratory, depending on the way the data are processed.

Measurement devices—instruments—are another component of a human relations laboratory. They are useful in providing theory-based data with which participants can work in evaluating and understanding their learning experience.

Rationale for Use

The lecturette, as the fourth major component included in a human relations design, can be used in several ways and for several purposes.

It can be delivered in large group sessions, commonly called "community" sessions. It can be used spontaneously in an intensive small-group session. It can be offered to participants before the laboratory or as handout material during the session.

The lecturette is a highly effective method of focusing a participant's learning from a structured experience or an intensive group meeting toward theoretical models. It can also provide a "cognitive map" for the experience that is to follow. It helps the participant transfer his learning to his everyday experiences by functioning as a guide to his behavior.

As a learning device for the participant and as a theoretical intervention for the facilitator, the lecturette is an excellent, direct, and useful means of infusing cognitive material into the laboratory experience.

FIVE COMPONENTS CONTRIBUTING TO EFFECTIVE INTERPERSONAL COMMUNICATIONS

Five interpersonal components offer clear distinctions between good communicators and poor communicators. These components are Self-Concept, Listening, Clarity of Expression, Coping with Angry Feelings, and Self-Disclosure.[1]

SELF-CONCEPT

The most important single factor affecting people's communication with others is their self-concept—how they see themselves and their situations. While situations may change from moment to moment or place to place, people's beliefs about themselves are always determining factors in their communicative behavior. The self is the star in every act of communication.

Everyone has literally thousands of concepts about himself: who he is, what he stands for, where he lives, what he does and does not do, what he values, what he believes. These self-perceptions vary in clarity, precision, and importance from person to person.

Importance of the Self-Concept

A person's self-concept is who he is. It is the center of his universe, his frame of reference, his personal reality, his special vantage point. It is a screen through which he sees, hears, evaluates, and understands everything else. It is his own filter on the world around him.

A Weak Self-Concept

A person's self-concept affects his way of communicating with others. A strong self-concept is necessary for healthy and satisfying interaction. A weak self-concept, on the other hand, often

distorts the individual's perception of how others see him, generating feelings of insecurity in relating to other people.

A person with a poor view of himself may have difficulty in conversing with others, admitting that he is wrong, expressing his feelings, accepting constructive criticism from others, or voicing ideas different from those of other people. In his insecurity he is afraid that others may not like him if he disagrees with them.

Because he feels unworthy, inadequate, and inferior, he lacks confidence and thinks that his ideas are uninteresting to others and not worth communicating. He may become seclusive and guarded in his communication, negating his own ideas.

Forming the Self-Concept

Even as a person's self-concept affects his ability to communicate, so his communication with others shapes his self-concept. As man is primarily a social animal, he derives his most crucial concepts of self from his experiences with other human beings.

Individuals learn who they are from the ways they are treated by the important people in their lives—sometimes called "significant others." From verbal and nonverbal communication with these significant others, each person learns whether he is liked or not liked, acceptable or unacceptable, worthy of respect or disdain, a success or a failure. If an individual is to have a strong self-concept, he needs love, respect, and acceptance from significant others in his life.

Self-concept, then, is a critical factor in a person's ability to be an effective communicator with others. In essence, an individual's self-concept is shaped by those who have loved—or have not loved—him.

[1]The five components are based on Dr. Millard J. Bienvenu's Interpersonal Communication Inventory, included in the Instrumentation section of this *Annual*.

LISTENING

Most communication education has focused on skills of self-expression and persuasion; until quite recently, little attention has been paid to listening. This overemphasis on the skills of expression has led most people to underemphasize the importance of listening in their daily communication activities.

However, each person needs information that can be acquired only through the process of listening.

Listening, of course, is much more intricate and complicated than the physical process of hearing. Hearing is done with the ears, while listening is an intellectual and emotional process that integrates physical, emotional, and intellectual inputs in a search for meaning and understanding. Effective listening occurs when the listener discerns and understands the sender's meaning: The goal of communication is achieved.

The "Third Ear"

Reik (1972) refers to the process of effective listening as "listening with the third ear." An effective listener listens not only to words but to the meanings behind the words. A listener's third ear, Reik says, hears what is said between sentences and without words, what is expressed soundlessly, what the speaker feels and thinks.

Clearly, effective listening is not a passive process. It plays an active role in communication. The effective listener interacts with the speaker in developing meaning and reaching understanding.

Several principles can aid in increasing essential listening skills.

1. The listener should have a *reason* or *purpose* for listening.
2. It is important for the listener to *suspend judgment* initially.
3. The listener should *resist distractions*—noises, views, people—and focus on the speaker.
4. The listener should *wait before responding* to the speaker. Too prompt a response reduces listening effectiveness.
5. The listener should *repeat verbatim* what the speaker says.

6. The listener should *rephrase in his own words* the content and feeling of what the speaker says, to the speaker's satisfaction.
7. The listener should *seek the important themes* of what the speaker says, by listening through the words for the real meaning.
8. The listener should use the time differential between the rate of speech (100-150 words per minute) and the rate of thought (400-500 words per minute) to *reflect* upon content and to *search* for meaning.
9. The listener should *be ready to respond* to the speaker's comments.

CLARITY OF EXPRESSION

Effective listening is a necessary and neglected skill in communication, but many people find it equally difficult to say what they mean or to express what they feel. They often simply assume that the other person understands what they mean, even if they are careless or unclear in their speech. They seem to think that people should be able to read each other's minds: "If it is clear to me, it must be clear to you, also." This assumption is one of the most difficult barriers to successful human communication.

A "Longer" Board

Satir (1972) tells of a family ruckus that occurred when the father sent his son to the lumber yard for a "longer" board. The child thought he knew what his father wanted and dutifully went to the lumber yard, but the "longer" board he brought back was still three feet too short. His father became angry and accused the boy of being stupid and not listening. The father had simply assumed that since *he* knew what he meant by "longer," his son would also know. He had not bothered to make himself clear or to check his meaning with his son.

The poor communicator leaves the listener to guess what he means, while he operates on the assumption that he is, in fact, communicating. The listener, in turn, proceeds on the basis of what he guesses. Mutual misunderstanding is an obvious result.

To arrive at planned goals or outcomes—from accomplishing the mundane work of everyday

126

life to enjoying the deepest communion with another person—people need to have a means for completing their communication satisfactorily.

An Effective Communicator

A person who can communicate his meaning effectively to others has a clear picture in his mind of what he is trying to express. At the same time he can clarify and elaborate what he says. He is receptive to the feedback that he gets and uses it to further guide his efforts at communication.

COPING WITH ANGRY FEELINGS

A person's inability to deal with anger frequently results in communication breakdowns.

Suppression

Some people handle their anger by suppressing it, fearing that the other person would respond in kind. Such people tend to think that communicating an unfavorable emotional reaction will be divisive. They may become upset even when others merely disagree with them.

I may, for example, keep my irritation at you inside myself, and each time you do whatever it is that irritates me, my stomach keeps score . . . 2 . . . 3 . . . 6 . . . 8 . . . until one day the doctor pronounces that I have a bleeding ulcer, *or* until one day you do the same thing that you have always done and my secret hatred of you erupts in one great emotional avalanche.

You, of course, will not understand. You will feel that this kind of over-charged reaction is totally unjustified. You will react angrily to my buried emotional hostility. Such a failure to cope with anger can end in homicide.

Expression

Expression of emotions is important to building good relationships with others. People need to express their feelings in such a manner that they influence, affirm, reshape, and change themselves and others. They need to learn to express angry feelings constructively rather than destructively.

The following guidelines can be helpful.

1. *Be aware* of your emotions.

2. *Admit* your emotions. Do not ignore or deny them.
3. *Own* your emotions. Accept responsibility for what you do.
4. *Investigate* your emotions. Do not seek for a means of rebuttal to win an argument.
5. *Report* your emotions. Congruent communication means an accurate match between what you are saying and what you are experiencing.
6. *Integrate* your emotions with your intellect and your will. Allow yourself to learn and grow as a person.

Emotions cannot be repressed. They should be identified, observed, reported, and integrated. Then people can instinctively make the necessary adjustments in the light of their own ideas of growth. They can change and move on with life.

SELF-DISCLOSURE

Sidney Jourard, author of *The Transparent Self* (1971) and *Self-Disclosure* (1971), says that self-disclosure—the ability to talk truthfully and fully about oneself—is necessary to effective communication. Jourard contends that an individual cannot really communicate with another person or get to know that person unless he can engage in self-disclosure.[2]

Indeed, this is a mutual process. The more I know about you, and the more you know about me, the more effective and efficient our communication will be.

A person's ability to engage in self-revelation is a symptom of a healthy personality. Powell (1969) puts it this way:

I have to be free and able to say my thoughts to you, to tell you about my judgments and values, to expose to you my fears and frustrations, to admit to you my failures and shames, to share my triumphs, before I can really be sure what it is that I am and can become. *I must be able to tell you who I am before I can know who I am. And I must know who I am before I can act truly, that is, in accordance with my true self* [p. 44].

---

[2]See the Self-Disclosure Questionnaire in the Instrumentation section of this *Annual.*

It can be argued that an individual will understand only as much of himself as he has been willing to communicate to another person.

Blocks to Self-Revelation

To know themselves and to have satisfying interpersonal relationships, people must reveal themselves to others. Yet self-revelation is blocked by many. For example (Powell, 1969):

> Powell: "I am writing a booklet, to be called *Why Am I Afraid to Tell Who I Am?*"
> Other: "Do you want an answer to that question?"
> Powell: "That is the purpose of the booklet, to answer the question."
> Other: "But do you want *my* answer?"
> Powell: "Yes, of course I do."
> Other: "I am afraid to tell you who I am, because if I tell who I am, you may not like who I am, and it's all that I have [p. 12]."

This conversation from real life reflects the fears and doubts that many people have—that they are not totally acceptable to others, that parts of themselves are unlovable, that they are unworthy. Cautious, ritualized communication behavior is the result.

Dynamics of Trust

The dynamics of fear can be exchanged for the dynamics of trust. No one is likely to engage in much self-disclosure in a threatening situation. Self-disclosure can be made only in an atmosphere of good will. Sometimes it takes one person's risk of self-disclosure to stimulate good will in other people. Trust begets trust; self-disclosure generates self-disclosure. The effective communicator is one who can create a climate of trust in which mutual self-disclosure can occur.

Being an effective communicator, then, is based on these five basic components: an adequate self-concept; the ability to be a good listener; the skill of expressing one's thoughts and ideas clearly; being able to cope with emotions, such as anger, in a functional manner; and the willingness to disclose oneself to others.

Myron R. Chartier

REFERENCES

Anastasi, T. E., Jr. *Face-to-face communication.* Cambridge, Mass.: Management Center for Cambridge, 1967.

Bienvenu, M. J., Sr. An interpersonal communication inventory. *The Journal of Communication,* 1971, 21, 381-388.

Carkhuff, R. R. *The art of helping.* Amherst, Mass.: Human Resource Development Press, 1972.

Combs, A. W., Avila, D. L., & Purkey, W. W. *Helping relationships.* Boston: Allyn and Bacon, 1971.

Jourard, S. *Self disclosure.* New York: Wiley-Interscience, 1971. (a)

Jourard, S. *The transparent self.* (Rev. ed.) New York: Van Nostrand Reinhold, 1971. (b)

Keltner, J. W. *Interpersonal speech-communication: Elements and structures.* Belmont, Ca.: Wadsworth Publishing, 1970.

LaBenne, W. D., & Greene, B. I. *Educational implications of self-concept theory.* Pacific Palisades, Ca.: Goodyear Publishing Co. Inc., 1969.

Powell, J. *Why am I afraid to tell you who I am?* Chicago: Peacock Books, Argus Communications Co., 1969.

Reik, T. *Listening with the third ear.* New York: Pyramid Publications, 1972.

Satir, V. *Conjoint family therapy.* (Rev. ed.) Palo Alto: Science and Behavior Books, 1967.

Satir, V. *Peoplemaking.* Palo Alto: Science and Behavior Books, 1972.

MAKING REQUESTS THROUGH METACOMMUNICATION

When we communicate with others, we do so on two levels. The first is the *denotative* level. This is the level dealing with what we say—our words, the straightforward verbal content of our messages. The second is the *metacommunicative* level. We communicate on this level whenever we communicate about our communication. Virginia Satir (1967), a well-known therapist, has suggested that we use communication about our communication to make requests of the person with whom we are interacting.

Metacommunications can be explicit and verbal, or they can be less obvious nonverbal cues. My tone of voice when I say, "Get out of my office" to someone tells him how to interpret my words. It tells him whether I am joking or serious. The nonverbal aspects of my voice indicate a request that he interpret my verbal, denotative message a certain way. By interpreting messages at both levels—denotative and metacommunicative—persons decide what they think we mean, then act on this basis.

Obviously there can be interpretation problems. Because so many metacommunications are nonverbal, meanings must be inferred. Another problem is that we may not know how we really feel about the other person. We may do things to confound him—because we're not sure ourselves what we want him to do or how we want him to interpret a message.

To amplify just a bit, let us presume that I really do not like a particular person, but that I also have difficulty rejecting people in general. This creates conflict in me. I want to reject the person, yet I do not want to reject him.

In such a situation, an interaction might go like this:

Me: Get out of my office (in a tone that says I'm serious).

Other: Oh, I didn't know you were busy. (He turns and starts to leave.)

Me: Wait a minute. (I feel guilty when I see he is leaving and feeling rejected.)

Other: Huh?

Me: Where are you going?

Other: You told me to get out.

Me: Oh, I was only kidding. (I deny the metacommunication given earlier.)

Other: (Confusion—What should he believe? My tone of voice earlier? Or my verbal message now? What should he do? Stay or go?)

This interaction is an example of *incongruent communication*, which occurs when two or more messages sent at different levels conflict seriously. Conflicting messages make things difficult for the person trying to interpret them. He wonders: "What does the other person really mean? Which of the requests should I believe?"

People vary in their capacities for sending requests clearly so that others do not need to guess much.

USELESS REQUESTS

Another point Satir (1967) makes is that some things cannot be requested. That is, it is useless to request the type of things people cannot produce. Here are examples of some useless requests:

1. We cannot ask others to feel as we do or as we want them to. Feelings are spontaneous. All we can do is try to *elicit* feelings. If we fail to elicit feelings, we can accept the situation, or try again.

2. We cannot ask others to think as we do. Thoughts also cannot be demanded. We can try to persuade. If that doesn't work, then we must accept the fact, compromise, or "agree to disagree."

3. We *can* demand that others do or say (or not do or not say) what we want. But if we succeed, the success is questionable. We

have shown only that we have power, not that we are lovable or worthwhile.

If we try to be more aware of our communicating and metacommunicating, we can change the way we make requests of others. If we increase our knowledge of ourselves and of what we want and how we feel about others, we are more likely to make clearer requests. We are less likely to put others in positions of conflict.

EXAMINING YOUR OWN REQUESTS

How congruent or incongruent are your communications? (If you don't know, ask others and then *listen closely* to what they say.) What kind of requests do you tend to make of others? Do you make useless requests? How clear are your requests? Do you confound others with conflicting requests or with denials that you ever make requests?

SUGGESTED ACTIVITIES

The following structured experiences, taken from J. W. Pfeiffer and J. E. Jones (Eds.), *A Handbook of Structured Experiences for Human Relations Training*, Volumes I and III, would be useful to the facilitator concerning the question of metacommunication.

Listening Triads (Vol. I, Structured Experience 8)

Verbal Progression (Vol. III, Structured Experience 65

Behavior Descriptions (Vol. III, Structured Experience 50)

Also applicable is J. E. Jones, "Communication Modes: An Experiential Lecture," in J. W. Pfeiffer and J. E. Jones (Eds.), *The 1972 Annual Handbook for Group Facilitators.*

Charles M. Rossiter, Jr.

REFERENCES

Pfeiffer, J. W. Conditions which hinder effective communication. In J. E. Jones and J. W. Pfeiffer (Eds.), *The 1973 annual handbook for group facilitators.* San Diego: University Associates, 1973, 120-123.

Satir, V. *Conjoint family therapy: A guide to theory and technique.* Palo Alto: Science Behavior Books, 1967.

FIGURE/GROUND

A common imperative in personal growth groups is to "stay in the 'here-and-now.' " Initially, this imperative was imposed to benefit group progress, but it often produces a stultifying effect. Energy is lost as the group attempts to understand the concept, filter out "there-and-then" data, and operate exclusively in the "here-and-now."

The Gestalt concept of figure/ground parallels the "here-and-now" time orientation in a personal and lively manner. Put simply, "figure" represents the person's current awareness; and "ground," short for background, is the scenery for that awareness. What is "figural" for an individual at any given moment is that person's here-and-now.

The person "forms" a figure, acts on the figure, destroys the figure, and repeats the cycle. A new figure cannot be clearly formed until the first is acted on.

Imagine, for example, that Tom is going to a personal growth group. He is driving through heavy traffic thinking about what will happen in the group. His thoughts concerning the group are foremost, or "figure." A dog runs in front of his car; he slams on the brakes. Now his group thoughts are "ground" and the dog incident is figure. But when he arrives at the retreat center, his "figure" is his expectant feeling about the group. Just as he enters the door, he smells the aroma of fried chicken. His figure now becomes his hunger, and his expectant feeling, ground. After dinner, his feeling of fullness is figure. He goes to the group room and seeks out the most comfortable seat. His figure—fullness—recedes into the background. The cycle continues.

It is important to note that action is necessary to "complete" figure. "Action," broadly interpreted, provides the energy to move figure to ground. Even the "action" of silently acknowledging figure can at times move it to ground. Of course, if the issue is potent, considerable energy or action may be required to move it to the background.

For example, when Marie arrived at the retreat center for the personal growth group, she was most concerned about her mother's impending surgery, and her concern was "figure." She did not even taste the fried chicken. After dinner she went to her room and silently acknowledged her feeling of concern. When the group began, her concern had become background. She now had made "space" for the group to emerge as figure.

The rhythmic flow of the figure/ground cycle occasionally becomes interrupted. Although there are several methods a person can use to interrupt the cycle, the most common is to "fuzz" the figure. Then, in order to reactivate the cycle, the figure must be clarified.

Mike is a member of the personal growth group. His figure is anger. He denies understanding his anger. To unblock and re-energize this figure, the facilitator may ask him:

1. What are you doing?
2. How are you doing that?
3. What do you want?
4. What do you need?
5. What are you imagining (pretending)?
6. What do you feel angry about?
7. Towards whom in this room do you feel most angry?

Once Mike has clarified his "figure," he may decide not to deal with his anger at this time. He may simply acknowledge it. Or he may arrange to have a confrontation with the object of his anger. Once he has made a decision to act on figure, his figure—anger—becomes ground.

Anne is another member of the group. She cannot identify her "figure." When the facilitator asks her what she is feeling, she shakes her head and says, "Nothing."

To clarify figure, it is essential to deal with the "here-and-now." How does Anne experience "nothing"? Where is "nothing" located in her body? Can she describe "nothing"? "Staying with the obvious" helps produce a clear figure.

Even when a person's figure is clearly nongroup material—an issue which is not part of the common experience of the group—he can be helped to act on his figure by himself, through such a method as silent acknowledgement or writing notes to himself.

The individual's ability to move nongroup figure into ground will depend on its intensity. Turning figure into ground to allow a new figure to emerge can be seen as a valid indication of personal power.

Although the figure/ground concept is but a small portion of Gestalt theory, its use can personalize and energize the "here-and-now" group concept. False issues and side issues are reduced as each member deals with his figure. Growth potential is increased.

SUGGESTED ACTIVITY

Dyadic interviews can be conducted between group members, following the questions above.

Judith James Pfeiffer

132

HIDDEN AGENDAS

Any group works on two levels: the level of the surface task with which the group is immediately concerned, and the level of the hidden, undisclosed needs and motives of its individual members. Participants' aspirations, attitudes, and values affect the way they react to the group's surface task. Such individual "hidden agendas" siphon off valuable energy that could be used for accomplishing the task at hand and for group maintenance.

Understanding how these hidden agendas work in the life of a group helps the group achieve its common goal more efficiently.

Individual Needs

A person joins a group in order to fulfill or express certain personal needs. His behavior as a member of that group is neither random nor haphazard: It is keyed to his personal motivations, which may be social or emotional, explicit or hidden to the group, known or unknown to the individual himself.

Needs, of course, take different forms and can be satisfied in different ways for different people. Physical and security needs are basic: An individual must have food, shelter, and warmth in order to maintain life; if he is not to be overwhelmed by anxiety, he must also achieve some security and stability in his environment.

When such basic survival needs are met, other needs press for satisfaction. An individual has social, ego, and self-fulfillment requirements as well. These are the needs that can best be fulfilled in a group situation; thus, their satisfaction is often the individual's motivation for joining a group.

As individuals seek acceptance from others, social needs become apparent; when these are filled, the person's ego presses for *its* satisfaction. Finally, as the individual begins to understand his own unique identity, he can become fully himself.

Hidden Needs

Hidden beneath the surface of the group's life are many individual, conflicting currents: its members' needs for belonging, acceptance, recognition, self-worth, self-expression, and productivity.

Such needs are personal and subjective, but they are not necessarily "selfish." Looking for the satisfaction of personal needs through group membership is both "normal" and "natural." We are not concerned here with the question of how or whether these needs should be satisfied, but with their effect on the group as a whole.

If *one* individual's needs block another from achieving *his* needs, or if such personal needs hinder the group from accomplishing *its* goals, then we become concerned. We want to legitimize the individual's fulfillment of his needs in ways that do not raise obstacles for other members of the group.

SOME SUGGESTIONS FOR LEADERS

The leader should keep in mind the fact that a group continuously works on both the hidden and the surface levels. Hidden agendas may prevent the group from moving as fast as participants would like or expect.

What can be done about hidden agendas:

1. The leader can look for hidden agendas and learn to recognize their presence.

2. A group member may help surface hidden agendas. He may say, for example, "I wonder if we have said all that we feel about the issue. Maybe we should take time to go around the table and ask for individual comments so that we can open up any further thoughts."

3. Hidden agendas can be brought into the open and discussed. But not all hidden agendas can be confronted successfully by a group; some are best left under the surface.

4. The leader should not criticize the group for the presence of hidden agendas; they are legitimate and must be worked with just like the surface task. The amount of attention that should be given to the hidden agendas depends on the degree of their influence on the group's task.
5. The leader should help the group find the means of solving hidden agendas. Problem-solving methods are needed, though techniques vary.
6. The group should spend some time evaluating its progress in handling hidden agendas. The last fifteen minutes of a meeting devoted to such evaluation is often very helpful.

Better and more open ways of dealing with hidden agendas should become apparent through experience. And as groups mature, hidden agendas are often reduced, thus increasing the amount of energy the group has to devote to its surface tasks.

SUGGESTED ACTIVITY

See *Vol. I*, Structured Experience 9.

THE INTERPERSONAL CONTRACT

The idea of contracting for change in intimate relationships tends to elicit negative reactions from most individuals. In our society, the word *contract* often connotes an impersonal process of tough bargaining in smoke-filled rooms between declared opponents. *Negotiation* evokes a picture of wily diplomats jostling for power through subterfuge, manipulation, and hints of armed intervention.

Neither of these scenes is readily applicable to personal relationships. Yet all relationships involve negotiated agreements which vary according to explicitness, duration, and restrictiveness. Husbands and wives, for example, develop pacts about household chores, while neighbors contract to form a car pool. Roommates reach agreements about visitors, paying bills, and study times. Teachers and students specify individual learning objectives.

Given its prevalence in our daily lives, the interpersonal contract might be described as the mortar that binds relationships; it lends predictability to our interactions and provides us with a basis for trust.

Implicit and Explicit Agreements

Most of the agreements individuals work out among themselves are implicit and are rarely verbalized. People normally function on the basis of unwritten compacts, seldom recognizing that they have indeed negotiated an agreement.

The most fulfilling means of facilitating change in a relationship, however, occurs when partners make a conscious and consistent effort to negotiate their expectations openly in an atmosphere of mutual trust and respect. In making a public commitment, both partners are more likely to carry out their agreements. Such explicit agreements are easily renegotiated and modified for the mutual benefit of participants.

Problem-Centered Perspective

People generally approach the process of contracting for change in their relationship from a problem-centered perspective: "We are doing all right, but we have a problem with...." The problem may be one of agreeing on family finances, learning how to express anger, or finding a satisfying means of completing a task. The situation is seen as lacking a necessary element or as an irritant to be remedied.

Though creative growth is seldom given equal attention, it too can serve as a subject for an interpersonal contract. Partners can use their contracts to determine how much energy they will spend on problem-solving and how much on creative development.

Two Approaches

Regardless of the circumstance that prompts them to seek change, partners can use one or both of two approaches in negotiating an interpersonal contract. They can develop a *mini-contract* to deal with situations that have a restricted time limit or scope, or they can seek the more comprehensive goals of a *developmental contract* to maximize the growth possibilities for both individuals and their relationship.

A mini-contract might, for example, specify acceptable means of expressing affection for members of the opposite sex, provide for completing job assignments on time, determine grading procedures, divide household tasks, set up a homework schedule, or designate the children's vacation bedtime.

The developmental contract is more comprehensive, involving decisions about how to implement the ideals of the partnership, how to provide for future changes, and how to work through problems. A couple, for instance, might develop a contract to enhance growth and intimacy in their marriage. Wanting to share in the process of learning together, they could contract to attend marriage-enrichment workshops and free university classes. They might seek to provide a renewed basis for intimacy in their relationship by contracting to spend one weekend a month as a couple—camping, visiting nearby cities, or having a "tryst" at a local hotel.

GUIDELINES FOR NEGOTIATING AN INTERPERSONAL CONTRACT

The Process

Negotiating an interpersonal contract can be a rewarding and illuminating experience, especially when both partners agree to negotiate in an atmosphere that is free of coercion and manipulation. Sitting down and talking things through—sharing your aspirations as individuals and partners—offers you new insights into yourselves, your values, feelings, priorities, and personal viewpoints. It can also help you find and realize rewarding new possibilities for your relationship.

If possible, find a quiet, private, *pleasant place*, free from outside disturbances, to negotiate and write your contract. While you are at it, be good to yourselves. Treat yourselves to a glass of wine, some freshly baked cookies, or any special treat.

Allow yourselves *ample time* to negotiate and write your contract; at least one hour per sitting is most helpful. Guidelines for implementing serious readjustments in a relationship are seldom developed in one sitting—take time over several sessions to let your ideas and feelings percolate and sort themselves out. Each of you could well spend some time alone defining, clarifying, and noting your personal behavioral goals before sharing them with your partner.

When you attempt to define and share your goals it is important that you consistently *check signals* with each other to make sure you have heard and understood what the other is saying. During the early stages of goal-sharing, you may practice the art of listening and responding by following the succeeding exercise.

Step 1: One person, Person A, takes responsibility for initiating a conversation about a specific topic; in this instance, "What I'd like our contract to do for us." As A talks, B becomes actively involved in the process of listening by nodding his head when he feels he understands, sitting forward in his chair, taking note of things he agrees or disagrees with, and sorting out what he understands from what he doesn't.

Step 2: After A completes his or her statement, B responds, "I heard you say . . ." and repeats what A has said. After B summarizes to A's satisfaction, they continue on to the next step.

Step 3: B attempts to clarify their communication further by expressing his understanding of the feeling aspect of A's message. He completes the sentence, "I think you mean (feel)...."

Step 4: After B has completed the process of summarizing and clarifying his feelings, A responds with his thoughts and reflections: "My response is...."

Step 5: The process is reversed and B then engages in a monologue on the same subject.

Tape recording your conversations may help promote effective communication between you and your partner, by giving both of you a more objective view of your interaction.

Most human behavior is guided by "self-fulfilling prophecies." We often get what we expect out of a relationship simply because our expectations guide our behavior in ways that produce complementary responses from others. For example, if a man sees himself as being unattractive to women, he more than likely will approach them in a way that communicates his expectations of himself—"You wouldn't want to go out with me, would you?"

Accordingly, as you enter your contract negotiations, it is important to consider your expectations for yourselves and each other and the influence they may have in determining the success or futility of your efforts. Some assumptions that facilitate or hinder interpersonal communication can be useful as a set of guidelines during your contract negotiations.

These are some assumptions that *facilitate* successful contract negotiations:

The Humility Assumption—I am not perfect, I would like to improve my interpersonal relationships and am willing to learn from you.[1]

The Human Dignity Assumption—I value you and feel you are equal to me.[1]

The Confidentiality Assumption—I will respect confidences which are entrusted to me.[1]

The Responsibility Assumption—I will share equally with you in building and maintaining our partnership.

The Changeability Assumption—I can change and am willing to try. Our relationship can change. We are not set in our ways.

Assumptions that *hinder* contract negotiations:

One (or both) of us "needs help," is mentally disturbed.

Our relationship is poor, hopeless, "on the rocks."[1]

My partner does not know what he's really like. I am going to get him to see the Truth about himself.[1]

All of our problems are my partner's fault. He is the one who needs to change.

My partner had better change, "or else."

My partner has hurt me. Now I am going to get even.

We are the way we are. There's no sense in stirring things up.

It seems apparent, then, that an atmosphere of trust, respect, and understanding, in which successful contract negotiations thrive, is most likely to occur when individuals are willing to listen and respond to each other without feeling that they are taking the risk of being manipulated or coerced.

The Product

When writing your contract, strive to avoid either extreme rigidity or excessive generalization in your statement.

Try to *determine your personal priorities* before specifying your goals. Identify your non-negotiables early in the process so you can work with or around them.

Very useful, especially during initial negotiations, is an *outline format*; it reads easily and encourages succinctness and clarity.

In writing each section, go from a *general objective* to the specific steps you will take to realize it. State your *action steps* so that both of you can understand your goal or purpose. Use *specific behavioral examples* to clarify what you mean. For instance, if you are experiencing difficulty in managing conflict, you might state "dealing with conflict" as a general objective. As action steps, you might list the following: "Both partners will define the issue before pursuing the argument"; "John/Margaret calls time out when he/she is no longer able to listen effectively"; "Margaret summarizes what has been said before presenting new information."

It is also helpful to visualize a *sequence of action steps*. In the example given above, "defining the issue" logically preceded the other steps since it is important to agree on the subject for argument before beginning to discuss it.

To avoid confusion, separate each general objective and the action steps connected with it, just as you would a clause in a contract. If you are developing a method for dealing with conflict in one section of your contract, for example, you should not include guidelines for completing chores, unless the chores are directly related to your conflict.

The best way to change is to act differently *now*. People have a tendency to postpone remedial actions, especially when they seem difficult or costly, but the past cannot be relived. Specify your action steps in *the present tense* and in the active voice, such as "summarizes," "clarifies," "asks," "takes," "names."

Have an objective outsider read your contract to make sure your goals and terms are clear. Remember, however, that your purpose should not be to persuade this person to take sides with either partner on an issue.

Finally, specify a time in the future *to review your contract* and renegotiate it if necessary. When reviewing your contract, you might ask some of the following questions:

Are the behaviors called for by the contract appropriate to the issue?

---

[1]This assumption and several of the others in this listing are taken from K. Hardy, *The Interpersonal Game* (Provo, Utah: Brigham Young University Press, 1967), p. 4.

Do the action steps adequately represent the behavior associated with the general objective?

Is the contract too rigid or too flexible?

As they are stated, are the objectives attainable?

Do the objectives agree with the philosophy of our relationship and with the aim of shared responsibility?

Contracting explicit, negotiated interpersonal contracts can be a very useful device for change in intimate relationships. The success of the process requires an atmosphere of mutual trust, time, helpful assumptions about each other, clear objectives, and a sequence of specific action steps toward the goal of mutual change.

SUGGESTED ACTIVITY

The facilitator presents the lecturette to a training group. (The participants can be given this material in written form.)

Group participants are then asked to discuss some of their goals for personal behavior change; to select a "partner" with whom they would like to share the process of negotiating and writing a contract; to share the basis of their "partnership" with the group; to read the "Guidelines"; and then to negotiate their contracts privately.

After negotiation, the entire group is reinformed to discuss and respond to the contracting process.

Clark Carney
S. Lynne McMahon

REFERENCE

Sherwood, J. J., & Glidewell, J. C. Planned renegotiation: A norm-setting OD intervention. In J. E. Jones & J. W. Pfeiffer (Eds.), *The 1973 annual handbook for group facilitators.* San Diego: University Associates, 1973, 195-202.

CONFLICT-RESOLUTION STRATEGIES

Conflict is a daily reality for everyone. Whether at home or at work, an individual's needs and values constantly and invariably come into opposition with those of other people. Some conflicts are relatively minor, easy to handle, or capable of being overlooked. Others of greater magnitude, however, require a strategy for successful resolution if they are not to create constant tension or lasting enmity in home or business.

The ability to resolve conflict successfully is probably one of the most important social skills that an individual can possess. Yet there are few *formal* opportunities in our society to learn it. Like any other human skill, conflict resolution can be taught; like other skills, it consists of a number of important subskills, each separate and yet interdependent. These skills need to be assimilated at both the cognitive and the behavioral levels (*i.e.*, Do I understand how conflict can be resolved? Can I resolve specific conflicts?).

RESPONSES TO CONFLICT SITUATIONS

Children develop their own personal strategies for dealing with conflict. Even if these preferred approaches do not resolve conflicts successfully, they continue to be used because of a lack of awareness of alternatives.

Conflict-resolution strategies may be classified into three categories—avoidance, defusion, and confrontation. The accompanying figure illustrates that avoidance is at one extreme and confrontation is at the other.

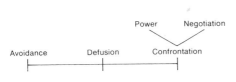

A Continuum of Responses to Conflict Situations

Avoidance

Some people attempt to avoid conflict situations altogether or to avoid certain types of conflict. These people tend to repress emotional reactions, look the other way, or leave the situation entirely (for example, quit a job, leave school, get divorced). Either they cannot face up to such situations effectively, or they do not have the skills to negotiate them effectively.

Although avoidance strategies do have survival value in those instances where escape is possible, they usually do not provide the individual with a high level of satisfaction. They tend to leave doubts and fears about meeting the same type of situation in the future, and about such valued traits as courage or persistence.

Defusion

This tactic is essentially a delaying action. Defusion strategies try to cool off the situation, at least temporarily, or to keep the issues so unclear that attempts at confrontation are improbable. Resolving minor points while avoiding or delaying discussion of the major problem, postponing a confrontation until a more auspicious time, and avoiding clarification of the salient issues underlying the conflict are examples of defusion. Again, as with avoidance strategies, such tactics work when delay is possible, but they typically result in feelings of dissatisfaction, anxiety about the future, and concerns about oneself.

Confrontation

The third major strategy involves an actual confrontation of conflicting issues or persons. Confrontation can further be subdivided into *power* strategies and *negotiation* strategies. Power strategies include the use of physical force (a punch in the nose, war); bribery (money, favors); and punishment (withholding love, money). Such tactics are often very effective from the point of view of the "successful" party in the conflict: He wins, the other person loses. Unfortunately, however, for the loser the real conflict may have only just begun. Hostility, anxiety, and actual physical damage are usual byproducts of these win-lose power tactics.

With negotiation strategies, unlike power confrontations, both sides can win. The aim of negotiation is to resolve the conflict with a compromise or a solution which is mutually satisfying to all parties involved in the conflict. Negotiation, then, seems to provide the most positive and the least negative byproducts of all conflict-resolution strategies.

NEGOTIATION SKILLS

Successful negotiation, however, requires a set of skills which must be learned and practiced. These skills include (1) the ability to determine the nature of the conflict, (2) effectiveness in initiating confrontations, (3) the ability to hear the other's point of view, and (4) the utilization of problem-solving processes to bring about a consensus decision.

Diagnosis

Diagnosing the nature of a conflict is the starting point in any attempt at resolution through negotiation. The most important issue which must be decided is whether the conflict is an ideological (value) conflict or a "real" (tangible) conflict—or a combination of both. *Value conflicts* are exceedingly difficult to negotiate. If, for example, I believe that women should be treated as equals in every phase of public and private life, and you believe they should be protected or prohibited in certain areas, it would be very difficult for us to come to a position that would satisfy us both.

A difference of values, however, is really significant only when our opposing views affect us in some real or tangible way. If your stand on women's place in society results in my being denied a job that I want and am qualified to perform, then we have a negotiable conflict. Neither of us needs to change his values for us to come to a mutually acceptable resolution of the "real" problem. For example, I may get the job but, in

return, agree to accept a lower salary or a different title or not to insist on using the all-male executive dining room. If each of us stands on his principles—maintaining our value conflict—we probably will make little headway. But if, instead, we concentrate on the tangible effects in the conflict, we may be able to devise a realistic solution.

The Israeli-Arab conflict provides a good example of this point. In order to settle the tangible element in the conflict—who gets how much land—ideological differences do not need to be resolved. It is land usage that is the area of the conflict amenable to a negotiated settlement.

It is important to determine whether a conflict is a real or a value conflict. If it is a conflict in values resulting in nontangible effects on either party, then it is best tolerated. If, however, a tangible effect exists, that element of the conflict should be resolved.

Initiation

A second skill necessary to conflict resolution is *effectiveness in initiating a confrontation*. It is important not to begin by attacking or demeaning the opposite party. A defensive reaction in one or both parties usually blocks a quick resolution of differences. The most effective way to confront the other party is for the individual to state the tangible effects the conflict has on him or her. For example: "I have a problem. Due to your stand on hiring women as executives, I am unable to apply for the supervisory position that I feel I am qualified to handle." This approach is more effective than saying, "You male chauvinist pig—you're discriminating against me!" In other words, confrontation is not synonymous with verbal attack.

Listening

After the confrontation has been initiated, the confronter must be capable of *hearing the other's point of view*. If the initial statement made by the other person is not what the confronter was hoping to hear, defensive rebuttals, a "hard-line" approach, or explanations often follow. Argument-provoking replies should be avoided. The confronter should not attempt to defend himself,

140

explain his position, or make demands or threats. Instead, he must be able to engage in the skill termed *reflective* or *active* listening. He should listen and reflect and paraphrase or clarify the other person's stand. When the confronter has interpreted his opposition's position to the satisfaction of the other person, he should again present his own point of view, being careful to avoid value statements and to concentrate on tangible outcomes. Usually, when the confronter listens to the other person, that person lowers his defenses and is, in turn, more ready to hear another point of view. Of course, if both persons are skilled in active listening, the chances of successful negotiation are much enhanced.

Problem-Solving

The final skill necessary to successful negotiation is the use of the problem-solving process to negotiate a consensus decision. The steps in this process are simply stated and easy to apply. (1) Clarifying the problem. What is the tangible issue? Where does each party stand on the issue? (2) Generating and evaluating a number of possible solutions. Often these two aspects should be done separately. First, all possible solutions should be raised in a brainstorming session. Then each proposed solution should be evaluated. (3) Deciding together (not voting) on the best solution. The one solution most acceptable to all

parties should be chosen. (4) Planning the implementation of the solution. How will the solution be carried out? When? (5) Finally, planning for an evaluation of the solution after a specified period of time. This last step is essential. The first solution chosen is not always the best or most workable. If the first solution has flaws, the problem-solving process should be begun again at step 1.

Since negotiation is the most effective of all conflict-resolution strategies, the skills necessary to achieve meaningful negotiation are extremely important in facing inevitable conflicts.

Suggested Activity

See also "Conflict Fantasy: A Self-Examination," in the Structured Experiences section of this *Annual*.

Joan A. Stepsis

REFERENCES

Gordon, T. *Parent effectiveness training*. New York.: Peter H. Wyden, Inc., 1971. This book outlines a similar approach to negotiating, emphasizing parent-child conflicts. It also contains several exercises relevant to a number of the skills discussed in this lecturette. The author is indebted to Gordon for his differentiation of "real" vs. "ideological" conflicts.

Wiley, G. E. Win/lose situations. In J. E. Jones and J. W. Pfeiffer (Eds.), *The 1973 annual handbook for group facilitators*. San Diego: University Associates, 1973, 105-107.

COG'S LADDER:
A MODEL OF GROUP DEVELOPMENT

The Cog's Ladder model consists of five steps of group development.

The first step is called the *Polite* stage. In this phase, group members are getting acquainted, sharing values, and establishing the basis for a group structure. The group members need to be liked.

The second step is *Why We're Here*. During this phase the group members define the objectives and goals of the group.

The third step consists of a *Bid for Power*. On this step of the ladder to maturity, group members attempt to influence one another's ideas, values, or opinions. This stage is characterized by competition for attention, recognition, and influence.

The fourth step is cooperative—the *Constructive* stage. In this phase, group members are open-minded, listen actively, and accept the fact that others have a right to different value systems. This stage might also be referred to as the "team-action" stage.

The fifth and final step is one of unity, high spirits, mutual acceptance, and high cohesiveness. It is the *Esprit* stage.

1. POLITE

The initial item on every group's agenda is to get acquainted, whether or not the leader of the group allows time for it. Generally, a T-group will begin with members introducing themselves. Name tags are provided to members of other groups to aid in the process of "getting to know you." Polite conversation includes information-sharing, which helps group members anticipate each other's future responses to group activities.

This lecturette is based on an article which previously appeared in *Advanced Management Journal*, Vol. 37, No. 1 (January, 1972), pp. 30-37.

During this phase, some group members rely on stereotyping to help categorize other members. A group establishes an emotional basis for future group structure. Cliques are formed which will become important in later phases. The items on the hidden agendas of group members stay hidden and do not usually affect behavior at this time. The need for group approval is strong. The need for group identity is low or completely absent. Group members participate actively, though unevenly, and usually agree that getting acquainted is important to the group. Conflict is usually absent in this phase.

Behavioral Rules

The rules of behavior seem to be to keep ideas simple; say acceptable things; avoid controversy; avoid serious topics; if sharing feelings, keep feedback to a minimum; avoid disclosure.

Nonverbal exercises are best to accelerate the Polite stage. By eliminating words, group members respond only to nonverbal behavior. Instead, when conversation and bodily gestures transmit conflicting signals, the Polite stage slows down because group members must spend time to sort out the signals from the noise.

2. WHY WE'RE HERE

When a group is ready to grow beyond the Polite stage, it usually enters the Why We're Here stage. Group members want to know the group's goals and objectives.

Some members demand a written agenda. A branch of managerial science (Management by Objectives) focuses on this step of group maturity. A task-oriented group needs to spend more time in this phase than a personal-growth group. For example, while T-groups will usually discuss establishing a purpose but will not agree on one, a team finds that agreement on goals is essential to group success.

Cliques

In the second phase cliques start to wield influence. Cliques grow and merge as clique members find a common purpose. Hidden agenda items begin to be sensed as group members try to verbalize group objectives most satisfying to themselves.

Identity as a group is still low. The need for group approval declines from what it was in the Polite stage as group members begin taking risks and displaying commitment. There is usually active participation from all members.

In a T-group, it is not uncommon for participants to look to the trainer to supply a group goal. Structure appears to evolve in this phase.

The time spent in this phase varies widely. Some groups omit it completely, while a few groups will give it most of their allotted time. Much seems to depend on the task to be done. The easier it is to define objectives, the faster a group appears to agree on them. When purpose comes from outside the group, the members will still discuss it in order to gain understanding and to build commitment. The group also needs to know that the purpose agreed on is important.

3. BID FOR POWER

The third stage of the model, Bid for Power, is characterized by competition.

In this phase a group member tries to rationalize his own position and to convince the group to take the action he feels is appropriate. Other members are closed minded and are accused of not listening. Conflict in the group rises to a higher level than in any other stage of group growth. A struggle for leadership occurs which involves active participation by all cliques, or subgroups. Typical attempts to resolve this struggle include voting, compromise, and seeking arbitration from an outside group.

The group does not feel a strong team spirit during this phase. Rather, some members may feel very uncomfortable as latent hostility is expressed. Some group members, who contribute willingly in earlier phases, remain completely silent in the Bid for Power phase. Other members relish the opportunity to compete and attempt to dominate the group. In T-groups these members may be accused of "bulldozing."

Cliques take on the greatest importance in this phase. Through cliques, the group members find they can wield more power.

Hidden agenda items cause a behavior change. Members who easily concealed their hidden agendas in earlier stages now find that other group members are becoming aware of these hidden items.

In T-groups, feedback in this phase can be stinging. Disclosure is cautiously attempted. The need for group approval declines below the level it has in step 2. Group members are willing to go out on a limb and risk the censure of the group. In all groups, creative suggestions fall flat because the group feels that the author wants credit (power) for the suggestion.

The group still does not build an identity in this phase. The range of participation by group members is the widest of any phase. That is, there is a greater difference between the speaking time of the least and the most talkative member in this phase than in any other phase.

The need for structure is strong. In T-groups the content during this phase may well be whether to elect a rotating chairman, a recording secretary, or a group leader. This process is, in reality, a bid for power.

Roles are important in third-phase activity. The group-building and maintenance roles are most important. The harmonizer, the compromiser, the gatekeeper, and the follower try to maintain an acceptable balance between the needs of individual group members and the needs of the group. The harmonizer seeks to reduce the level of conflict to offset the tendency that the aggressor will raise the conflict levels.

Some groups never mature past this stage. Nevertheless, they can fulfill their task, even though the data indicate that solutions arising out of third-phase activity are not optimum solutions; they never satisfy all group members and, at best, are products of compromise.

4. CONSTRUCTIVE

The transition from the third stage (Bid for Power) to the fourth stage (Constructive) is characterized by an attitude change. Group members give up their attempts to control and substitute an attitude of active listening.

In the Constructive stage, group members are willing to change their preconceived ideas or opinions on the basis of facts presented by other members. Individuals actively ask questions of each other. A team spirit starts to build. Cliques begin to dissolve. Real progress toward the group's goals becomes evident. Leadership is shared. Group identity begins to be important to the group members. The range of participation by members narrows. When conflict arises it is dealt with as a mutual problem rather than a win-lose battle. At this point in a group's growth, it may be difficult to bring in a new member.

Because of members' willingness to listen and to change, a group in this phase will often use the talents of any individual who can contribute effectively. Practical creativity can be high because the group is willing to accept creative suggestions. Furthermore, creative suggestions are solicited by the group, listened to, questioned, responded to, and, if appropriate, acted on.

Depending on the talents of the group members and the problem to be solved, an optimum solution or decision—almost always better than any offered by a single group member—can result from fourth-phase interaction. For this reason some businesses are attempting to organize for "team" group activity.

Any group exercises which enhance the basic values of group cooperativeness are appropriate for groups in this phase, such as those based on sharing, helping, listening, anticipating group needs, questioning, and building. Competitive exercises at this point tend to disrupt group growth, as they apply gentle pressure to regress to phase 3 (Bid for Power).

Group leaders can be most effective in this phase by asking constructive questions, summarizing and clarifying the group's thinking, trusting the group to achieve its maximum potential, trying to blend in with the group as much as possible, and refraining from making any comments that tend to reward or to punish other group members. An effective group leader will also be tolerant of group members' widely varying abilities to contribute to the group's goals.

5. *ESPRIT*

The fifth and final phase of group growth is the *Esprit* phase. Here the group feels a high group morale and an intense group loyalty. Relationships between individuals are empathetic. The need for group approval is absent because each group member approves of all others and accepts them as individuals. Both individuality and creativity are high. The overall feeling is that "we don't always agree on everything but we do respect each other's views and agree to disagree." A nonpossessive warmth and a feeling of freedom result. Cliques are absent.

The group may create an identity symbol. The members participate as evenly as they ever will. The need for structure depends on whether the group is an action group or a learning group; learning groups have no need for structure if they have evolved to this phase.

At this stage, the group is strongly "closed." If a new member is introduced, the feelings of camaraderie and *esprit* will be destroyed, since the group must regress to an earlier stage and then grow again to the *esprit* stage, carrying the new member along in the process.

A group in this phase continues to be constructive and productive. In fact, such a group usually achieves more than is expected or than can be explained by the apparent talents of the group members.

Hidden Agendas

Although hidden agenda items are present in this phase, they do not seem to detract from the *esprit* and group loyalty. Perhaps group members have granted to themselves and to one another the *right* to have hidden agendas provided it is productive to do so—for the individual and for the group. Or, the trust level may have risen so high that the group trusts each member not to misuse the group loyalty. By this time, the group may be well aware of each member's hidden agenda and may recognize that it holds no threat.

INTERRELATIONSHIPS

Reasons prompting a group to move, or not to move, from one phase to another vary. For example, the transition from phase 1 (Polite) to phase 2 (Why We're Here) seems to occur when any single group member desires it. He can simply say, "Well, what's on the agenda today?" and the group will usually move to phase 2.

The ability to listen has been found to be the most important human trait in helping groups move from phase 3 (Bid for Power) to phase 4 (Constructive). In some cases, where the group as a whole desired to relate in the fourth phase while several members stayed rooted in the third phase, groups have been observed to reject these members.

On the other hand, the transition from phase 3 to phase 4 can be permanently blocked by a strong, competitive group member or by his clique.

The transition from phase 4 (Constructive) to phase 5 (Esprit), however, seems to require unanimous agreement among group members.

Group cohesiveness seems to depend on how well the group members can relate in the same phase at the same time. A group will proceed through these five stages only as far as its members are willing to grow. Each member must be prepared to give up something at each step in order to make the move to the next stage.

To grow from stage 1 (Polite) to stage 2 (Why We're Here), for example, each member must relinquish the comfort of nonthreatening topics and risk the possibility of conflict.

In the move from stage 2 to stage 3 (Bid for Power), he must put aside a continued discussion of the group's purpose and commit himself to a purpose with which he may not completely agree. Further, he must risk personal attacks, which he knows occur in phase 3.

Growing from phase 3 to phase 4 (Constructive) requires individuals to stop defending their own views and to risk the possibility of being wrong. Phase 4 demands some humility.

The step from phase 4 to phase 5 (Esprit) demands that a member trust himself and other group members. And to trust is to risk a breach of trust.

SUGGESTED ACTIVITY

See "Cog's Ladder: A Process-Observation Activity" in the Structured Experiences section of this Annual.

George O. Charrier

REFERENCES

Blake, R. R., & Mouton, J. S. The managerial grid. Houston: Gulf Publishing, 1964.

Cartwright, D., & Zander, A. Group dynamics. New York: Harper & Row, 1953.

Culbert, S.A. The interpersonal process of self-disclosure: It takes two to see one. NTL Institute of Applied Behavioral Science, 1968.

Del Vecchio, A., & Maher, W. Interact. National Council of Catholic Men, 1970.

Haiman, F. S. Group leadership and democratic action. Boston: Houghton Mifflin, 1950.

Hall, E. T. The silent language in overseas business. Harvard Business Review, 1960 (May-June).

Luft, J. Group processes: An introduction to group dynamics. Palo Alto: National Press, 1963.

McGregor, D. The human side of enterprise. New York: McGraw-Hill, 1960.

Pfeiffer, J. W., & Jones, J. E. (Eds.) A handbook of structured experiences for human relations training, Vols. I and II. San Diego: University Associates, 1969, 1970.

Tuckman, B. W. Developmental sequence in small groups. Psychological Bulletin, 1965, 63 (6), 384-399.

Zenger, J. H. A comparison of human development with psychological development in T-groups. Development Journal, 1970 (July).

THE "SHOULDIST" MANAGER

An individual may experience his world and communicate his experiences in different ways. Gestalt theory contrasts three of these ways: *About*ism, *Should*ism, and *Is*ism. In the approach called Aboutism, the individual abstracts his contact with his environment. He *talks about* his life instead of *experiencing* it here and now.

Shouldism is another way of experiencing life. When a person is "shoulding" he continually measures his actions and thoughts against a particular mental set of standards, in an attempt to conform to the image he holds of himself.

Yet another approach, in direct contrast to Shouldism, is Isism. In this approach, the individual tries to become as aware as possible of his own feelings (whatever they may be) and to act accordingly. The "is-istic" mode values spontaneity, naturalness, and freedom, in contrast to Shouldism's deliberation, good manners, and self-control.

All of these concepts apply, of course, to organization life as they do to most other areas of our lives. Shouldism, particularly, often affects managers in special ways. A person may have a set of ideas about proper managerial behavior—"how I ought to act as a manager"—gathered from a number of sources.

For example, a formal, prescribed set of rules may be provided by the organization. In some companies these rules may deal not only with situations at work, but also with personal conduct off the job. Usually, however, the manager's "shoulds" are accumulated from other sources as well—his sense of the traditions of good management, his observations (which may be incomplete or distorted) of senior managers, a stereotype of the executive. Or the manager may have gathered his set of shoulds from a management training program. (Such a program, incidentally, often includes the rules of appropriate interpersonal behavior learned in human relations training sessions.)

However he has acquired his shoulds, the manager combines these with his personal way of behaving that he has been developing since infancy into an elaborate system of what he thinks is acceptable behavior. In other words, he restricts his way of experiencing and reacting to his world. He becomes inhibited; he does not allow himself to be spontaneous, to be "himself," to live in the is-istic mode. His subordinates model their behavior on his, and another generation of "shouldist" managers results.

For a number of decades, the emphasis in organizations has been on planning and control. Of course, the complexity of present-day organizational requirements demands planned action—and this has been a largely successful approach to organizational needs. However, the emphasis on deliberation and planning has often been carried to the point of insisting on moderated and predictable behavior. Indeed, one of the more radical proposals anyone dealing with organizational theory could make today would be to increase spontaneity in organizations.

This emphasis on control has had its costs: a decrease in spontaneity and excitement, an inability to enjoy. In stressing shouldist aims, the values of Isism have been neglected.

In their attempt to find a "better way" of dealing with people, managerial training programs—especially those that are human relations oriented—try to prescribe certain managerial principles for effective and positive relationships with subordinates, superiors, and peers.

Often—probably far too often—these programs set up a model of "*the* best manager" and try to shape managers to that model. This can have unfortunate results. Many of the managers being trained may simply not relate to the principles implicit in the model except as theoretical information.

Often, however, a manager may attempt to behave in the prescribed way without having accepted or even recognized the values behind such behavior. The result, of course, is incongruous—and it will be quickly perceived as such by the people with whom the manager deals. If the manager finds that he is not rewarded with the improved performances or better relationships that he anticipated, he may, out of a sense of failure, reject human relations theories altogether.

Many managers interpret such theories as manipulative in purpose. Their idea of human relations is "to get people to do what you want them to do, but to make them think it was their idea."

However, the manager bent on manipulation will discover, as Lincoln said, that "you can fool all of the people some of the time and some of the people all of the time, but you can't fool all of the people all of the time." A manager simply encounters the people he works with too frequently and in too many different situations for manipulative strategies to be truly effective.

Most behavioral science theoreticians would, of course, renounce manipulation as a goal. Nevertheless, many theoreticians do not fully recognize an important fact: When an individual follows *any* set of principles that he has not integrated into his own character, he is being manipulated—even if only by himself. In fact, self-manipulation may be the most subtle, and the most limiting, form of manipulation. If you act in certain ways because you think it is "appropriate" or "effective," you are not being "yourself" but are following an image of what you think you *should* be.

Even when a manager is actually convinced, after extensive human relations training, that it is better to treat people according to Theory Y than Theory X, and he "changes" his behavior accordingly, self-manipulation may still be present. He may be spending considerable amounts of his energy trying to repress his natural behavior in favor of a more "effective" approach. As indicated before, under such circumstances the manager is unlikely to achieve successful results and may soon revert to his old behavior patterns.

This does not mean that a manager cannot be helped to learn various techniques and approaches for specific tasks such as running a meeting, organizing work to be done, sensing what is happening among his subordinates, and so on. First, however, he must understand himself and his own particular behavioral characteristics. Then he can learn to adapt helpful techniques to fit his own character, rather than adapt his character to fit the techniques.

After all, it is obvious that successful and well-liked managers may differ tremendously in their personal styles and approaches. This is true at every level of management, in every industry, and even in the same company in the case of managers who succeed one another on the same job. A manager is not wholly defined by what he says or how he acts in a given situation at a specific time to achieve a particular purpose. He is also what he is seen to be by others in unplanned moments, at ease or under stress, when his guard is down.

Just as most of us appreciate a variety of people, with often contradictory characteristics, so we react toward a manager not merely in terms of the way he exercises his managerial role, but in terms of his entire character and outlook.

If a manager's authentic, individual style turns out not to be well suited to a managerial role, then the manager ought to consider changing his specialty. Such a shift would probably be most satisfactory not only for those he deals with, but also for the "shouldist" manager's own self-esteem and personal satisfaction.

The contrast between the Gestalt concepts of Shouldism and Isism is clear. In organization life—and the manager's role, particularly—there might well be a renewed emphasis on the spontaneous values of Isism.

Stanley M. Herman

PERSONAL AND ORGANIZATIONAL PAIN: COSTS AND PROFITS

We have no choice whether life will be painful. We cannot do away with stress, conflict, apprehension, disconfirmation, hurt, failure, and loss in social interchange; it is unlikely that we can reduce very much the overall number of occasions for pain without reducing the opportunities for interpersonal interaction itself.

Practitioners of organization development (OD) sometimes seem almost to promise their clients that an OD "treatment," so to speak, will erase the personal pains ordinarily encountered in organizational life. Some practitioners in the field express the hope that this will happen. Both the promise and the hope should be foregone.

Increasing the Profit of Pain

Despite the fact that we probably cannot reduce by much the total amount of pain with which we must cope, we can do a great deal to increase the profit we get from our pains. Much of our pain—certainly most of our psychological pain—is pain we give each other, and it is within our power to redistribute the occasions upon which pain arises. We can, through explicit agreement about responsibilities and the careful practice of new sorts of collaboration, share more equally the burden of pain. More than that, we can deliberatively and collaboratively choose the *purposes* for which we shall expose ourselves to pain, instead of finding ourselves ambushed by pain dumped on us by others; we can agree with our colleagues on what we hope to purchase with our pain.

To give a commonplace example, we can buy greater satisfaction in the work we do with our colleagues if we are willing to pay the cost in admitting to certain ineptitudes, learning some new role patterns, and persevering in the face of rebuffs. On the other hand, we can avoid risk, rebuff, and stumbling relearning if we are willing to pay the price in joyless work and in shrivelling withdrawal from our colleagues.

In short, we can often purchase longer-lasting satisfactions with shared pain than we can usually buy with hidden pain. Finally, once the necessity for honest pain is openly agreed upon, and once the risk is jointly undertaken with colleagues, we can learn that pain need not be seen as shameful and that it need not cripple action.

What OD can do is to move pain from one occasion to another and from one person to another. This is no small achievement. Our society is built to concentrate pain on certain segments of society and in certain behavior settings. Medical and psychological treatment is much more available to the rich than to the poor. The president's chair is more softly padded than the clerk's.

Necessity of Pain

Without saying very much about it, we all recognize the fact that the conduct of human business must cause pain among those who carry it on. In any large-scale engineering project such as erecting a building, a bridge, or a dam, it is taken for granted by the engineers that a certain number of people will be crippled and a certain number will die. When a large engineering project is completed without a death, engineers congratulate one another. When a stretch of highway is built, it is built with the firm knowledge of all concerned that some of the workmen will be hurt; beyond that, all know that the highway will soon be stained with the blood of some of its users.

People enter the profession of medicine with the sure knowledge that a certain number of them must catch the diseases of their patients. People enter business schools and go into high-pressure occupations under the known risk of psychosomatic ailments and various neuroses. Schools are built with the sure knowledge that those who "fail" in them will be psychologically damaged and marked for life.

Inappropriate Pain

We expect people to encounter pain and damage of certain sorts in certain places: miners in mines, executives in meetings, students in classrooms, spouses in families, motorists on the highways, and soldiers in war. But we do not expect that executives will suffer from cave-ins, spouses from failures on examinations, students from shrapnel wounds, or miners from psychosomatic ulcers; and when they do, we feel that something has gone awry. We are especially likely to be outraged, in brief, when a certain kind of pain occurs in an unaccustomed setting.

What OD Can Do

Organization development alters the settings in which pains appear and the persons upon whom they descend. Furthermore, OD raises questions about the propriety of the previously existing *distribution* of pain. Beyond that, it challenges the old ways of *coping* with pain.

When undertaking to change the distribution of pain and the ways of coping with it, OD begins with what may be the hardest lesson of all; it begins by asking participants to expose their personal pains in the work group. This in itself, if only because it violates existing norms, is painful. Describing personal pains requires the participants to consider explicitly both in words and actions what sort of pain is being paid for what sort of gain, and by whom. Significant OD cannot occur except through this step.

Another way to say all this is that OD does not and cannot merely "improve" organizations in the sense of making the wheels turn a little more quietly. It cannot leave organizations unchanged in their structure or norms and still make them "better."

Practitioners of OD are sometimes challenged (and properly) on the point of whether they are merely making life more comfortable for the bosses—merely giving management still more subtle ways to keep employees pacified. To the extent that practitioners go through superficial motions—such as arranging meetings where the employees are allowed to talk but where pains are not allowed to be shown—the charge is accurate.

Change—Cost and Reward

To the extent that members of the organization are enabled to uncover their reciprocal human resources, despite the risk of exposing the long resentment of an unproductive task or the grief of revealing a talent long wasted, the work will get done more surely. It will bring deeper satisfactions to workers—but only at the cost, if cost it is, of new relations and a new sharing of duties and powers between workers and bosses.

If the worker is to put "more of himself" into his work, he can do so only by finding satisfactions for more of his needs. This deeper transformation of the individual's relation to his work can occur only if it is supported by a corresponding transformation in the norms and processes of the organization.

This deeper transformation puts inevitable stresses on the old ways by which members of organizations have adapted themselves to organizational life. The change will inevitably be painful. And after the change, many people will find themselves facing new pains in new places.

Organization development, if effective, will not merely "improve" organizations—it will change them. It will produce new kinds of behavior settings, new kinds of norms, new potentialities, a new scope for achievement. The new way of life, the new collaboration, the new sharing of achievement and defeat, of joy and sorrow, will be exhilarating and fulfilling beyond what most people have known. But the new way will not be placid nor will it arrive comfortably; its price will be the acceptance of pain in unaccustomed places and the effort of learning to use pain in new ways.

Philip J. Runkel

COMMUNICATION PATTERNS IN ORGANIZATION STRUCTURE

Anyone who has contact with organizations cannot escape the omnipresent phenomenon of organization structure. A new employee comes face-to-face with the imposed condition of structure as soon as he is told, "You report to Mr. Smith." Structuring the organization is generally accepted as an important factor influencing how people perform their vital functions.

In one sense, *structure* means the relatively fixed relationships among the members of an organization. (The typical organization chart is a diagram of fixed relationships.) However, factors which affect interaction patterns and coordination efforts cannot be illustrated with a typical, static chart. Therefore, in another sense, structure can be a diagram of interpersonal processes drawn at a particular point in time.

IDENTIFYING STRUCTURE

Structure may be imposed. Or it may emerge as a group of persons interacting over time. If structure is imposed, it usually is called *formal* structure. If structure emerges from interpersonal interaction, it is sometimes called *informal* structure. In addition, structures that emerge within a formally structured organization may be called *operating* structures. The demands of task, people, and setting involved in performance-supporting interaction usually give rise to operating structure, particularly when the formal structure is insufficient, unrealistic, inefficient, or out of date. Thus, identifying the operating structure is crucial in understanding performance.

Many managers today are concerned whether patterning of relations significantly influences group or organization performance and the social reactions of members. In some organizations, sequential work-flow and assembly-line arrangements have caused problems involving performance, productivity, and satisfaction.

EXPERIMENTS INVESTIGATING STRUCTURE

Insight into problems created or facilitated by various structures has been gained from laboratory experiments, utilizing the concept of a *communication pattern*, to investigate effects of structure on performance and morale. These studies showed that:

1. The structure of a communication pattern affects accuracy of messages communicated.

2. The structure of a communication pattern affects task performance of groups.

3. The structure of a communication pattern affects satisfaction of group members.

Four communication patterns investigated are called Radial, Hierarchical, "Y," and Leader-Centered. In the diagrams following, each letter represents a person and each line a potential communication link. For example, in the radial pattern, person A may communicate with persons B and E but not with person C or D.

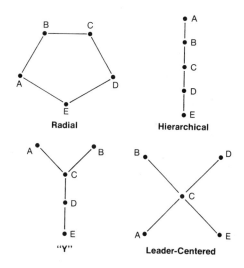

Radial | Hierarchical

"Y" | Leader-Centered

One way of characterizing communication patterns is by centrality. Centrality measures an individual's closeness to other individuals in a particular pattern. The most central position is the position closest to all other positions. Position C has the greatest centrality within the Hierarchical, "Y," and Leader-Centered patterns. In these, position C has the greatest degree of centrality in the Leader-Centered pattern, less in the "Y," and still less in the Hierarchical pattern. No position in the Radial pattern has greater centrality than any other. Within any pattern, centrality limits the independent action of some group members and, therefore, primarily determines the leadership role, variation of activity, and group member satisfaction.

In a star pattern (Leader-Centered) group, for example, the only person who may be enjoying the situation is the leader, person C; the others will probably feel bored and left out. In a circle (Radial) group pattern, however, almost any member can, at one time or another, be the "leader."

A Leader-Centered group is likely to be faster at a specific task than a Radial group. But the Radial group is likely to demonstrate higher morale and more enthusiasm than the Leader-Centered group. A Radial group also seems more capable of coping with change (Leavitt, 1972, pp. 192-193).

Knowledge of patterns can aid a leader in developing an accurate and task-oriented pattern which influences job satisfaction positively. Formal and informal communication patterns in real organizations do have many characteristics discovered and analyzed by researchers. However, one must remember that the regulation of communication flow and the imposition of restrictions in a laboratory setting are *techniques*, not intended to be a close analog of particular groups or organizations. Communication patterns are important potential tools for investigation. However, insight into other aspects of structure—such as span of control, formalization, specialization, and organization size—should complement an understanding of communication-link patterns.

Dave Ford
Ord Elliott

REFERENCES

Davis, J. H. *Group performance.* Reading, Mass.: Addison-Wesley, 1967.

Gibson, J. L., *et al. Organizations: Structure, processes, behavior.* Dallas: Business Publications, 1973.

Hall, R. H. *Organizations: Structure, and process.* Englewood Cliffs: Prentice-Hall, 1972.

Leavitt, H. J. *Managerial psychology.* (3rd ed.) Chicago: University of Chicago Press, 1972.

INTRODUCTION TO THE
THEORY AND PRACTICE SECTION

In leadership and management development, in organization development, in the consulting process, in the whole human relations training field, we believe that the most critical component is the personal, *human* element. Theory, technique, and research are important and invaluable, but they should be seen in perspective, against a framework of the human, the personal, the individual, the practical, the *real*.

**DIMENSIONS OF
FACILITATOR EFFECTIVENESS**

The Person

Empathy	Congruence
Acceptance	Flexibility

Skills

Listening	Responding
Expressing Oneself	Intervening
Observing	Designing

Techniques

Structured	Confrontations
Experiences	Interventions
Instruments	(Verbal and
Lecturettes	Nonverbal)

Theories

Personality	Systems
Group Dynamics	Community Behavior
Organizational Behavior	

The Person

Social ills continue to plague us despite our current, incredible, brilliant technology. We need to learn more about our own interpersonal relationships—and this is what human relations training is about. The common denominator is the *person*. To become better as a facilitator one must become better as a person.

One of the significant personal dimensions is the ability to *feel empathy* for another person. Complete empathy is not possible, of course; we can never experience someone else's situation exactly as he does. But we can try to see things from another person's perspective; this effort is critical.

Acceptance is another important personal dimension—allowing another person to be different, to have a different set of values and goals, to behave differently. Rogers calls this Unconditional Positive Regard (UPR).

Congruence and *flexibility* determine two additional aspects of the person. A congruent person is aware of himself and what he is feeling and is able to communicate that self to another person in a straightforward way. He is healthy and psychologically mature. A flexible person is not dogmatic, opinionated, rigid, or authoritarian. As a consultant he should be able to deal with another person at that person's pace.

If people have these personal attributes, they are therapeutic. Just being around them makes others feel good; they help by being well-integrated persons themselves.

The most meaningful direction a consultant can take is toward improving his own personal development, furthering his own understanding of his values, attitudes, impulses, desires. Two major interpersonal conflicts that a facilitator must be able to resolve for himself are his capacity for intimacy and his relation to authority.

Important as the personal dimension is, however, there are other components involved in successful human relations training.

Skills

Certain basic communication skills are necessary in order to promote individual, group, and organizational growth. A facilitator needs to develop his ability to *listen*, to *express* himself (both verbally and nonverbally), to *observe*, to *respond* to people, to *intervene* artfully in the group process, and to *design* effective learning environments that make efficient use of resources.

Techniques

One can also heighten and improve the effect of human relations training through certain techniques. Structured experiences, instruments, lecturettes, confrontations, verbal and nonverbal interventions are all useful in increasing a facilitator's effectiveness.

Theories

Theory is a resource. It is one of the components a facilitator uses to develop and improve himself as a practitioner.

Theories abound in the human relations field: personality theory, group dynamics, theory of organizational behavior, community behavior, systems theory. Systems theory, for example, has some interesting implications for OD in that it points out that all systems are interdependent and no one can be dealt with in isolation.

Practice

At the moment, human relations practitioners are far ahead of theorists: the tendency is to try out an idea and see if it works first, and then to find the research underpinnings necessary for its justification. Explanation follows practice.

Theory and research are inextricably intertwined with practice—one requires the other. Yet if the choice had to be made between a brilliant theorist thoroughly grounded in technique and theory and a stimulating, effective consultant with a well-integrated personal self—our choice would be the latter.

It is with this emphasis and personal perspective that the Theory and Practice section of this *Annual* is presented.

THE MESSAGE FROM RESEARCH

Jack R. Gibb

Trainers, consultants, and practitioners of human relations training have frequently asked me pertinent questions about research studies in the field. While writing a book on human relations training, I found I had collected a large quantity of materials, from which some impressions, generalizations, and answers could be distilled. I narrowed my list of materials to 344 studies ("A Bibliography of Research on Group Training," listed at the end of this article), which represent the most readily available published studies or completed doctoral dissertations in English that have quantitative data relevant to their stated hypotheses and use group training as the independent variable. In making my selection, I excluded therapy and counseling groups, organizational-change studies, and didactic sessions—except in cases where these studies dealt with an especially relevant issue. I did try, however, to include all studies that met my criteria. Although my list is not complete, it is representative of the research on group training during the quarter century since T-groups were first used by NTL in 1947.

I am very much aware of the difficulty of distilling such a body of reference material in limited space. It has been necessary to list references by number only, to cite in each instance only a few of the most relevant studies, and often to make oversimplified statements about complex issues with conflicting data. Thus, in offering my comments and interpretations, I invite the reader to consult the original sources. They are very rich, heuristic, and full of detail.

My survey, then, leads me to the following conclusions about nineteen of the most frequently asked questions concerning research in group training.

How much research has been done on group training? The following table makes it clear that

there is a great deal more than even the most favorable critics have mentioned. This research is growing rapidly (104, 105), and, judging from the great volume of prepublication drafts and informal papers that I have seen, I would guess that the growth will continue. Particularly impressive in light of earlier academic opposition to group training is the great number of doctoral studies from a wide variety of academic disciplines, indicating a breadth of acceptance and support that may lead to greater quality and integration of research.

Research Studies on the Effects of Group Training During the Period 1947-1972

Years	Doctoral Dissertations	Other Studies	Total
1947-48	1	0	1
1949-50	0	0	0
1951-52	3	2	5
1953-54	0	2	2
1955-56	2	3	5
1957-58	4	5	9
1959-60	2	2	4
1961-62	1	6	7
1963-64	3	8	11
1965-66	10	20	30
1967-68	20	15	35
1969-70	82	27	109
1971-72	75	43	118
Total	203	133	336

Is the current research of sufficient quality to be considered seriously? Yes. It is true that group training research has been justifiably criticized (39, 137) for methodological inadequacies such as poor design, the lack of appropriate comparison groups, irrelevant or unreliable measures, and overgeneralization, but the quality is improving considerably. Some promising long-range efforts are those of Bebout and his associates (15). However, what seems especially limiting, to me, is the frequent lack of representative design. For instance, it is common to provide a sample of 136 participants, say, and then to "sample" one or perhaps two trainers in each condition, comparing trainer style or training method! There is likely to be as much variation in trainers as in other group members. The same flaw holds true in selecting one company, one school, or one group and then making generalized statements about, say, industrial work groups from a sample of one. Nevertheless, I think the quality of research is much better than it is reported to be. More academic support, more adequate research training, and more cross-fertilization with other fields are encouraging developments. Unfortunately, it is academically fashionable to make blanket rejections of the research in this field. Helpful and critically valid are incisive articles such as those by Campbell and Dunnette (39) and Harrison (127), and these have already had a salutary effect on later studies.

Does group training produce changes in participants? Yes; most group training produces changes in many group members.

What kinds of changes are produced? Of what psychological significance? Do they endure? Do they transfer? What kinds of training are most effective? How many people change? What mechanisms account for the changes? The answers to these more significant questions are complex and detailed.

As more than 300 different dependent variable measures were used in the studies I examined, the results can only be summarized here. Investigators report statistically significant increases in such variables as risk-taking, expressed warmth and caring, empathy, internal control, self-esteem, congruence in self- and ideal-concept, interpersonal sensitivity, problem-solving skills, expressiveness, trust, spontaneity, democratic behavior, number of innovations, genuineness, etc. Statistically significant decreases are reported in such variables as feelings of anxiety, rigidity, racial prejudice, discomfort with

feelings, dogmatism, and alienation. Measurements in the studies are taken largely on proximal, perceptual, and affective states; little attention is paid to changes in behavior on the job or in the home, presumably because of the many financial and procedural difficulties of such research. Standardized tests are most often used, the most frequently employed being the Personal Orientation Inventory (27 studies), the Tennessee Self-Concept Scale (22 studies), and the *FIRO-B* (21 studies).

The results, however, are by no means always statistically significant. Self-acceptance, for instance, was measured as a dependent variable in 41 studies, showing positive changes in 21 studies and no change in 20 studies. Individual studies are difficult to interpret. Often there are important discrepancies. Or, perhaps, the control group may make comparable gains. Three studies, for instance, found that the training group did significantly less well than the control group. The differences obtained may be caused by such things as test wisdom, regression toward the mean, random variations in test scores, or rater bias. Similarly, the lack of differences may be due to little "real" difference between conditions, insufficient time in training, a lack of competence of the trainer, insensitive measures, the measurement of tangential variables, or a host of other factors.

Are there negative effects? Yes. The research shows that some participants, following training, report changes that they or others perceive as negative: more irritability on the job or in the family; less tendency to be open with others (327); a greater sense of rebellion towards or discomfort with authority (98); unrealistically increased levels of aspiration and expectation (107); reduced feelings of confidence and security (66); less conformity to an organizational role; more requests for therapy and counseling (183); increased defensiveness (216, 250).

There is, however, evidence linking these negative outcomes to specific flaws or inadequacies in the training situation itself. We do have some clues about the trainer behaviors, group states, or member-member relationships that lead to negative effects: feedback at inappropriately early stages of the group; a very

156

brief training period; insufficient structure, especially at early stages of the group; a tightly controlling leader style; or certain dysfunctional compositional groupings.

Nevertheless, because group training produces more affect than most other types of education and training, it apparently involves some risks. Certain forms of disruption, discomfort, or other negative feelings *may* lead to later growth; others may not.

Are there extreme effects, either positive or negative? There are few hard data. In my opinion there is good clinical evidence of enduring and extreme *positive* effects: dramatic changes in life style, new creativity, greatly increased personal productivity, and the like. Except for the Armor qualitative study (6) of peak experiences, however, little attention is paid to the issue in the studies reported here.

There is considerably more attention to extreme *negative* effects. Reports, frequently undocumented, cite psychotic breaks, divorces, job losses, suicides. While it is not likely that such dramatic negative or positive effects are produced by the brief training experiences evaluated here, training-group experiences, or a succession of them, may, however, trigger certain behaviors or attitudes. Groups such as the quasi-therapeutic "West Coast" encounter groups or intensive personal-growth groups—especially when directed by aggressively stimulating or tightly controlling leaders—may produce highly negative effects. A recent study (183) provides such evidence in the case of college student volunteers. But it seems much less likely to expect these extreme effects from, for instance, process-oriented training groups conducted with adults who are seeking leadership training, improvement of executive skills, or professional growth.

We need, I think, to discover more about the effects of tension level, feeling expression, confrontation, withdrawal, and other member-group states that presumably mediate extreme effects. Some studies suggest profitable directions for future research. One study, for instance, shows that T-group tension triggered less anxiety than was aroused by the pre- and post-tests taken by the participants (148). Another study (194)

found that stress in T-groups did not reach a "deviant" level, while it did in perceptual-isolation student groups.

Do the effects last? We do not know. There are few significant data on this question. It is commonly assumed that the effects dissipate quickly and, in any event, do not endure over long periods of time. Only about a third of the studies made follow-up measurements. Most of these did find that statistically significant results identified immediately at the end of training persisted at least until the follow-up measures, usually performed from one week to six months following training. A few studies made measurements over a longer period of time (one, after 2½ years), but there is no consistency in the results.

Much needed are follow-up studies that measure changes over longer periods, perhaps several years. It is likely that the brief training periods used in the studies are too short to produce enduring effects. We need to know whether "booster shots" make a difference and whether longer periods of training create more lasting change. And perhaps we need further development of measuring techniques and a greater understanding of mediating mechanisms before we can attempt to calculate long-term effects with any precision.

Is group training worth doing? There are some relevant data comparing group training with alternative methods for effecting individual and organizational change. Thirty-six studies compared training groups (sensitivity training, encounter groups, T-groups) with content-centered didactic groups. For most purposes and on most measures, training groups were significantly and consistently superior to didactic groups in the case of attitudinal, perceptual, and self-concept variables, and they were occasionally superior as well in informational outcomes. For instance, when compared with didactic control groups, group training produced more comfort with feelings (2), greater empathy and expressed warmth (318), less submissive behavior (187), better interpersonal relations with peers (102), and higher inner-direction scores (119). On some outcomes, however, didactic groups did better. For instance (136), after case discussion, members changed positions on advocacy papers, whereas training group people did not. Also, lecture-discussion groups were more effective in learning about methods (211). Some studies showed no significant differences between training groups and didactic groups (e.g., 307, 337, 339, 177).

Group training was compared with other models of experiential training (systematic skill training, counseling, etc.) in 22 studies. In ten of the studies the group training outperformed the experiential training, which appeared to be more structured—though it is not always possible to tell from the experimental reports. In five cases the more structured training was superior. Thus, interaction analysis training (227), role-playing (281), and a communications skills workshop (285) were each superior to the training groups in generating measured outcomes. In some studies neither condition improved and in some studies both conditions improved.

More precise measures and long-range "engineering" studies will provide better comparisons of the effectiveness of unstructured group training and of alternative methods of producing organizational change, personal growth, social action, attitude change, and other hoped-for outcomes. Nevertheless, research studies reported here do show that group training can be an effective method of producing significant outcomes in such activities as reducing prejudice (265, 266), training religious leaders (40, 67), working with delinquents (328), race relations (3, 8, 309), marriage relations (36, 236), Job Corps training (319), police-officer training (234), retirement-community work (150), and a host of similar activities relating to social action. Again, however, there are many examples of nonsignificant outcomes when group training is used in similar programs: Catholic nuns (327), prison inmates (215), a black-awareness program (190), adult leaders in the church (297, 31), race-relations programs (188, 197, 141, 306), and male-female relations (97).

Clearly, not all "group training" is alike by any means. From the research results it seems that there are six critical variables to be considered in predicting the effectiveness of a group-training program: the general macroenvironment in which the training occurs, the behavior and leader style of the trainer or consultant, the nature of the feedback, the amount of training,
the group state, and perhaps the technique or method used.

Who participates in the training groups? Persons selecting training are likely to be "special" in some way. In some studies, they have been found to be less self-assured and less well adjusted than the average individual (280), to have less self-esteem, and even, in one study (250), to be in the pathological range on the Tennessee Self-Concept Scale. Other studies have found selectors to be no different from nonselectors (108). Even though the possible relationship between maladjustment in selectors and negative and dysfunctional reactions to group training has been the concern of a number of investigators, there is clearly not enough data on this significant issue. Still, the data do suggest that both researchers and practitioners might well consider selection and screening procedures in composing their training groups.

Who can profit from group training? The studies are not clear on this issue. Researchers, in interpreting their data, have mentioned each of the following classes of people as responding least well to their group experiences: those who have a high need for structure or have high F scores; low verbal participators; nonvolunteers; work mates or team members; hospitalized psychotics; and those who hold nonparticipatory attitudes on management. Other studies, to the contrary, have reported successful group training with each of these groups. My guess, from little hard data, is that some leaders, with appropriate styles, can work well with any of the above groups of people.

How do we compose groups for optimal effects? There is a considerable body of research on this question, with nineteen of the listed studies providing information. Many of the research studies have chosen rather homogeneous groups (e.g., all diabetics, all black female sophomores), but they have no control groups and are interested in other-than-composition variables. Most of the groups, however, are heterogeneous volunteers. Experimental attempts to compare heterogeneity with homogeneity are heuristic but inconclusive: work-oriented or person-oriented members (128); predisposition to a Bionic modality (182); high or low trust on the Rotter test

(238); and *FIRO-B* predispositions (276, 256, 254, 242, 241). There are strong indications that compatible groups may outperform incompatible groups on selected measures, that group atmospheres are influenced by composition, and that there are individual differences in reactions to homogeneity. These reactions may depend on trainer variables (242).

How long should individual group sessions be? There are few hard data. In the experiments, individual sessions have lasted from 5 minutes (!) to over 30 hours. Marathons show significant outcome changes in some studies (88, 168, 240) and not in others, just as weekly two-hour sessions show comparable changes. The few studies that compare spaced and massed training time show no clear differences. There is some evidence, however, that a combination of massed (at the beginning and at the end) and spaced sessions is slightly best (11). In view of the strong interest in this issue and its practical importance, it is surprising that there is not more research. What evidence there is indicates that what goes on in the session is far more important than how long it may last.

How long should the training period last? Again, we have little data to go on. The total training time in the studies varied from one hour to about 60 hours, but a surprising number of studies used only 1 to 12 hours of total training time, a length considered too short by the investigators themselves. One study showed that a three-week laboratory was superior to a two-week laboratory (33), especially when overt behavioral changes are measured. Another study (29), comparing 3-day, 5-day, and 8-day sessions, found little difference between them, but it did find that loss of sensitivity was less after the 8-day than the 3-day experience. Clearly, we need more information.

Are stages of group development significant for learning? The data are sparse. The search for consistent and predictable stages of group development is a continuing one, but as yet not very profitable. Groups differ widely. There seems to be little consistency in developmental trends (194). Promising data indicate that some changes, under some conditions, do take place over time: rated level of trust (70); increases in

interdependence (169); predictable shifts in mood (13); sequences of group themes (184); process movement (210); development of Tuckman's stages (268); and type of work and emotionality (18). Significant work is continuing (72, 200), but the findings at this point are of little help to the practitioner.

What trainer styles or behaviors are most effective? Warm, supportive styles of leadership are consistently found to be effective, leading to high learning. Studies in therapy and counseling concur with this finding.

A variety of sources provides evidence that an effective leader offers some low and flexible, but not controlling or arbitrary, structure. Structured leadership in the early stages may cause less resistance (197) and better decision-making (316). Reducing the structure may cause increased problem-solving ability (74) and increased feeling expression (139).

Can group training be effective without leaders present? Thirty-eight studies used some kind of leaderless condition, with 21 studies employing the programmed Encountertapes. An impressive indication is that groups without leaders physically present showed gains similar to those of leader-led groups, outperformed leader-led groups on several occasions (63, 175, 267), and usually showed fewer decrements or negative outcomes (107, 183, 37, 169). Nevertheless, leader-led groups seem superior for some purposes. When direct comparisons are made, leader-led groups come out best more often than do the tape groups (52, 202, 258, 261, 308, 313). It is significant, however, that the Encountertape groups and Management Grid groups are leader-surrogate groups, that they do provide "structure," and that they are, indeed, often more structured than leader-led groups. Therefore, the critical factor of "leaderlessness" can be tested only when groups are not programmed with tapes, instruments, or instructions. In studies approximating these conditions, groups showed positive gains (37, 107, 169, 244).

Is it possible to train trainers? The evidence on this question is very indirect and inconclusive. Seldom is it gathered from experiments where clear comparisons are made among trained, less trained, and untrained leaders. Some studies do show that training produces gains in expressive warmth and support, which are proven characteristics of effective group leaders. It is assumed that training programs are producing more effective trainers, but the evidence is not clear. We certainly need more data.

What mechanisms lead to participant learning? A recent and promising research direction is toward a more theory-based examination of the mechanisms associated with high or low learning and change. There is illuminating research—with practical applications for group leaders—concerning the following mechanisms, each proposed by researcher or theorist as a primary factor in the learning of participants: therapeutic qualities or behaviors of leaders, members, or relationships (9, 16, 43, 47, 48, 58, 62, 75, 102, 123, 187, 232, 271, 290, 334); group development states (13, 70, 72, 133, 169, 184, 194, 200, 210, 268, 302, 303); formation of TORI trust processes (37, 49, 70, 94, 97, 99, 107, 154, 169, 176, 244, 270); quality and amount of feedback (49, 76, 79, 82, 91, 92, 106, 113, 164, 186, 222); experiencing and sharing of affect in an interactive situation (2, 29, 60, 150, 182, 211); development of self-esteem (31, 34, 46, 50, 54, 73, 139, 173, 233); cognitive integration of the experience (7, 10, 103, 111, 136, 173, 228, 306, 315); and reciprocal disclosure (23, 60, 119, 155, 177, 192, 273, 291, 318).

Each of these formal or informal orientations has led to differential research decisions about overall design, measures of dependent variables, the selection of comparison groups, the analysis of data, and the interpretation of results. In many cases, studies are successively built upon one another, and the collection of data has led to theory reformulation and engineering application. I have discussed these relationships in detail in other publications (104, 105, etc.). The interested reader is referred to the various studies indicated in the bibliography.

Does group training lead to institutional and societal change? Because of space limitations I have omitted from the bibliography the extensive research literature evaluating the application of group training technologies to organization development and institutional change. (This research is discussed in 105.) The evidence is incomplete and often conflicting, but there is strong support for the following conclusion: When routinely applied to institutions, T-groups and encounter groups are ineffective *unless* they are integrated into long-range efforts that include such elements as a total organizational focus, system-wide data collection, provision for feedback and information flow, organization-focused consultation over an extended time, and data-supported theory. Earlier efforts toward group-centered organizational change have often produced little or no change. Recent studies, however, look more promising.

A BIBLIOGRAPHY OF RESEARCH ON GROUP TRAINING

1. Ackerman, P. H. A staff group in a women's prison. *International Journal of Group Psychotherapy*, 1972, **22**, 364-373.

2. Alderfer, C. P., & Lodahl, T. M. A quasi experiment on the use of experimental methods in the classroom. *Journal of Applied Behavioral Science*, 1971, **7**, 43-69.

3. Allan, T. K., & Allan, K. H. Sensitivity training for community leaders. *Proceedings of the Annual Convention of the American Psychological Association*, 1971, **6**, 577-578.

4. Anzalone, A. P. Personality characteristics relevant to research in human relations training. Unpublished doctoral dissertation, University of Nevada, 1972.

5. Argyris, C. Explorations in interpersonal competence—II. *Journal of Applied Behavioral Science*, 1965, **1**, 255-269.

6. Armor, T. H. Peak-experiences and sensitivity training groups. Unpublished doctoral dissertation, University of California, Los Angeles, 1969.

7. Aronson, S. R. A comparison of cognitive vs focused-activities techniques in sensitivity group training. Unpublished doctoral dissertation, University of Connecticut, 1971.

8. Bagdassarroff, B. J., & Chambers, N. E. An evaluation of the encounter group process through assessment of value shifts and patterns of black and white educators. Unpublished doctoral dissertation, United States International University, 1970.

9. Baker, F. S. A comparison between two methods of teaching prospective counselors to provide high therapeutic conditions. Unpublished doctoral dissertation, Case Western Reserve University, 1970.

10. Baldwin, B. A. Change in interpersonal cognitive complexity as a function of a training group experience. *Psychological Reports*, 1972, **30**, 935-940.

11. Bare, C. E., & Mitchell, R. R. Experimental evaluation of sensitivity training. *Journal of Applied Behavioral Science*, 1972, **8**, 263-276.

12. Bass, B. M. Reactions to "12 Angry Men" as a measure of sensitivity training. *Journal of Applied Psychology*, 1962, **46**, 120-124. (a)

13. Bass, B. M. Mood changes during a management training laboratory. *Journal of Applied Psychology*, 1962, **46**, 361-364. (b)

14. Baumgartel, H., & Goldstein, J. W. Need and value shifts in college training groups. *Journal of Applied Behavioral Science*, 1967, **3**, 87-101.

15. Bebout, J., & Gordon, B. The value of encounter, L. N. Solomon & B. Berzon (Eds.), *New perspectives on encounter groups*. San Francisco: Jossey-Bass, 1972, 83-118.

16. Bellanti, J. The effects of an encounter group experience on empathy, respect, congruence, and self-actualization. Unpublished doctoral dissertation, Pennsylvania State University, 1971.

17. Ben-Zeev, S. Comparison of diagnosed behavioral tendencies with actual behavior. In D. Stock & H. A. Thelen (Eds.), *Emotional dynamics and group culture*. Washington, D.C.: National Training Laboratories, 1958, 26-34. (a)

18. Ben-Zeev, S. Sociometric choice and patterns of member participation. In D. Stock & H. A. Thelen (Eds.), *Emotional dynamics and group culture*. Washington, D.C.: National Training Laboratories, 1958, 84-91. (b)

19. Berlin, J. I. Program learning for personal and interpersonal improvement. *Acta Psychologica*, 1964, **13**, 321-335.

20. Berzon, B., Pious, C., & Farson, R. E. The therapeutic event in group psychotherapy: A study of subjective reports by group members. *Journal of Individual Psychology*, 1963, **19**, 204-212.

21. Berzon, B., Reisel, J., & Davis, D. P. Peer: An audio tape program for self-directed small groups. *Journal of Humanistic Psychology*, 1969, **9**, 71-86.

22. Berzon, B., & Solomon, L. N. Research frontier: The self-directed therapeutic group—three studies. *Journal of Counseling Psychology*, 1966, **13**, 490-497.

23. Bidwell, W. W. A study of openness as a factor in the human relations training of preservice teachers. Unpublished doctoral dissertation, Ohio State University, 1966.

24. Bitner, J. A. Diabetes, self-concept, and an encounter group: A pilot study using phenomenological analysis and the Tennessee Self Concept Scale. Unpublished doctoral dissertation, United States International University, 1972.

25. Blake, R. R., & Mouton, J. S. Some effects of managerial grid seminar training on union and management attitudes toward supervision. *Journal of Applied Behavioral Science*, 1966, **2**, 387-400.

26. Bobele, H. K. An exploratory study of the use of body-movement as a personal growth adjunct in sensitivity training. Unpublished doctoral dissertation, University of California, Los Angeles, 1970.

27. Bolman, L. Laboratory versus lecture in training executives. *Journal of Applied Behavioral Science*, 1970, **6**, 323-336.

28. Bolman, L. Some effects of trainers on their T groups. *Journal of Applied Behavioral Science*, 1971, **7**, 309-326.

29. Bramson, R. M. Changes in social sensitivity in group training. Unpublished doctoral dissertation, University of California, Berkeley, 1969.

30. Brenner, A. M. Self-directed T groups for elementary teachers: Impetus for innovation. *Journal of Applied Behavioral Science*, 1971, **7**, 327-341.

31. Brook, R. C. Self concept changes as a function of participation in sensitivity training as measured by the Tennessee Self Concept Scale. Unpublished doctoral dissertation, Michigan State University, 1968.
32. Brown, L. D. "Research action": Organizational feedback, understanding, and change. *Journal of Applied Behavioral Science*, 1972, 8, 697-712.
33. Bunker, D. R., & Knowles, E. S. Comparison of behavioral changes resulting from human relations training laboratories of different lengths. *Journal of Applied Behavioral Science*, 1967, 3, 505-523.
34. Bunker, G. L. The effect of group perceived esteem on self and ideal concepts in an emergent group. Unpublished master's thesis, Brigham Young University, 1961.
35. Burke, R. L., & Bennis, W. G. Changes in perception of self and others during human relations training. *Human Relations*, 1961, 14, 165-182.
36. Burns, C. W. Effectiveness of the basic encounter group in marriage counseling. Unpublished doctoral dissertation, University of Oklahoma, 1972.
37. Byrd, R. E. Self-actualization through creative risk taking. Unpublished doctoral dissertation, New York University, 1970.
38. Calliotte, J. A. The effect of basic encounter groups on student teachers' personality traits and subsequent teaching behaviors. Unpublished doctoral dissertation, St. Louis University, 1971.
39. Campbell, J. P., & Dunnette, M. D. Effectiveness of T-group experiences in managerial training and development. *Psychological Bulletin*, 1968, 70, 73-104.
40. Carney, E. A measurement study of passively defensive persons in communication work-shops. *Dissertation Abstracts International*, 1971, 31, 12.
41. Carron, T. J. Human relations training and attitude change: A vector analysis. *Personnel Psychology*, 1964, 17, 403-424.

42. Cecere, G. J. Change in certain personality variables of counselor education candidates as a function of T-groups. Unpublished doctoral dissertation, Rutgers State University, 1969.
43. Cerra, P. F. The effects of T-group training and group video recall procedures on affective sensitivity, openmindedness, and self-perception change in counselors. Unpublished doctoral dissertation, Indiana University, 1969.
44. Cherlin, D. L. Anxiety and consultant differences in self-study groups. Unpublished doctoral dissertation, Yale University, 1967.
45. Cimbolic, P. The effects of sensitivity training upon black clients' perceptions of counselors. Unpublished doctoral dissertation, University of Missouri, 1970.
46. Cirigliano, R. J. Group encounter effects upon the self-concepts of high school students. Unpublished doctoral dissertation, St. John's University, 1972.
47. Clark, J. V., & Culbert, S. A. Mutually therapeutic perception and self-awareness in a T-group. *Journal of Applied Behavioral Science*, 1965, 1, 180-194.
48. Clark, J. V., Culbert, S. A., & Bobele, H. K. Mutually therapeutic perception and self-awareness under variable conditions. *Journal of Applied Behavioral Science*, 1969, 5, 65-72.
49. Clarke, J. F. Some effects of nonverbal activities and group discussion on interpersonal trust development in small groups. Unpublished doctoral dissertation, Arizona State University, 1971.
50. Cleveland, S. E., & Morton, R. B. Group behavior and body image: A follow-up study. *Human Relations*, 1962, 15, 77-85.
51. Connolly, W. J. Participation in a communication training laboratory and actualizing changes in church leaders. Unpublished doctoral dissertation, United States International University, 1970.

52. Conyne, R. K. Facilitator-directed and self-directed sensitivity models: Their effect on self-perceptual change. Unpublished doctoral dissertation, Purdue University, 1970.
53. Cooper, C. L. The influence of the trainer on participant change in T-groups. *Human Relations*, 1969, 22, 515-530.
54. Cooper, C. L. T-group training and self-actualization. *Psychological Reports*, 1971, 28, 391-394.
55. Cooper, C. L. An attempt to assess the psychologically disturbing effects of T-group training. *British Journal of Social & Clinical Psychology*, 1972, 11, 342-345. (a)
56. Cooper, C. L. Coping with life stress after sensitivity training. *Psychological Reports*, 1972, 31, 602. (b)
57. Cooper, C. L., & Oddie, H. Group training in a service industry: Improving social skills in motorway service area restaurants. *Interpersonal Development*, 1972, 3, 13-39.
58. Costinew, A. E. The basic encounter group as an innovation in counselor education. Unpublished doctoral dissertation, Wayne State University, 1970.
59. Counseling Center Staff. Effects of three types of sensitivity groups on changes in measures of self-actualization. *Journal of Counseling Psychology*, 1972, 19, 253-254.
60. Culbert, S. A. Trainer self-disclosure and member growth in two T-groups. *Journal of Applied Behavioral Science*, 1968, 4, 47-73.
61. Culbert, S. A., Clark, J. V., & Bobele, H. K. Measures of change toward self-actualization in two sensitivity training groups. *Journal of Counseling Psychology*, 1968, 15, 53-57.
62. Danish, S. J. Factors influencing changes in empathy following a group experience. *Journal of Counseling Psychology*, 1971, 18, 262-267.
63. Davies, M. M. A comparison of the effects of sensitivity training and programmed instruction on the development of human relations skills of beginning nursing students in an associate degree program. Unpublished doctoral dissertation, St. Louis University, 1970.
64. Delaney, D. J., & Heimann, R. A. Effectiveness of sensitivity training on the perception of non-verbal communications. *Journal of Counseling Psychology*, 1966, 13, 436-440.
65. Delaney, E. T. The effects of a group experience on the self-awareness of supervisor trainees and teacher trainees in supervision. Unpublished doctoral dissertation, University of Illinois, 1970.
66. DeMichele, J. H. The measurement of rated training changes resulting from a sensitivity training laboratory of an overall program in organization development. Unpublished doctoral dissertation, New York University, 1966.
67. Dietterich, P. M. An evaluation of a group development laboratory approach to training church leaders. Unpublished doctoral dissertation, Boston University, 1961.
68. Diller, J. V. The encounter group as a means of reducing prejudice. Unpublished doctoral dissertation, University of Colorado, 1971.
69. Dodson, J. P. Participation in a bi-racial encounter group: Its relation to acceptance of self and others, racial attitudes, and interpersonal orientations. Unpublished doctoral dissertation, Purdue University, 1970.
70. Draeger, C. Level of trust in intensive small groups. Unpublished doctoral dissertation, University of Texas, Austin, 1968.
71. Dunnette, M. D. People feeling: Joy, more joy, and the "slough of despond." *Journal of Applied Behavioral Science*, 1969, 5, 25-44.
72. Dunphy, D. C. Phases, roles, and myths in self-analytic groups. *Journal of Applied Behavioral Science*, 1968, 4, 195-226.
73. Dyer, R. D. The effects of human relations training on the interpersonal behavior of college students. Unpublished doctoral dissertation, University of Oregon, 1967.
74. Easton, C. W. The effect of the structure and emphasis of group training methods on communication skills attitude change and problem-solving ability. Unpublished doctoral dissertation, Rutgers State University, 1971.

75. Edwards, D. D. Effects of an extended encounter group experience upon counselor facilitation of client self-exploration. Unpublished doctoral dissertation, North Illinois University, 1971.

76. Egelhoff, E. A. Encounter group feedback and self-perception change. Unpublished doctoral dissertation, University of Texas, 1970.

77. Eisenbeiss, M. J. The effect of sensitivity group experience on counselors-in-training and their understanding of counselee communication. Unpublished doctoral dissertation, University of Wyoming, 1972.

78. Eisenstadt, J. W. An investigation of factors which influence response to laboratory training. *Journal of Applied Behavioral Science*, 1967, 3, 575-578.

79. Elbert, W. E. Changes in self-concept, self-actualization, and interpersonal relations as a result of video feedback in sensitivity training. Unpublished doctoral dissertation, East Texas State University, 1969.

80. Elliott, A. L. Fostering self actualization of high school students through general semantics training in encounter groups. Unpublished doctoral dissertation, United States International University, 1969.

81. Elliott, G. R. The effects of the T-group method upon the communication and discrimination skills of counselor trainees. Unpublished doctoral dissertation, Kent State University, 1971.

82. Fadale, V. E. An experimental study of the effects of videotape feedback in a basic encounter group. Unpublished doctoral dissertation, East Texas State University, 1969.

83. Fennell, N. W., & Kenton, R. W. Some effects on personality of a basic encounter group in a community college class. Unpublished doctoral dissertation, United States International University, 1970.

84. Fenwick, D. D. An evaluation of a planned program of human relations development for college students. Unpublished doctoral dissertation, University of Nebraska, Teachers College, 1967.

85. Fisher, I. S. The relationship between selected personality characteristics and the effects of training to develop small group productivity skills and interpersonal competence. Unpublished doctoral dissertation, University of Miami, 1970.

86. Force, E. J. Personal changes attributed to human relations training by participants, intimates and job colleagues. Unpublished doctoral dissertation, Michigan State University, 1969.

87. Foster, B. W. An investigation of changes in levels of dogmatism, self-concept, needs for inclusion, affection, and control, as a result of encounter group experiences with selected graduate students. Unpublished doctoral dissertation, University of South Dakota, 1972.

88. Foulds, M. L. Effects of a personal growth group on a measure of self-actualization. *Journal of Humanistic Psychology*, 1970, 10, 33-38.

89. Foulds, M. L. Changes in locus of internal-external control: A growth group experience. *Comparative Group Studies*, 1971, 2, 293-300.

90. Foulds, M. L., Dirona, R., & Buinan, J. F. Changes in ratings of self and others as a result of a marathon group. *Comparative Group Studies*, 1970, 1, 349-355.

91. Freid, J. B. The effects of input and feedback on accuracy of self descriptions in short-term sensitivity training. Unpublished doctoral dissertation, University of South Carolina, 1970.

92. French, J. R. P., Jr., Sherwood, J. J., & Bradford, D. L. Change in self-identity in a management training conference. *Journal of Applied Behavioral Science*, 1966, 2, 210-218.

93. Friedlander, F. The impact of organizational training laboratories upon the effectiveness and interaction of ongoing work groups. *Personnel Psychology*, 1967, **20**, 289-308.

94. Friedlander, F. The primacy of trust as a facilitator of further group accomplishment. *Journal of Applied Behavioral Science*, 1970, **6**, 387-400.

95. Friedman, V. S. The effects of sensitivity training on students at a major metropolitan university. Unpublished doctoral dissertation, St. Louis University, 1969.

96. Gage, N. L., & Exline, R. V. Social perception and effectiveness in discussion groups. *Human Relations*, 1953, **6**, 381-396.

97. Gamez, G. L. T-groups as a tool for developing trust and cooperation between Mexican-American and Anglo-American college students. Unpublished doctoral dissertation, University of Texas, 1970.

98. Gamez, K. B. Transfer of learning from T-groups to other groups. Unpublished doctoral dissertation, University of Texas, 1970.

99. Garner, H. G. Effects of human relations training on the personal, social, and classroom adjustment of elementary school children with behavior problems. Unpublished doctoral dissertation, University of Florida, 1970.

100. Gassner, S. M., Gold, J., & Sandowsky, A. M. Changes in the phenomenal field as a result of human relations training. *Journal of Psychology*, 1964, **58**, 33-41.

101. Geisler, J., & Gillingham, W. The effects of a personal growth experience. *National Catholic Guidance Conference Journal*, 1971, **15**, 183-186.

102. Geitgey, D. A. A study of some effects of sensitivity training on the performance of students in associate degree programs of nursing education. Unpublished doctoral dissertation, University of California, Los Angeles, 1966.

103. Gibb, J. R. Effects of role playing upon (a) role flexibility and upon (b) ability to conceptualize a new role. Paper presented at the meeting of the American Psychological Association, Cleveland, September 1953.

104. Gibb, J. R. The effects of human relations training. In A. E. Bergin & S. L. Garfield (Eds.), *Handbook of psychotherapy and behavior change*. New York: Wiley, 1971, 839-862.

105. Gibb, J. R. A research perspective on the laboratory method. In L. B. Benne, J. R. Gibb, & R. Lippitt (Eds.), *The laboratory method of changing and learning*. New York: Wiley, 1974.

106. Gibb, J. R., Smith, E. E., & Roberts, A. H. Effects of positive and negative feedback upon defensive behavior in small problem-solving groups. Paper presented at the meeting of the American Psychological Association, San Francisco, September 1955.

107. Gibb, L. M., & Gibb, J. R. Effects of the use of "participative action" groups in a course in general psychology. Paper presented at the meeting of the American Psychological Association, Washington, D.C., September 1952.

108. Gilligan, J. F. Personality characteristics of selectors and non-selectors of sensitivity training and the relationship between selector characteristics and training outcomes. Unpublished doctoral dissertation, University of Idaho, 1972.

109. Gilliland, S. F. Some effects of a human relations laboratory on moral orientation. Unpublished doctoral dissertation, Boston University, 1971.

110. Gold, J. S. An evaluation of a laboratory human relations training program for college undergraduates. Unpublished doctoral dissertation, Columbia University, 1967.

111. Goldberg, R. M. Changes in self-ideal discrepancies in sensitizers and repressors as a function of a sensitivity training experience. Unpublished doctoral dissertation, University of Cincinnati, 1970.

112. Goldstein, S. R. Differential effects of physical and nonphysical encounter group techniques on dimensions of self-esteem, interpersonal relations and defense. Unpublished doctoral dissertation, Temple University, 1970.

113. Golembiewski, R. T., & Blumberg, A. Confrontation in complex organizations: Attitudinal changes in a diversified population of managers. *Journal of Applied Behavioral Science*, 1967, 3, 525-547.

114. Golembiewski, R. T., Carrigan, S. B., Mead, W. R., Munzenrider, R., & Blumberg, A. Toward building new work relationships: An action design for a critical intervention. *Journal of Applied Behavioral Science*, 1972, 8, 135-148.

115. Gordon, R. D. A quantitative investigation of selected dynamics and outcomes of the basic encounter group. Unpublished doctoral dissertation, University of Kansas, 1971.

116. Grant, S. J. The effects of a basic encounter group experience on supervision by supervisor trainees. Unpublished doctoral dissertation, University of Illinois, 1970.

117. Grater, H. Changes in self and other attitudes in a leadership training group. *Personnel Guidance Journal*, 1958, 37, 493-496.

118. Green, F. The effects of a task-encounter work-shop on the administrative staff of a public school system. Unpublished doctoral dissertation, United States International University, 1970.

119. Green, J. G. A study of expressed behavior changes occurring as a result of exposure to filmed classroom situations and T-group sensitivity training. Unpublished doctoral dissertation, Washington State University, 1969.

120. Greiner, L. E. Organizational change and development. Unpublished doctoral dissertation, Harvard University, 1965.

121. Haiman, F. S. Effects of training in group processes on open-mindedness. *Journal of Communication*, 1963, 13, 236-245.

122. Hall, J., & Williams, M. S. Group dynamics training and improved decision making. *Journal of Applied Behavioral Science*, 1970, 6, 39-68.

123. Hammann, K. A. Trainer orientation, member experience, and empathy: A true experiment exploring the source and kinds of impact of sensitivity training. Unpublished doctoral dissertation, University of Michigan, 1970.

124. Harpel, R. L. The effect of encounter group composition upon social and political attitudes. Unpublished doctoral dissertation, University of Colorado, 1970.

125. Harrison, R. Impact of the laboratory on perceptions of others by the experimental group. In C. Argyris, *Interpersonal competence and organizational effectiveness*. Homewood, Ill.: Irwin, 1962, 261-271.

126. Harrison, R. Cognitive change and participation in a sensitivity training laboratory. *Journal of Consulting Psychology*, 1966, 30, 517-520.

127. Harrison, R. Research on human relations training: Design and interpretation. *Journal of Applied Behavioral Science*, 1971, 7, 71-86.

128. Harrison, R., & Lubin, B. Personal style, group composition, and learning. *Journal of Applied Behavioral Science*, 1965, 1, 286-301.

129. Harrow, M., *et al.* The T-group and study group laboratory experiences. *Journal of Social Psychology*, 1971, 85, 225-237.

130. Heck, E. J. A training and research model for investigating the effects of sensitivity training for teachers. *Journal of Teacher Education*, 1971, 22, 501-507.

131. Heiner, H. G. An application of T-group method to the teaching of family relationships. Unpublished doctoral dissertation, University of Washington, 1970.

132. Hellebrandt, E. T., & Stinson, J. E. The effects of T-group training on business game results. *Journal of Psychology*, 1971, 77, 271-272.

133. Hill, W. F. The influence of sub groups on participation in human relations training groups. Unpublished doctoral dissertation, University of Chicago, 1955.

134. Himber, C. Evaluating sensitivity training for teen-agers. *Journal of Applied Behavioral Science*, 1970, **6**, 307-322.

135. Hipple, J. L. Effects of differential human relations laboratory training designs on the interpersonal behavior of college students. Unpublished doctoral dissertation, University of Iowa, 1970.

136. Holloman, C. R., & Hendrick. H. W. Effect of sensitivity training on tolerance for dissonance. *Journal of Applied Behavioral Science*, 1972, **8**, 174-187.

137. Holmes, C. B. The effect of sensitivity training on counseling behavior. Unpublished doctoral dissertation, University of Toledo, 1971.

138. Howard, R. D. The effects of structured laboratory learning on the inter-personal behavior of college students. Unpublished doctoral dissertation, University of Oregon, 1969.

139. Hull, D. The effect of laboratory training on self concept and self actualization. Unpublished doctoral dissertation, University of Missouri, 1971.

140. Hull, W. F. Changes in world-mindedness after a cross-cultural sensitivity group experience. *Journal of Applied Behavioral Science*, 1972, **8**, 115-121.

141. Innis, M. N. An analysis of sensitivity training and laboratory method in effecting changes in attitudes and concepts. Unpublished doctoral dissertation, University of Houston, 1970.

142. Jacobson, E. A., & Smith, S. J. Effect of weekend encounter group experience upon interpersonal orientations. *Journal of Consulting & Clinical Psychology*, 1972, **38**, 403-410.

143. Jeffers, N. E. An examination of new techniques for enhancing human growth experiences. Unpublished doctoral dissertation, Claremont Graduate School, California, 1971.

144. Jepson, P. Some effects of self-actualizing growth on teen-agers. Unpublished doctoral dissertation, United States International University, 1969.

145. Johnson, D. L. The relationships between human relations training for educational administrators and changes in their leader behavior. Unpublished doctoral dissertation, University of Maryland, 1969.

146. Johnson, D. L., Hanson, P. G., Rothaus, P., Morton, R. B., Lyle, F. A., & Moyer, R. Follow-up evaluation of human relations training for psychiatric patients. In E. H. Stein and W. B. Bennis (Eds.), *Personal and organizational change through group methods*. New York: Wiley, 1965, 152-168.

147. Johnson, D. L., Rothaus, P., & Hanson, P. G. A human relations training program for hospital personnel. *Journal of Health and Human Behavior*, 1966, **7**, 215-223.

148. Johnson, D. W., Kavanagh, J. A., & Lubin, B. T-groups, tests, and tension. *Small Group Behavior*, 1973 (February), 81-88.

149. Johnson, L. K. The effect of trainer interventions on change in personal functioning through T group training. Unpublished doctoral dissertation, University of Minnesota, 1966.

150. Johnson, R. F. The effects of encounter groups on selected age related variables in a volunteer geriatric population. Unpublished doctoral dissertation, University of Miami, 1970.

151. Johnston, J. J. Some effects of three kinds of groups in the human relations area. Unpublished doctoral dissertation, University of California, Los Angeles, 1967.

152. Joure, S. A., Frye, R. L., Green, P. C., & Cassens, F. P. Examples of overuse of sensitivity training. *Training & Development Journal*, 1971, **25**, 24-26.

153. Kassarjian, H. H. Social character and sensitivity training. *Journal of Applied Behavioral Science*, 1965, **1**, 433-440.

154. Kegan, D. L. Trust, openness, and organizational development: Short-term relationships in research and development laboratories and a design for investigating long-term effects. Unpublished doctoral dissertation, Northwestern University, 1971.

155. Kelley, H. H. First impressions in interpersonal relations. Unpublished doctoral dissertation, Massachusetts Institute of Technology, 1948.

156. Kelley, H., & Pepitone, A. An evaluation of a college course in human relations. *Journal of Educational Psychology*, 1952, *43*, 193-209.

157. Kennedy, T. F. An exploration of the effects of sensitivity training upon selected personality traits. Unpublished doctoral dissertation, St. John's University, New York, 1972.

158. Kepes, S. Y. Experimental evaluations of sensitivity training. Unpublished doctoral dissertation, Michigan State University, 1965.

159. Kernan, J. P. Laboratory human relations training: Its effect on the "personality" of supervisory engineers. Unpublished doctoral dissertation, New York University, 1963.

160. Khanna, J. L. A discovery learning approach to inservice training. Paper presented at the meeting of the American Psychological Association, San Francisco, September 1968.

161. King, W. R. The effects of a T-group experience on teacher self-perception and classroom behavior. Unpublished doctoral dissertation, Stanford University, 1970.

162. Klingberg, H. E. An evaluation of sensitivity training effects on self-actualization, purpose in life, and religious attitudes of theological students. Unpublished doctoral dissertation, Fuller Theological Seminary, California, 1971.

163. Koile, E. A., & Draeger, C. T-group member ratings of leader and self in human relations laboratory. *Journal of Psychology*, 1969, *72*, 11-20.

164. Kolb, D. A., Winter, S. K., & Berlew, D. E. Self directed change: Two studies. *Journal of Applied Behavioral Science*, 1968, *4*, 453-471.

165. Komins, A. S. An analysis of trainer influence in T-group learning. Unpublished doctoral dissertation, Boston University, 1972.

166. Koziey, P. W., Loken, J. O., & Field, J. A. T-group influence on feelings of alienation. *Journal of Applied Behavioral Science*, 1971, *7*, 724-732.

167. Kraus, W. A. Laboratory groups: Effect on the tolerance scale of the California Psychological Inventory. Unpublished doctoral dissertation, Ohio University, 1970.

168. Krear, M. L. The influence of sensitivity training on the social attitudes of educational leaders or racially-imbalanced schools. Unpublished doctoral dissertation, United States International University, 1968.

169. LaBoon, S. TORI: A theory of community growth. Unpublished master's thesis, United States International University, 1971.

170. Lakin, M., & Carson, R. C. Participant perception of group process in group sensitivity training. *International Journal of Group Psychotherapy*, 1964, *14*, 116-122.

171. Lasalle, A. J. The effects of encounter and programmed group treatments on self-concept. Unpublished doctoral dissertation, State University of New York, 1970.

172. Lee, R. E. Relationship between basic encounter group and change in self concepts and interpersonal relationships of college low achievers. Unpublished doctoral dissertation, United States International University, 1969.

173. Lee, W. G. Differences in self-concept changes among three educative treatments. Unpublished doctoral dissertation, Florida State University, 1971.

174. Lee, W. S. Human relations training for teachers: The effectiveness of sensitivity training. *California Journal of Educational Research*, 1970, *21*, 28-34.

175. Leiterman, P. R. Attitudinal and behavioral changes in self-directed and leader-directed personal growth groups. Unpublished doctoral dissertation, University of Kentucky, 1970.

176. Leon, J. E. Attitude change, as a result of T-group sessions, in a pre-teaching population. Unpublished doctoral dissertation, Case Western Reserve University, 1972.

177. Levy, S. J. An empirical study of disclosing behavior in a verbal encounter group. Unpublished doctoral dissertation, Yeshiva University, 1971.

178. Levy, S. J., & Atkins, A. L. An empirical investigation of disclosing behavior in a verbal encounter group. *Proceedings of the Annual Convention of the American Psychological Association*, 1971, 6, 297-298.

179. Lieberman, M. A. The relationship between the emotional cultures of groups and individual change. Unpublished doctoral dissertation, University of Chicago, 1958. (a)

180. Lieberman, M. A. The relation of diagnosed behavioral tendencies to member-perceptions of self and of the group. In D. Stock & H. A. Thelen (Eds.), *Emotional dynamics and group culture*. Washington, D.C.: National Training Laboratories, 1958, 35-49. (b)

181. Lieberman, M. A. Sociometric choice related to affective approach. In D. Stock and H. A. Thelen (Eds.), *Emotional dynamics and group culture*. Washington, D.C.: National Training Laboratories, 1958, 71-83. (c)

182. Lieberman, M. A. The influence of group composition on change in affective approach. In D. Stock and H. A. Thelen (Eds.), *Emotional dynamics and group culture*. Washington, D.C.: National Training Laboratories, 1958, 131-139. (d)

183. Lieberman, M. A., Yalom, I. D., & Miles, M. B. *Encounter groups: First facts*. New York: Basic Books, 1972.

184. Liebowitz, B. A method for the analysis of the thematic structure of T-groups. *Journal of Applied Behavioral Science*, 1972, 8, 149-173.

185. Link, S. L. A study of degree of change in self-concept as a result of participation in a marathon T-group. Unpublished doctoral dissertation, University of Oregon, 1971.

186. Lippitt, G. L. Effects of information about group desire for change on members of a group. Unpublished doctoral dissertation, American University, 1959.

187. Lippitt, L. L. Participant learnings resulting from a human relations training experience for teacher trainees. Unpublished doctoral dissertation, University of Michigan, 1971.

188. Little, F. W. The effect of a personal growth group experience upon measured self concept of a selected group of black college freshmen. Unpublished doctoral dissertation, Purdue University, 1971.

189. Livingston, D. G. The effects of varying group organization upon perception of power and benefit. Unpublished doctoral dissertation, University of Kansas, 1951.

190. Livingston, L. B. Self-concept change of black college males as a result of a weekend black experience encounter workshop. Unpublished doctoral dissertation, Arizona State University, 1971.

191. Lohman, K., Zenger, J. H., & Wescler, I. R. Some perceptual changes during sensitivity training. *Journal of Educational Research*, 1959, 53, 28-31.

192. Loper, M. D. Videotaped feedback and changes in self-concept during and after sensitivity training. Unpublished doctoral dissertation, University of California, Los Angeles, 1970.

193. Lubin, B., & Zuckerman, M. Affective and perceptual-cognitive patterns in sensitivity training groups. *Psychological Reports*, 1967, 21, 365-376.

194. Lubin, B., & Zuckerman, M. Level of emotional arousal in laboratory training. *Journal of Applied Behavioral Science*, 1969, 5, 483-490.

195. Lumpkin, M. A. The effect of an encounter group experience on the role anxiety and therapeutic competence of student therapists. Unpublished doctoral dissertation, Texas Technological University, 1971.

196. Lundgren, D. C. Interaction process and identity change in T-groups. Unpublished doctoral dissertation, University of Michigan, 1968.

197. Lundgren, D. C. Trainer style and patterns of group development. *Journal of Applied Behavioral Science*, 1971, 7, 689-709.

198. Lynch, A. Q. The effects of basic encounter and task training group experiences on undergraduate advisors to freshmen women. Unpublished doctoral dissertation, University of Florida, 1968.

199. Lynn, A. W. Measures of self-actualization changes and their relationship to interaction preferences among encounter group participants. Unpublished doctoral dissertation, University of Southern California, 1972.

200. Mann, R. D. The development of the member-trainer relationship in self-analytic groups. *Human Relations*, 1966, 19, 84-117.

201. Marchand, R. H. A comparison of T-group and practicum approaches to the training of undergraduate resident assistants. Unpublished doctoral dissertation, Florida State University, 1972.

202. Maroun, T. J. Differential effects of two methods of encounter group training on the personal growth of counselor candidates. Unpublished doctoral dissertation, Indiana University, 1970.

203. Mase, B. F. Changes in self-actualization as a result of two types of residential group experience. Unpublished doctoral dissertation, Northwestern University, 1971.

204. Massarik, F., & Carlson, C. The California Psychological Inventory as an indicator of personality change in sensitivity training. Unpublished master's thesis, University of California, Los Angeles, 1960.

205. Mates, M. E. The effects of trainer personality on trainer behavior and on participant personality change in a sensitivity training experience. Unpublished doctoral dissertation, George Peabody College for Teachers, 1972.

206. Mathis, A. G. Development and validation of a trainability index for laboratory training groups. Unpublished doctoral dissertation, University of Chicago, 1955.

207. Maxey, J. H. The effects of interaction analysis training and sensitivity training on the verbal teaching behavior of pre-service teachers. Unpublished doctoral dissertation, University of Michigan, 1970.

208. McFarland, G. N. Effects of sensitivity training utilized as in service education. Unpublished doctoral dissertation, George Peabody College for Teachers, 1970.

209. McGee, R. D. A study of sensitivity training as a method of changing self concept. Unpublished doctoral dissertation, University of Tennessee, 1969.

210. Meador, B. D. Individual process in a basic encounter group. *Journal of Counseling Psychology*, 1971, 18, 70-76.

211. Merriam, M. L. The effects of two group methodologies on interpersonal behavior. Unpublished doctoral dissertation, Pennsylvania State University, 1970.

212. Michael, E. M. The effect of the human relations training upon the academic achievement of pre- and early adolescent children. Unpublished doctoral dissertation, Wayne State University, 1968.

213. Miles, M. B. Changes during and following laboratory training: A clinical-experimental study. *Journal of Applied Behavioral Science*, 1965, 1, 215-242.

214. Miller, G. M. The effects of sensitivity training design and personality factors upon the attitudes of group participants. Unpublished doctoral dissertation, Case Western Reserve University, 1969.

215. Miller, J. H. Sensitivity training with incarcerated criminals: Personality correlates of participant duration and an assessment of therapeutic value. Unpublished doctoral dissertation, Auburn University, 1971.

216. Mindes, S. The differential effect of a modified encounter group experience on the achievement test performance of high and low-defensive pupils. Unpublished doctoral dissertation, New York University, 1970.

217. Minter, J. R. The effects of sensitivity training on self concept and attitudes of student teachers. Unpublished doctoral dissertation, East Texas State University, 1969.

218. Mitchell, M. D. Machiavellianism, control, and social desirability: Their relation to certain outcomes of human relations training. Unpublished doctoral dissertation, Purdue University, 1967.

219. Mitchell, R. R. An evaluation of the relative effectiveness of spaced, massed, and combined sensitivity training groups in promoting positive behavior change. Unpublished doctoral dissertation, University of California, Los Angeles, 1969.

220. Morton, R. B. The organizational training laboratory—some individual and organization effects. Advanced Management Journal, 1965, 30, 58-67.

221. Moscow, D. T-group training in the Netherlands: An evaluation and cross-cultural comparison. Mens en Onderneming, 1969, 23, 345-362.

222. Myers, G. E., Myers, M. T., Goldberg, A., & Welch, C. E. Effect of feedback on interpersonal sensitivity in laboratory training groups. Journal of Applied Behavioral Science, 1969, 5, 175-186.

223. Myrick, R. D., & Paré, D. D. A study of the effects of group sensitivity training with student counselor-consultants. Counselor Education & Supervision, 1971, 11, 90-96.

224. Nadler, E. B., & Fink, S. L. Impact of laboratory training on sociopolitical ideology. Journal of Applied Behavioral Science, 1970, 6, 79-92.

225. Nance, E. E. The effects of human relations training on selected personality variables. Unpublished doctoral dissertation, Western Michigan University, 1971.

226. Nath, R. Dynamics of organizational change: Some determinants of managerial problem solving and decision making competences. Unpublished doctoral dissertation, Massachusetts Institute of Technology, 1964.

227. Nye, L. S. K. The development and implementation of two pre-practicum training approaches and an evaluation of their effects upon counseling performance. Unpublished doctoral dissertation, Purdue University, 1971.

228. Orsburn, J. D. Sensitivity training versus group lectures with high school problem students. Unpublished doctoral dissertation, Kent State University, 1966.

229. Osborne, G. E. The relationships between sensitivity training, self-perception and student teaching behavior in a program for elementary education student teachers. Unpublished doctoral dissertation, Purdue University, 1970.

230. Oshry, B. K., & Harrison, R. Transfer from here-and-now to there-and-then: Changes in organizational problem diagnosis stemming from T-group training. Journal of Applied Behavioral Sciences, 1966, 2, 185-198.

231. Parker, C. C. The effects of the group process experience on rigidity as a personality variable. Unpublished doctoral dissertation, Ball State University, 1971.

232. Parry, K. A. The effect of two training approaches on counselor effectiveness. Unpublished doctoral dissertation, University of Missouri, 1969.

233. Peters, D. R. Self-ideal congruence as a function of human relations training. Journal of Psychology, 1970, 76, 199-207.

234. Pfister, G. C. An investigation of the effectiveness of laboratory training in increasing interpersonal communication skills with police officers. Unpublished doctoral dissertation, University of Washington, 1970.

235. Pickhardt, C. E. Perceptions by self and others of female black and white teachers from segregated and desegregated schools before and after a six week training institute. Unpublished doctoral dissertation, University of Texas, 1970.

236. Pilder, R. J. Some effects of laboratory training on married couples. Unpublished doctoral dissertation, United States International University, 1972.

237. Pino, C. J. Illinois Institute of Technology interaction in sensitivity training groups. Unpublished doctoral dissertation, Illinois Institute of Technology, 1969.

238. Piper, W. E. Evaluation of the effects of sensitivity training and the effects of varying group composition according to interpersonal trust. Unpublished doctoral dissertation, University of Connecticut, 1972.

239. Poe, B. J. The effect of sensitivity training on the relationship between risk taking and other selected behavioral factors. Unpublished doctoral dissertation, East Texas State University, 1971.

240. Pollack, D., and Stanley, G. Coping and marathon sensitivity training. Psychological Reports, 1971, 29, 379-385.

241. Pollack, H. B. Change in homogeneous and heterogeneous sensitivity training groups. Journal of Consulting and Clincial Psychology, 1971, 37, 60-66.

242. Powers, J. R. Trainer orientation and group composition in laboratory training. Unpublished doctoral dissertation, Case Institute of Technology, 1965.

243. Pratt, W. M. The effectiveness of the use of the T-group laboratory method as an adjunct to a developmental approach to teaching. Unpublished doctoral dissertation, East Texas State University, 1969.

244. Pressman, M. L. A study of an intensive TORI weekend group experience and its effects on interpersonal skills. Unpublished master's thesis, University of Utah, 1970.

245. Psathas, G., & Hardert, R. Trainer interventions and normative patterns in the T-group. Journal of Applied Behavioral Science, 1966, 2, 149-169.

246. Pyke, S. W., & Neely, C. A. Evaluation of a group communication training program. Journal of Communication, 1970, 20, 291-304.

247. Rand, L. P., & Carew, D. K. Comparison of T-group didactic approaches to training undergraduate resident assistants. Journal of College Student Personnel, 1970, 11, 432-438.

248. Rankin, R. C. Attitudinal perceptions of black students and white students as influenced by an instrumented laboratory experience. Unpublished doctoral dissertation, Arizona State University, 1971.

249. Reddy, W. B. Sensitivity training as an integral phase of counselor education. Counselor Education & Supervision, 1970, 9, 110-115. (a)

250. Reddy, W. B. Sensitivity training or group psychotherapy: The need for adequate screening. International Journal of Group Psychotherapy, 1970, 20, 366-371. (b)

251. Reddy, W. B. Interpersonal compatibility and self-actualization in sensitivity training. Journal of Applied Behavioral Science, 1972, 8, 237-240. (a)

252. Reddy, W. B. On affection, group composition, and self-actualization in sensitivity training. Journal of Consulting & Clinical Psychology, 1972, 38, 211-214. (b)

253. Reddy, W. B. The impact of sensitivity training on self-actualization: A one year follow-up. Comparative Group Studies, in press.

254. Reddy, W. B., & Byrnes, A. The effects of interpersonal group composition on the problem solving behavior of middle managers. Journal of Applied Psychology, 1972, 56, 516-517.

255. Reisel, J. A search for behavior patterns in sensitivity training groups. Unpublished doctoral dissertation, University of California, Los Angeles, 1959.

256. Riley, R. An investigation of the influence of group compatibility on group cohesiveness and change in self-concept in a T-group setting. Unpublished doctoral dissertation, University of Rochester, 1970.

257. Ring, B. Recognized similarity: An investigation of significant events reported by encounter group participants. Unpublished doctoral dissertation, Boston University, 1972.

258. Rios, R. M. The comparative effects of tape-led, led, and leaderless groups. Unpublished doctoral dissertation, University of Southern California, 1972.

259. Rosenthal, D. Perception of some personality characteristics in members of a small group. Unpublished doctoral dissertation, University of Chicago, 1952.

260. Rothaus, P. Instrumented role playing in a psychiatric training laboratory. *Archives of General Psychiatry*, 1964, 11, 400-410.

261. Rothaus, P., Johnson, D. L., & Blank, G. Changing the connotations of mental illness in psychiatric patients. *Journal of Counseling Psychology*, 1967, 14, 258-263.

262. Rothaus, P., Johnson, D. L., Hanson, P. G., Brown, J. B., & Lyle, F. A. Sentence-completion test prediction of autonomous and therapist-led group behavior. *Journal of Counseling Psychology*, 1967, 14, 28-34.

263. Rothaus, P., Johnson, D. L., Hanson, P. G., Lyle, F. A., & Mayer, R. Participation and sociometry in autonomous and trainer-led patient groups. *Journal of Counseling Psychology*, 1966, 13, 68-76.

264. Rothaus, P., Morton, R. B., Johnson, D. L., Cleveland, S. E., & Lyle, F. A. Human relations training for psychiatric patients. *Archives of General Psychiatry*, 1963, 8, 572-581.

265. Rubin, I. The reduction of prejudice through laboratory training. *Journal of Applied Behavioral Science*, 1967, 3, 29-50. (a)

266. Rubin, I. Increased self-acceptance: A means of reducing prejudice. *Journal of Personality and Social Psychology*, 1967, 5, 233-238. (b)

267. Rudman, S. Positive changes in self-concept as a function of participation in encounter groups and encountertape groups. Unpublished doctoral dissertation, Memphis State University, 1970.

268. Runkel, P. J., Lawrence, M., Oldfield, S., Rider, M., & Clark, C. Stages of group development: An empirical test of Tuckman's hypotheses. *Journal of Applied Behavioral Science*, 1971, 7, 180-193.

269. Russell, W. J. A study of changes in measures of inner-direction, open-mindedness, and intraception during laboratory training designs of the Methodist church. Unpublished doctoral dissertation, Syracuse University, 1968.

270. Rutan, J. C. Self acceptance change as a function of a short term small group experience. Unpublished doctoral dissertation, Boston University, 1971.

271. Sales, A. P. Rehabilitation counselor candidate change resulting from sensitivity group experiences. Unpublished doctoral dissertation, University of Florida, 1971.

272. Santucci, A. A. The effects of T-group process and study skill training on self-confidence levels of economic opportunity fund college freshmen. Unpublished doctoral dissertation, Lehigh University, 1972.

273. Scherz, M. E. Changes in self-esteem following experimental manipulation of self-disclosure and feedback conditions in a sensitivity laboratory. Unpublished doctoral dissertation, George Peabody College for Teachers, 1972.

274. Schmuck, R. A., Runkel, P. J., & Langmeyer, D. Improving organizational problem solving in a school faculty. *Journal of Applied Behavioral Science*, 1969, 5, 455-482.

275. Schubert, P. W. Personality type and self-perceived change resulting from sensitivity group experience. Unpublished doctoral dissertation, Purdue University, 1971.

276. Schutz, W. C., and Allen, V. L. The effects of a T-group laboratory on interpersonal behavior. *Journal of Applied Behavioral Science*, 1966, **2**, 265-286.

277. Schwartz, R. I. An experimental study of massed and spaced encounter. Unpublished doctoral dissertation, State University of New York, 1971.

278. Seashore, C. N. Attitude and skill changes in participative action training groups. Unpublished master's thesis, University of Colorado, 1955.

279. Sebring, R. H. The effects of human relations training on selected student teacher personality variables, attitudes, and behaviors. Unpublished doctoral dissertation, Pennsylvania State University, 1970.

280. Seldman, M. L. An investigation of aspects of marathon-encounter group phenomena: Types of participants and differential perceptions of leaders. Unpublished doctoral dissertation, Temple University, 1971.

281. Shapiro, J. L. An investigation into the effects of sensitivity training procedures. Unpublished doctoral dissertation, University of Waterloo, 1970.

282. Shapiro, J. L., & Diamond, M. J. Increases in hypnotizability as a function of encounter group training: Some confirming evidence. *Journal of Abnormal Psychology*, 1972, **79**, 112-115.

283. Shapiro, J. L., and Ross, R. R. Sensitivity training for staff in an institution for adolescent offenders. *Journal of Applied Behavioral Science*, 1971, **7**, 710-723.

284. Sherwood, J. J. Self identity and referent others. *Sociometry*, 1965, **28**, 66-81.

285. Shilling, L. E. The differential effect of two small group training procedures upon the acquisition of interpersonal communication skills and the extinction of interpersonal anxiety. Unpublished doctoral dissertation, University of Georgia, 1970.

286. Shinn, R. The effects of sensitivity training on oral communication competence among secondary school social studies student teachers. Unpublished doctoral dissertation, University of California, Los Angeles, 1969.

287. Sikes, W. W. A study of some effects of a human relations training laboratory. Unpublished doctoral dissertation, Purdue University, 1964.

288. Skinner, W. W. Effects of systematic human relations training on the organizational and performance characteristics of a medical unit. Unpublished doctoral dissertation, University of Georgia, 1971.

289. Slager, J. B. Leader personality type as a factor of change in T-groups. Unpublished doctoral dissertation, Purdue University, 1972.

290. Smith, D. J. A comparison of the effects of short-term individual counseling, group counseling, and sensitivity training on the self-concepts of male college students. Unpublished doctoral dissertation, Boston College, 1971.

291. Smith, O. P. Changes in self-actualization and self-concept as a result of the use of visual feedback in marathon sensitivity training. Unpublished doctoral dissertation, East Texas State University, 1970.

292. Smith, P. B. Attitude changes associated with training in human relations. *British Journal of Social and Clinical Psychology*, 1964, **3**, 104-112.

293. Smith, P. B., & Honour, T. F. The impact of Phase I managerial grid training. *Journal of Management Studies*, 1969, **6**, 318-330.

294. Smith, W. D. A study of the effects of sensitivity training on the self-concept of student teachers. Unpublished doctoral dissertation, University of New Mexico, 1970.

295. Snortum, J. R., & Myers, H. F. Intensity of T-group relationships as a function of interaction. *International Journal of Group Psychotherapy*, 1971, **21**, 190-201.

296. Solomon, L. N., Berzon, B., & Davis, D. P. A personal growth program for self-directed groups. *Journal of Applied Behavioral Science*, 1970, **6**, 427-452.

297. Spehn, M. R. Relationship between an intensive group experience and change in church leaders' religious attitudes. Unpublished doctoral dissertation, *Dissertation Abstracts International*, 1971, **31**, 12.

298. Steele, F. I. The relationship of personality to changes in interpersonal values effected by laboratory training. Unpublished doctoral dissertation, Massachusetts Institute of Technology, 1965.

299. Steele, F. I. Personality and the "laboratory style." *Journal of Applied Behavioral Science*, 1968, 4, 25-45.

300. Steele, F. I., Zand, D. E., & Zalking, S. S. Managerial behavior and participation in a laboratory training process. *Personnel Psychology*, 1970, 23, 77-90.

301. Stinson, J. E. The differential impact of participation in laboratory training in collaborative task effort on intact groups and fragmented groups. Unpublished doctoral dissertation, Ohio State University, 1970.

302. Stock, D. The relation between the sociometric structure of the group and certain personality characteristics of the individual. Unpublished doctoral dissertation, University of Chicago, 1952.

303. Stock, D., & Ben-Zeev, S. Changes in work and emotionality during group growth. In D. Stock and H. A. Thelen (Eds.), *Emotional dynamics and group culture*. Washington, D.C.: National Training Laboratories, 1958, 192-206.

304. Stockton, R. A. An investigation of the effect of sensitivity training on the attitudes of teacher education students. Unpublished doctoral dissertation, Ball State University, 1969.

305. Stone, P. A. Comparative effects of group encounter, group counseling and study skills instruction on academic performance of underachieving college students. Unpublished doctoral dissertation, University of South Dakota, 1972.

306. Stone, W. O. A study of pre-recorded relaxation training, rational-emotive and personal growth group counseling intervention techniques in the reduction of state anxiety in black multi-occupational trainees. Unpublished doctoral dissertation, Florida State University, 1971.

307. Stoudt, C. L. The comparative effects of sensitivity training, didactic training, and no training on the rating of responses to the Wisconsin counselor education selection. Unpublished doctoral dissertation, University of Wisconsin, 1970.

308. Sutfin, A. B. An evaluation of activities in a human relations training experience. Unpublished doctoral dissertation, Purdue University, 1971.

309. Tallant, W. J. Changes in pre-service teachers involved in a multi-cultural training program utilizing formal presentations, sensitivity training, planned social activities, and a cooperative living arrangement. Unpublished doctoral dissertation, East Texas State University, 1970.

310. Taylor, F. C. Effects of laboratory training upon persons and their work groups. Paper presented at the meeting of the American Psychological Association, Washington, D.C., September 1967.

311. Tchack, E. Self-actualization and clarity of perception of self and others during sensitivity training. Unpublished doctoral dissertation, Columbia University, 1972.

312. Terleski, D. R. The relationship between unstructured and structured sensitivity group experiences and self-perceived changes of group members. Unpublished doctoral dissertation, Purdue University, 1970.

313. Thomas, M. D. Developing human potential through group interaction: A study of changes in personality factors, personal attitudes, and group functioning in university students participating in human relations training. Unpublished doctoral dissertation, University of Kansas, 1970.

314. Tilly, G. T. An evaluation of personality factors associated with changes following laboratory training. Unpublished doctoral dissertation, Louisiana State University, 1971.

315. Tolela, M. Effects of T-group training and cognitive learning on small group effectiveness. Unpublished doctoral dissertation, University of Denver, 1971.

316. Tompkins, D. S. Group effectiveness as a function of leadership style moderated by stage of group development. Unpublished doctoral dissertation, Ohio State University, 1972.

317. Treppa, J. A., & Frickie, L. Effects of a marathon group experience. *Journal of Counseling Psychology*, 1972, **19**, 466-467.

318. Trotzer, J. P. Process comparison of encounter groups and discussion groups using videotape excerpts. *Journal of Counseling Psychology*, 1971, **18**, 358-361.

319. Tucker, M. F. An experimental investigation of human relations laboratory training among disadvantaged Job Corpsmen. Unpublished doctoral dissertation, University of Utah, 1969.

320. Uhes, M. J. Expression of hostility as a function of an encounter group experience. *Psychological Reports*, 1971, **28**, 733-734.

321. Underwood, W. J. Evaluation of laboratory-method training. *Training Directors Journal*, 1965, **19**, 34-40.

322. Vail, J. P. The effects of encountertapes for personal growth on certain specific aspects of the intellectual, behavioral, and self-concept development of culturally disadvantaged Negro girls. Unpublished doctoral dissertation, University of Georgia, 1970.

323. Valiquet, M. I. Individual change in a management development program. *Journal of Applied Behavioral Science*, 1968, **4**, 313-326.

324. Varner, E. B. Impact of basic group encounter on self-actualization of junior college students. Unpublished doctoral dissertation, University of Florida, 1969.

325. Vogt, J. F. A cross-cultural study (Lebanon and United States) of perceptual, attitudinal, and behavioral effects of the laboratory method in a teacher education course. Unpublished doctoral dissertation, University of Michigan, 1970.

326. Wagner, A .B. The use of process analysis in business decision games. *Journal of Applied Behavioral Science*, 1965, **1**, 387-408.

327. Walker, R. E., Shack, J. R., Egan, G., Sheridan, K., & Sheridan, E. P. Change in self-judgments of self-disclosure after group experience. *Journal of Applied Behavioral Science*, 1972, **8**, 248-253.

328. Washburn, R. W. Human relations training for confined delinquents. Unpublished doctoral dissertation, Colorado State University, 1968.

329. Wedel, C. C. A study of measurement in group dynamics laboratories. Unpublished doctoral dissertation, George Washington University, 1957.

330. Weigel, R. G. Outcomes of marathon group therapy and marathon group topical discussion. Unpublished doctoral dissertation, University of Missouri, 1968.

331. Weissman, H. N., Seldman, M., & Ritter, K. Changes in awareness of impact upon others as a function of encounter and marathon group experiences. *Psychological Reports*, 1971, **28**, 651-661.

332. Weldon, F. A. The effects of a value seminar group experience in relation to selected student teacher needs, level of self-esteem and attitudes. Unpublished doctoral dissertation, University of Montana, 1971.

333. Wheeler, W. F. Effects of encounter group methods upon selected measures of the body image. Unpublished doctoral dissertation, University of Southern California, 1971.

334. Wilker, P. B. The effect of sensitivity training on specific counseling skills. Unpublished doctoral dissertation, Rutgers State University, 1971.

335. Willis, R. J. A search for predictors of growth through interpersonal interaction. Unpublished doctoral dissertation, United States International University, 1972.

336. Wolfe, W. W. A study of a laboratory approach to in-service development programs for school administrators and supervisors. Unpublished doctoral dissertation, University of Texas, 1965.

337. Wyse, M. Sensitivity training versus group lectures with elementary school problem students. Unpublished doctoral dissertation, Case Western Reserve University, 1969.

338. Young, J. R. The effects of laboratory training on self-concept, philosophies of human nature, and perceptions of group behavior. Unpublished doctoral dissertation, George Peabody College for Teachers, 1970.

339. Zacker, J. W. The effects of experimental training upon empathy, interpersonal sensitivity, cynicism, and alienation in police recruits. Unpublished doctoral dissertation, City University of New York, 1971.

340. Zand, D. E., Steele, F. I., & Zalking, S. S. The impact of an organizational development program on perceptions of interpersonal, group, and organization functioning, *Journal of Applied Behavioral Science*, 1969, 5, 393-410.

341. Zener, A. E. Human relations training and job corps adjustment. Unpublished doctoral dissertation, University of Utah, 1971.

342. Zenger, J. H. The effect of a team human relations training laboratory on the productivity and perceptions of a selling group. Unpublished doctoral dissertation, University of Southern California, 1967.

343. Zimet, C. N., & Fine, H. J. Personality changes with a group therapeutic experience in a human relations seminar. *Journal of Abnormal and Social Psychology*, 1955, 51, 68-73.

344. Zullo, J. R. T-group laboratory learning and adolescent ego development. Unpublished doctoral dissertation, Northwestern University, 1972.

THERAPEUTIC INTERVENTION AND THE PERCEPTION OF PROCESS

Anthony G. Banet, Jr.

Group psychotherapists have compared their function in the psychotherapy group to the work of an orchestra conductor, a catalyst, a detective, a midwife, a captain of a ship. They have called themselves parents, teachers, guides, facilitators, healers, helpers, coaches, social engineers.

However this complex and difficult leadership position is regarded, the group psychotherapist's primary task function is to work those immediate process issues that offer the greatest promise for group members' growth and behavior change. "Working the issues" involves three major components: accurate perception of the unfolding of the group process; appropriate and helpful intervention designed to produce change; and follow-through with the diverted process after change has been initiated.

Despite alleged differences (whether real or apparent) between psychotherapy groups and other varieties of personal growth and training groups, it is hoped that this discussion of the leadership function will be widely applicable to many groups, psychotherapeutic or not.

The psychotherapy group is a small group of persons (six to twelve members) which employs a trained psychotherapist to help individuals in the group overcome personal deficiencies and make constructive changes in their behavior. Some special characteristics of the psychotherapy group: (a) the members feel that they need help in personal, interpersonal, marital, or vocational areas; (b) members are selected by the psychotherapist to participate; (c) the relationship between group members and the psychotherapist is contractual, with the psychotherapist assuming primary leadership responsibilities; (d) the group meets on a regular basis over a period

of time; (e) verbal interaction is the group's usual, but not exclusive, mode of working.

The group psychotherapist's mission is to provide an environment in which the individual group member can accomplish his aims: develop *awareness* of what he is doing, accept or *own* responsibility for his own behavior, and *act* in accordance with his newly discovered awareness and ownership.

THE GROUP PROCESS

At any given moment in the life of a group, a variety of events is occurring. One member yawns; another is preoccupied with resentment towards his wife. The psychotherapist is impatient. All but two members are seated on the floor. Another member debates whether to disclose the information he gave his individual psychotherapist yesterday. Two members discuss in whispers their scorn for a popular newspaper advice column.

Much is happening. A member addresses the group; attention now focuses on the speaking member. Private events give way to interaction, which is a prime attribute of the psychotherapy group and the reason for its existence.

Group process is the interaction, over time, of two or more of the elements classified in Table 1. More specifically, as defined by Foulkes and Anthony (1957), it is "the interaction of the elements of the (group) situation in their reciprocal relationships and communications, verbal and nonverbal."

Table 1 classifies the various internal and external forces which have impact on the group process and which are to be monitored by the group psychotherapist. The elements reflect the

Table 1. Classification of Process Elements Which Compose the Momentary Field of Active Influences on Group Life*

GROUP	MEMBER	CONTEXTUAL
Interaction System: The pattern of interpersonal behavior and communication among members	**Behavior Style:** How the member tends to behave and communicate while in the group	**Physical and Social Contacts:** The pattern of behavior and communication outside the group with group members or others
Group Emotion: The predominant mood or feeling in the group; the feeling relations among members	**Personal Feeling State:** The needs, drives, urges being experienced	**Emotional Relations:** The type and quality of the feeling relations between group members and outsiders
Normative System: The set of shared ideas about how members, as a group, should feel and behave while in the group	**Internalized Norms:** The degree to which a member incorporates the group norms into his own system	**Contractual Relations:** Relationships between group members and outsiders (spouses, children, parents, employers, etc.) which have obligations attached
Group Culture: The collectively defined preferences and standard operating procedures for working in the group	**Beliefs and Values:** Explicit and implicit definitions of reality; preferences for given ideas, philosophies, world views	**Cultural Interchange:** Feelings about the way group membership is perceived by others; how the group culture can/does interact with the outside world
Executive System: The group's capabilities for developing consciousness; how group leadership is defined and regarded; feelings of members toward the leader and his feelings toward them	**Ego:** The person's capabilities for assessing realities; his strengths, genetic endowment, self-concept; how he feels about himself; his ability to plan and his change potential; intrapsychic events	**Freedom-Control Relations:** How members interact with outside authority figures; degree of dependence on the outside world for nurturance, safety, etc.

*Adapted from Mills (1967).

fact that any group member is an individual who exists in a permanent system outside the group and who joins a temporary system—the psychotherapy group—to change his way of being in the permanent system.

In Lewinian terms, the elements of process compose a momentary field of all forces that actively influence the group life at any given point in time (Lewin, 1935). Behavioral elements, most visible and measurable, are at the top of each of the three categories in Table 1; the elements listed toward the bottom of each section are more covert and inferential. Some elements are always of importance in the psychotherapy group, others only rarely; but, as Mills (1967) emphasizes, there is "no naturalistic nor *a priori* grounds for excluding sectors of elements" if the group is to become an environment for change.[1]

Group Elements

These refer to phenomena which occur while the group is meeting. The *interaction system* is the pattern of interpersonal behavior and communication between members; it is *how* interaction happens in the group. It includes how members are addressed, how they cluster or pair off, whether they speak to individual members or to the entire group, etc. The *group emotion* is the feeling tone, the emotional climate: groups may be playful, angry, fearful, hard at work, depressed, excited. The group emotion may be collectively produced or may be the result of the special influence of one or two powerful members. The *normative system* consists of the set of shared ideas about how members should feel, think, and behave. Group norms may be heavily influenced by the psychotherapist, especially if he sanctions certain types of behavior and discourages others. The *group culture* is separate from the set of group norms. It includes preferences and standard operating procedures, such as sitting on the floor, asking permission to go to the bathroom, touching each other, making "inside" jokes: the degree of formality or informality. The *executive system* includes how group leadership is defined and regarded, how or whether leadership functions are shared, members' feelings for (or about) and perceptions of the psychotherapist, his feelings for (or about) and perceptions of members. The group's capacity to develop consciousness of itself, that is, to become its own leader, is also part of the executive system.

Member Elements

Process events generated by individual group members while they are in the group meeting are member elements. The member's *behavior style* includes his methods of verbal and nonverbal communication, body posture, speech habits; tendencies toward self-disclosure or self-projection, monopolizing or withdrawing, etc. The behavior style may or may not reflect the *personal*

[1] I am indebted to Mills (1967) for his cogent discussion of the sociological aspects of group interaction. Table 1 is a modification of his classification, appropriate to psychotherapy groups.

feeling state, the *needs, drives, or urges* that the member experiences while in the group meeting. There may be considerable variation among individual members in their awareness of body sensations, expectations, comfort level, impulses, wishes and fears. *Internalized norms* refer to the set of group "shoulds" incorporated by the individual member. For the psychotherapy group member, group norms may conflict with norms gathered from other settings. Norms govern specific behaviors, while *beliefs and values* are explicit or implicit definitions of reality (self, the group, outside events) which indicate the ideas or philosophies that the member prizes, prefers, fears, or rejects. The *ego* refers to the member's capabilities for assessing reality, diagnosing his current situation, and altering his style, habits, feelings, and beliefs according to new circumstances. It includes the member's self-concept and self-regard, his strengths, intelligence, genetic endowments, defense system, and level of vulnerability.

Contextual Elements

Often screened out by the here-and-now focus of the training group, contextual elements may assume considerable importance in the psychotherapy situation. The context is the environment in which the group member experiences his difficulties and distortions most painfully: It is here that he wants to change his behavior. Because the psychotherapy group meets only periodically, the "back-home" situation of members is an ever-present reality.

It is usually assumed in group work that a member's behavior in the group corresponds closely to his behavior outside the group. Because of his knowledge of the member's history and context, the psychotherapist can help the member see the parallels between his group behavior and his behavior in his context. Interventions which associate current group events with contextual phenomena have high therapeutic potential.

Contextual elements include events that occur among group members when the group is not in session, as well as interactions with persons unrelated to the group. It is common for social and sexual relationships to develop among group members, and such contextual events may acquire critical importance during the succeeding group sessions.

Physical and social contacts refer to interactions with persons (other group members or nonmembers) outside the group setting. *Emotional relations* are the member's feelings about affective relationships with group members or others outside the group. These include such attitudes as inadequacy and suspicion and ideas of reference. *Contractual relations* are relationships with obligations attached: with spouse, children, parents, employers, or legal authorities, including also a member's financial obligations. *Cultural interchange* refers to the member's position in his culture—whether he feels included, excluded, or alienated; how he feels his membership in the group (*i.e.*, being labeled "sick" or a "patient") is regarded by others outside the group—and the relationship between the culture of the group and the culture of the context. Another cultural aspect is the member's inclusion in outside groups (class, socioeconomic, racial, religious) which may influence his or others' behavior within the group meeting. *Freedom-control relations* represent a member's attitudes toward authority and responsibility and the influence these perceptions have on his and other members' behavior.

PERCEPTION OF GROUP PROCESS

The elements of process constitute a field of bewildering complexity. They vary widely in their significance, visibility, and *pragnanz*.[2] The psychotherapist, in order to perform his vital function for the group, must be able to coordinate his perceptions of process elements and to focus on those which are, at the same time, sufficiently ripe, visible, and important.

What makes the task of the psychotherapist so difficult is that he must be able to perceive what lies under the surface and to form judgments and take action on the basis of his perceptions. Like the video director, he must choose one image

---

[2] A German term meaning "readiness," used in Gestalt therapy.

from several pictures presented by several different cameras. The decision is difficult, but the psychotherapist does have a variety of tools to aid his perception of group process.

Objectives

Much has been written in praise of objectives (Mager, 1962); a precise objective allows a group to know when it has reached its goal. Unfortunately, however, the goals of psychotherapy groups rarely are clearly defined: "setting people free," "working through a neurosis," "reconstructing a defense system." Psychotherapy groups also may be designed to serve specific *functions*—such as support, remotivation, emotional re-education, or socialization—rather than to meet specific *objectives*.

Psychotherapeutic objectives are often vague because few people come to psychotherapy with a clearly stated objective. Psychotherapists sometimes regard a group member's ambiguities as a license to aim at the total reconstruction of the member's personality. But such an overwhelming objective may promote interminable group membership.

A therapeutic contract (Egan, 1970, 1972) is a useful way for a psychotherapy group to specify its objectives. The contract allows the therapist to describe which process variables he will focus on, which variables he will screen out, and what his expectations are. It also allows members to set time limits for decisions and to circumscribe specific areas of behavior change.

Group members' objectives are rarely unanimous. Great disparity in objectives is prized by some psychotherapists and avoided by others. Generally, the more explicit the objectives, the sharper the focus of the group, allowing the psychotherapist to concentrate intensely on one or two elements of process. Precise objectives, of course, do not automatically reduce the importance of all other process elements. Some events may acquire such intensity that they cannot be ignored. For instance, social or sexual contacts between group members outside the group may so influence the process of the group meeting that contracted objectives cannot be pursued. In this situation, objectives can be suspended temporarily or renegotiated.

Theory

The psychotherapist uses theory as a set of lenses to enhance his perception of process. A comprehensive theory can aid his immediate observation and help him to predict future process; it may also guide him to appropriate interventions.

Group Theory

A set of formal or informal assumptions about group life gives the psychotherapist a chance to predict how individuals will behave in the group, what group phenomena are likely to occur, and how the group will grow and develop over time. A group theory reveals order and pattern in a seemingly random or chaotic situation.

Most theories of psychotherapy groups describe the group meeting in metaphorical terms that indicate what is happening in the group, what will happen, and how the psychotherapist will perceive and interpret the happening.

The group as family is a prevalent metaphor in psychoanalytic literature. The psychotherapist may construct the group to heighten transferences to family figures—mother, father, or siblings. The group-as-family becomes a setting in which members relive past events and receive corrective emotional experiences, this time guided by the parent-psychotherapist. In such a group, process elements such as behavior style or group culture may be unimportant, while ego-context interactions may be highly significant.

The group as primal horde—the Tavistock model originated by Bion—focuses only on group and contextual elements, completely ignoring individual member process elements, thus producing an intense examination of authority relations and other "basic assumptions" of the group.

The group as a community of learners is a metaphor which allows the group to see itself as a safe and supportive community in which members can learn about themselves and the process of change. In this model, contextual process elements may be of little or no importance.

The group as theatre—Gestalt therapy—focuses on one-to-one interaction between psychotherapist and individual group member while other group members become observers. As the primary interactive event is the transaction between the leader and a member's ego, such a group may never focus on group elements.

Not all metaphors for the psychotherapy group are explicit; some psychotherapy groups resemble classrooms, others seem to be quasi-religious in character. For some therapists, the model may change from session to session. Group metaphors determine how the psychotherapist conceives his task and which process elements he regards as critical. A psychotherapist may be eclectic, but never atheoretical.

Developmental Theory

Group movement over time, usually occurring in phases, is the concern of developmental theory. Issues crucial in the first few meetings (such as safety, confidentiality, and influence) give way to other issues (degree of self-disclosure, interdependence) as the life of the group proceeds.

Developmental theories differ in particulars (Bennis & Shepard, 1970; Kaplan & Roman, 1963; Rogers, 1970), but there is considerable agreement in the perception of phases. Generally, initial phases of development are concerned with power, authority, and dependency relationships; later phases revolve around questions of intimacy and autonomy. The therapist who is aware of the group's probable development will heighten the accuracy of his perceptions.

Table 2 indicates the perceptual focus given to the elements of process by various representative theories and objectives. Elements within the *unshaded area* are seen as important and critical; elements within the *shaded area* are ignored, controlled, or specifically excluded. The initials referring to process elements are keyed to the elements of process as categorized in Table 1. (For example, "IS" refers to "Interaction System," which appears at the top left of Table 1.)

Table 2. Major Group Approaches Classified According to Process Elements

IS	BS	PSC
GE	PFS	ER
NS	IN	CR
GC	BV	CI
ES	E	F-CR

A. Communications Skills Workshop

IS	BS	PSC
GE	PFS	ER
NS	IN	CR
GC	BV	CI
ES	E	F-CR

B. Classic Psychoanalytic Group Psychotherapy

IS	BS	PSC
GE	PFS	ER
NS	IN	CR
GC	BV	CI
ES	E	F-CR

C. Gestalt Therapy

IS	BS	PSC
GE	PFS	ER
NS	IN	CR
GC	BV	CI
ES	E	F-CR

D. Tavistock Model

IS	BS	PSC
GE	PFS	ER
NS	IN	CR
GC	BV	CI
ES	E	F-CR

E. Classic T-Group

IS	BS	PSC
GE	PFS	ER
NS	IN	CR
GC	BV	CI
ES	E	F-CR

F. Group as Community of Learners

IS	BS	PSC
GE	PFS	ER
NS	IN	CR
GC	BV	CI
ES	E	F-CR

G. Value Clarification Focus

IS	BS	PSC
GE	PFS	ER
NS	IN	CR
GC	BV	CI
ES	E	F-CR

H. Transactional Analysis

IS	BS	PSC
GE	PFS	ER
NS	IN	CR
GC	BV	CI
ES	E	F-CR

I. Classic Basic Encounter Group

Key to Abbreviations

IS	(Interaction System)	BS	(Behavior Style)	PSC	(Physical and Social Contacts)

IS (Interaction System)
GE (Group Emotion)
NS (Normative System)
GC (Group Culture)
ES (Executive System)

BS (Behavior Style)
PFS (Personal Feeling State)
IN (Internalized Norms)
BV (Beliefs and Values)
E   (Ego)

PSC (Physical and Social Contacts)
ER (Emotional Relations)
CR (Contractual Relations)
CI (Cultural Interchange)
F-CR (Freedom-Control Relations)

Ground Rules

The psychoanalyst Sandor Ferenczi, it is reported, instructed his analysands to eat, drink, urinate, and defecate as infrequently as possible between analytic sessions, so that all possible energy could be reserved for their time together. Limitations such as these can be hazardous, but many group workers find it advantageous to set some ground rules, primarily to sharpen the perception of process. A therapist may forbid contact between members outside the group. He may refuse to see clients individually while they are members of the psychotherapy group, or he may decide to see each group member in individual sessions.

Most behavioral guidelines for group participants (many produced in training-group practice: Pfeiffer, 1972)—such as speaking for yourself, avoiding probing questions, looking at the person you're talking to—are aimed at clarifying communication and heightening encounter between group members.

Ground rules also help a group use its time efficiently, enabling it to concentrate on work in those cells of the Hill Interaction Matrix (Hill, 1973) where personal and interpersonal confrontations occur. In terms of process perception, ground rules sharpen the images that the psychotherapist receives from the group.

One ground rule—maintaining a here-and-now (rather than there-and-then) focus—has acquired considerable importance. Such an emphasis greatly enriches the psychotherapeutic potential of the group and saves the group from dreary recapitulations of past events.

Amplification

Since many process elements occur below the surface, the psychotherapist often finds it helpful to intensify, or amplify, the process event to make it visible to all members of the group. Amplification also allows the psychotherapist to check the accuracy of minimal cues.

Repetition of words, feedback checks for distortion, and nonverbal expression are all ways of intensifying process elements not clear to the group. Such clarification is the purpose of many exercises used in human relations training, and

these experiences—trust exercises, influence line-ups, and "making the rounds"—can be useful in the psychotherapy situation as well.

Amplification is not the process element itself; it merely heightens awareness of the element. For example, cohesion does not occur because group members are touching one another; rather, they touch to manifest more intensely the psychological cohesion that is present. If amplification fails to increase awareness, the psychotherapist must reconsider his reading of cues.

Explicit objectives, theory, ground rules, and amplification lighten the task for the group psychotherapist. In a seven-member group, at any given moment, there are at least 966 potential interactions between process elements; with tools to aid perception, the psychotherapist can reduce the number to three or four.

THERAPEUTIC INTERVENTION

The psychotherapist's efforts to communicate his perceptions to the group members are *facilitative interventions* aimed at helping the group develop a consciousness of itself and its behavior. For a group of learners or trainees, heightened awareness can be sufficient to initiate change and the sharing of leadership functions. For members of a psychotherapy group, however, heightened awareness, although necessary, is usually insufficient.

Not every grunt uttered by the psychotherapist is an intervention. The therapist may make contributions as a member of the group, ranging from small talk through maintenance functions to working his own issues. As a participant-observer, he may make facilitative interventions to heighten group awareness. As the leader, the most prestigious and powerful individual in the group, his primary function, of course, is to provide help.

Therapeutic interventions are a therapist's strong statements of confrontation or support of significant behaviors; these statements are designed to modify, halt, accelerate, or divert the direction of the group process so that group members can move from awareness to ownership and action.

Cohen and Smith (1972) discuss intervention in terms of "critical incidents" occurring in the group process and provide a model for the varieties of leader response to such incidents. A critical incident is a group phenomenon "judged important enough by a group leader to consider, consciously and explicitly, a decision to act in a way assumed to have an important impact on the group."

A modified version of Cohen and Smith's "intervention cube" model is presented in Figure 1. The intervention cube is a method of classifying the dimensions of facilitative interventions according to focus, type, and level. In their training of trainers, these theorists have found the intervention cube useful in investigating and categorizing the different styles of leadership intervention. As they see it, the leader's "awareness of an intervention style may lead [him] to adopt a more healthy mix of interventions as well as allow him to experiment with new styles and chart his progress."

Focus

The target to which the therapist directs his intervention is its focus. He may intervene with an individual, into an interaction between several group members, or with the group as a whole.

Type

The type of intervention describes both its content and the way it is communicated to its target. The therapist may use several different types of intervention.

Figure 1. The Intervention Cube: A Classification of Therapeutic Interventions According to Type, Focus, and Level*

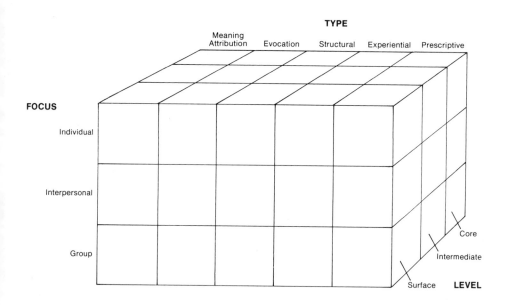

---

*Modified from Cohen & Smith (1972).

186

Meaning Attribution

This type of intervention describes or suggests a definite meaning to the process event targeted. The meaning may be in terms of theory ("Whenever Charlie shows his Child, your Parent gets hooked"), association ("You're doing with Marleen what you do with your wife—raising hell and then withdrawing"), or metaphor ("The group wishes to murder its leader but fears the chaos that would follow in his absence"). Meaning attribution attempts to connect here-and-now events with significant events in the member's past or context.

Evocation

Therapist behaviors sometimes are attempts to elicit specific emotional responses from the group. Asking a member to "stay with" his anxiety or requesting the group to report the fears that perpetuate a silence are examples.

Structural

All varieties of a therapist's nonverbal or physical behavior are structural interventions—such as holding, shaking, or wrestling with a group member. Or a therapist may urge a member to experiment with body movements or physical contact. Structures—ad hoc exercises to carry awareness through to action—also include role-plays or simulations.

Experiential

This type of intervention is a direct report of the therapist's inner experiences and feeling responses to events occurring in the group. Such feedback is especially powerful because of the therapist's role potency.

Prescriptive

When the therapist instructs members of the group to test new behavior in their contextual fields and report the results back to the group, he is using a prescriptive intervention. His purpose is to motivate group members to action beyond the group session.

Level

The third dimension of the intervention cube concerns the level of the intervention. Level refers to the visibility of process elements, ranging from highly visible, measurable behaviors at one end of the spectrum (the process elements in the top row of Table 1—Interaction System, Behavior Style, and Physical and Social Contacts) to inferential, intrapsychic phenomena on the other end (the process elements in the bottom row of Table 1—Executive System, Ego, and Freedom-Control Relations). Level is not a measure of the importance of the target element, but only of its perceptual availability. The *surface level* refers to publicly observable behavior (such as a speech pattern), the *intermediate level* to complex chains of behavior (such as value systems or group culture), and the *core level* to hidden events which the psychotherapist, based on his understanding of human behavior, infers. A fuller discussion of the importance of choosing the appropriate level of intervention can be found in Harrison (1968).

Style

After classifying therapeutic interventions according to focus, type, and level, there is still the question of therapist style—which means the therapist's preference for (or habit of) making certain kinds of interventions in the group process. Some styles may be rather fixed—as, for example, with a psychoanalytic therapist whose interventions are consistently on a core level. A Gestalt therapist may initiate his interventions with evocative, surface statements to an individual and then move toward structured core interventions, while a Tavistock-trained therapist may make group-focused, attributive core interventions. Other, more eclectic, therapists may make widely varying interventions during a single group meeting.

The therapist's style of intervention has important consequences. Intervention at the surface level may miss troublesome forces or hidden agendas. Consistent use of an individual focus may hinder group cohesion, whereas overuse of core-level interventions may create unwanted dependence on the expertise of the therapist.

A therapist's ability to classify his interventions is a measure of his awareness of his own behavior in the group; it does not suggest that the therapist should be calculating. Knowledge of the variety of interventions possible can, instead, help develop his flexibility. A useful self-inventory on style can be found in Wile (1972).

Matching accurate process perceptions with effective therapeutic responses requires all the skill, invention, and experience that the psychotherapist has. This part of his function depends less on his training than on the creative powers he possesses.

FOLLOWING-THROUGH

No matter how powerful, timely, or precise the psychotherapist's intervention, it does not heal. It only invites the individual group member to grow and change. It is not growth and change.

Some new behaviors need to be learned only once, but for the member of the psychotherapy group, change is difficult. Because of this, the responsibilities of the group psychotherapist continue. The follow-through of therapeutic intervention involves reinforcing a group member's decision to change and facilitating his new awareness. Following-through expresses the therapist's continuing care for those who look to him for help. For the psychotherapist, it means living with the impact of his interventions and observing their outcome.

REFERENCES

Bennis, W. G., & Shepard, H. A. A theory of group development. In R. Golembiewski & A. Blumberg, *Sensitivity training and the laboratory approach.* Itasca, Ill.: Peacock Publishers, 1970.

Cohen, A. M., & Smith, R. D. The critical-incident approach to leadership intervention in training groups. In W. G. Dyer, *Modern theory and method in group training.* New York: D. Van Nostrand, 1972.

Egan, G. *Encounter: Group processes for interpersonal growth.* Belmont: Brooks/Cole, 1970.

Egan, G. Contracts in encounter groups. In J. W. Pfeiffer & J. E. Jones (Eds.), *The 1972 annual handbook for group facilitators.* San Diego: University Associates, 1972, 185-196.

Foulkes, S. H., & Anthony, E. J. *Group psychotherapy: The psychoanalytic approach.* (2nd ed.) Gannon, 1957.

Harrison, R. Some criteria for choosing the depth of organizational intervention strategy. Paper delivered to the Fourth International Congress of Group Psychotherapy, Vienna, 1968.

Hill, W. F. Hill Interaction Matrix (HIM): A conceptual framework for understanding groups. In J. E. Jones & J. W. Pfeiffer (Eds.), *The 1973 annual handbook for group facilitators.* San Diego: University Associates, 1973.

Kaplan, S., & Roman, M. Phases of development in an adult therapy group. *International Journal of Group Psychotherapy,* 1963, 13, 10-26.

Lewin, K. *A dynamic theory of personality.* New York: McGraw-Hill, 1935.

Mager, R. F. *Preparing instructional objectives.* Palo Alto: Fearon, 1962.

Maslow, A. *Motivation and personality.* (2nd ed.) New York: Harper and Row, 1970.

Mills, T. M. *The sociology of small groups.* Englewood Cliffs: Prentice-Hall, 1967.

Pfeiffer, J. W. Guidelines for group member behavior. In J. W. Pfeiffer & J. E. Jones (Eds.), *The 1972 annual handbook for group facilitators.* San Diego: University Associates, 1972.

Rogers, C. R. *Carl Rogers on encounter groups.* New York: Harper & Row, 1970.

Wile, D. B. Nonresearch uses of the group leadership questionnaire (GTQ-C). In J. W. Pfeiffer & J. E. Jones (Eds.), *The 1972 annual handbook for group facilitators.* San Diego: University Associates, 1972, 87-106.

LIFE/WORK PLANNING

Art and Marie Kirn

Our interest in life/work planning had its origin in our own life/career transitions: on the one hand, from an academic church career as a priest, philosopher, and teacher to a consulting career, marriage, and a family. On the other hand, from involvement in college administration, the poverty program, a monastic retreat center, and innovation in education to human potential consulting, marriage, and a family.

These transitions were slow and painful, involving two distinct phases. The first involved coming to some sense of who we were. In the second phase, we had to decide what we were going to do now that we knew ourselves well enough to make some choices.

This double experience provided the stimulus for a rationale, a design, and a set of practical guidelines for reproducing some of the essential conditions that made possible our own life/career transitions.

Our experiences showed us that all the institutions we had experienced—church, education, government, business—were based on the Theory X assumptions that people lack ambition, dislike responsibility, and prefer to be led, and that the institution's responsibility is to manage people's lives to its own advantage. Along with the vast majority of people, we have found it only too easy to let circumstances and the objectives of others control our lives.

In the development of a group program in life and career planning over the last three years, we have evolved a philosophy about the process—a collection of assumptions, conclusions, and values which form the rationale for the training design we have worked out and used extensively. At this writing, about one thousand persons have experienced Life/Work Planning, some with us and others with leaders we have trained.

RATIONALE FOR THE PROGRAM

1. Vast, Untapped Potential

Most of us possess many unused resources that lie dormant most of the time. Many people secretly nurture fantasies of a second (and sometimes a third, fourth, or fifth) career. We are all Walter Mittys at heart.

It is thought that 95 percent of the human race lives on 5 percent of its potency. Maslow's (1962) studies of self-actualizing people reveal immense creative resources, quite apart from specific talents, in very ordinary people. The creativity curve in most children levels off at six, seven, or eight years, when school experiences and socialization effectively close them down. Transactional Analysis describes the stance of everybody early in life as "You're OK, I'm not OK." Indeed, the entire human potential movement is based on the assumption that the capacity to grow is largely untapped in most people.

2. Fear of Potency

Many people are afraid of their own power. Too common in our culture are such working assumptions as "pride goeth before a fall." Many people are much more comfortable with negative criticism than with praise, because they are more used to feeling bad than good about themselves. Getting in touch with one's own strengths and resources often evokes a wave of guilt at not having used them as one might. Otto (1972) has written extensively about how these negative feelings tend to immobilize us and about some of the training issues involved in getting in touch with them and working with them.

3. Responsibility for Self

The key to successful life/career planning is the willingness to take responsibility for oneself. This implies that it is indeed possible for an individual to take control of his life in the midst of the forces around him. In any organizational or life situation a person has three choices—change it, love it, or leave it. Change it—he must change his behavior, goals, or circumstances. Love it—he must recognize that it is his choice to stay with it, for whatever set of reasons. Leave it—he must find another environment for his energies. Feeling forced to stay with it and hating it is not a viable and productive human alternative. When choice is removed, violence results. Prisoners are subject to violence. A man "trapped" in his job ("look at what they've done to me") has given up something of his humanness. He is not in the same situation as someone who *chooses* to do what he does not like for whatever reason he might have.

4. Resistance to Responsibility

Many people tend in practice to resist taking responsibility for themselves. This statement is not an acceptance of the Theory X assumptions underlying authoritarian management practices; it simply describes the way many people in fact behave. In addition to the factors which build up fear of one's own potency, institutional life as we know it heavily encourages dependence, conformity, submission, role-playing, and lack of responsibility. Gibb (1972) has pointed out how this defensive and submissive behavior in the individual is a direct expression of fear. He has also shown that fear and the behaviors flowing from it are largely matters of choice. Too many people too often *choose* fear and defensiveness.

Theory Y, which supports more participative management practices, assumes that people are capable of *not* choosing fear—that they naturally prefer trust and the authentic, spontaneous, and open behavior that flows from it. Certainly, some of our institutions (the U.S. Constitution is a fine example) were conceived in the belief that people will take responsibility for themselves.

5. Resentment of Loss of Control

Even if most people resist taking responsibility for themselves, they resent their own sense of impotence and loss of control when somebody assumes responsibility for them. This is a paradox for a designer-trainer. Its real meaning seems to be that the deeper dynamic in people is the urge to grow, to change, and to take charge of their own lives. But sometimes growth and change are painful. Forcing, provoking, helping, controlling, persuading, and strategizing sometimes work, but more often these strategies tend to heighten fear and deepen resistance.

6. Enthusiastic Response

When people begin to experience trust and openness and to realize that they are truly free to set and achieve their own goals, they tend to respond with enthusiasm and ingenuity. Patience and some degree of risk are required for a trainer to trust that others will grow when they are ready to. Participants may need some time to test the credibility of a situation in which, perhaps for the first time, the responsibility is fully theirs. Nevertheless, the reward of crossing the crisis point together is an exhilarating release of energy which makes a participant of the leader and leaders of the participants.

7. Change a Constant

Many people—and organizations—are uncomfortable with change or at least the blinding rate of change in these times. They find it confusing, unsettling, taxing. But change is a constant, both around us and within us.

Our assumption is that people do not need to be changed or influenced nearly as much as they need to develop their ability to handle change around them as it happens. This is mostly a matter of realizing and utilizing their own resources. It does not always require that a person change his goals or career; an adjustment of behavior or circumstances may suffice. It is often enough to accept full responsibility for a personal career choice and its implication in order to mobilize one's energies to cope with change.

8. Unprecedented Opportunities

Opportunities to grow, to find interesting work, to vary one's life and work experience, to travel and live in different places exist in our society today to an unprecedented degree. We do not imply that we live in a perfect or a perfectly just world, merely that the freedom and opportunity to realize one's potential are relatively rich and available to a relatively large proportion of people. Blacks, women, the aged, the poor, the young, and many other minority or disadvantaged groups have a greater scope for choice than ever before. Conformity in dress, in organizational standards of behavior, in social customs, even in economic patterns, is under heavy pressure. We must continue to work to make our choices even wider, but we must also actively pursue the possibilities we do have.

9. Organization of Self-Knowledge

Moving effectively towards significant goals in one's life requires more than personal insight. It is, of course, an essential part of any life/career planning experience, but by itself it is not enough to produce results. Self-knowledge must be organized and focused in order to contribute to practical progress. If we are to choose a direction or course of action wisely, then systematic approaches to self-diagnosis, goal-setting, generating new alternatives, decision-making, planning and anticipating future problems are clearly in order. Without these ways of organizing self-knowledge, valid insights may never bear fruit.

THE LIFE/WORK PLANNING DESIGN

Given the richness of human resources, the rapid rate of change, and the multiplicity of opportunity, it is paradoxical that so many are afraid of their potency, resistant to change, and blind to opportunity. This paradox is the central issue to a facilitator working in the arena of life and career planning. He can take heart, however, from the fact that the paradox can be broken by the very resources that people have and fear. The facilitator need only encourage people to share their fears and their problems for a climate of mutual support, trust, and openness to develop, permitting people to focus on the positive in themselves and each other. Then the way is open to growing self-realization, autonomy, and interdependence. People begin to use their own and each other's resources freely. The effect is a synergistic burst of energy.

The central objective of our Life/Work Planning design (summarized below) is to initiate and foster this mobilization of self in a group setting by providing frameworks for developing a data profile for oneself (Phase I) and for organizing that data to achieve the goals one identifies as significant (Phase II).

Scope of the Design

PHASE I: Finding Out About Your Work and Your Life

To the Participant: Overview

1. Where are you? Statement of your life/work situation.
2. An introduction to learning from your own experience. Microlab.
3. Where have you been? Your lifeline.
4. What is a peak work experience?
5. What is important? What can you do without?
6. What can you do? An inventory.
7. Who are you? A self-inventory.
8. Who are you? Two self-portraits.
9. Your work preferences. Some hard choices.
10. Who needs you? Redefining your work.
11. What do you see? The newspaper exercise.
12. A conversation with Peter F. Drucker.
13. Profile of the '70s.
14. Marshall McLuhan on work.
15. What do you like to do? An inventory.
16. What means most to you? An inventory.
17. What do you want to be doing? A look at your future.
18. Obituary and epitaph.
19. Summing up. The life/work checklist.
20. Interconnections. A grid.

PHASE II: Putting It All Together

Introduction to Phase II

21. Where are you now? Restatement of your life/work situation.

22. What comes first? Priority-setting.
23. What's going for and against you? Force-field analysis.
24. Where are you taking yourself? Trend analysis.
25. What next? Decision-making.
26. How do you get there? Planning.
27. What can go wrong? Getting ahead of trouble.

Wrap-up

Phase I provides a series of closely timed and carefully structured activities for reflecting on and sharing experience, values, and reactions. They cut across past, present, and future; focus on aspects of self image; and use a variety of approaches and media for stimulating perception. The pace is rapid and varied.

The result is a low-key atmosphere in which critical behavioral or personal issues are not dealt with by open-ended encounter. Rather, the expectation is that significant issues will come up again and again, each time from a different point of view. This produces a cumulative effect—themes and conclusions tend to emerge. There is a large block of time at the end of Phase I for more extended exploration of particular issues.

At the end of Phase I, Life/Work Planning participants typically find themselves in one of three types of situations. They need further diagnosis, clarification, or ordering of their goals; they need to make one or more basic choices of goals or means of attaining them; or they need to plan how to achieve them.

Conceptual Tools

To facilitate thinking through these situations, Phase II adapts for individual use conceptual tools long in use by managers and administrators for handling similar situations in organizational settings. Each of the following tools is presented in an instrumented manner.

- *Priority-setting* assesses the relative seriousness, urgency, and growth potential of goals, tasks, or concerns.
- *Force-field analysis* assesses the feasibility of a proposed goal or course of action by laying out the forces for and against it, analyzing the importance and probability of these

forces, and establishing actions to minimize negative forces.

- *Trend analysis* scans past behaviors for positive or negative trends and factors in outside circumstances and makes projections on where behavior patterns are leading. The outcome is to adjust goals and/or behaviors and/or circumstances. It is a useful tool for clarifying goals.
- *Decision-making* presents a matrix for comparing how well alternatives meet objectives on the one hand, and what elements of risk are involved in each alternative on the other. On the basis of this information an informed choice is possible.
- *Planning* helps one think through objectives, assumptions, resources, constraints, and key decision points, before detailing and scheduling tasks or action steps.
- *Getting ahead of trouble* systematically identifies specific high-priority potential problems along with their likely causes, and establishes actions both to prevent them from becoming actual and to cope with them if they do. These actions become a means of improving plans.

These tools afford a continuing and much-used resource for thinking through situations as they arise in a participant's life long after the workshop. No one uses all of them at the time of the workshop, but over a year or two, one would probably find all of these conceptual tools useful at one time or another.

PRACTICAL REFLECTIONS ON DESIGN AND EXECUTION

We hope that some comments on our experiences with this design will be useful to those building their own designs, using others, or undertaking the Life/Work Planning design.

Trust-Building

We place heavy emphasis in the opening activities on trust-building. Several activities invite participants to share descriptions of their life/work situations, and reactions, feelings, and observations about a series of questions which focus on key issues of life and work. As they share, trust begins to grow.

We encourage participants from the start to take responsibility for the choices they make—the pace and depth of their participation, the issues they wish to deal with, the people with whom they wish to interact. We urge participants to "pass" at any given point if they so wish. We ask that they are clear about why they make this choice, but we do not demand that they defend their choice to others.

Freedom from coercive group norms encourages people to be more open and responsible than they might otherwise be. When they see others beginning to be proactive, they are encouraged to be so themselves. When they see that others are not there to "help" them, they find it easier to relax and take responsibility for helping themselves. They also see that nobody is going to act for them and that nothing will happen if they do not act for themselves.

Positive Emphasis

Throughout the program there is an emphasis (although not an exclusive one) on positive experiences and perceptions. What has been your *peak* work experience? What are the things you *can* do? What means *most* to you? What do you *like* to do? What do you *like* about yourself? As people get into this positive mode, some of the fears they have about their abilities begin to dissolve. But because looking at the positive side of oneself is a potential threat, it is important that trust be sufficiently established early in the life/work program.

Avoidance

The fact that no one need feel constrained to deal with what he does not wish to produces some avoidance. But a strong counterforce toward movement is the realization that avoiding the issue is self-defeating.

It has been our experience, often repeated, that even people who seem to be avoiding reality or who are being highly defensive are really learning.

Refraining from "Helping"

In the course of prolonged and disciplined experience with refraining from "helping" participants to deal with what we think they ought to do, our respect for people's ability to know their own priorities and to act on them has grown immeasurably.

We assume that people are capable of taking charge of their own lives. Any behavior which contradicts that assumption, no matter how well intentioned, is ultimately counterproductive.

The exciting corollary of this is that it leaves the leader free to administer the program and to interact spontaneously out of his own needs and goals. Authentic behavior of this kind is, in fact, often very helpful, besides being more interesting, productive, and enjoyable for the leader.

Subgroups

Vital to the momentum of proceeding through a long series of structured experiences is the play between the dynamics of the subgroup and the total group.

The largest total group we have experienced so far is sixty-five. The only limitation seems to be logistical: Can a facilitator be heard and seen, and can the group function in the available space?

An ideal size for subgroups is four or five, large enough for good interaction but small enough to give everyone air time on a tight schedule.

Space

A space large enough for the total group to meet together and to break down into subgroups when needed makes it easy for the leader to move around, answer questions, clarify procedures, and participate where or when he wants to. It makes for an easily varied and well-paced flow between activities done in the total group and in subgroups and makes it easy for anyone to switch groups if he wishes. It also facilitates ending one activity and starting another.

Groups tend to become sensitive to the need for pacing themselves reasonably. The single large room allows the group to keep in touch with what is going on elsewhere in the total group. On occasion, some of the total group activities generate very powerful and intense experiences for participants. Finally, the large room makes it easy for the leader to take quick readings of the group's needs and priorities, against which he can make adjustments in the choice, sequence, or pace of the activities.

Administering a Program

We have found the distinction between leading a group and administering a structured program to a group very useful and liberating. In the latter case, the group is leaderless. When we are free of a leader or helper role, we find that administering the program does not get in the way of our participating actively and spontaneously.

Subgroup Membership

Assuming responsibility for oneself is most critical in the choice of membership in subgroups. The initial choice comes after enough introductory activities to give some data. Choices are not irrevocable, and people feel easier if they realize they can switch later. However, subgroups tend to get involved and find it difficult to give up the common data base they quickly build together.

Occasionally subgroups or individuals find themselves working less productively or with unwanted obstacles. The most effective resolutions are generally those which the total group designs for itself, often very informally—an easier process in larger groups and much facilitated by having a single large working area for the entire program.

Group vs. Individual Experience

The group dimension of Life/Work Planning gives it several powerful advantages over one-to-one or individual (private) experiences. The group provides the trust and support needed to face difficult situations and to explore one's growth frontier. Participants find comfort in the fact that others share similar difficulties. The group affords exposure to values and experiences other than one's own and the chance to compare perceptions with others. The group is a rich source for new ideas and potential problem solutions.

Materials

Immeasureable aids to the pace and changing focus of the program are duplicated materials in a binder. They provide the instruments for many activities, but, more important, they provide a log for perceptions, insights, information of all kinds. The response of participants to "putting it down on paper" is almost uniformly positive, even when one discounts the fact that such a log strongly reflects the time and circumstances when it was written.

One pitfall to the use of written materials—indeed, to the use of structured activities at all—is the tendency many people have to respond to them in ways they feel they "ought" to. This tendency usually diminishes when attention is called to it and when it becomes evident that the responses are for sharing and learning among group members. The key here is the individual's realization that he truly has responsibility for his own experience and growth.

Some Results

We have observed rather consistently over the last three years that participants tend to see Life/Work Planning not as an event but as an introduction to a continuing process. Occasionally someone comes back to repeat the program in a new time and location and has a totally different experience from his first. Many have stayed in touch with us, offering evidence of continued growth and the use of their learning and, particularly, of the Phase II tools.

It is the combination of the human relations approach in Phase I and the practical, results-oriented conceptual approach in Phase II that seems to make these results possible. We have observed the same combination at work in successful organization development projects (as opposed to training events) where the objective is a continued engagement with organizational growth linked with the achievement of organizational results.

REFERENCES

Bolles, R. N. *What color is your parachute? A practical manual for job-hunters and career changers.* Berkeley: Ten Speed Press, 1972.

Connor, S. R., & Fielden, J. S. Rx for managerial 'shelf sitters.' *Harvard Business Review*, 1973 (Nov.-Dec.), 113-120.

Ford, G. A., & Lippitt, G. *A life planning workbook.* Fairfax, Va.: NTL Learning Resources Corporation, 1972.

Gibb, J. R. TORI theory and practice. In J. W. Pfeiffer & J. E. Jones (Eds.), *The 1972 annual handbook for group facilitators.* San Diego: University Associates, 1972.

Hall, M. H. A conversation with Peter F. Drucker. *Psychology Today*, 1968 (March), 21 ff.

Kepner, C. H., & Tregoe, B. B. *The rational manager.* New York: McGraw-Hill, 1965.

Kirn, A. G. *Life work planning.* Trainer's Manual and Workbook. Pittsburgh, 1971. Available from the author, 106 North Beacon, Hartford, Conn. 06105.

Life-planning program. In J. W. Pfeiffer & J. E. Jones (Eds.), *A handbook of structured experiences for human relations training*, Vol. II (Rev. ed.) San Diego: University Associates, 1974, 103-112.

Maslow, A. *Toward a psychology of being.* Princeton: D. Van Nostrand, 1962.

Otto, H. A. *Group methods to actualize human potential.* Beverly Hills: Holistic Press, 1972.

Robinson, A. J. McGregor's theory X—theory Y model. In J. W. Pfeiffer & J. E. Jones (Eds.), *The 1972 annual handbook for group facilitators.* San Diego: University Associates, 1972, 121-123.

Simon, S. B., et al. *Values clarification: A handbook of practical strategies for teachers & students.* New York: Hart, 1972.

CYBERNETIC SESSIONS:
A TECHNIQUE FOR GATHERING IDEAS

John T. Hall and Roger A. Dixon

The term "cybernetic session" is used here to identify a technique for generating and gathering ideas, quickly and effectively, from people in moderate-sized to large groups.

We will describe our *objectives* (what it is we think we are doing). Then we will describe our *process* (what we are doing), our *uses* of the technique, its range of possibilities, and some of its benefits.

OBJECTIVES

The technique described here is called "cybernetic" because of the way things appear to happen when it is used. Just as the human brain can manage a myriad of complex relationships, and the computer can keep track of and classify a large volume of inputs in an incredibly brief span of time, so the cybernetic session allows us to bundle many variables and a large volume of input into a concise time frame. This technique works by collecting input and feedback from individuals arrayed in a variety of configurations. As the collection process proceeds, synthesis and evaluation also occur, the primary value of the technique being the ease with which it allows us to comprehend and gather complex ideas from groups of people.

Through the dynamics of capture, feedback, and recapture of thoughts in a changing interpersonal environment, users get much closer to the reality or at least to the shape of group opinions and ideas—closer, certainly, than any survey or questionnaire techniques we have used or seen used in the management field.

The cybernetic technique can be compared in a rather simplistic way with the usual approach to gathering ideas and opinions.

Normally, a collection of random group ideas is reduced to a structured format, which lists alternatives to that particular question. Instead, with the cybernetic approach, the collection of data is approached in a self-organizing fashion; the usual rigid format is not imposed. By *not* making the usual assumption that participants speak the same language, the cybernetic self-organizing approach produces a much less standardized result.

PROCESS

The design for a cybernetic session includes these steps:

1. Classifying concerns of an activity (*e.g.*, how to organize) into four areas or questions. These areas may overlap but should allow enough latitude to embrace the universe of the particular concern.

2. Constituting the questions as stations.

3. Assigning an itinerary for each participant by filling out a card (Figure 1) which shows the participant where he should be (station) and when he should be there (period). The itinerary card is derived from the table in Figure 2.

4. Assigning a person to each station to record data and to review what has been said previously as new participants come to the station. The recorder is not a discussion leader.

By following the itinerary card, each participant works at each of the four stations and interacts with other participants in eight different participant configurations. At eight- to fifteen-minute intervals half of the people at each station move to a new station. The remaining half maintain the continuity of the discussion. The new members bring fresh ideas. The departing members do not move as a body but disperse so

Figure 1. A Cybernetic Session Itinerary Card

		Participant 6	
Period	*Station*	*Period*	*Station*
1	F	5	N
2	X	6	B
3	X	7	B
4	N	8	F

Figure 2. Cybernetic Session Matrix: 4 Sessions, 8 Periods, and up to 48 Participants

Participant Number

	1	2	3	4	5	6	7	8	9	10	11	12	13	14	15	16	17	18	19	20	21	22	23	24
Period												**Station**												
1	N	N	B	B	F	F	X	X	N	N	X	X	B	B	F	F	B	B	F	F	N	N	X	X
2	N	B	B	F	F	X	X	N	N	X	X	B	B	F	F	N	B	N	F	X	N	F	X	B
3	B	B	F	F	X	X	N	N	X	X	B	B	F	F	N	N	N	N	X	X	F	F	B	B
4	B	F	F	X	X	N	N	B	X	B	B	F	F	N	N	X	N	F	X	B	F	X	B	N
5	F	F	X	X	N	N	B	B	B	B	F	F	N	N	X	X	F	F	B	B	X	X	N	N
6	F	X	X	N	N	B	B	F	B	F	F	N	N	X	X	B	F	X	B	N	X	B	N	F
7	X	X	N	N	B	B	F	F	F	F	N	N	X	X	B	B	X	X	N	N	B	B	F	F
8	X	N	N	B	B	F	F	X	F	N	N	X	X	B	B	F	X	B	N	F	B	N	F	X

Participant Number

	25	26	27	28	29	30	31	32	33	34	35	36	37	38	39	40	41	42	43	44	45	46	47	48
Period												**Station**												
1	F	F	B	B	N	N	X	X	X	X	N	N	F	F	B	B	B	B	N	N	X	X	F	F
2	F	B	B	N	N	X	X	F	X	N	N	F	F	B	B	X	B	X	N	B	X	F	F	N
3	B	B	N	N	X	X	F	F	N	N	F	F	B	B	X	X	X	X	B	B	F	F	N	N
4	B	N	N	X	X	F	F	B	N	F	F	B	B	X	X	N	X	F	B	X	F	N	N	B
5	N	N	X	X	F	F	B	B	F	F	B	B	X	X	N	N	F	F	X	X	N	N	B	B
6	N	X	X	F	F	B	B	N	F	B	B	X	X	N	N	F	F	N	X	F	N	B	B	X
7	X	X	F	F	B	B	N	N	B	B	X	X	N	N	F	F	N	N	F	F	B	B	X	X
8	X	F	F	B	B	N	N	X	B	X	X	N	N	F	F	B	N	B	F	N	B	X	X	F

that interpersonal conflicts are not carried forward from station to station. The direct products of the sessions, usually completed in one to two hours, are gathered from the recorder at each station.

Advantages

In most instances our use of the cybernetic session has obtained these advantages:

1. A great deal of information is gathered in a relatively small amount of time.

2. Group opinions and concerns are shaped or self-organized. This shaping process has the obvious advantage of distilling random thoughts into ideas which can be acted upon, but it also works as an educational experience: People develop a fuller understanding of the whole area of concern through self-expression and listening to others.

3. Many people are "in" on things from the beginning.

4. Supervisors and subordinates, perhaps because the cybernetic experience is new for both, are in a better position to influence each other than they would be in a structured discussion or a committee with a leader.

5. Later interviews with people involved in the session are especially fruitful because of (a) the fuller understanding of the whole area of concern mentioned above and (b) a willingness to discuss views openly. Because the interviewer is able to come directly to the point in the follow-up interview, much less time is spent in gathering information.

6. A feeling of involvement (*we* need to solve the problem) develops.

USES OF CYBERNETIC SESSIONS

In the applications we have attempted, the most impressive results have been the variety and volume of output captured by the recorders. Our first practical experiment, designed to elicit questions regarding management functions at a government agency, produced a list of seventy-eight distinctly formulated inputs from twenty-five or thirty participants. Next we began to use the technique on a larger scale: getting specific user requirements for the agency's Management

Information System; studying the needs of an organization's clerical-secretarial staff; and redesigning an organization's financial management systems. In these sessions the participants were for the most part employees at lower organizational levels, who would not normally be consulted, even about matters that had considerable impact on the performance of their jobs.

A Case Study

An experiment in the use of a Theory-Y approach to management was a critical test of the cybernetic technique. The experiment was requested by one of the technical divisions following a presentation of Douglas McGregor's Theory X (authoritative)—Theory Y (participative) concept of management.

The experiment began with a cybernetic session involving the professional staff of the technical division. We developed four stations which we felt would increase the probability of achieving both ideas and a self-organizing movement: Station N—Objectives; Station B—External Coupling; Station F—Internal Relationships; and Station X—Internal Structure. Figure 3 shows an excerpt from the notice which each participant received prior to the session.

Over eighty percent of the division's professional staff participated in the session, which was introduced by the senior management analyst responsible for the entire Theory Y experiment. As the session proceeded, the four recorders (members of the Management and Organization Division) noted each item introduced—*i.e.*, idea, viewpoint, opinion, complaint—with, of course, no source identification. The session lasted eighty minutes. Twenty-five hours later, each recorder had assembled the input material from his station and relayed it to the division chief and his staff. In this case, the cybernetic session generated responses to the question "What's wrong with this division?"

This experiment of the cybernetic process was a success. It proved for us the value of the cybernetic technique, which we had been experimenting with for two years, as an input device. We found we had an untapped reservoir of ideas for

Figure 3. Notice to Participants of Cybernetic Session

Cybernetic Session
Friday, July 25—9:30
Lecture Room C

Station	*Discussion Area*
N	Are the objectives of the Technical Division clearly defined to you? Are they the correct objectives? If not, what should they be?
B	What are the appropriate external relationships (groups) for the Division? Are those relationships being adequately maintained? Are there outside groups that the office should be using or serving that it is not?
F	What are appropriate internal relationships between the Division and other divisions within the organization? Is there capability or expertise within the organization that the Division should be using?
X	Does the internal structure of the Division foster dynamic working relationships? What new methods of disseminating information would improve communications?

---

program improvements. We also had a clear insight into individuals' views of the objectives and internal structure of the organization, together with a better view of the strengths and weaknesses of the way this structure operated.

The input from the cybernetic session was followed by subsequent interviews. A number of rather easily implemented changes resulted in a significant increase in the morale and productivity of the organization. Confidence also was established in the cybernetic session as a stimulus for bringing about change.

Range of Possibilities

We have also used this technique in a broad range of subjects, such as determining user needs for management information, developing policies and procedures for equipment and space management, and managing financial resources. For these subjects we distribute a general invitation to the staff. Input is then used by the particular design team or task force to structure its

own work approach and to develop interview/questionnaire material following the standard approach.

Figure 4 shows an invitation issued for a cybernetic 'session on managing financial resources. The results became a major input to a task force on financial management. Recommendations from the task force then determined several major changes in the organization's financial management policies.

Extra-Work Use

Members of a church retreat used a cybernetic session to determine ways to implement previously established goals. The morning was spent in the cybernetic session; during the lunch period the recorders assembled the ideas from the sessions into related areas. The afternoon session began with a presentation of the results to the whole group. Each member then chose the area on which he would like to work, and the group organized itself into several smaller groups (task

Figure 4. Invitation for Cybernetic Session

TO SECTION CHIEFS AND PROJECT LEADERS: **June 27**

The Financial Management Task Force #1, "Allocation of Funds for Administrative and Technical Support," is preparing recommendations and alternatives for the Executive Staff on ways to improve the management of financial resources at the project, section, program, division, institute, and organization levels.

A number of cybernetic sessions will be conducted on July 2 and July 8 in Lecture Room B, Administration Building. Section Chiefs, Project Leaders, and other interested staff members are invited to provide inputs to the task force. Each workshop session will last one hour and forty minutes.

We seek input on such questions as these:
1. What should be your financial authority and responsibility?
2. What financial information do you need to carry out your technical work?
3. How should overhead costs be supported by technical projects?
4. To what degree must section chiefs and project leaders be involved in estimating costs for other agency work?

If you wish to attend one of these design/workshop sessions, please complete the form below and return it to us in the enclosed envelope.

To: Financial Management Task Force #1
       A902 Administration Building

Participant: Name _____ Bldg. & Room _____

                   Extension _____ Div. & Sec. _____

Session preferred (please check)

July 2   9 a.m._____   3 p.m._____

July 8   9 a.m._____   3 p.m._____

---

forces) to work on specific problems. One of the task forces divided again when its members felt that their area of concern was too broad. Specific assignments were made, and the task forces met again to follow up on the action taken.

A high degree of commitment resulted, perhaps because people felt a definite sense of openness during the sessions. One person said, "I've said things today I've wanted to say for years, but I never felt I could."

In another instance, the technique was used first to develop an entire year's social program for a church group and then to plan each activity. Planning sessions were held on a quarterly basis, with the chairman for each activity acting as recorder at the station concerned with his activity. The fourth station was used to gather feedback about activities of the previous quarter. When the sessions were used to gather ideas for monthly meetings and programs, enough good ideas were generated for two years. An interesting idea, suggested but not yet tried, was to have a "cybernetic social."

Cybernetic sessions were also used to determine the best way to raise funds for the construction of a church. After the usual gathering of ideas, one member of the planning group classified the suggestions according to return and risk. The committee then selected several ideas which were presented to the congregation for a vote. Building and selling a house was the method chosen. Through the process of the cybernetic session, the idea was developed and carried out. With the successful result of this first project, the group now plans to build a house each year until the new church can be financed.

Student Use

The technique has also been used in working with high school students. In this case, the subject was social situations that challenged personal moral standards, and all participants and recorders were peers. Through the cybernetic device, the students attempted to determine a "correct" course of action. Many students commented that this was their first opportunity to talk about such things in a positive way, and several said that the discussions brought out alternatives which had not occurred to them before.

BENEFITS

Our use of the cybernetic session has shown that the specific advantages derived from the session vary according to the type of group involved and the presence of a comprehensive strategy for the session. This process does not evaluate the ultimate worth of the ideas generated; it is a technique of exploration.

In addition to the data gathered through recorders, benefits include a positive morale boost through participation in a leveled employee-supervisor relationship. Also, ancillary benefits result from developing new interpersonal relationships. We have found that not only do people convey to one another a significant amount of useful information on matters outside the scope of the sessions, but that new relationships develop as a result of the contact between individuals.

"DON'T YOU THINK THAT . . .?": AN EXPERIENTIAL LECTURE ON INDIRECT AND DIRECT COMMUNICATION

J. William Pfeiffer and John E. Jones

EXPERIENTIAL ACTIVITIES

This paper attempts to set forth certain theoretical concepts concerning indirect and direct communication. In order to integrate theory with practice, six activities are interspersed throughout this paper. These activities are designed to add the dimension of experiential learning to the theoretical concepts discussed.

Each of the six activities described is inserted at the exact point in the lecture at which the activity is designed to occur. Activity 1, for example, should take place before any theoretical concepts are introduced. The activities can accommodate an unlimited number of participants.

Activity 1

A. *The facilitator has the group form quartets. No talking is allowed.*

B. *Each person in each quartet writes down the first* two *things that he would communicate to each of the other people in his group. Again, no talking is allowed.*

C. *The facilitator gathers and publishes information concerning how many of the twenty-four items generated in each group are questions.*

D. *Participants are directed to "discard" the items they have generated; they will be asked to "communicate" later.*

THEORETICAL CONCEPTS

One basic focus of the human relations movement is on the effective utilization of communication. Many people fear taking risks in interpersonal relationships, yet since they need to feel that they are articulate and adept at "communication," they often engage in what we can call "pseudo communication."

In reality, they try to direct the risk of interpersonal communication away from themselves. They fear to present their own opinions, ideas, feelings, desires.

The individual who fears taking risks may want to manipulate others into fulfilling his own desires or expectations. Thus he would be saved from being rejected or from exposing his vulnerability to others. His motive may also be to control others without apparently assuming authority.

This paper attempts to illustrate several common varieties of indirect, pseudo communication and to suggest some alternatives to these misdirected patterns of communication.

NONCOMMUNICATION

One way that people engage in noncommunicative discourse is by speaking as if they represented other people, in an attempt to get illegitimate support for their points of view. For example, a person who prefaces his remarks by saying, "I agree with Fred when he says . . ." or "I think I speak for the group when I say . . ." is not communicating. He is simply attempting to borrow legitimacy.

PSEUDO QUESTIONS

Perhaps the most frequently misused communication pattern is the question. In fact, most questions are pseudo questions. The questioner is not really seeking information or an answer to his "question." Rather, he is offering an opinion—a statement. But because he does not want to risk having his idea rejected, he frames it as a question, hoping to force the other person to agree with him.

With few exceptions, we could eliminate *all* questions from our communications with others. Since most questions are *indirect* forms of communication, they could be recast as statements, or direct communications. By replacing pseudo questions with genuine statements, we would come much closer to actual communication with each other.

Before we can achieve the aim of *direct* communication, however, we must be able to identify the varieties of pseudo questions that people tend to use. There are eight basic types of pseudo questions. Specific examples of each of these types of *indirect* communication are noted.

Co-Optive Question

This pseudo question attempts to narrow or limit the possible responses of the other person. "Don't you think that . . .?" is a classic example of this type. Or, "Isn't it true that . . .?"; "Wouldn't you rather . . .?"; "Don't you want to . . .?"; "You wouldn't want that, would you?" The questioner is attempting to elicit the response he wants by building certain restrictions into his question.

Punitive Question

When he uses a punitive question, the questioner really wants to expose the other individual without appearing to do so directly. For example, a person may be proposing a new theoretical model in training and his listener, knowing that the theory has not been properly researched, may ask him what the experimental evidence indicates. The purpose of the questioner is not to obtain information but to punish the speaker by putting him on the spot.

Hypothetical Question

In asking a hypothetical question, a person again resorts to a pseudo question. "If you were in charge of the meeting, wouldn't you handle it differently?" He does not actually want to know how the individual would handle it. He may wish to criticize the meeting, or he may be indirectly probing for an answer to a question he is afraid or reluctant to ask. Hypothetical questions typically begin with "If," "What if," or "How about."

Imperative Question

Another type of pseudo question is the one that actually makes a demand. A question such as "Have you done anything about . . .?" or "When are you going to . . .?" is not asking for information. Rather it implies a command: "Do what you said you were going to do and do it soon." The questioner wants to impress the other person with the urgency or importance of his request (command).

Activity 2

A. *The facilitator assigns one category of pseudo questions to each member of each quartet. The quartet is given five minutes to "communicate," with each person restricted to initiating "his" assigned category of pseudo questions.*

B. *No processing time is allowed at this point.*

Screened Question

The screened question is a very common variety of pseudo question. The questioner, afraid of simply stating his own choice or preference, asks the other person what *he* likes or what *he* wants to do, hoping the choice will be what the questioner himself secretly wants.

For example, two acquaintances decide to go out to dinner together. One individual, afraid to take the risk of making a suggestion that he is not sure will be accepted, resorts to a screened question: "What kind of food do you prefer?" Secretly he hopes the other person will name his own favorite food, say Chinese. Or he frames his question another way: "Would you like to have Chinese food?" Both questions screen an actual statement or choice, which the questioner fears to make: "I would like to have Chinese food."

One result of the screened question is that the questioner may get information he is not seeking. If the other person misinterprets the question about what kind of food he prefers, for example, he may tell the questioner about exotic varieties of food he has experienced in his travels—not what the questioner wanted to know at all.

On the other hand, the screened question may sorely frustrate the person being questioned. He is not sure how he should answer in order to give the "correct" response, and he feels under pressure to "guess" what the questioner really wants him to say.

The questioner, too, may find the results of a screened question frustrating. If the other person takes him at his word, the questioner may find himself trapped into a choice (Italian food, for example) that he does not like but cannot escape because he did not have the courage to state his own desires clearly from the beginning. Worse, both individuals may be unable to "risk" a suggestion and end up eating Greek food, which neither likes.

In marriage, the screened question may be used by one partner to punish or control the other. One individual may seem generously to offer the other "first choice," while he/she actually poses the question in such a way that he/she can reject the partner's suggestions and then offer, as a compromise, his/her own choice, which he/she wanted all along. Thus he/she gets what he/she wants by manipulating the partner into the position of offering all the "wrong" choices.

Set-Up Question

This pseudo question maneuvers the other person into a vulnerable position, ready for the axe to fall. One example of the set-up question is "Is it fair to say that you . . .?" If the person being questioned agrees that it is fair, the questioner

has him "set-up" for the kill. Another way set-up questions are introduced is by the phrase "Would you agree that . . .?" The questioner is "leading the witness" in much the same way a skillful lawyer sets up a line of response in court.

Rhetorical Question

One of the simplest types of the pseudo question is the rhetorical question, which comes in many forms. The speaker may make a statement and immediately follow it with a positive phrase that assumes approval in advance: "Right?" or "O.K.?" or "You see?" or "You know?" He is not asking the other person to respond; indeed he wishes to forestall a response because he fears it may not be favorable. Often, an insecure person may acquire the habit of ending almost all his statements with "Right?" as an attempted guarantee of agreement.

Or the questioner may precede his statements or requests with such negative phrases as "Don't you think . . .?"; "Isn't it true that . . .?"; "Wouldn't you like . . .?" In either case, the individual who fears risking his own opinion is trying to eliminate all alternatives by framing his "question" so that it elicits the response he wants.

A supervisor may say to a staff member, "Don't you think it would be a good idea to finish the report tonight and have it out of the way?" He phrases his question so as to make it appear that the decision to work late was a joint one. The staff member may not approve of the suggestion, but he has little or no alternative but to agree.

"Got'cha" Question

A "got'cha" question is derived from Eric Berne's *Games People Play* (1964): "Now I got'cha, you son-of-a-bitch." Related to the set-up question, a "got'cha" question might run something like this: "Weren't you the one who . . .?"; "Didn't you say that . . .?"; "Didn't I see you . . .?" The questioner's joy in trapping the other person is fairly palpable. He does not want an "answer" to his "question"; he wants to dig a pit for the respondent to fall into.

CLICHÉS

Pseudo questions are one method of indirect communication; clichés are another. When people use clichés they really don't want to communicate with another person—or they want to feel they are "communicating" without sharing anything of significance. Thus they resort to routinized, pat, standardized, stylized ways of responding to each other.

Examples of clichés abound. "You could hear a pin drop." "If you've seen one, you've seen them all." "He hit the nail on the head." "He took the bull by the horns." "He has us over a barrel." "We got our bid in just under the wire." "It's an open-and-shut case." "He left no stone unturned in his search." "Better late than never." "The early bird gets the worm." "He can't see the forest for the trees." "I've been racking my brains over the problem." "His kind of person is few and far between." "He is always up at the crack of dawn." "Let's get it over and done with." "His mind is as sharp as a tack." "Better safe than sorry." "She's as cute as a button."

No one can avoid using clichés occasionally. But the frequent use of tired, worn-out phrases diminishes the effectiveness of communication.

EFFECTS OF INDIRECT COMMUNICATION

If, then, we have established that clichés and pseudo questions are forms of indirect (and, therefore, ineffective) communication, it is important to know some of the effects that such indirect communication has on dealings between people.

Guesswork

We can note five major effects generated by indirect communication. First, it encourages each individual to make guesses about the other. Without direct, open patterns of communication, people cannot get to know each other successfully; what they do not know, they will make guesses about. Such "guessing games" further inhibit or obstruct true communication.

Inaccuracy

If one person is forced to guess about another, he may often be wrong. Yet he communicates with that person on the basis of his assumptions, the accuracy of which he is unable to check. Obviously, communication based on inaccurate assumptions is not clear or direct.

Inference of Motives

Indirect communication also increases the probability that people will be forced to infer the motives of each other. They will try to "psych" each other: Why is he doing that? What is his intention behind that? By communicating through clichés and pseudo questions, we hide our true motivations.

Game-Playing Behavior

Further, indirect communication encourages people to "play games" with each other: to deceive, to be dishonest, not to be open or straightforward. Clearly, such behavior leads away from the basic aims of human relations training. When the questioner is playing a "got'cha" game, for example, his behavior may be contagious.

Defensiveness

One of the surest effects of indirect communication is defensiveness. Since there is an implied threat behind a great deal of indirect communication, individuals tend to become wary when faced with it. Their need to defend themselves only widens the gap of effective communication even further.

Defensiveness can be recognized in several different postures, all characteristic results of indirect communication: *displacement, denial, projection, attribution,* and *deflection.*

Activity 5

A. *Participants form "new" triads.*

B. *The members of each triad communicate with each other for ten minutes* without *using questions or clichés.*

C. *Five minutes of processing time follows.*

DIRECT (EFFECTIVE) COMMUNICATION

In contrast to indirect (ineffective) communication, direct (effective) communication is marked by the capacity for taking certain risks in order to understand and be understood.

Characteristics

Communication is effective when it has certain characteristics.

It is *two-way* communication, with ideas, opinions, values, attitudes, beliefs, and feelings flowing freely from one individual to another.

It is marked by *active listening*, by people taking responsibility for what they hear—accepting, clarifying, and checking the meaning, content, and intent of what the other person says.

It utilizes *effective feedback.* Not only does each person listen actively, he also responds to the other individual by telling that person what he thinks he is hearing. The process of feedback tests whether what was heard is what was intended.

It is *not stressful.* Communication is not effective if people are concerned that they are not communicating; when this happens, it is a key that the communication is not functioning properly.

It is *clear* and unencumbered by mixed or contradictory messages (verbal, nonverbal, or symbolic) that serve to confuse the content of the communication. In other words, it is *direct.*

Any communication always carries two kinds of meanings: the content message and the relationship message. We not only hear *what* other people say to us, we also hear implications about our mutual relationship. If we are so preoccupied with detecting cues about the latter, we may distort the content message severely or lose it altogether. When communication is effective, both messages are clearly discernible; one does not confuse or distract the other.

Approaches

Confrontation is one of five major approaches that can foster direct communication. Each person can learn to confront the other in a declarative rather than an interrogative manner. We can attempt to eliminate almost all our pseudo questions by formulating them into direct statements.

Active listening can be encouraged. This is a powerful antidote to indirect communication. We can learn to paraphrase, empathize, reflect feelings, test the accuracy of our inferences, and check our assumptions in order to produce clearer, more straightforward communication with others.

Owning is a third means of fostering direct communication. If individuals can learn to accept their legitimate feelings, data, attitudes, behavior, responsibility, etc., then they can learn to reveal themselves more directly to other people. Owning what we *are*, what we are *feeling*, and what *belongs* to us is a first step toward communicating more effectively.

Locating, a fourth approach toward direct communication, is a way of finding the context of a question. Some questions we cannot answer because we do not know their "environment," so to speak. We need to learn to locate these questions before we can respond to them. Questions are usually more effective if they are preceded by an explanation of where they are "coming from."

Sharing is the final, and perhaps most important, point directing us toward effective communication. All communication is a sharing process: In attempting to communicate with others, we are sharing our views, beliefs, thoughts, values, observations, intentions, doubts, wants, interests, assumptions, strengths, and weaknesses.

For any of these approaches to be useful, we must, as we indicated earlier, be ready to take risks and to work toward a genuine sharing of a common meaning with the other person. If we are not prepared to risk, we will not attain successful, effective, direct communication.

Activity 6

A. *The participants form sextets.*

B. *The learning of the experience is processed in terms of back-home applications.*

C. *Each participant contracts to find out what has happened with his spouse or with a fellow worker without using questions.*

REFERENCES

Berne, E. *Games people play: The psychology of human relationships.* New York: Grove, 1964.

Jones, J. E. Communication modes: An experiential lecture. In J. W. Pfeiffer & J. E. Jones (Eds.), *The 1972 annual handbook for group facilitators.* San Diego: University Associates, 1972.

Jones, J. E. Risk-taking and error protection styles. In J. W. Pfeiffer & J. E. Jones (Eds.), *The 1972 annual handbook for group facilitators.* San Diego: University Associates, 1972.

Pfeiffer, J. W. Conditions which hinder effective communication. In J. E. Jones & J. W. Pfeiffer (Eds.), *The 1973 annual handbook for group facilitators.* San Diego: University Associates, 1973.

Pfeiffer, J. W. Risk-taking. In J. E. Jones & J. W. Pfeiffer (Eds.), *The 1973 annual handbook for group facilitators.* San Diego: University Associates, 1973.

Pfeiffer, J. W., & Jones, J. E. Openness, collusion and feedback. In J. W. Pfeiffer & J. E. Jones (Eds.), *The 1972 annual handbook for group facilitators.* San Diego: University Associates, 1972.

MODELS AND ROLES OF CHANGE AGENTS

Marshall Sashkin

Models for inducing change within an organization may have different orientations. Some that are concerned with producing specific change might be labeled *adoptive* models. Others oriented toward producing "changingness," a general state conducive to change, may be called *adaptive* models.

The differences between them boil down to these: Is the aim to get the client to change in certain specified ways, to adopt certain new practices, to use certain new technological devices? If so, an adoptive model is appropriate.

Is the aim to help the client become more adaptable, more open to change, and able to change in needed ways (whatever the specifics as defined by the client might be)? To accomplish this aim, the client uses internal and external resources for change, rather than relying on outside help. An adaptive model is appropriate.

ADOPTIVE MODELS

Three major approaches center on the diffusion and adoption of technological and social inventions or changes. All are oriented toward researchers developing knowledge which could be beneficial once put into practice. Thus, the question raised by all three models is: "Researchers have developed some new device, mechanism, process, or procedure. How can potential users be convinced to put it into practice?"

Research, Development, and Diffusion (RDD)

The first and oldest model is generally called Research, Development, and Diffusion. RDD is devoted to making sure that he who builds a "better

In part, this paper, prepared by Marshall Sashkin, summarizes concepts more fully developed by M. Sashkin, W. C. Morris, and L. Horst (1973). It was originally prepared as part of a book in process, "A Resource Book for Training and Planned Change," by R. Lippitt, M. Sashkin, *et al.*

mouse trap" beats a path to the doors of the world. (We now know that, in reality, the world rarely beats a path to the inventor's door, even when the invention not only works but works better.)

Basic to RDD is production of an innovation or invention through institutional research by a corps of trained research scientists. The innovation is tested and developed by a lengthy process. Then, the innovation is ready for "diffusion" to users. Adoption occurs when diffusion is effectively carried out. This means that the innovation must be presented to potential users appropriately, at the right time, and by the "correct" type of communication. Careful study of the user population is necessary to determine these factors.

RDD is technologically oriented and concerned primarily, though not exclusively, with how to get individuals, groups, and organizations to adopt and use such innovations as auto seat belts, new breakfast foods, or an improved assembly method for welded machinery. RDD can also be applied to adoption of social-behavioral innovations, such as management practices or educational methods. But such application is not common. Effective use of RDD depends essentially on sophisticated marketing methods. However, the evidence we have on the use and results of RDD indicates that the model does not seem to be very effective, generally.

Social Interaction and Diffusion (SID)

Social Interaction and Diffusion is concerned with behavior change to a greater degree than RDD is. But it does retain emphasis on adoption of technological innovations, such as acceptance of new drugs by physicians. The primary orientation, however, is the same as that of RDD: how people can be persuaded to adopt and use an innovation. The SID model is based on the large body of evidence that certain "opinion leaders" set trends and others follow. The followers adopt innovations after contact with opinion leaders who have already done so and recommend that others do so as well.

The change strategy is to identify opinion leaders and to direct specific information, education, demonstration, and persuasion efforts toward them, rather than toward followers (the "general public").

Various problems arise, however. There are no "general" opinion leaders. For each innovation specific leaders must be identified. "Fashion" opinion leaders, for example, are not the same people as "voting" opinion leaders. Furthermore, identification is not always easy. Sometimes opinion leaders are unaware of their social role or, more frequently, they do not want to be identified.

Another problem is that this leader-identification approach is individually oriented. It does not use the great norm-setting power of organized groups, formal and informal. Thus, in dealing with an organization like a YMCA, an auto-assembly plant, or a local men's club, the SID model may be quite inefficient compared to other approaches—even if it does produce some results.

Linkage

This third, more sophisticated model focuses much more on the process of adoption. Linkage, developed by Havelock (1968), basically is concerned with the roles of the disseminator who links the research source with the user(s) of innovations. The "linker" may not be a person but a procedure or a group of people. The Linkage model considers significant the user (client-system) learning how to obtain and use information *externally* (where and how to ask so that the external resource can understand, etc.) and *internally* (how to draw on knowledge resources within). Still, the model places primary emphasis on the adoption of specific innovations rather than on the adoptive *capacity* of the user.

Although Linkage is not limited to either "hard" or "soft" technological innovation, it does not seem to place sufficient emphasis on adaptivity. Adaptivity is the focus of any model concerned with producing long-range, survival-facilitating change. Next, three such adaptive models are examined.

ADAPTIVE MODELS

All three adaptive models are oriented toward development of adaptive capacity in a client system—the ability to become aware of needs for change and to plan, implement, and evaluate action changes.

Second, all stress client participation in specific change efforts. The client learns to use the change model by applying it to specific real problems, with the help of an external change agent.

Third, all three models are based, to differing degrees, on an approach developed by Kurt Lewin called "action-research."

Intervention Theory and Method (ITM)

Intervention Theory and Method is a model described by Chris Argyris (1970). It differs from the other two adaptive models in many minor ways and in two major ways.

First, this model is oriented exclusively toward changes in internal processes. The interventionist is relatively unconcerned with technological or structural change. He does not help the client go outside of the system for change resources (information, expert help, and such), with the possible exception of calling in another change agent who possesses certain specialized process skills.

Second, there is less emphasis, in practice, on generation of research knowledge relevant to the change process. Although there is considerable emphasis on collecting and analyzing data within the client system and on monitoring effects of actions, the aim is to provide the client with skills for accomplishing activities which create effective, adaptive internal changes. In practice, if not in theory, there is no aim to generate experimental knowledge on the process of change or to build better behavioral science theories about the change process. This, of course, fits with the first emphasis on the internal processes of the client system.

Planned Change (PC)

This second model is by Lippitt, Watson, and Westley (1958).

PC differs substantially from ITM in two ways: First, change resources outside of the client system, as well as within, receive attention. Furthermore, the model is not oriented solely toward process change, although this type of change does receive most of the focus.

Second, more specific attention goes to evaluating action changes. The PC model concentrates more than the ITM model on measuring effects to support effective change and further planning. However, as in the case of the ITM model, generation of behavioral science knowledge on change process is not emphasized in practice.

Action-Research (AR)

Not only does the AR model combine the attributes of ITM and PC, it also adds the emphasis lacking in these two—the generation of new, useful knowledge about the process of change, about specific change methods or techniques, about specific changes (of a technical, structural, or process nature), or about the resolution or means of resolving certain social problems.

In other words, the AR model creates specific changes which develop client resources for self-change and future adaptability. These changes include client training in the research methods needed for data collection, in problem understanding, and in evaluation of change attempts. The results are increased behavioral science knowledge about change.

To accomplish this, the change agent fulfills three roles—those of consultant, trainer, and researcher. Following is a brief examination and comparison of these roles as they are employed (or omitted) in all six of the change models discussed here.

CHANGE-AGENT ROLES

The change agent using each of the six models described here assumes different roles.

In RDD, the change agent is really a *consultant*, aimed at helping the client adopt and use certain innovations.

In ITM, the interventionist is primarily a *trainer*, showing the client how to use the ITM approach to alter client system processes. Part of the role is training the client in certain research skills—data-gathering and analysis methods.

The AR model includes consultant and trainer roles, plus that of *researcher*. The researcher's task is to generate new behavioral science knowledge, which can be used by other change agents as well as by academicians primarily involved in developing and refining theory and understanding.

The chart that follows (Figure 1) compares roles in all six models more specifically.

The three adoptive models focus on the consultant role of the change agent. Some training may occur with the SID model, and a limited type of training (in information-retrieval skills) is likely with Linkage. Although some research has been done on all three adoption models (especially SID and Linkage), research is not an integral part of their operation.

The three adaptive models emphasize consultation and training roles, although the nature of these roles differs somewhat. ITM includes consultation on process issues, not on specific content problems. PC and AC emphasize process consultation, but often include consultation around content problems.

All three adaptive approaches train the client in use of the model to produce change. For ITM, this training is the primary emphasis; PC and AC are more balanced in focus. In the ITM model, research has a heavy conceptual emphasis but an apparently weak practical emphasis, except for client training in skills needed to generate valid information. PC goes somewhat further in noting the importance of research for evaluation of change, as well as data-gathering and diagnosis. AR is the only model with a basic part generating new behavioral science knowledge, as well as client training in research skills for data collection, diagnosis, and evaluation.

Figure 1. Comparison of Six Change Models in Terms of the Roles of the Change Agent

ADOPTIVE CHANGE MODELS	ROLES		
	Consultant	Trainer	Researcher
RDD	Primary emphasis; the major function of the change agent is facilitating adoption of some specific innovation.	Not included; however, some training may take place, in the sense that the client may be taught how to obtain similar knowledge in the future.	Research may be accomplished but this is rare and is not a part of the change process or necessary to it.
SID	Primary emphasis; the major function of the change agent is facilitating adoption of some specific innovation or practice.	Not included; however, certain members of the client system may be made more aware of their roles as resources for new knowledge and other members may learn to seek them out and use them more effectively.	Research is not a primary focus and not part of the change process, although research done on this model has been used to "refine" it.
Linkage	Primary emphasis; the major function of the knowledge linker—the change agent—is effective diffusion of specific innovation (technical or social) by creating linkages between the knowledge source and the user; such linkages may be made permanent through roles carried out by an individual linker or by a linking group or as institutionalized procedures.	Training may occur in that the client learns more effective methods for getting information from external resources; in addition, the client may learn better internal data-retrieval procedures.	Research is not a focus, although considerable research has been done on the model and on the diffusion and utilization processes; however, the model itself does not contribute to such research as a part of its normal operation.

ADAPTIVE CHANGE MODELS	ROLES		
	Consultant	Trainer	Researcher
ITM	Consultation on process only, not on content problems; however, the interventionist does introduce the client to new methods of data-gathering, analysis, decision-making.	Primary emphasis on training the client in new skills and methods (process oriented).	Emphasized to the extent of training the client in research skills needed for generation of valid information prior to and during the change process; research for development of new behavioral science knowledge is emphasized conceptually, but does not seem an integral part of the model.
PC	Consultation on process primarily, but also on content; for example, the derivation-utilization conference introduces the client to new content knowledge resources.	Major emphasis on training the client in skills and methods for creating adaptive changes.	Emphasized mostly in evaluation of effects of specific changes and client training in certain research skills needed for data collection and diagnosis; the importance of the generation of new behavioral science knowledge is noted, but it is not an operational part of the model.
AR	Consultation on process is emphasized, but content consultation also occurs.	Major emphasis on training for development of internal resources for change.	Major emphasis on research as the basis for action, an important area of client training, and the source of new knowledge about change which can be used by behavioral science practitioners and theorists.

CONCLUSION

The difference between adoptive and adaptive change models in general is far more significant than differences among the three models of each type. This is particularly true for the adaptive models: Their differences are really minor and all three are generally useful.

We suggest that the three adoptive models, particularly SID and Linkage, are useful in certain circumstances, with Linkage being the most generally useful of the three. However, effective change is based primarily on the three adaptive models, Intervention Theory and Method, Planned Change, and Action-Research.

REFERENCES

Argyris, C. *Intervention theory and method.* Reading, Mass.: Addison-Wesley, 1970.

Frohman, M. A., Sashkin, M., & Kavanagh, M. J. Action research as an organization development approach. Unpublished manuscript, 1973.

Havelock, R. G. Dissemination and translation roles. In T. L. Bidell & J. M. Kitchell (Eds.), *Knowledge production and utilization in educational administration.* Eugene, Ore.: University Council for Educational Administration and Center for the Advanced Study of Educational Administration, University of Oregon, 1968.

Havelock, R. G., Guskin, A. E., Frohman, M. A., Havelock, M., Hill, M., & Huber, J. *Planning for innovation.* Ann Arbor, Mich.: Center for Research on Utilization of Scientific Knowledge, Institute for Social Research, University of Michigan, 1969.

Katz, E. The two-step flow of communication: An up-to-date report on a hypothesis. *Public Opinion Quarterly,* 1957, 21, 61-78.

Katz, E., & Lazarsfeld, P. *Personal influence.* Glencoe, Ill.: Free Press, 1955.

Lewin, K. Group decision and social change. In T. M. Newcomb and E. L. Hartley (Eds.), *Readings in social psychology.* New York: Holt, Rinehart, and Winston, 1947.

Lewin, K. *Resolving social conflict.* New York: Harper's, 1947.

Lippitt, R., Watson, J., & Westley, B. *The dynamics of planned change.* New York: Harcourt, Brace, & World, 1958.

Olmosk, K. E. Seven pure strategies of change. In J. W. Pfeiffer & J. E. Jones (Eds.), *The 1972 annual handbook for group facilitators.* San Diego: University Associates, 1972, 163-172.

Sashkin, M., Morris, W. C., & Horst, L. A comparison of social and organizational change models: Information flow and data use processes. *Psychological Review,* 1973, 80.

Whyte, W. F., & Hamilton, E. L. *Action research for management.* Homewood, Ill.: Irwin-Dorsey, 1964.

INDIVIDUAL NEEDS AND ORGANIZATIONAL GOALS: AN EXPERIENTIAL LECTURE

Anthony J. Reilly

One of the main objectives of human relations training is to coordinate *what is known* about human behavior with *what actually takes place* in the working world. Behavioral scientists have generated a wealth of knowledge about man and the way he relates to his work environment.

This paper presents a framework for introducing a number of theoretical orientations around three work-related topics: individual needs, the psychological contract, and managerial style.

There are many ways to explore with managerial and staff personnel various concepts and approaches that can be used to develop the human potential of organizations. This paper considers each of its topics both experientially and theoretically. Specific experiences are emphasized to allow participants to become personally involved in the concepts discussed and to discover and validate certain aspects of human behavior theory.

No effort, however, has been made to present in-depth theoretical positions. Instead, the facilitator is referred to a number of investigators who have done significant research relating to the concepts discussed. The facilitator is encouraged to supplement the activities suggested here with additional appropriate theory.

HUMAN RESOURCE DEVELOPMENT

The human relations consultant, whether he functions as an internal consultant or as an external facilitator to an organization, is concerned with human resource development. Individual needs must be meshed with organizational goals. In working with organizations, the consultant generally sees individuals as possessing much

more potential than is ever actualized in most settings. If it is properly tapped, this potential—which includes physical skills as well as creative energy—can lead to greater satisfaction for the individual as well as to improved organizational effectiveness.

The identification of individual needs and organizational needs and the relationship between these two sets of needs are the central issues of this paper. The concept of the psychological contract seeks to mesh individual and organizational needs, thus bringing into play the component of leadership behavior—getting work accomplished through people.

INDIVIDUAL NEEDS

This activity is designed to clarify what individuals want from their work.

Goals

1. To make individuals aware of their personal work needs and how they vary in intensity.
2. To allow participants to discover the relationships between their needs and their opportunities to meet those needs.
3. To highlight theory related to people's needs in organizations.

Process

The time required for this activity is approximately one hour.

1. *Individual list.* Participants are asked to write short phrases answering the question "What do individuals want from their work?"

2. *Group list.* Representative items generated by individual participants are then listed on a

piece of newsprint. The group's list should indicate the major dimensions of all the individual lists. Some of the items that generally emerge on this topic:

Good salary
Promotion potential
Sense of achievement
Good working conditions
Job security
Freedom of self-expression
Feeling "in" on things
Being with other people
Challenge
Supportive supervision

3. *Rank-ordering specific needs.* The next step is to ask participants to copy the group list and rank-order each need as it applies to themselves in their present work situation. Number 1 would indicate "most importance," and so on. Participants are told that they will be sharing their rankings with another person in the group.

4. *Rank-ordering the availability of opportunity.* After rank-ordering the list, participants are asked to fold their sheets so that they cannot see the rank-order they just completed. Then they rank-order each item on the list again, this time in terms of the amount of opportunity available in their present work for meeting that particular need. Number 1 again would indicate "most opportunity" and so on. The following is a typical response pattern:

Importance	Individual Need	Opportunity
3	Good salary	3
7	Promotion potential	4
2	Sense of achievement	5
5	Good working conditions	1
6	Job security	2
1	Freedom of self-expression	6
8	Feeling "in" on things	9
10	Being with other people	7

Importance	Individual Need	Opportunity
4	Challenge	10
9	Supportive supervision	8

5. *Sharing of rankings.* A number of short activities may be used at this point to involve participants.

   a. For each item, the participant should determine the difference between his ranking for "importance" and his ranking for available "opportunity."

   b. Participants can be paired to exchange their ranking sheets and discuss similarities and differences that they perceive between needs and opportunities. Older and younger participants, long-tenured and short-tenured persons, and management and nonmanagement personnel are possible pairings of participants.

6. *Participant learnings.* Next, a group discussion is conducted in which participants are asked to share their personal learnings. One way to focus the discussion is to ask each participant to offer to the group the one most significant point that resulted from his discussion with his partner. A poster can be made by the facilitator listing the points made by participants.

Theory

The work of three well-known motivational theorists may be introduced to participants (Maslow, 1968; Herzberg, 1973; and McClelland, 1967).

If, for example, the facilitator chooses to present Maslow's Need Hierarchy and his general approach to human needs, he may ask participants to classify each work need generated by the group into Maslow's hierarchy. The results might look like this:

Self-Actualization Needs
Freedom of self-expression
Challenge

Ego-Status Needs
Promotion potential
Sense of achievement

216

Belonging Needs
Feeling "in" on things
Being with other people
Supportive supervision

Safety Needs
Job security

Basic Needs
Good salary
Good working conditions

Herzberg has extended Maslow's thinking by applying it to a work setting. Further, he has contributed his own theory concerning work needs and has done considerable research in the area of motivation and its relation to work.

A theory of need achievement which also may be tied in to human work needs is McClelland's (1967) contribution to research about this topic. The facilitator can introduce the idea of the need for achievement by showing how it is reflected in the need list of the participant.

Application

If this activity is to be successful, it is important that the facilitator consider how the participants' learnings may be applied on a day-to-day basis. He may discuss such points as self-awareness, the understanding of individual differences and similarities, and the implications for job assignments.

THE PSYCHOLOGICAL CONTRACT

This topic deals with the meshing of individual needs with organizational goals.

Goals

1. To have participants identify specific expectations that organizations have of workers.
2. To contrast "people" needs with the needs of organizations.
3. To introduce the notion of the psychological contract.

Process

This experience requires approximately thirty minutes. It is a natural extension of the activity on individual needs.

1. *Listing organizational needs.* The entire group generates a list of specific wants that organizations have of their employees, and a poster is made of these expectations.

The following is a representative list that could emerge:
High quality work
Loyalty to the company
Growth for employees
Employee satisfaction
Commitment to the organization's objectives
Conformity
Creative ideas
Risk-taking behavior
Status-quo
Cooperation

2. *The psychological contract.* In the next step, the list of individual needs is posted side by side with the list of organizational needs, thus highlighting the interdependence of the two lists. This introduces the idea of the psychological contract, an implicit agreement concerned with meeting each set of needs as fully as possible. The two lists might then appear like this:

Individual Needs	*Organizational Needs*
Good salary	High quality work
Promotion potential	Loyalty to the company
Sense of achievement	Growth for employees
Good working conditions	Employee satisfaction
Job security	Commitment to the organization's objectives
Freedom of self-expression	Conformity
Feeling "in" on things	Creative ideas
Being with other people	Risk-taking behavior
Challenge	Status-quo
Supportive supervision	Cooperation

Theory

In numerous organizations, formal, explicit contracts exist between management and nonmanagement personnel. These contracts aim at meeting workers' needs and at the same time guarantee that the organization will continue to thrive and be productive. Historically, formal contract negotiations are cast in terms of a win-lose model, which can have costly effects on organizational life.

Management "wins" a labor arbitration or the union "wins" a pay increase. In reality, however, the losers wield considerable power. Management may "win" a labor dispute, but workers can join hands and make life miserable for management. On the other hand, management can lay off the very workers who have "won" a pay increase. Such win-lose struggles abound.

In contrast, the psychological contract that exists between an individual and the organization for which he works is *implicit*, although it can be made quite explicit. The contract is concerned with meshing individual and organizational needs in such a way that both sides "win."

Kolb *et al.* (1971) have some good insights into this mutual influence:

> The dynamic quality of the psychological contract means that individual and company expectations and individual and company contributions mutually influence one another. High expectations on the part of the company can produce increased individual contributions, and great contributions will likewise raise expectations. From the company's point of view, the question becomes "How can we manage our human resources so that we can maximize individual contributions?" "How can we socialize our members to accept our expectations and norms as legitimate?" For the individual the questions are "How can I get the satisfaction and rewards that I want from this organization?" "How can I manage my personal growth and development?" [p. 8]

Several other investigators have studied related variables (Argyris, 1970; Schein, 1965; and McGregor, 1960). Their research carries important concepts which can well be introduced at this point.

The work of Argyris relates directly to this activity. He has made in-depth studies in various organizational settings, and he states that both labor unions and management have missed the main point with regard to individual employee needs. He agrees with Herzberg's findings that needs centering around pay, job security, and benefits are necessary but not sufficient for today's workers.

Today's frustrations, Argyris feels, center on the underutilization of employees' talents. He sees a direct, interdependent relationship between individual needs and organizational needs.

Schein has investigated the effects of an individual's early experience with an organization and has written extensively about the socialization of individuals in organizations.

McGregor, generally regarded as being one of the most influential behavioral scientists of our times, is probably also one of the most misquoted. He has contributed widely to the field and is especially noted for clarifying and translating behavioral science research into practical implications for managers.

Application

Participants may be encouraged to share the results of this activity—especially the idea of the psychological contract—with their own supervisors. A supervisor might find the activity very helpful in the orientation of new employees. Its value in this context is that both individual and organizational needs can be made clear, specific, and concrete.

The activity could also be used as a selection tool, matching organizational and individual needs with job requirements. Usually, prospective employees—and employers—attempt simply to make a favorable impression on each other. Seldom are real needs discussed. An activity such as the Psychological Contract can set the stage for rewarding exchanges between employer and prospective employees.

MANAGERIAL STYLE AND THE IMPLEMENTATION OF THE PSYCHOLOGICAL CONTRACT

Goals

1. To coordinate a person's managerial style with individual and organizational needs as reflected in the psychological contract.
2. To give participants feedback about management style.
3. To consider concepts related to management style.

Process

Approximately one hour is required for this topic.

1. *Choice of instrument.* The consultant chooses one of several instruments which yield information about a person's management style. Pfeiffer and Heslin (1973) review a number of such instruments which are applicable.

2. *Administration of instrument.* After the instrument is administered, the consultant presents some leadership theory which relates to the chosen instrument.

Theory

Because of the nature of the psychological contract, it is the responsibility of both the individual and the organization to see that the contract is implemented.

The manager represents the organization. It is his job to see that organizational needs are met. Indeed, management's key function is to accomplish work through and with people—*i.e.*, to mesh organizational needs with individual needs.

Likert (1967) and Hall (1968) are two theorists who have published widely in the area of leadership behavior.

Likert has studied the long-term effects of leadership style on organizational effectiveness. His concept of a "supportive relationship" respects individual needs and values, while matching high demands of employees.

Hall has approached leadership theory in a practical way through a number of instruments which provide feedback to individuals about their leadership styles. His matrix approach places individual needs along one dimension and organizational needs along a second dimension in such a way as to allow an individual to see how his leadership philosophy and behavior condition his response to each set of needs.

Application

The idea of leadership style is directly relevant to day-to-day events in the life of any manager or supervisor who must accomplish work by means of other people. Feedback from an instrument on style can easily be translated into specific events related to participants' jobs.

CONCLUSION

For work efficiency and employee satisfaction, both organizational needs and individual needs must be met. If people are to be productive and to have the sense that their talents are being utilized, it is important that their needs be clearly known to their organization. On the other hand, organizational needs must also be specified and clearly communicated to employees.

One of the aims of human relations consultants is to coordinate these two, often differing, sets of needs in ways that meet the requirements of both employer and employee, thus leading to improved work situations for all involved.

REFERENCES

Argyris, C. *Intervention theory and method: A behavioral science view.* Reading, Mass: Addison-Wesley, 1970.

Hall, J. *Styles of leadership survey.* Teleometrics, Inc., 1968.

Herzberg, F. *Work and the nature of man.* New York: New American Library, 1973.

Herzberg, F., Mausner, B., & Snyderman, B. *The motivation to work.* (2nd ed.) New York: Wiley, 1959.

Kolb, D. A., Rubin, I. M., & McIntyre, J. M. *Organizational psychology: An experiential approach.* Englewood Cliffs: Prentice-Hall, 1971.

Likert, R. *Human organization: Its management and value.* New York: McGraw-Hill, 1967.

Maslow, A. H. *Toward a psychology of being.* (2nd ed.) New York: Van Nostrand Reinhold, 1968.

McClelland, D. C. *Achieving society.* New York: McGraw-Hill, 1967.

McGregor, D. *Human side of enterprise.* New York: McGraw-Hill, 1960.

Pfeiffer, J. W., & Heslin, R. *Instrumentation in human relations training.* San Diego: University Associates, 1973.

Schein, E. H., & Bennis, W. G. *Personal and organizational change through group methods.* New York: Wiley, 1965.

BASIC CONCEPTS OF SURVEY FEEDBACK

David G. Bowers and Jerome L. Franklin

Perhaps the most common misconception about survey feedback pivots upon the failure to distinguish the *process* and what it represents from the *data* and what they represent. For the unwary, a rush to action based upon this misconception all too often results in damage to the recipient and disillusionment for both him and the purveyor.

Survey feedback is not a sheet of tabulated data, nor is it the simple return of such data to some representative of the respondents. Instead, it is a relatively complex guidance *method* which draws upon the device of the questionnaire survey to upgrade and make more complete, rational, and adequate a process inherent in social organizations.

THE NATURE OF FEEDBACK

At the root of survey feedback, as with any guidance device, are several fairly fundamental properties: (1) *purposiveness*, (2) *a flow of events* through time, and (3) *periodic discrepancies* of what occurs from what was desired or intended. The first of these refers to the perhaps obvious fact that "feedback" in the absence of some aim, objective, target, or purpose is meaningless. The recitation of stock market quotations may be eminently meaningful to a broker or to an investor eagerly or anxiously anticipating his gains or losses; it has no meaning for a person who has no stake in it, does not understand it, and for whom it is simply "feed" (*i.e.*, noise).

The second basic property points to what must be implicit in the term "feedback," namely that a number of events occur sequentially across time. They flow from an action by the potential recipient to an end-state about which he hopefully gets information on how well the sequence has gone.

The third fundamental condition simply states that for feedback to be useful (*i.e.*, to result in mid-course corrections), one must assume that some difference or discrepancy exists from time to time between what has been desired or intended and what has actually occurred.

Building upon these three basic properties, one is able to distinguish feedback from other forms of information input. Information which is novel and extraneous to accepted purposes, while potentially quite useful, is different from feedback. Information which refers to events now complete and not likely to recur is not feedback and, for guidance purposes, is as likely to be without value as is information which conveys no difference from what was intended (*i.e.*, leads to no action).

Descriptive or Evaluative Feedback

At a somewhat more concrete level, much is often made in interpersonal settings of the value of providing feedback that is descriptive, rather than evaluative. To the extent that this precept refers to avoiding the debilitating effects of threat and punishment, one can only concur. Both research and experience indicate that fear, resentment, and excessive anxiety at best can be counterproductive, at worst paralyzing and highly destructive.

However, this is a different genre of issue from that which arises if one insists that feedback, when provided, must be unconnected to value judgments of goodness and badness, usefulness, desirability, and the like. In fact, the heart of any feedback process is precisely that: a reading, returned to the actor, on how well or how poorly things are going in relation to what he has done. In this sense, feedback (including survey feedback) *is* evaluative.

Its highly desirable property of descriptiveness is therefore determined not by the extent to which it avoids evaluations (it does not and cannot), but by the extent to which it encompasses in its message information about the flow of events leading to the outcome. As such, it must be connected, in a way clearly understood, accepted, and believed by the actor, to a model of those events which includes cause-effect relationships.

In form, it is built around the notion that if the actor does A, it results in B, which in turn produces C. Although feedback that lets the actor know only that he has not attained in his most current attempt(s) the desired state of C certainly possesses some utility, feedback that tells him as well that his A was inappropriate, or that it did not lead to a sufficient B, permits him to revise his actions and perhaps the model itself on something more than a trial-and-error basis. It is in this sense that another property commonly felt to be desirable in feedback—that it be *helpful*—reflects a great deal of truth. However, helpfulness resides more in what the feedback permits the actor to do constructively than in the demeanor or tone of the purveyor.

Turning to the specific case of survey feedback, the substance of these points is that it must:

- be built around a model which has a maximum likelihood of being correct (that is, around principles of behavior and organization derived and verified scientifically as appropriate to the situation);
- be clearly tied, through this model, to outcomes which are positively valued; and
- provide a return of model-valid information relevant to more than merely the outcomes of the process represented by the model.

Previous Endorsement of Model

Finally, an obvious corollary is that the principles, ideas, and concepts which make up the model must be accepted and endorsed by the actor *before*, not merely after, he receives the information intended as feedback. A survey feedback operation launched without this prior acceptance, but in the hope that the information fed back will itself be persuasive, is foredoomed to

failure for those same reasons mentioned in the earlier stock market quotations illustration: The input will be meaningless and therefore rejected. Where the principles and concepts contained in the model and operationalized in the survey are not understood or accepted in advance, the leader, change agent, or facilitator is well advised to proceed no further until, by training or planned experience, he has implanted that understanding and acceptance.

THE CHARACTER AND QUALITY OF DATA FOR SURVEY FEEDBACK

Understanding the causal sequences—let alone measuring them—involves us in an immediate paradox. If we say, for example, that A causes B, we have to assume two mutually contradictory things: that both A and B occurred at exactly the same point in time (since no event can be caused by something that it is not in contact with), and that A must have preceded B (since a cause must occur before its effect). In everyday life, we solve this problem by *storing* large numbers of connected $A \rightarrow B$ events and looking at them for some period of time.

The same practice holds true for the survey. In describing in a questionnaire the behavior of their leader, the behavior of their fellow members, or the conditions present in the larger organization of which their group is a part, respondents summarize a large number of specific acts and events, some of which have caused others. The picture which results in the tabulated data, although taken at one point in time, is a composite photograph of the person, group, and/or organization as it has persisted over some period of weeks or months. By the changes observed in the picture from one administration and feedback to the next, movement is depicted in much the same way as in a motion picture.

Accuracy of the Picture

The accuracy of the resulting picture depends upon the care which goes into those several aspects of the process and upon the instrument which reflects their design: the accuracy and adequacy of the body of principles and concepts upon which both the model and the instrument have been built (are they the result of rigorous research, or of armchair extractions from experience?); the reliability and validity of the questionnaire instrument and its measures (does it measure dependably and accurately what it purports to measure?); and the conditions under which the data are collected (trust, confidence, care, and clarity of procedures).

Beyond the conventional indicators of validity, the procedure employed in survey feedback relies upon the consensual validation implicit in collecting multiple perceptions of the same events from several persons. Those who view and report about the same phenomenon should substantially agree in their perception and differ from other persons perceiving other events.

A Representation of Reality

What results, of course, is a representation in abstract symbols (numbers) of the organizational reality in which respondents live. Events have been summarized by each respondent across some period of time considered by him to be appropriate, translated by the survey into numbers, and summarized in the tabulation across all members of the group. Their subsequent ability, in the feedback process, to translate this back into a common experience base about which joint conclusions can be drawn depends upon the clarity and concreteness of the original questionnaire items. Clear, concrete, descriptive items are more readily converted in the discussion back into clear, concrete examples than are fuzzy, abstract ones. *It is precisely this translation-summarization-conversion process, resulting in a shared view of problems and strengths, which lies at the heart of survey feedback's payoff potential.*

Perception of Threat

Confidentiality of individual responses also plays a considerable role in the validity question. Survey feedback is seldom undertaken in other than hierarchical organizational settings. The differences in positions, roles, status, and power which this fact implies make each respondent vulnerable in some respect to being held accountable in punitive terms for having expressed

himself. If the threat is real, and applicable to the majority of respondents, the facilitator's attempt to use survey feedback to develop constructive problem-solving obviously faces a situation of model nonacceptance.

However, more common, and in some ways critical, is the real *perception* of an unreal threat, and it is this anxiety which the confidential treatment of individual responses helps allay. Even though it is obvious to respondents that some handful of personal background items could identify him, there is considerable reassurance in not having to place his name upon his questionnaire. "Taking attendance," scrutinizing a respondent's questionnaire as he hands it in, and peering over his shoulder are similarly to be avoided, as is the practice of including immediate superiors and their subordinates in the same questionnaire-completion session.

Observing these cautions, together with aggregating data across all respondents in the group and into summary indices geared to the group's size (a mean response preserves confidentiality in small groups, whereas a percentage spread does not), helps guarantee that the results will be truly consensually valid and reasonably free from distortions attributable to a threatened position.

CRITICAL ASPECTS OF THE FEEDBACK PROCESS

The usefulness of the survey data depends as much upon the nature of the feedback process as upon the character and quality of the actual data. Although a complete treatment would involve a consideration of specific aspects of this process, we will focus at present upon only four additional major issues: (1) the role of a resource person in the process; (2) the pre-existing role relationships of persons in the groups; (3) feedback sequencing for groups at different hierarchical levels within social systems; and (4) the place and value of the survey feedback process.

Effectively done, survey feedback is a complex process requiring special knowledge and skills. Its success depends largely upon the ability of the individuals involved to understand and subsequently use the data as the basis for altering conditions and behaviors. In most cases the recipients of survey feedback require the help of a resource person who provides expertise and skill in several areas and who serves as a link between these persons and those other resources (e.g., knowledgeable persons) which serve as a potential energy source for the group's development.

The Resource Person's Role

The resource person's expertise must include an understanding of organizational processes and techniques of data aggregation and statistical analyses. In addition, this person must be skilled in helping the recipients understand and use the feedback data constructively. Abilities related to these functions include those of formulating meaningful pictures of social interactions on the basis of quantitative information and interacting with individuals and groups to facilitate the constructive use of the data.

It should by now be apparent that the resource person's role is not an easy one. To be useful to the process, he must know the group's data *thoroughly* prior to any feedback-related contact with its members or its leader. Only a thorough grounding in data analysis and interpretation can provide this skill, and only extensive practice can perfect it. In the group's discussion, he must be able to distinguish the elaboration and refinement of otherwise tabulated reality from the frequently exciting, but obfuscating, attempts by the group to provide the consultant with what it is they think he wants to hear and work with. He must be able to intervene in the process to keep it on track with the model and with what he knows represents a profitable course for the group. Yet he must do so in ways that avoid his being perceived as "laying it on," telling them what to do, or solving their problems for them.

Group-Member Relationships

Through all of this, he must remember that the feedback group meeting or training session is an artificial setting for the group's members. The fact that, in survey feedback, they are and ordinarily have been for some time imbedded in a network of relationships, roles, and functions means that, for them, *the greater part of their organizational reality exists outside that setting and is more closely aligned to the data than to the*

process which he has stimulated. This fact requires that, prior to the *group* session, he present and discuss the data privately with the group leader or supervisor and counsel him as to the meaning of the data. Only then can that leader, who must himself chair the group session, be expected to cope constructively with the stresses and strains of meeting his subordinates.

"Waterfall" Design

Although this latter principle is extended by some to augur for what is known as a "waterfall" design of survey feedback (beginning the process at a subordinate echelon only after it is complete in several sessions at the echelon above), this would appear to be an unnecessary elaboration. The modeling, which is presumed to be an advantage, seems in fact to be less important than the reassurance which is provided by having had an exposure as a subordinate in the group above. This seems to be largely accomplished during the first or early session. Adhering to a "top-down" design, yet pushing to as nearly simultaneous feedback to all levels as possible, would appear from experience and such evidence as exists to be an optimal strategy.

The Place and Value of Survey Feedback

The point has been made that the survey feedback process ordinarily is attempted within complex social systems. This point cannot be overstressed; it is this fact, principally among others, which ordinarily complicates even further what must seem to the reader as an already complicated process. Survey feedback is a method, procedure, or technique which often occurs within a broader paradigm termed "Survey-Guided Development." This latter and broader procedure encompasses, in addition to survey feedback, the use of survey data to diagnose the organization as a functioning social system; it also establishes the proper sequencing of inputs—determined through diagnosis—of a (nonfeedback) informational, skill, and structural-change variety.

A person proposing to move, as a facilitator or change agent, into a survey-guided development effort cannot hope to do so without first understanding the processes of survey feedback.

REFERENCES

Alderfer, C. P., & Ferriss, R. Understanding the impact of survey feedback. In W. W. Burke & H. A. Hornstein (Eds.), *The social technology of organizational development.* NTL Learning Resources Corp., 1972, 234-243.

Bowers, D. G. *Change in five plants: An analysis of the current state of development efforts in the GM-ISR program.* Ann Arbor, Mich.: Institute for Social Research, 1971, 33-36.

Bowers, D. G. OD techniques and their results in 23 organizations: The Michigan ICL study. *Journal of Applied Behavior Science,* 1973, 9 (1), 21-43.

Bowers, D. G. *System 4: The ideas of Rensis Likert.* Scranton, Pa.: Basic Books, in press.

Bowers, D. G., & Franklin, J. L. Survey-guided development: Using human resources measurement in organizational change. *Journal of Contemporary Business,* 1972, 1 (3), 43-55.

Franz, V. R. W., Holloway, R. G., & Lonergan, W. G. The organization survey feedback principle as a technique for encouraging workers' involvement in organizational improvement. Paper presented to the Second World Congress of the International Industrial Relations Association, Geneva, Switzerland, 1970.

Katz, D., & Kahn, R. Organizational change. In *The social psychology of organizations.* New York: John Wiley & Sons, 1966, 390-451.

Klein, S. M., Kraut, A. I., & Wolfson, A. Employee reactions to attitude survey feedback: A study of the impact of structure and process. *Administrative Science Quarterly,* 1971, 16 (4), 497-514.

Mann, F. C. Studying and creating change: A means to understanding social organization. In C. M. Arensberg *et al.* (Eds.), *Research in industrial human relations: A critical appraisal.* New York: Harper, 1957.

Mann, F. C., & Baumgartel, H. *The survey feedback experiment: An evaluation of a program for the utilization of survey findings.* Ann Arbor, Mich.: Institute for Social Research, 1954.

Miles, M. B., Hornstein, H. A., Callahan, D. M., Calder, P. H., & Schiavo, R. S. The consequence of survey feedback: Theory and evaluation. In W. G. Bennis, K. D. Benne, & R. Chin (Eds.), *The planning of change.* New York: Holt, Rinehart & Winston, 1969, 457-468.

Neff, F. W. Survey research: A tool for problem diagnosis and improvement in organizations. In S. Miller & A. Gouldner (Eds.), *Applied sociology.* Riverside, N.J.: Free Press, 1965, 23-38.

Taylor, J. C., & Bowers, D. G. *Survey of organizations: A machine scored standardized questionnaire instrument.* Ann Arbor, Mich.: Institute for Social Research, 1972.

TEAM-BUILDING

Anthony J. Reilly and John E. Jones

If a creature came from another planet to study earth civilization and returned to give a report, a "fair witness" about us would be, "They do almost everything in groups. They grow up in groups, learn in groups, play in groups, live in groups, and work in groups." Facilitators working in organizations understand that the basic building blocks of human systems are interdependent groups of people, or teams.

Some of the most exciting things about organization development (OD) are the many different, potentially useful activities and interventions that are available in this field. Many of these are oriented toward the individual working in the organization: career planning, one-to-one coaching and counseling, job enrichments, life planning. In this focus, the individual looks at himself in relation to his organization.

Another class of interventions, however—equally significant to an organization's growth—focuses on groups within the organization. This direction includes such activities as problem-solving at the group level, confrontation meetings, diagnostic meetings, and goal-setting sessions.

A TEAM EFFORT

Team-building—another intervention at the group level—is an activity that appeals particularly to group facilitators because of their intensive growth-group background and also because it generates considerable excitement among team members.

We, along with a number of other writers in the human relations field, contend that team-building activities represent the most important single class of OD interventions.

This paper considers team-building in depth: what it is, its goals, how it differs from other OD activities, the steps that have to be taken to

assure that it is done well, specifics about conducting team-building sessions.

"Team," as it is used here, pertains to various kinds of groups. Most typically, it refers to intact, relatively permanent work groups, comprised of peers and their immediate supervisor. But there are other kinds of teams, which may be more temporary in nature, whose charter is to come together for the purpose of accomplishing a particular task. Committees, task-forces, "start-up" groups—each of these may be a team. For a group to function effectively as a team, several important elements must be present. (1) The group must have a charter or reason for working together; (2) members of the group must be interdependent—they need each other's experience, abilities, and commitment in order to arrive at mutual goals; (3) group members must be committed to the idea that working together as a group leads to more effective decisions than working in isolation; (4) the group must be accountable as a functioning unit within a larger organizational context.

In this light, team-building is seen as a vital part of an OD effort. It affords a work group the opportunity to assess its strengths, as well as those areas that need improvement and growth. A group's team-building effort has definite implications for the total effectiveness of the entire organization.

Team-Building Goals

Certain task and interpersonal issues impede a team's functioning. *Team-building aims at improving the problem-solving ability among team members* by working through these issues. This major goal includes a number of subgoals:

1. A better understanding of each team member's role in the work group;

2. A better understanding of the team's charter—its purpose and role in the total functioning of the organization;
3. Increased communication among team members about issues that affect the efficiency of the group;
4. Greater support among group members;
5. A clearer understanding of group process—the behavior and dynamics of any group that works closely together;
6. More effective ways of working through problems inherent to the team—at both task and interpersonal levels;
7. The ability to use conflict in a positive rather than a destructive way;
8. Greater collaboration among team members and the reduction of competition that is costly to individual, group, and organization;
9. A group's increased ability to work with other work groups in the organization;
10. A sense of interdependence among group members.

The final aim of team-building, then, is a more cohesive, mutually supportive, and trusting group that will have high expectations for task accomplishment and will, at the same time, respect individual differences in values, personalities, skills, and idiosyncratic behavior. Successful team-building should nurture individual potential.

Team-Building vs. Training and Skill-Building

The activities and norms developed in team-building sessions are different but complementary to those characteristic of management training and skill-building sessions. Concepts such as leadership styles, decision-making, communication patterns, motivation, competition, and morale are all relevant to the process of team development.

However, management training may encourage sameness rather than difference in individuals' approach to work and the organization. Instilling company values and philosophy into an individual's work personality does promote company loyalty. Nevertheless, we contend that such an approach can reach the point of diminishing returns; if it neglects the development of the individual employee, it will ultimately become costly to the organization (Reilly, 1973).

The Consultant's Role

The consultant working with a group in a team-building effort has a key task: "response-ability"—the skill of responding to the group and of intervening in the group's life in such a way as to facilitate its problem-solving capability. Thus the consultant's allegiance is to the entire group, not to the boss or to a particular clique within the team. This must be clear before the team-building venture begins. Of course, the consultant does not ignore the man in charge! Indeed, he may need special counsel from the consultant outside the formal team-building session. But, in order to function in the best way possible, the consultant must be his own person, free to respond equally to each team member.

We see the consultant's role in team-building as a "process" consultant rather than an "expert" consultant. It is his responsibility to develop the process awareness by which the team can take a meaningful look at itself, its functions, its method of working, and its goals for change.

The process consultant in team-building should help the group solve its own problems by making it aware of its own group process and the way that process affects the quality of the team's work. In other words, his aim is to work himself out of a job.

With this approach, the strength of the facilitator's influence in team-building is not obvious to either himself or to members of the team. Yet we find that the consultant's skills and values generally carry considerable weight in the work group's opinion. It is his responsibility to be aware of his own impact on the group.

The Role of Games and Simulations

Since the focus of team-building centers on real-life issues and concerns which the work group faces on a day-to-day basis, inventories, simulations, or structured experiences generally play a minor role in team-building sessions. They are best used when there is a need to generate data which the team uses to get a clearer understanding of its own process. Inventories such as *FIRO-B*, for example, may serve as excellent interventions to focus upon behaviors of group members. Or a structured experience aimed at discerning group-leadership functions may prove very helpful in uniting the group.

We find that an exercise or inventory can be especially useful in team-building sessions for the following purposes:

1. To help team members diagnose where they are as a group—what they do well or poorly;
2. To aid in the understanding of group members' communication patterns, decision-making approaches, and leadership styles;
3. To surface latent or hidden issues;
4. To focus an issue which the team understands but seems unable to investigate deeply;
5. To demonstrate specific techniques that group members can use to improve the quality of their time together.

However, using exercises and simulations in team-building sessions can have potential pitfalls. A group may spend valuable time working on issues unrelated to their day-to-day work as a group; or a facilitator may get caught up in the excitement which comes as a result of participating in simulations and inventories of an introspective type, even though such learnings are not the main objectives of team-building. The facilitator must be able to balance both the concerns of team-building and the learning needs of team members.

Issues

A number of issues are important in beginning a team-building effort. Since many facilitators approach team development from T-group and/or clinical backgrounds, it is worthwhile to consider some special concerns about working with intact groups.

Climate-Setting. Expectations about the differences in a group's way of working together at the completion of a team-building endeavor should be explored with the manager or supervisor of a group. In team-building, the overall objective is to improve the team's performance and satisfaction through looking at its process and resolving conflicting situations. The kind of climate or atmosphere established in the group is affected by the group's new behaviors: communicating candidly, confronting and dealing with issues, utilizing each group member's resourcefulness. Once a climate is created, it is important that it be supported and nourished.

It is critical that the consultant help the group leader understand the implications of the group's climate. For example, the supervisor may be accustomed to interacting with subordinates in an authoritarian manner. As a result, team members may harbor resentment towards him and also feel that they are underutilized in the group. If a norm of openness becomes established as the team-building progresses, chances are that the supervisor will get this feedback. Therefore, it is vital to the success of the sessions that the supervisor enter the activity with a good understanding of the implications of opening up communications within the group.

Establishing Expectations. By devoting special time to examining its own workings, a group generally raises its expectation of improvement. This is usually realistic. However, it is easy for group members to develop unrealistic expectations. They may assume that as a result of a three- or four-day meeting, their group will be cured of all its ills. Such a notion, if not dealt with, can lead to considerable strain for the consultant and can frustrate team members so that they lose confidence in the team-building process.

It is the consultant's job to help the group set realistic and attainable objectives for its session. At the end of the meetings, participants should be able to evaluate the extent to which they have accomplished their aims. It is important that group members take responsibility for what they accomplish as well as for what they fail to accomplish in their team-building session.

At the same time, the consultant must be aware of the degree of responsibility he is willing to assume for the group's working through its issues. It is foolish for a consultant to guarantee that a group's problems will be solved. Rather, the facilitator's contract is to help develop a process which gives members the potential to work through their own problems.

The self-fulfilling prophecy is apparent here: If the consultant and group members set high but realistic expectations for themselves, they often accomplish their goals; on the other hand, if they expect to accomplish little, chances are they will accomplish little.

One-Shot Efforts. Ideally, team-building is not a one-time experience. It can help a group develop to a higher level of functioning by strengthening group members' functional behaviors and deleting dysfunctional ones.

The effectiveness of most team-building efforts is increased if there is some follow-through after the initial sessions. This may be done formally by way of additional sessions or less formally by continuing to build upon norms developed during the initial session. In either case, the consultant should stress the need for continuity in the team—that together the group is involved in an on-going process. Such follow-up helps to insure that action steps are implemented to resolve the issues focused during the session. Also the group is able to reassess where it is and exactly how it is functioning differently as a result of its earlier experience.

As an isolated event, then, team-building decreases the learning potential for the group. It is most effectively carried out as part of a well-planned OD effort.

Systemic Effects. It is safe to assume that an intact group does not function independently of other work groups. What is done to one group more often than not affects the affairs of other groups. Team-building often does have systemic effects. For example, to go into an organization and work with one district within a region is likely to affect the entire region. Persons who have experienced successful team-building are apt to want to share their enthusiasm with colleagues from other districts. By establishing new norms of working together more effectively, a particular work group can have quite a significant impact on the lives of other groups. Similarly, if a group has an unsuccessful experience, the negative fallout may affect the entire system.

Inherent in team-building is a potential for change in specified areas. It is assumed that one team cannot change without affecting, at least indirectly, the functioning of other teams.

The consultant must be aware of the impact of his intervention on the immediate group with whom he works as well as on related groups in the organization. Such awareness can mean the difference between success and failure.

Task vs. Interpersonal Focus. Just as it is important for a consultant to have an understanding of the climate of the groups with which he works, so in team-building sessions it is vitally important for the consultant and his client groups to agree upon the kinds of issues around which the group focuses its efforts. Identifying needs and designing effective interventions through which the group can meet its needs are the consultant's prime tasks.

It is difficult, but extremely important, to consider the balance between task and interpersonal concerns prior to the team-building session. The consultant's job is to state his own biases and help the group define workable boundaries.

Some teams consciously decide not to work at an interpersonal level during a team-building session, while other teams decide to invest considerable energy at this level.

We have found it helpful to work those interpersonal conflicts which interfere with the group's accomplishment of its task goals. It may be desirable to negotiate a contract with the group to determine what data will be considered out of bounds. A group whose members have had intensive growth-group experience may profitably wrestle with issues concerning their feeling reactions to each other's behavior.

Touchy-Feely. Most individuals become members of work groups to meet goals other than intrapersonal or interpersonal development. Therefore, it is usually inappropriate for the facilitator to advocate such growth in a team-building session. It is particularly unwise, in our judgment, to use techniques commonly associated with "sensitivity training" with persons who must work together on a day-to-day basis.

Effective Problem-Solving

Process awareness is, to our mind, the essence of team-building. When it understands and monitors its own process, a group is better able to accomplish its tasks and to utilize the talents of its

230

group members. Each process dimension—such as sharing ideas in the group, making decisions, the feeling tone of the group, its morale—needs to be focused upon as the opportunity arises in the group.

Norms of trust and openness. As a result of their increased ability to confront what develops in a group, members often grow towards a greater sense of trust and openness with each other. "Trust" and "openness" are two of the softest terms used in all of human relations training—and two of the hardest dimensions to cultivate in a group of individuals who work closely together. But it is our contention that greater trust and openness provide a greater potential for group task accomplishment as well as for personal satisfaction.

Trust and openness also lead to a climate in which conflicts are seen as healthy and productive. Dealing with conflict in a direct and forthright manner energizes groups. People say what they want to other individuals and expect other individuals on the team to do the same.

Feedback. Effective team-building leads to more effective feedback to group members about their contributions to the work group. Individuals learn the value of being willing to give, solicit, and utilize feedback from their colleagues. This can lead not only to increased overall effectiveness for the group, but also to personal development and growth for team members.

Prelude to Intergroup Problem-Solving

Before two groups meet jointly to improve their "interface," it is vitally important that each team first experience team-building as an intact work group. Each group should have its own house in order before attempting to join other groups to explore mutual problems. This is not to say that a group should be functioning "perfectly." Rather, it means that group members should be able to listen effectively to one another and to approach problems straightforwardly.

Some of the variables that help pave the way for successful intergroup exchanges include being able to identify problems, to engage in feedback processes in a relatively nondefensive

manner, to be authentic and not play the game of one-upmanship.

One of the most helpful and effective interventions in getting groups prepared for an intergroup meeting is an exercise commonly referred to as an organization mirror, or image exchange. Briefly, it is an exercise whereby each group writes down adjectives or phrases which describe its perceptions of itself and of the other group. Group members also predict the other group's perceptions of them as a group. These lists are generated by the two groups separately. The consultant may help each group prepare to accept and react to the feedback or exchange perceptions it is about to receive.

In our experience, Group A generally predicts that Group B sees it much more negatively than Group B actually does. Further, Group B often sees Group A more positively than Group A sees itself. Such discoveries quickly dispel a lot of ogres and nonproductive anxiety.

PREPARING FOR THE MEETING

It is important for the consultant to prepare participants for what will happen during the session. The sensing interview—which will be covered in more depth later in this paper—provides an opportunity for expectations to be clarified. The consultant can describe in general what the meeting will be about. Expectation gaps can be checked out and worked through if they exist. Participants usually want to know exactly what kind of interactions they can anticipate in the meeting. For the consultant to withhold responses to such legitimate inquiries can generate nonproductive anxiety.

Planning the Team-Building Session

Another relevant concern has to do with the physical environment surrounding the team-building session. At least two days of uninterrupted time away from the day-to-day work distractions are essential. Being away from the telephone and office interruptions can generate or free significant energy. It is also imperative that participants commit themselves to the entire team-building session. For several persons to come and go over the course of the event spells potential disaster for the experience. It almost goes without saying, of course, that the team leader must be present for the entire session.

Sensing

One of the best ways for a consultant to make certain that he at least partially understands an intact work group is to talk with each member before the team-building session. Face-to-face interviews, or "sensing," enable the facilitator to do a number of specific things in preparation for the team-building session (Jones, 1973).

First, sensing enables the consultant to gather diagnostic information about the group in its members' own words, information which is quite subjective, since it represents personal opinions. Secondly, sensing enables the consultant to clarify his own perceptions of how the team functions collectively. It serves as a supplement to other available sources of information about the group. And thirdly, sensing increases the psychological ownership of the information used in the team session, since it is generated by the actual group members.

We find the following guidelines helpful in conducting sensing interviews:

1. Sensing interviews should remain anonymous but not confidential. Since it is a frustrating experience for a consultant to receive confidential data that he cannot discuss in the session, we prefer to set an expectation of nonconfidentiality. Whatever information a team member shares with the interviewer becomes legitimate information for the session. We do, however, maintain anonymity. Thus, a team member can discuss a concern without his name being attached to it.

2. Only information which might realistically be dealt with over the course of the team-building session should be generated. To collect more data than can be processed may lead to false expectations and frustration.

3. Sensing is a rapport-building opportunity for the consultant. He has to make contact with each team member and vice-versa.

4. During the interview the consultant should be quite open about answering questions about the session, its objectives, format, flavor—whatever may be of importance to the individual participants.

5. It is vital that sensing data not be shared with participants before the session begins, even though it is sometimes tempting to confirm what one person has said through probing with another.

6. Taking notes during the interviews is helpful. By writing down verbatim a group member's response to a question, individual quotes can be used to substantiate general points during the session. Doing this increases ownership of the data for the team members.

7. It is important that persons being interviewed be told how the information that they share with the consultant is to be used. They may not ask directly, but they do want to know.

Sensing interviews are usually far more desirable than questionnaire-type surveys. The personal contact between consultant and participants can pave the way for an effective team-building session. The two approaches, sensing interviews and surveys, can be used together to good effect.

Preparing Data Feedback

Once sensing interviews are completed, it is the consultant's job to make some sense out of the data collected. He may note common themes, which become major categories for feedback to the group.

We find it useful to make a series of posters depicting the general themes of the data, including specific quotes, to make the data come alive. Posters may be made representing different categories of feedback: feedback for each team member; team members' perceptions of how the group makes decisions; and goal statements for the session. The exact nature of the posters depends upon the consultant's judgment of the group's level of readiness for working at a particular level. This reality should be kept in mind when designing the feedback session.

232

Coaching the Team Leader

Of all the individuals participating in the team-building session, it is the supervisor (boss, chairman, leader, etc.) who probably has the most, potentially, to gain or to lose from the experience. Often it is he who suggests team-building. Making the proposal for a session is a significant intervention in a group's life. It is bound to cause group members to react, varying from enthusiastic support to indifference to overt resistance.

It is crucial that the supervisor be adequately prepared for the session, since it is he who is most likely to be a target of feedback in the team-building session. To help make this a growth experience for both the supervisor and his subordinates, the consultant should attend to several dimensions during the planning phase.

One guideline we firmly adhere to is that the consultant should never surprise the boss. Nothing can destroy trust faster than for the consultant to make a big intervention for which the supervisor is completely unprepared. For example, if the leader expects nothing but positive and supportive feedback in the session—however unrealistic this expectation may be—and the consultant confronts him with heavily negative feedback, one can well imagine the probable outcomes: hurt, defensiveness, disbelief, the feeling of being betrayed. To safeguard against this result, the consultant is wise to prepare the supervisor for the meeting.

However, the leader must not conclude, from this function of the consultant, that the consultant is "his man"—that the consultant's role is to protect him from the feedback of his team members. Rather, the consultant's job is to work for the entire group, not to be partial to any one individual or to any subgroup. The client is the team, not the supervisor. In an OD effort, the real client is the organization of which the team is a part.

The method used to prepare the supervisor depends upon who actually takes charge of and conducts the session, the supervisor or the consultant. Some consultants prefer for the supervisor to run the meeting. In this case, he must be given the results from the sensing interviews in enough detail so that he can present data to his group. The consultant, then, generally will serve as a process observer, encouraging the group to take a look at its methods of working during the session.

Another option is for the consultant to conduct the majority of the session. In this case, it is of utmost importance that he know exactly what is going on with the group and exactly what outcome he wants the group to reach at the end of the session. If he does not have this background or knowledge, it is better for the consultant to concentrate on functioning as a reactive observer to the group's behavior.

Our own preference takes both options into account. That is, we prefer that the supervisor conduct his own staff meeting, while we observe the process and assist the group in studying its own process. But we also structure into the session specific activities, aimed at clarifying problems and working through to solutions.

Regardless of the format followed, the supervisor should be encouraged to be open to feedback and not to be defensive. Group members pay close attention to his receptivity, and his behavior is powerful in setting expectations. It is necessary, too, that he be authentic, that he not fake, for example, being receptive when actually he is feeling defensive. The norm should be one of strategic openness (Pfeiffer & Jones, 1972).

THE MEETING ITSELF

Expectations

It is helpful to begin the opening session by talking about what is actually going to take place. There should be no big surprises for anyone. One effective way to begin is to have both group members and the consultant specify their expectations for the meeting. In this way expectation gaps can be dealt with early.

One strategy is to have members list specifically what they want to happen and what they do not want to happen. The consultant may ask, "What is the best thing that could happen here, and what is the worst thing?"

Publishing the Sensing Data

After obtaining expectations, the data gained from the sensing interviews should be published in some form. During the presentation it is important that the team not begin to process the data. Team members should, however, be encouraged to ask for clarification so that everybody understands what the data say.

Agenda-Setting

The group's next task is to set its agenda, focusing on the data at hand. This should be done within the time constraints of the meeting. If a group commits itself to a five-day agenda for a two-day meeting, the result can only be a frustrating experience.

Setting Priorities

Having an agenda to work on, problem areas should then be determined in order of priority. It is important that the group (especially if it is undergoing its first team-building experience) be encouraged to start with a problem that can be solved. Members can then experience a feeling of success and begin to feel that they are a part of a team that is pulling together.

Problem-Solving

We consider problem-solving to be a pervasive and cyclical phenomenon which occurs throughout the team-building process. To assure its effectiveness, we find two techniques, used between cycles, to be helpful. One is to have the group critique (or process) its own style in working each problem on the list of priorities. That is, the group works one round, processes its functioning, and then takes on another problem. Such an approach provides an opportunity for the group to improve its problem-solving effectiveness over the course of a work session. Members can reinforce each other for their helpful behaviors and work through or lessen their dysfunctional behaviors.

Another technique is to post charts. These may include points of view about a problem, solutions, and action decisions. Such an approach enables the group to monitor its own progress or lack thereof. The chart serves as public "minutes" of the meeting, including problem statements, solutions, deadlines, and persons responsible for implementing solutions.

Planning Follow-Up

The purpose of this phase of team-building is to assure that the work begun by the group does not die once the group ends its formal team-building session.

It is helpful to have the group summarize the work accomplished during the team-building session: to take stock of decisions made during the session, and to reiterate which people are responsible for implementing which decisions within specific time parameters.

Within a month following the session a follow-up meeting should be held so that group members can assess the degree to which they have carried out expectations and commitments made during the team session.

DYSFUNCTIONAL BEHAVIORS

During a team-building session it is likely that a consultant will have to assist a team in confronting dysfunctional team behaviors. Listed below are the commonly observed behaviors that tend to obstruct team development, including ways of coping with and working the behaviors in a productive way.

Saboteur

This is a person who engages in behaviors designed to destroy or significantly impair the progress made by the team. Examples: "Got'cha" behavior; "Wait until J.B. sees what you're up to," "Yes, but . . .," and "This will never work!"

Sniper

A person who takes cheap shots at group members (whether they are present or not) by throwing verbal or nonverbal "barbs" is likely to lessen the productivity of the group. For example, the "sniper" might say, "When we were talking about plant expansion, old J.B. (who always ignores such issues) made several points, all of which were roundly refuted."

Assistant Trainer

This is a team member who wants to demonstrate his awareness of group process by making interventions in order to "make points" with the consultant. He may make procedural suggestions to the point of being obnoxious. One of his favorite interventions is, "Don't tell me what you think, tell me how you feel!"

Denier

This person plays the "Who, me?" game. When confronted, he backs off immediately. He may also ask many questions to mask his statements or points of view, and he generally refuses to take a strong stand on a problem.

Quiet Member

Members may be quiet for innumerable reasons. It has been remarked about silence: "It is never misquoted, but it is often misinterpreted."

Anxious Member

He may engage in such counter-productive behaviors as smoothing over conflict, avoiding confrontation, doodling, "red-crossing" other members, and protecting the leader.

Dominator

Some team members simply take up too much air time. By talking too much, they control the group through their verbosity.

Side-Tracker

This person siphons off the group's energy by bringing up new concerns ("deflecting") rather than staying with the problem being worked. Under his influence, groups can rapidly generate an enormous list of superfluous issues and concerns and become oblivious to the problem at hand. The game he plays is generally something like, "Oh, yeah, and another thing . . . ."

Hand-Clasper

Legitimacy and safety can be borrowed by agreeing with other people. For example, this person says, "I go along with Tom when he says . . . ."

Polarizer

A person who points out differences among team members rather than helping them see sameness in the ownership of group problems can prevent the development of group cohesion. He is a person likely to have a predisposition toward seeing mutually exclusive points of view.

Attention-Seeker

This behavior is designed to cover the group member's anxiety by excessive joking, horsing-around, and drawing attention to himself. He may do this very subtly by using the personal pronoun "I" often. He may also be a person who describes many of his own experiences in an attempt to look good to other group members.

Clown

This person engages in disruptive behavior of a loud, boisterous type. He may set a tone of play rather than of problem-solving.

Confronting Dysfunctional Behaviors

The characters described briefly above have one common theme: Each inhibits and distracts the group from working at an optimal level.

In dealing with such dysfunctional roles, the consultant will find it helpful to follow three general steps.

1. He should draw attention to the dysfunctional behavior itself but avoid the trap of labeling or classifying the person as, for example, a "sniper" or a "hand-clasper." Such evaluative labeling only elicits defensiveness from the individual. Instead, the behavior that is getting in the group's way should be described.
2. The consultant should spell out what appear to be the specific dysfunctional effects of the behavior. This should not be done in a punitive fashion, but in a supportive, confrontive manner. Often the person distracting the group is unaware of the negative impact of his behavior. Sometimes he really wants to be making a contribution and does not know how to be an effective team member.
3. Alternative behaviors should be suggested which will lead to a more productive and satisfying climate for the disruptive person and his colleagues.

FACILITATOR INTERVENTIONS

Process Interventions

Centering around the on-going work of the group as it engages in problem-solving activities, process interventions include ones aimed at improving the team's task accomplishment as well as helping to build the group into a more cohesive unit.

Process interventions to heighten task accomplishment include the following examples:

* having the group translate an issue into a problem statement;
* observing that the group is attending to several problems simultaneously rather than sticking to one problem at a time;
* observing that a decision was made out of a "hearing-no-objections" norm and having the group deal with this posture;
* inviting the group to develop action plans related to a problem solution;
* suggesting that the group summarize what has been covered within a given problem-solving period;
* helping the group to monitor its own style, using its resources;
* using instruments, questionnaires, and ratings to assess the group's position on a particular topic.

Process interventions aimed at group maintenance or group building include the following examples:

* pointing out dysfunctional behaviors which keep the group from achieving a cohesive climate;
* encouraging group members to express feelings about decisions the group makes;
* encouraging group members to *respond* to one another's ideas and opinions verbally, whether in terms of agreement or disagreement;
* confronting behaviors that lead to defensiveness and lack of trust among group members, *e.g.*, evaluative feedback and hidden agendas;
* verbally reinforcing group-building behaviors such as gatekeeping, harmonizing, etc.

Structural Interventions

Another class of interventions is termed structural because it deals with the way group members are arranged physically as a group. Structural interventions include the following:

* having group members work privately—making notes to themselves, for example—before they discuss the topic jointly as a total group;
* having members pair off to interview each other about the problem;
* forming subgroups to explore the different aspects of the problem and then share their work with the remainder of the group;
* forming a group-on-group design, to enable an inner group to work independently of an outer group, which, in turn, gives process feedback to inner-group members.

FACILITATOR EFFECTIVENESS

The technology behind effective team-building is vitally important. Of greater importance, however, is the facilitator's own personal uniqueness. To become more complete as a facilitator means to become more complete as a person.

Managing one's own personal growth is an important precondition to effectiveness in facilitating team-building sessions. If a facilitator is aware of his own needs, biases, and fears, he is less likely to project these onto the groups with which he works. Consequently, he is able to concentrate on the needs of the group.

A consultant can increase his team-building skills by working with different kinds of groups. Seeking out experiences in various organizations, with different types of clients, can be a creative challenge for the facilitator.

It is important that, whenever feasible, two persons co-facilitate team-building sessions. Doing so serves as a source of perception checks for each facilitator. It also gives each the opportunity to support and enrich the personal and professional growth of the other.

Team-building is an exciting activity for the facilitator. Intervening in the life of work groups affords both challenges and opportunities for direct application of behavioral science concepts.

REFERENCES

Jones, J. E. The sensing interview. In J. E. Jones & J. W. Pfeiffer (Eds.), *The 1973 annual handbook for group facilitators.* San Diego: University Associates, 1973.

Pfeiffer, J. W., & Jones, J. E. Openness, collusion and feedback. In J. W. Pfeiffer & J. E. Jones (Eds.), *The 1972 annual handbook for group facilitators.* San Diego: University Associates, 1972.

Reilly, A. Three approaches to organizational learning. In J. E. Jones & J. W. Pfeiffer (Eds.), *The 1973 annual handbook for group facilitators.* San Diego: University Associates, 1973.

THE SHADOW OF ORGANIZATION DEVELOPMENT[1]

Stanley M. Herman

Much current theory and practice in organization development (OD) derives from what might be called conventional human relations assumptions. These underlying values, powerful though often unexpressed, affect both clients and consultants. They are primarily derived from a set of biases in favor of "positive" emotions and attributes. As a result, other aspects of human interaction that involve "negative" emotions and attributes have been neglected. I believe this bias has been a severe limitation on the OD field.

"POSITIVE" AND "NEGATIVE"

In the Gestalt orientation (the theoretical base for the OD approach advocated here), the "negative" emotions are not neglected. Through concepts of polarization and integration, a person's whole range of emotions is valued. The integrated individual is able to experience both love and hate. He can exert dominance without being or thinking himself a tyrant; he can experience submission without feeling crushed. If individuals and organizations are to realize their potential for vitality and growth, they need to be aware of both their "negative" and "positive" aspects.[2]

OD Values

Conventional human relations values current in OD include:

- Logic and rationality
- Trust and openness
- Collaboration and participation
- Affection and responsiveness
- Group interest

While these values are appropriate and important, OD has frequently neglected or designated values at the other end of the spectrum of human interaction. For example:

- Authority and control
- Caution and reserve
- Autonomy and separateness
- Competition and aggressiveness
- Dislike and resistance
- Self interest

This sometimes-explicit, sometimes-implicit renunciation of the "negative" or "shadow" qualities has weakened a good deal of organization development effort by depriving it of the vigor and energy that are frequently inherent in the negative thrust. Equally important, this tendency has, I believe, only increased clients' guilt feelings and their inability to cope with the "tough" parts of their worlds.

In contrast, in the Gestalt approach to OD negative behavior is not denied. The client is encouraged to become fully aware of what he *is* experiencing (rather than what he or the consultant thinks he *should* be experiencing) and to work out viable relationships based on his own unique qualities and dynamics instead of on the consultant's idea of good human relations practice. (See "The 'Shouldist' Manager" in the Lecturettes section of this *Annual*.)

---

[1]The concept of the Shadow is used in the psychology of C. G. Jung to characterize those aspects of an individual's personality that he has not integrated into his self-image. The Shadow thus often contains characteristics that seem negative, alien, and threatening to the individual, and he frequently rejects them. In so doing, he denies part of himself: He is incomplete and unbalanced, using important life energy in an internal struggle against himself. Since the struggle to repress the Shadow can never be completely successful, he is also troubled by its intermittent appearance in his behavior.

I want especially to express my thanks to Dr. Irving Polster of the Gestalt Institute of Cleveland for his helpful criticism of this paper.

[2]For the sake of clarity and emphasis, this contrast is made in strong terms (Gestalt fashion). It may seem extreme to some readers. There has been, however, movement toward a broader and more realistic approach to human dynamics on the part of some organization development consultants and practitioners.

Full exchanges that acknowledge the reality and health of the "negative" as well as the positive aspects of human behavior are encouraged. Genuine behavior change (rather than "acted change") requires that the individual become completely aware of his present behavior and responsible for it.[3]

CHANGE IN INTERPERSONAL RELATIONSHIPS

In the Gestalt framework, change in interpersonal problem relationships occurs in a variety of ways.

Change in other people's reactions to an individual's behavior occurs when they understand his behavior more clearly and are willing to deal with him in his context.

For example, in one team-building session, a powerful and vocal manager, who was seen by many of his subordinates as harshly critical and punitive, was encouraged to intensify his behavior even further in the group setting. It soon became clear to all that he was expressing his own frustrations ("It keeps me from getting ulcers," he later explained) rather than punishing his subordinates.

In another case, a manager intensely involved in his own specialty was perceived by his peers to be totally unwilling to listen to their points of view. After they had expressed their complaints fully, they recognized that his intensity was also a strength for their team.

Change in the individual's views of himself (e.g., lessened feelings of self-contempt or failure) occurs when he fully experiences and acknowledges his own behavior. When a person feels better about himself, it is likely that others feel better about him too.

For example, an organization member who was accused by his peers and his manager of being both sarcastic and aloof first denied the charge. As we worked together, however, he acknowledged that his sense of humor was ironic, and that in trying to control it, he only made himself appear aloof as well.

When he was asked to dramatize his ironic humor with group members, he was delighted with his own performance. The others were too. In this case, a positive change in relationships continued long after the group session. The manager still made ironic (or sarcastic) comments, but he was no longer seen as aloof and most people appreciated his wit.

Change in actual behavior occurs when the "unfinished business' (e.g., old resentments) stimulating that behavior is cleared up, allowing new and clearer perceptions of others to emerge.

In one case, a long conflict between a department head and his senior subordinate had developed. The subordinate finally acknowledged that he resented his department head because he believed that he himself should have been promoted to that position several years before. In a "two-chair polarization" exercise in which he played both his own and his manager's parts, he slowly and steadily struggled through his unfinished resentments (of *himself* primarily) and later began to make real contact with his boss.

Change in the response of the individual to others results when their expectations of him are clarified. The individual recognizes for the first time that he is being asked for help and cooperation and not being criticized.

There may be an *acceptance of the status-quo* resulting in no substantive change but less tension. Often such acceptance, by reducing pressures, actually seems to precipitate later real change.

Most frequently, of course, there may be *a combination* of two or more of the above.

CONTRASTS BETWEEN CONVENTIONAL HUMAN RELATIONS (CHR) AND GESTALT (G) APPROACHES

Group vs. Individual

CHR: Focus on group-helping and team-building

G: Focus on recognition and mobilization of individual strength

In conventional human relations (CHR) theory, the emphasis is on building mutual understanding and cooperative behavior. People are

---

[3]Stanley M. Herman, "A Gestalt Orientation to Organization Development," *Contemporary Organization Development* (NTL Inst. of Applied Behavioral Science, 1972) pp. 69-89.

encouraged to help each other. Stronger members of the team look after "weaker" members. Roles such as "gatekeeper" and "summarizer" are encouraged. Group pressure is applied to dominant members of the group, especially when their domination seems to inhibit the less aggressive members. Group members take responsibility for each other's welfare.

In the Gestalt (G) orientation, each individual is encouraged to take responsibility for himself. "Helping weaker members" is not encouraged. Each person takes charge of his own action (or inaction) and discovers his capacity for initiating (and suppressing) behavior. Instead of discouraging a dominant member through pressure, attention is directed toward the passive member so that he may interrupt the dominant member and *get what he wants for himself through his own action*. Oversimplified, this approach attempts to strengthen the "weak," rather than weaken the "strong." As a result, the entire group is strengthened.

An example may serve as clarification. In a typical CHR consulting intervention, if the consultant observes that one member of the group is having a difficult time expressing himself in an exchange with a dominant member, the consultant points out to the dominant member the effect of his style of expression on the more passive member. Very frequently this intervention, especially when bolstered by others' feedback, produces a feeling of guilt in the dominant member and an effort to restrain his strong and expressive style. However, since the natural forces in him are unchanged, this effort not only takes a great deal of his energy but is frequently unsuccessful as well.

A G-oriented consultant would first focus on the reluctant team member. He might ask the member whether he has something he wants to say. If so, he might then ask the passive individual what it is that stops him from expressing himself. If the reluctant member reponds that he has a difficult time doing so, faced with the strongly dominant member, the consultant asks him to consider the consequences to himself if he were to be more expressive. The passive member is not, however, forced to be more expressive. The following dialog is an example.

Consultant: John, I am concerned that you haven't been saying anything, even though we have been discussing your area.
John: Yes, I know.
Consultant: Is there anything you want to say on this subject?
John: I guess so, but Dick comes on so strong that I'm a little reluctant to speak up.
Consultant: What is it that makes you stop yourself from saying what you want to say?
John: Well, I guess I just don't want to interrupt.
Consultant: What's your objection to interrupting?
John: I don't know. I guess maybe it seems impolite to do that.
Consultant: To whom would it be impolite?
John: To Dick, I guess.
Consultant: So you would rather keep yourself from saying what you want to say than be impolite. Is that it?
John: Well, I don't know. When I think about it that way, maybe not.
Bill (another group member): It doesn't seem to me that Dick holds himself back by being afraid of being impolite.
John: No, that's true. I never thought about it that way.
Consultant: It seems to me that you have to make the choice. You have to take responsibility for yourself and decide whether you are going to say what you want to say or not.
John: Yes, I guess I do. And I guess I will. I do have something to say. (Turns to Dick and addresses him.)

Why vs. How

CHR: Examination of situational elements of the interaction process: emphasis on *why*

G: Emphasis on what the individual does and *how*

In the CHR approach, the consultant helps those involved in their attempts to explain the situation by examining various interpretations, suggestions, and solutions. The approach is sequential and rational.

The G-oriented approach, on the other hand, is seldom analytical. It emphasizes the *now* and the *how* rather than the *then* and the *why*. Since there are almost invariably multiple explanations for every phenomenon in behavior, an intellectual understanding of why something happened frequently does little to help change perceptions or behavior.

In the G orientation, the consultant encourages the parties to become aware of what they are doing and what they are avoiding. For example, in the preceding dialogue, a CHR-oriented consultant might have asked John whether he was inhibited because he saw Dick as being in a stronger organizational position. Or the consultant might have explored John's past relationships with Dick and others in the group. If the consultant were psychoanalytically oriented, he might also have questioned John about his past relationships with authority figures.

Analysis vs. "Dramatization"

CHR: Analysis of "problem behavior" and methods for correcting it

G: Intensification or dramatization of "problem behavior" until a change in relationship occurs

In the CHR-oriented group, "problem behavior" patterns are highlighted and explicitly identified (usually through feedback). The individual receives proposals for changing his behavior. Even though these proposals are often offered as suggestions (*i.e.*, the consultant makes it clear that there is, of course, no compulsion for the group member to change his style), the disadvantages of the old style are made clear.

Not only is such an approach manipulative, but the behavior change that comes from it is frequently forced. Often the suppressed feeling is apparent in body tension, restlessness, or other signs. It would seem that restrained irritation or affection is seldom healthy for the individual or the group.

In the G-oriented group, members are encouraged to be aware of their feelings and behavior, and to emphasize where they are rather than where they "ought" to be. The consultant urges them to dramatize the polarities in themselves, rather than to analyze and solve their "problem behavior."

Leveling vs. Vitalizing

CHR: Aggressiveness and conflict seen as negative forces in system; manifest conflict seen as a sign of openness but something to be resolved as soon as possible

G: Aggressiveness and conflict valued as vitalizing forces; aggressiveness essential for creativity

In the CHR-oriented group, expressions of aggression or conflict are primarily seen as indications of trust and openness ("leveling"). However, in this approach, efforts are quickly directed toward analyzing the causes of disagreement and resolving them in a rational "problem-solving" manner.

Competitive behavior is not valued except when it is focused outside the group. Within the organization, the emphasis is almost invariably on cooperative and collaborative behavior.

Group aggressiveness and conflict are considered both natural and valuable in the G-oriented group. Rather than moving very quickly into problem-solving (which often increases the likelihood of a later recurrence of the conflict), the G group attempts to polarize and further sharpen differences and conflict elements.

With the help of a consultant to highlight the issues, individuals are encouraged to express their feelings and beliefs, even to exaggerate them if necessary. People find that full argument is less embarrassing and "damaging" than they had imagined. Equally important, new perspectives emerge from this process.

In working with a situation of conflict, the "two-chair" approach mentioned earlier may be used in which the individual conducts a dialogue with himself, portraying both protagonist and antagonist.[4] In this way, he is able to become aware of his resentments against the alienated parts of himself and thus to eventually re-own those alienated parts. When both parties in the situation have had an opportunity to explore each other's position, they are then in a better position to deal with each other and with the remaining *real* issues between them.

---

[4]For illustrations see Perls, F. A., *Gestalt Therapy Verbatim*, Real People Press, 1969.

For example, in a conflict situation involving a recently appointed high level manager, who was black, and two of his peers, who were white, it was only after the black manager recognized that some part of his antagonism grew out of a feeling of being patronized as a black man that he and his white peers were really able to deal with more substantive issues between them.

External vs. Internal Feedback

CHR: Emphasis on others' feedback

G: Emphasis on an individual's own internal feedback

The cycle of interaction generally proceeds as follows in the typical CHR-oriented group: The individual acts; he receives feedback about his actions and their effect on others; he then has the choice of whether or not to modify his behavior in response to this feedback, particularly if it is negative.

A number of training programs throughout the country use this approach in managerial development. As noted in a recent brochure advertising sensitivity training: *The age-old continuing wish of men and women to see themselves as others see them has the most practical basis for those who supervise or serve in key roles in our society. To increase the effectiveness of our relationships with others, we need to know more accurately how they see us—what we do that is useful and what we do that detracts from our usefulness.*

Thus, others' feedback may be used as a guide by the recipient in modifying his behavior and thereby increasing his effectiveness. If the individual is not ready to make such behavior modification, however, the changes frequently prove to be forced, temporary, and ineffective.

In the G-oriented group, the feedback of others is de-emphasized and the focus placed on the individual's own awareness of his behavior.

For example, in a CHR group, an individual might get this feedback: "Joe, I feel frustrated. You seem very evasive and that produces a negative reaction in me. I wish you would be more direct." In the G group, Joe could well be encouraged by the consultant to be *more* evasive with others in the group, but in a deliberate way.

One member of a management group spoke in halting, theoretical generalizations. When, at the consultant's suggestion, he *consciously* communicated with other members of the group in the most abstract and theoretical way he could, his voice, manner, and delivery showed increasing strength and then humor. He became quite animated and energetic, much to his own pleasure and the enjoyment of his peers.

Later he became aware that he used his hesitancy and abstract manner to avoid being challenged. He also discovered his own capacity to use a more direct style when he wished to do so.

In the G-oriented group, the consultant looks at current behavior not as something to be corrected or changed, but rather as something that needs emphasis and increased awareness on the part of each individual. If such behavior is dysfunctional, change will occur naturally.

Interdependence vs. Autonomy

CHR: Emphasis on interdependence

G: Emphasis on individual autonomy and competence: the capacity to choose independent, competitive or collaborative behavior

Interdependence may very well be a requirement in some organizations, particularly if the organization is responsible for complex technology systems. However, it is not, or ought not to be, a goal in itself.

Often, groups are exhorted by consultants and CHR-educated managers to work together and to find the synergy in their cooperation. This striving sometimes contributes to considerable frustration when the actual requirements of the task do not require interdependence.

In the G-oriented approach, interdependence is recognized when it is a requirement of the situation or task to be done. However, when it is not required, the group is not encouraged to strain for interdependence. What is important is increasing the ability of the individual or the group to operate independently, cooperatively, or competitively—whichever is appropriate.

Open vs. Up-Front

CHR: "Open" values

G: "Up-front" values (which may also be "closed")

The CHR-oriented group approach places a high value on trust and openness, and quite frequently group pressures toward openness and intimacy are very strong.

While the G-oriented group does not discourage openness in relationships, neither does it discourage individuals from being "closed" when that is their explicit choice. If, under these circumstances, the group applies pressure on the individual to be more sharing, the consultant often will support the individual's right to remain separate and to restrict his sharing. When the individual recognizes that he can choose to say "no," he can then say "yes" more fully and freely when that is what he wants to do.

Experimentation vs. Awareness

CHR: Learning and experimenting with new concepts and new behavior

G: Increasing awareness of present behavior and its completion

In the CHR-oriented group, members are encouraged to learn, primarily from feedback, and then to try out new methods of behaving and interacting with one another. Attention is focused on such areas as the improvement of communication, active listening, nondefensiveness, etc. The search for the "right way" or the "most effective way" of interacting often encourages systematized behavior in accordance with some particular prescribed model such as Theory Y or "the manager's role."

In the G-oriented group, spontaneous behavior is highly valued, rather than the fulfillment of prescribed role behavior. Thus, in allowing himself to be authentic, the individual may well behave from time to time in ways that are less than "ideal." But an authentic exchange between human beings who allow themselves to be as they are—"good" and "bad"—brings about more genuine and more satisfying relationships. There is surely room for a great deal of diversity in behavior styles.[5]

[5]I do not really take most "problem behaviors" very seriously. Whether a style is polite or harsh is not terribly important. What counts, as the saying goes, is whether or not you've "got your shit together." And to *that* I do pay a great deal of attention.

Observer vs. Advocate

CHR: Consultant as a neutral and objective observer of process

G: Consultant as activist, director, and participant

The consultant in a CHR-oriented group frequently feels (especially in dealing with conflict issues) that he should be objective, fair, uninvolved, and, at best, do as little leading of the group as possible. CHR-oriented consultants frequently speak of "the group's needs," and they believe it is inappropriate to pursue their own needs. Many of these consultants indicate considerable concern that group members may become dependent upon them.

In the G-oriented group the consultant is much more likely to take an active part and to act and react impulsively, not merely as a model to others, but also to suit his own needs. His assumption, particularly when working with industrial groups comprised of people with relatively high ego strengths, is that group members need not be unduly protected. He does not fear that they will become dependent upon him, if he is freely himself in the group, allowing them to see his own strengths and weaknesses. Since he has no special image to maintain because of his particular professional function, he may allow himself to experience and express the full range of emotions—including anger, affection, confusion, pride, inadequacy—just as the other members of the group may. With this attitude, members recognize him for what he is, an ordinary human being with a special set of traits and particular skills.

Another contrast worth noting is that most CHR-oriented consultants, while encouraging the expression of emotion in personal growth groups and work groups, generally treat the expressed feelings as "data" to be considered rationally—a kind of intellectualization of emotion. The G-oriented consultant relies less on intellectual theory and more on intuition (his and others') and on his faith in the high value of authentic behavior.

Organizational Culture vs. Individual Competence

CHR: Focus on changing organization's culture

G: Focus on increasing individual's competence, whatever the culture

A frequent phrase heard among many OD consultants is "changing the organization culture." Sending managers off to human relations training is not enough, say the consultants; we need to affect the norms and values back at the organization. If patterns are not changed in the "back-home" culture, the consultants warn, the manager returning from his positive experience at a sensitivity lab will be confronted with lack of support or even rejection from his fellow managers because of his new, more open style.

This means that the organization must find ways to encourage modes similar to those developed in the training group. The demise of more than one company's OD effort has been attributed to its failure to do just that.

In the CHR framework certain underlying assumptions are clear. First, the desired and encouraged direction of change is toward the "positive" emotions, especially group support, interdependence, and participation. Second, it is generally assumed that these values are better for the organization than the "negative" emotions—frequently in terms of both humanitarian and efficiency criteria. Third, it is also assumed that making these new values operable in the organization requires consensual support by others, i.e., that it is too dangerous to be open, sharing, and collaborative if others are not. Thus, the individual manager can change only if the "system" can be altered to support him.

It will come as no surprise that the G-oriented approach is more individualistically focused, encompassing the negative as well as the positive emotions as sources of human energy and vitality. Few business or government organizations could seriously be categorized as tyrants. (It is likely that people who run that kind of organization do not often hire OD consultants anyway.)

Styles of management can, however, vary significantly on the spectrums of permissiveness-control, participation-directiveness, etc. One side of the continuum is not necessarily better than the other, either from the standpoint of effectiveness or humanitarianism.

With this set of assumptions, then, the G-oriented consultant is less likely to focus on changing the "culture"[6] and more likely to help his clients identify *what they want, what prevents them from getting what they want,* and *what alternatives are available to them.* When these questions have been addressed, the client may deal with greater clarity and vigor with others in the organization, and he may do so in whatever style he finds most promising, given the present "culture" and his own requirements of himself.[7]

One implication of this point is that effective development of team members does not always require that all meet together in dealing with their concerns and conflicts. The individual may recognize and mobilize his strength through private consultations and transfer his improved effectiveness back into his working environment.

CONCLUSION

The values of today's CHR practitioners derive, I believe, from liberal-democratic biases and traditions. In reaction against the mass exploitation and mechanistic outlook of the early days of industrialization, we have fostered and justified gentility, participation, and rationality. In so doing we have often neglected or denied power, directiveness, and impulse, and these "negative" aspects are as vitally important to being a complete person as are their more comfortable, "positive" counterparts.

[6]While I acknowledge that in the organization development context "culture" may be a useful term, I also find it, and other words like it, to be lifeless abstractions frequently used in "behavioral science conversations" as substitutes for specific situations. In the G-oriented framework, abstracting can be a way of avoiding.

[7]I believe that for the most effective development of organization relationships, as well as for the individual himself, it is important for the client first to become aware of his own stance, including his fears, projections, alienations, etc. He frequently discovers that many of his worries become far less terrifying when reduced to concrete action possibilities than as vague abstractions.

POSTSCRIPT

Selfishness

I heard a woman on the beach
  say to her little girl
Don't be selfish
What sad advice

I would give her better
Be selfish, little girl
Love yourself well
Love yourself first
Then will you love others
  far, far better

Not with grudging show
Nor with unfeeling ritual
Or numb duty, or self-congratulating
  sacrifice
Or stuttering terror of loss

Be selfish, little girl
Be best to yourself
And rest assured that you
  will always be
Joyfully, unstintingly
And if you will give to others
Give them most
Help to be best
  to themselves too.

Freedom 1

No one grants you freedom
You are free if you are free

No one enthralls you
You enthrall yourself
And when you have
You may hand your tether
  to another
  to many others
  to all others, or
  to yourself

Perhaps the last is worst of all
For that slave master is hardest to see
And hardest to rebel against
But he is easiest to hate
  and to damage

I do not know how to tell you to be free
I wish I did
But I do know some signs of freedom
One is in doing what you want to do
  though someone tells you not to
Another is in doing what you want to do
  even though someone tells you to do it.

Stanley M. Herman

For other poems by Stanley M. Herman, see "Notes on Freedom" in the 1972 *Annual*.

INTRODUCTION TO THE
RESOURCES SECTION

The Resources sections of the *Annuals* are intended to complement each other. Together they comprise a growing reference source.

Reference Sources

'72 Annual
Professional associations
Sources of games and simulations (annotated)
Films

'73 Annual
OD glossary
Bibliography (annotated)
Growth centers

'74 Annual
Training in the UK and Europe
AHP Growth Center list

The books reviewed in the *Annuals* are intended as an emerging "basic book shelf" of significant publications in human relations training. Each title chosen is selected with this rationale in mind.

Reviewers are required (1) to be familiar with the particular area covered by the book and (2) to be practitioners in the field. As in the rest of the *Annual*, the emphasis in the Resources section is on practicality. Thus, reviewers are asked to react to a book from the point of view of a practitioner, not a scholar.

Book Reviews

'72 Annual
W. C. Schutz. *Here Comes Everybody*
C. R. Rogers. *Carl Rogers on Encounter Groups*
G. Egan. *Encounter: Group Processes for Interpersonal Growth*
R. T. Golembiewski and A. Blumberg. *Sensitivity Training and the Laboratory Approach*

P. Runkel, R. Harrison, and M. Runkel (Eds.). *The Changing College Classroom*

The Addison-Wesley Series on Organization Development:
W. G. Bennis. *Organization Development: Its Nature, Origins, and Prospects*
R. Beckhard. *Organization Development: Strategies and Methods*
P. R. Lawrence and J. W. Lorsch. *Developing Organizations: Diagnosis and Action*
R. R. Blake and J. S. Mouton. *Building a Dynamic Corporation Through Grid Organization Development*
R. E. Walton. *Interpersonal Peacemaking: Confrontation and Third Party Consultation*
E. H. Schein. *Process Consultation: Its Role in Organization Development*

'73 Annual
M. James and D. Jongeward. *Born to Win: Transactional Analysis with Gestalt Experiments*
Baba Ram Dass. *Be Here Now*
C. Argyris. *Intervention Theory and Method: A Behavioral Science View*
R. W. Budd and B. D. Ruben. *Approaches to Human Communication*
A. Maslow. *The Farther Reaches of Human Nature*
N. O'Neill and G. O'Neill. *Open Marriage: A New Life Style for Couples*

'74 Annual
G. Egan. *Face to Face*
P. Hill. *Toward a New Philosophy of Management*
R. A. Schmuck and M. B. Miles (Eds.). *Organization Development in Schools*

R. A. Schmuck, P. J. Runkel, S. L. Saturen, R. T. Martell, and C. B. Derr. *Handbook of Organization Development in Schools*

J. W. Pfeiffer and R. Heslin. *Instrumentation in Human Relations Training*

D. G. Lake, M. B. Miles, and R. B. Earle, Jr. (Eds.). *Measuring Human Behavior*

M. A. Lieberman, I. D. Yalom, and M. B. Miles. *Encounter Groups: First Facts*

HUMAN RELATIONS TRAINING IN THE UK AND CONTINENTAL EUROPE

Cary L. Cooper

THE UNITED KINGDOM

For many years in England, people involved in sensitivity training, encounter groups, OD, and social-change techniques were generally divided into two camps. The main division during the 1960s was between the activities of the Tavistock Institute of Human Relations and those of the University of Leeds. In the former, a number of behavioral scientists emerged whose group work and organizational activities were linked to Bion's theory and to the sociotechnical system developed by Trist and his associates.

The University of Leeds group, which was spearheaded by Galvin Whitaker in the Department of Management Studies (of which, incidentally, I am a product), was the center of sensitivity training and allied social-change innovations, based primarily on the American West Coast Model á la Bob Tannenbaum and Fred Massarik.

Any real contact between the two groups was minimal and consisted of very little cooperation in introducing joint training and change programs in the country, or in providing a platform for exchanging information.

In the late '60s and early '70s another development took place—the encounter group movement, or as many antagonists in England called it, "the touchy-feelies." This development introduced another split in the group relations movement in England, this time between OD adherents and the encounter group contingent (including people involved in body-awareness training, Gestalt therapy, bioenergetics, etc.).

Each of these groups regarded the other with "less than" understanding, the OD group deprecating the lack of professionalism among encounter group leaders, and the encounter group advocates criticizing what appeared to them to be the capitalistic orientations and personal inhibitions of the OD people. Therefore, by 1970 we had two divisive elements in the group relations field, one based on differences in theoretical approach or orientation, and the other based on differences in degree of person-centeredness and in focus (*i.e.*, organizations or persons).

Sometime in 1966, a number of individuals, primarily from Leeds, began to hold mini-conferences on group work topics. Several residential conferences were arranged at Leeds over the next few years. Unfortunately, the turnout was small and the participants were, for the most part, confined to Leeds-oriented sensitivity trainers. In 1969, this loosely organized group tentatively moved closer to formalizing its organization and some of its activities and subsequently became known as the Group Relations Training Association (GRTA).

In 1970 it was decided that GRTA would attempt to provide a means of including all the various approaches and subcultures within the group work field in the United Kingdom. The mechanism was to be the GRTA Annual Conference in September 1971 at the London Business School. The conference was to become an experiential market place with a large number of alternative activities scheduled for each half-day session over a four-day period. For example, after the opening session of the conference, which included a specially designed mini-laboratory to get people acquainted with one another, the first evening included the following events: marathon encounter group, ERGOM[1] management exercise, encounter tape session, OD and research,

---

[1] European Research Group on Management.

and commercial psychological games. The next morning included: training for creativity, the Blake and Mouton marriage grid, Coverdale training, and a demonstration of encounter group facilitator style. The afternoon consisted of a Gestalt awareness demonstration, a community experience, a demonstration of the Tavistock trainer style, psychodrama, and a seminar in "mini-society" training methods. The conference was organized for four days, and the participants were encouraged to wander around and participate in whatever activities interested them.

By creating an opportunity for all the disparate groups to come together and discuss their approaches and "wares," it seemed as if greater tolerance was nurtured among the participants. The attendance was overwhelming, including nearly all the people in the group relations field from the UK and a number from Ireland, Holland, Belgium, France, Denmark, Sweden, and over a dozen Americans. All in all, it was the biggest and most comprehensive conference held in Europe to date.

The success of the conference—the integration of the different approaches into a "sharing organization"—was fully realized on the last day when the GRTA held its annual meeting. Participants representing the different schools of group work were elected to the Executive of the Association. The Executive's task was to plan future training programs within the community, trainer-development activities, specialist workshops, future conferences, etc. Now, the GRTA Executive more truly reflected the various approaches and activities in the UK group world.

The GRTA is run primarily by the Executive as a group. Events and activities are generally initiated by those members on the suggestion of the membership at large. In addition, any GRTA member can initiate an activity (for example, a lab for community-development workers), and get GRTA financial support by simply submitting in detail his ideas and plans. The GRTA is nonprofit-making, although some activities make profits which subsidize other events.

Since 1971 the GRTA has grown stronger, greatly increasing its membership and activities, which now extend into Continental Europe. A large number of Irish, Dutch, French, Danish,

Swedish, and Japanese trainers have recently joined the Association, and more intercultural activities are planned for the future. GRTA established a low-cost open lab for people in the helping professions (*i.e.*, social workers, probation officers, clergy, nurses, psychiatrists, etc.) which is now run biannually. Mini-society labs are run once a year with varying populations. A trainer-development program has been organized, and specialist workshops on a variety of topics have been arranged throughout the year for GRTA members. In addition, "couples" labs and labs for selected groups in the community (*e.g.*, teachers) are planned for the future.

In 1972, in conjunction with the Association of Humanistic Psychology, the GRTA held a conference in London with the theme of Creative Change in Higher Education. This event was once again very successful on two counts: first, in terms of attendance; and second, in introducing group relations training to the field of education. University teachers, polytechnic lecturers in teacher training colleges, and primary and secondary teachers all joined the GRTA members in exploring the problems peculiar to educational institutions. Opportunities were provided for people to listen to reports about different experiential techniques which had been used in teaching and OD in universities and schools. In addition, exercises and demonstrations were held on some of these devices, including a demonstration of co-counseling for students within a student counseling service context; an OD program for primary schools demonstrated by role-playing techniques; an experimental classroom group to illustrate how these groups had been used and could be used to enhance creativity among art and architecture students at polytechnics and universities; a conflict-resolution model for dealing with conflict between university students and administration, with an accompanying exercise to demonstrate how it operates in practice; and many other similar activities. As a result of this conference, the GRTA membership in the education field grew enormously and, as a result, a number of activities have been organized to cope with the specialist needs of this group.

Finally, the GRTA held its four-day 1973 conference at the Polytechnic of Central London during September. This conference borrowed the notion of the market place generated by the 1971 conference but incorporated an important difference. There were three choices of activity events for each half-day period: an experiential session, an application session, and a theoretical session. A participant could opt to take part in an encounter group, or listen to how these groups have been applied, or listen to and participate in a discussion on the theoretical aspects of encounter groups. If the same subject area was explored in all three, they were usually staggered so that an interested person could, during the course of the day, attend all three. In addition, a slot of time was established which people could use as an opportunity to meet each other and exchange ideas about the events of the conference or other extraconference agenda.

Many of the events during this conference were organized around topical social problems and issues. For example, one session was devoted to a community and OD program between various groups in Northern Ireland; another session focused on the efforts of an Anglican vicar to work with groups of blacks and whites in South Africa; another concentrated on working with labor relations in the UK, etc. It was at this conference that one could see the beginning of a shift in direction: toward problems in society and toward social change.

In addition to providing opportunities for personal growth, or in designing programs of growth and development within large multinational organizations, there is now a new impetus to utilize change-agent skills to help with immediate social problems, particularly in areas where the issues have a long and unresolved history. It seems to me that a growth from obsession with intergroup professional rivalry to social concern is a healthy one, one that symbolizes the coming of age of group work in the UK.

CONTINENTAL EUROPE

In the early 1960s an organization was formed called the European Institute for Transnational Studies in Group and Organizational Development (E.I.T.). It seemed from its early meetings in Holland in 1963 and Paris in 1964 that the European scene would now have a central focus for human relations training. Its declaration of intent was "to bring into being a transnational body of professional and social sciences under conditions which will foster the development of a distinctive competence in the undertaking of research, training, and consulting activities concerning intergroup and cross-cultural phenomena and problems arising in transnational organizations and environments."

Unfortunately, the original founding fathers of E.I.T. restricted the membership so severely that the great bulk of European trainers were excluded; what remained were a few of the older, more established trainers. This image of E.I.T. as an "exclusive club" has persisted, and its membership and activities have not grown substantially.

The basic philosophy or orientation of the E.I.T. trainers is different from human relations training in the U.S. and in most of the UK. Many of the E.I.T. trainers draw heavily from Bion (1959) and tend to use many of his quasi-psychoanalytic concepts. This particular emphasis focuses on group as opposed to individual behavior, explores in greater depth the "authority" issue, and avoids the developments in personal growth and sensory-awareness training. The trainers are also primarily interested in organizations and institutional groups. This, of course, is not the case for every member of E.I.T.; there are some very clear exceptions. However, many of the E.I.T. members are perceived by most other European trainers in this way.

The Dutch Experience

A number of other European developments have taken place, the most notable of which is the Dutch experience. In Holland, the Dutch trainers established a very sizable professional association called Trainers in Social Relations (T.S.R.). It was formed from within the Netherlands Institute of Preventive Medicine in Leiden, which has provided the group with the institutional support for long-term development. It has one of the best trainer development programs in Europe, which was designed to include not only an intensive training course for potential trainers but also cotraining experiences, as well as an elaborate mechanism for professional development which provides its constituents with continuous feedback on their training skills as perceived by their T.S.R. colleagues.

Most of the activities of T.S.R. are described in a monthly house magazine entitled *Wizzel Woking*, which is written in Dutch and English. In addition to T.S.R.'s interests in professional trainer development, it runs training programs for industry, for hospitals, and for the social services. The group is particularly noted for its work with the Dutch Roman Catholic Church.

The Dutch trainers are also very keen on intercultural collaboration, and wherever there is a European training event, you will see a strong Dutch contingent present. The Dutch trainers have been strongly influenced by American human relations training. They have adopted and culturally adapted many of the techniques and approaches of NTL and, to some extent, the methods of West Coast trainers (particularly those at UCLA).

Other European Developments

The other developments in Europe are much more limited than either E.I.T. or T.S.R. and usually focus on one or two persons in particular countries. Gunnar Hjelholt of Denmark stands out as a leading figure in the development of the mini-society.

The mini-society[2] is an attempt to study, in a microcosm, the subtle sociological and psychological forces that lie beneath the problems of our present life in society. It has many similarities to the usual classical sensitivity training or human relations laboratories: (1) it is held at an isolated place (Gunnar runs his on a peninsula in a large lake in Southern Sweden); (2) it is limited in time; (3) there is a staff; (4) the participants are divided into groups by the staff in advance; and (5) it is expected that people experiment with behavior and explore relationships within the community.

The mini-society differs from the usual laboratories in that (1) there is a greater variation in the backgrounds of participants; that is, efforts are made to ensure a representative sample of society at large, particularly in terms of socio-economic status, age, and sex; (2) the groups are homogeneously composed; (3) the focus of attention is on the relationship of an individual group to other groups within the mini-society.

The mini-society concept has begun to take hold in the UK and elsewhere on the Continent, as the integration of Europe through the EEC becomes an economic necessity and the inevitable intergroup conflicts between EEC countries become a daily event.

Another strictly European development is the International Institute for Organizational and Social Development (IOD), which was set up by Lee Vansina in Belgium. IOD sponsors a number of European activities, particularly in the organization and management development areas. It also organizes ERGOM, which runs the Bass Management Development group exercises throughout the whole of Western Europe. In addition to the ERGOM exercises, Vansina and colleagues do a great deal of group and organizational work in a variety of European languages.

Very little work has been reported from Germany, but some exciting work is being done in France by Max Pages of the *Association pour la Recherche et l'Intervention Psychosociologue* and by Jaques Ardoine of the *Association Nationale pour le Development des Sciences Humaines Appliques*. In addition, some work in the OD and planned-change fields has been instituted in Bratislava, Czechoslovakia, by Ivan Perlaki. He is using a series of specially designed instrumented laboratories for "family" groups, and has been a frequent visitor to the West to seek advice and support.

SUMMARY

Most of the extensive human relations training and research developments have taken place in the UK and Holland, with occasional individual achievements and innovations in other European countries.

---

[2]This approach and many other European training experiences for individual and organizational growth can be found in a book edited by the author entitled *Group Training for Individual and Organizational Development*, published by S. Karger AG, Arnold-Bocklin-Strasse 25, 4000 Basel 11, Switzerland.

No mention has been made of the work in Southern European countries such as Italy, Spain, Greece, etc. The reason for this should be apparent. Very little work has been done in any of these countries, and the number of people actively engaged in human relations training is almost nonexistent. At the very least, their activities have not been publicized in the more active countries in Europe. It may be that there is a relationship between social-change techniques and economic development such that developed countries have a greater need for improving human relations; perhaps they even possess the facilities for such innovations. Meanwhile, the developing countries are stuck at the lower levels of the Maslowian hierarchy, and improved human relations is a luxury they cannot afford.

One can see more and more that the developed European countries are moving toward closer liaison. This can be gauged by the increasing network of GRTA; by the publication of the quarterly Swiss journal *Interpersonal Development* (which publishes European, as well as North American, articles on sensitivity training, group therapy, and OD); by the increasing research cooperation between different countries (*i.e.*, ERGOM); and by the cross-fertilization of new approaches, such as the mini-society (between the UK and Denmark), and the use of intergroup and institutional group designs (between the UK and Austria).

Agenda Items for the Future

I would like to conclude with some of the hopes and concerns of the people involved in the human relations movement in the UK and Continental Europe. One of our main hopes for the next decade is that we find the means of integrating and sharing the knowledge acquired within our own local communities for the wider use of European training as a whole. We also hope to provide opportunities both locally and within the European community to encourage the improvement of the human relations movement by creating programs for trainer development (a major concern and goal of most European trainers). It is our wish to create opportunities for genuine social change in the institutions within Europe that will one day govern all that was once a group of culturally isolated, inward-looking countries.

REFERENCES

Berger, M. L., & Berger, P. J. (Eds.) *Group training techniques*. London: Gower Press, 1972.

Cooper, C. L. (Ed.) *Group training for individual and organizational development*. Basle, Switzerland: S. Karger AG, 1973.

Cooper, C. L., & Mangham, I. L. *T-Groups: A survey of research*. London: John Wiley & Sons, 1971.

Davies, I. K. *The organization of training: A behavioural science approach*. London: McGraw-Hill, 1972.

Hacon, R. (Ed.) *Personal and organizational effectiveness*. London: McGraw-Hill, 1971.

van der Vegt, R. *Training and evaluating*. Utrecht, Holland: Drukkerij Elinkwijk, 1973.

Walton, H. (Ed.) *Small group psychotherapy*. London: Penguin, 1971.

AHP GROWTH CENTER LIST
January 1974

Association For Humanistic Psychology
325 Ninth Street, San Francisco, California 94103

AHP, by listing these growth centers, in no way endorses them. Caveat experiensor! The list is brought up to date periodically in the AHP Newsletter, available to AHP members. A duplicated sheet is also available. There is no easy way to keep up with the comings and goings of growth centers. Some listed may not exist any more; others certainly have come into existence since the preparation of this issue. We urge centers to let us know of new addresses. The list itself is geographically oriented for quick reference. The names given are those of people to contact, not necessarily the heads of the centers.
° = Listed in '73 but did not respond to '74 questionnaire.

The Association for Humanistic Psychology invites requests for its other lists, which are available free or at cost: for example, a humanistic book list, a humanistic schools list, a humanistic education resources list. An AHP member (membership applications are available on request) receives all of these lists automatically.

Australia

Australian Institute
of Human Relations
c/o Janet Clarke Hall
Royal Parade, Parkville 3052
Melbourne, Victoria
3477692
Tony Andreatta

Coonardoo Centre °
6 Oaks Avenue
Cremorne N.S.W.
Sydney, 2090
90-5548 (Sydney)
Marjorie P. Holburn

Human Development Centre
P.O. Box 179
St. Ives, NSW
2075
450-1504
Louis E. Herbst

Human Interaction Seminars °
Box 4984, G.P.O.
Sydney 2001 NSW
450-1504
Louis E. Herbst

Belgium

Interaktie-Akademie
Mortselsesteenweg 78
2540 Hove
03-55-57-67
Ferdinand Cuvelier

Canada

Canadian Institute
of Psychosynthesis °
29, Avenue Winchester
Montreal, Quebec
514-488-4494
Martha Crampton

Centennial Acres Inc. °
Box 960
Bracebridge, Muskoka
Ontario
705-385-2289
A. Barbara Steven

Center for the Whole Person
Box 67
MacTier, Ontario
416-961-1212
William Swartley

Center for the Whole Person
76 Dupont Street
Toronto, Ontario
416-961-1212
Judi Greene

Centre de Psychologie
Conjugale et Familiale
1256 Sherbrooke est
Montreal 133, Quebec
522-7088
Jean-Guy and Madeleine
  Leclerc-Bonin

Centre of Movement
121 Avenue Road
Toronto, Ontario
416-961-6978
Ruth Bernard

Claremont Centre
for Human Potential
85 Spadina Road
Toronto, Ontario
416-921-7777
Anna Palo-Heimo

Cold Mountain Institute
Manson's Landing
Cortez Island, British Columbia
Richard Weaver

Cold Mountain Institute °
2527 West 37th Avenue
Vancouver 13, British Columbia
604-263-3533
Wendy Barrett

Eidetic Center
c/o Evering Consultants
43 Eglinton Avenue East
Toronto, Ontario
416-481-6419
Henry Evering

Encounter
380 St. George Street
Moncton, New Brunswick
506-854-2200

Reprinted from *AHP Growth Center List*, January 1974, by permission of the Association for Humanistic Psychology, 325 Ninth Street, San Francisco, California 94103.

Gestalt Institute of Canada °
Box 779
Chemainus, British Columbia
604-246-3450
Jerry Rothstein

Gestalt Institute of Quebec
3590 Ridgewood, Apartment 404
Montreal 247, Quebec
514-731-6742
Don Horne

*I.F.G.: Croissance
personnelle*
831 Rockland
Montreal, Quebec
735-5171
Andre Lafrance

*Institut des Relations
Humaines Inc.*
2120 Sherbrooke est., Suite 208
Montreal 133, Quebec
522-1518
Guy Majeau

*The Institute for Studies in
Psycho-Physical Science* °
14 Medici Court
Scarborough 702, Ontario
416-266-8816
Dan Farmer

Nemaya Farm Growth Center
543 St. Clements Avenue
Toronto, Ontario, M5N 1M3
416-483-1777
Sy Silverberg

New Values Association
47 Prince Charles Drive
Toronto, Ontario MGA 241
416-783-8437
Gershon Matheus

Anthony Paplauskas-Ramunas
187 Carling Ave.
Ottawa 1, Ontario
Canada

Shalal Institute °
P.O. Box 2196
Vancouver, British Columbia
604-687-7148
Alan Tolliday

Strathmere °
R.R. #3, North Gower
Ontario
613-692-4111
Alex Sim, Eleanor Sim,
   Marsha Bracewell

Synergia
P.O. Box 1685
Station B
Montreal 110, Quebec
Marie Brewer

Yasodhara Ashram
Box 9
Kootenay Bay
British Columbia
604-277-9220
Swami Rhada

*York University, E.G.O.
(Education and Growth
Opportunities) Programme*
4700 Keele Street
Downsview 463, Ontario
416-667-3276
Sy Silverberg

England

Ananda Centre, Ltd. °
Eisley Court
20/22 Gt. Titchfield Street
London, W.1
01-636-3491

Bristol Encounter Centre
28 Drakes Way
Portishead, Bristol
Portishead 847490
Ken Waldie, John Crook

Centre for Bio-Energy
18 Hanover Park
London SE IS 545
01-639-4675

Centre for Human Communication
63 Abbey Road
Torquay, Devon
Kevin Kingsland

Centre for Humanistic Studies
18a Allingham Court
Haverstock Hill
London, NW 3
Jacob Stattman, Michael Barnett

The Churchill Centre
22 Montague Street
London W1
01-402-9475

Community
6 Harley Road
London NW 3
01-586-3545
Michael Barnett

*Consultants in Humanistic
Psychology*
18a Allingham Court
Haverstock Hill
London NW 3
Jacob Stattman, Michael Barnett,
   William Grossman

*The Hallam Clinic for
Transactional Analysis*
11 Stumperlowe Pack Road
Sheffield 510 3QP
Alan Bryon

Interface
P.O. Box 28
Wilmslow, Cheshire
Trevor Mumby

Manchester Encounter Centre
7 Oak Avenue
Chorlton-Cum-Hardy,
Manchester

Quaesitor °
187 Walm Lane
London NW 2
01-452-8489
David and Sandy Blagdon

Staines Growth Centre
The Flat
36a Kingston Road
Staines

France

*Centre de Developpement
du Potentiel Humain*
25 rue de la Bienfaisance
Paris 8

*Groupe Francais d'Etudes
de Sociometrie*
Centre Montsouris, 8
villa Montsouris
75014 Paris
589.55.69
Francois Tosquelles,
   Anne Ancelin Schutzenberger

Insight
64 rue de Condorcet
Paris 9

Aline Mantel Graf
79 Avenue de la République
Paris 11

Vacances 2000
18, avenue de l'Opéra
Paris 1

Germany

Zist
8122 Penzberg
Wolf Büntig

Israel

Tivyon Growth Centre
P.O. Box 808
Kfar Shmaryahu
03-937358
Michael Bernet

Republic of South Africa

Prod °
P.O. Box 65
Horison, Transvaal
011-763-1299
Eoin O'Leary

Venezuela

Encuentro
Apartado 51855
Caracas 105, Venezuela 740954
Dr. Jose Geller

Eastern Area, USA

*Adirondack Mountain Humanistic
Education Center*
Springfield Road
Upper Jay, New York 12987
518-946-2206
Howard Kirschenbaum

Aegis Institute
Box 238
Haverford, Pennsylvania 19041
215-649-7894
Grace Stern, Larry Phillips

Anthos
24 East 22nd Street
New York, New York 10010
212-673-9067
Martin Shepard, Steve Gelman

Associates for Human Resources
P.O. 727, 191 Sudbury Road
Concord, Massachusetts 01460
617-259-9624
Registrar

Atlantis Foundation°
181 Willard Avenue
Newington, Connecticut 06111
213-233-1712
Thomas Penrose, Jack Cohen

Atlanta Training Network
2744 Peachtree Road NW
Atlanta, Georgia 30305
Gordon H. Mann

Canberra Institute
1323 Avenue N
Brooklyn, New York 11230
212-339-2810

Casaelya
350 Elmwood Avenue
Buffalo, New York 14222
716-882-2828
Gene W. Brockopp

*Center for Applied
Social Science°*
Boston University
270 Bay State Road
Boston, Massachusetts 02215
617-353-2770
Helene Nemzoff

*Center for Development of
Individual Potential°*
NTL Institute for Applied
   Behavioral Science
1201 16th Street, NW
Washington, D.C. 20036
212-833-4363

Center for Experiential Living
235 East 49th Street
New York, New York 10017
212-751-4389

Center for Family Interaction
Ten Hatter's Court
Hatbord, Pennsylvania 19040
215-672-7877
Dick Jontry, Ruthann Pippenger

Center for Human Development
221 Shady Avenue
Pittsburgh, Pennsylvania 15206
412-361-1400
Bunny Kramer

*Center for Human Development,
Group Effectiveness, and
Leadership Education*
Association Island
Henderson Harbor, New York 13651
315-938-5022
Richard W. Billings

Center for Human Potential
Maple Hill-East Monkton
RD #2, Box 238
Bristol, Vermont 05443
802-453-3660
John D. Perry, Jr.

Center for Human Potential
120 West 69th Street
New York, New York 10023
H. C. Frank Keeton

Center for the Whole Person
Route 1, Box 84
Mays Landing, New Jersey 08330
609-625-1611
Penny Burton

Center for the Whole Person
1 Pine Drive
Roosevelt, New Jersey 08555
609-448-5727
Bobbi Feldman

Center for the Whole Person
52 Bolton Lane
Willingboro, New Jersey 08046
609-871-3671
Cal Marques

Center for the Whole Person
304 West 105th Street
New York, New York 10025
212-222-9445
David Freundlich

Center for the Whole Person
517 South 22nd Street
Philadelphia, Pennsylvania 19146
215-985-0638
Mike Broder

Center of Man
P.O. Box 14126

Center on the Ridge
4763 Ormonde Drive
Cazenovia, New York 13035
315-655-3393
Robert Bolton

Central Counseling Service
4 West 76th St.
New York, New York 10023
799-9460
Ted Smith

Cornucopia
3205 S.W. 27th Avenue
Miami, Florida 33133
305-446-4900
John A. Self, Fran Johnston

Creativity Laboratories, Inc.
463 West Street
New York, New York 10014
212-989-1826
Edward Eichel

Creative Resources Association
1625 W. Montgomery Avenue
Villanova, Pennsylvania 19085
215-525-6498
C. B. Nolte

Dialogue House Associates
45 West Tenth Street
New York, New York 10011
212-228-9180

Discovery—A Human Relations Center
428 Market Street, Box 1089
Camden, New Jersey 08101
609-365-9496
Mark L. Krell

*Encounters—Workshops in Personal
and Professional Growth*
5225 Connecticut Avenue, NW
   Suite 209
Washington D.C. 20015
301-530-4485 or 212-363-3033
Lawrence Tirnauer

Gainesville, Florida 32601
904-466-3351
Ted Landsman

Generation One
345 West 85th Street, Suite 46
New York, New York 10024
Don Fass, Sharlee Cohen,
   Dick Hoffmann

*Gestalt Institute of
Western New York*
350 Elmwood Avenue
Buffalo, New York 14222
716-882 2828
Gene W. Brockopp

Gestalt Psychotherapy Associates
211 Central Park West
New York, New York 10024
212-362-1212
Michael Kriegsfeld

Grow °
312 West 82nd Street
New York, New York 10024
212-595-5330
Mildred C. Smith

Growth Groups °
7 West 73rd Street
New York, New York 10023
212-787-2136 or 828-2316
Toni Gabriel, Bob Guglielmo

Habitat: A Center for
Pre-Retirement Planning
Madaket Road
Nantucket Island
Nantucket, Massachusetts
603-432-3707
Michael K. Jones

Human Development Growth Center °
350 Northern Boulevard
Great Neck, New York 11021
516-829-9443
Abraham H. Seidman

Human Dimensions Institute °
4380 Main Street
Buffalo, New York 14226
716-839-2336
Jeanne Pontius Rindge

Human Resources Center
of Connecticut
210 Prospect Street
New Haven, Connecticut 06511
562-6189
Ella Fierman

Humanist Society of
Greater New York
2109 Broadway at 73rd Street
New York, New York 10023
212-799-0191
Joseph Ben-David

Humanistic Psychology Center
of New York
285 Central Park West
New York, New York 10024
Carmi Harari

Institute for Experiential
Learning and Development
1687 Lawrence Road
Trenton, New Jersey 08638
609-882-6815
Doris Rothman

The Institute for Human Relations
Laboratory Training
Box 233, Kensington Station
Brooklyn, New York 11218
212-941-1917
Jerome Gold

Institute for Living, Inc. °
2309 Delancey Place
Philadelphia, Pennsylavnia 19103
215-546-7344
Kurt Konietzko

Institute for Psychoenergetics °
7 Harvard Square
Brookline, Massachusetts
617-653-6022
Buryl Payne

Institute for Rational Living
45 East 65th Street
New York, New York 10021
212-535-0822
Janet L. Wolfe

Institute for Sociotherapy °
Division of Community Education
39 East 20th Street
New York, New York 10003
212-260-3860
Mary Watson

The Institute for
Structural Awareness
1625 West Montgomery Avenue
Villanova, Pennsylvania 19085
215-525-6498
Dorothy L. Nolte

Integro °
112 Hunter Lane
North Wales, Pennsylvania 19454
215-368-0767
Joe Kovatch

Interface, Inc. °
2714 27th Street, NW
Washington, D.C. 20008
202-466-2255
Ed Elkin

Island °
Route 1, Box 86
Madison, Virginia 22727
703-948-6244
Donovan Thesenga

Laurel Institute, Inc.
2010 Pine Street
Philadelphia, Pennsylvania 19103
215-545-2800
Barton Knapp, Marta Vago

The Lindisfarne Association
P.O. Box 1395
Southampton, New York 11968
516-283-8210
Gene Fairly, William Thompson

Maitri
RFD
Elizabethtown, New York 12932

Mid-Atlantic Training Committee
1500 Massachusetts Avenue, NW
Suite 325
Washington, D.C. 20005
202-223-0582
John Denham

Mid-State Oasis
226 West Southey Avenue
Altoona, Pennsylvania 16602
814-942-9684
Louis D. Goodfellow

New England Center for Personal
and Organizational Development
Box 575
Amherst, Massachusetts 01002
413-549-0886
Jack Canfield,
    Judy Ohlbaum-Canfield

The New Haven Center for
Human Relations
400 Prospect Street
New Haven, Connecticut 06511
203-776-1333
Gelen Eliasoph, Bob Singer

Northeast Institute for
Self Development
1730 Welsh Road
Philadelphia, Pennsylvania 19115
215-676-5293
Paul Hannig

Number Nine °
Youth Crisis/Growth Center
266 State Street
New Haven, Connecticut 06511
203-787-2127
Dennis Jaffe, Shelia Fox-Gage

Open House
412 Linn Street
Ithaca, New York 14850
607-273-1137

P.E.A.C. Institute °
495 West End Avenue
New York, New York 10024
212-663-2119
Theo Skolnik

Personal Growth Center
10 Ipswich Avenue
Great Neck, New York 11021
516-487-8130
Gladys Osrow

The Piedmont Program
Box 6129
Winston-Salem, North Carolina
    27109
919-725-9850
John Woodmansee

Plainfield Consultation Center °
831 Madison Avenue
Plainfield, New Jersey 07060
201-757-4921
Lawrence Kesner

Primal Experiences Center
22 East 17th Street
New York, New York 10003
212-243-1704
Alice Sharron

Quest Center for Human Growth °
4933 Auburn Avenue
Bethesda, Maryland 20014
301-652-0697
Robert D. Caldwell

The Red Barn Workshop Center
Litchfield, Connecticut 06759
203-567-8763
Renée Nell

The Red Barn Workshop Center
Westerly, Rhode Island 02891
401-322-1214
Robert Bettinger

Ricorso
The City College of New York
138th Street and Convent Avenue
New York, New York 11753
212-621-2294
Jerome Gold

The Roscoe Center, Inc.
645 West End Avenue
New York, New York 10025
212-595-0996

*Sage Institute of
Applied Philosophy*
549 Longfellow Avenue
Virginia Beach, Virginia 23462
804-499-1831
Roy W. Black

Seven Oaks
Route 1, Box 86
Madison, Virginia 22727
703-948-6244
Donovan Thesenga

Sky Foundation
10 South Front Street
Philadelphia, Pennsylvania 19106
215-925-8038
V. Pratap

*Sono Institute for
Human Potential*
5417 Walnut Street
Pittsburgh, Pennsylvania 15232
412-421-2206
Jack B. Kauffman

Stepping-Stone
Four Potter Park
Cambridge, Massachusetts 02138
617-864-6838
Dan Menkin

Training for Living, Inc.
487 Park Avenue
New York, New York 10022
212-832-1444
Virginia Van Bokkelen

*Wainwright Center for
the Development of
Human Resources*
260 Stuyvesant Avenue
Rye, New York 10580
914-967-6080
Alfred Sunderwirth

*W.I.L.L. (Workshop Institute
for Living-Learning)* °
100 Colony Square, Suite 933
1175 Peachtree Street, NE
Atlanta, Georgia 30309
404-892-0232
Paul P. Hirschfield

*Workshops in Spontaneous
Art Expression* °
3901 Alton Place, NW
Washington, DC 20016
202-966-8556
Mala Betensky

Central Area, USA

All the Way House, Inc. °
1507 S. Stewart Avenue
Lombard, Illinois 60148
312-627-3623
Scott Mason, Carolyn Sylva

*Alverna (Center for
Human Development and
Spiritual Growth)*
8140 Spring Mill Road
Indianapolis, Indiana 46260
317-257-7339
Maury Smith, Donald Betz

*Almare: The Institute of
Human Relatedness*
P.O. Box 108
Bowling Green, Ohio 43402
419-352-0698
Jim Guinan

Ananda Marga Yoga Society °
3455 East 12th Street
Wichita, Kansas 67208
316-684-0001
Dick Griffin

Blood, Bob and Margaret
2005 Penncraft Court
Ann Arbor, Michigan 48103
313-769-0046

Cambridge House, Inc. °
1900 North Cambridge Avenue
Milwaukee, Wisconsin 53202
414-273-6333
Sandra A. Badtke

Centre for Creative Change
9378 Olive Boulevard
St. Louis, Missouri 63132
314-991-0427
Barry Schapiro

Communication Center # 1 °
1001 Union Boulevard
St. Louis, Missouri 63113
314-863-7297
Mel R. Spehn

Community House
2420 South Taylor Road
Cleveland Heights, Ohio 44118
216-321-4608
Carolyn Olds

Dallas Gestalt Therapy Institute
6526 L.B.J. Freeway
Dallas, Texas 75240
H. Weiner or J. R. Allen

*Forest Hospital
Postgraduate Center* °
555 Wilson Lane
Des Plaines, Illinois 60016
312-827-8811, Extension 175
Robert Willford, Erika Danilovich

Foundation Growth Center °
12700 Southwest Highway
Palos Park, Illinois
312-448-0780
Jack E. Van Liew

Gestalt Institute of Cleveland °
12921 Euclid Avenue
Cleveland, Ohio 44112
216-421-0469
Harriet Schenker

Hara, Inc. °
P.O. Box 28177
Dallas, Texas 75228
214-279-6868
M. Kovich

*Human Resource
Developers, Inc.*
112 West Oak Street
Chicago, Illinois 60610
312-644-1920
Dean C. Dauw

Humanistics
511 Beryl Drive
Kent, Ohio 44240
216-673-8729
Ansell Woldt

Independence Counseling Center
3675 S. Noland Road, Suite 115
Independence, Missouri 64055
816-833-0408 or 833-0409
John W. Johnston

Institute for Advanced
Pastoral Studies
380 Lone Pine Road
Bloomfield Hills, Michigan 48013
313-646-9375
Jack Biersdorf

Jonesboro Counseling Center
114 East Oak
Jonesboro, Arkansas 72401
935-7100
Glenn A. Galtere

Laboratories for
Human Development
9661 Gans Avenue
Canton, Ohio 44721
Bryce A. Kramer

The Laos House °
4100 Red River
Austin, Texas 78751
512-452-0117
Robert R. Bryant

The Lawrence Growth Center
Box 3331
Lawrence, Kansas 66044
913-842-9322
Paul and Mary Friedman

Live Oaks Workshops
2437 Vineville Avenue
Macon, Georgia 31204
912-746-2726
Robert E. Taylor

Logos Institute: A Center
on Religion and
Human Potential °
Chicago Theological Seminary
5757 University Avenue
Chicago, Illinois 60637
312-752-5757
Philip Anderson, Arthur Foster

Michiana Growth Center
1920 Bond Road
Niles, Michigan 49120
616-684-3752
Dot Bowland

Midwest Institute for Human
Understanding, Inc. °
572 West Market Street, Suite #1
Akron, Ohio 44303
216-762-9056
William H. Holloway

Oasis: Midwest Center
for Human Potential °
20 East Harrison Street
Chicago, Illinois 60605
312-922-5964
DeLacy Brubaker

Oklahoma Growth Center
1523 Glenwood
Oklahoma City, Oklahoma 73190
J. R. Allen

Oklahoma Growth Center, Inc.
3312 North Cardinal Drive
Oklahoma City, Oklahoma 73121
405-424-6341
Barbara Lundy

The Place °
1546 Spruce Drive
Kalamazoo, Michigan 49008
616-344-4771
Neil Lamper

A Place for
Human Understanding
5850 Lincoln Avenue
Chicago, Illinois 60659
312-275-3600
Larry Kokkelenberg

Prairie View °
P.O. Box 467
Newton, Kansas 67114
316-283-2400
Merrill F. Raber

Primal Awareness
Education Center
1240 Ashland Avenue
St. Paul, Minnesota 55104
612-646-3242
N. A. Ewald

Shadybrook House °
King Memorial Road, Box 98
Mentor, Ohio 44060
216-255-3406
William J. Weinland

Sunergos Institute Inc.
4909 Forest Avenue
Downers Grove, Illinois 60515
Maurice Paulson, Genevieve Paulson

Tuwaqachi (A Gestalt Center)
2103 121st Avenue, Route 2
Allegan, Michigan 49010
616-667-6992
Neil Lamper

Western Area, USA

Academy of Creative Education °
P.O. Box 877
San Jacinto, California 92383
714-654-2625
James C. Ingebretsen

ALPHA-PSIgenics Research
Institute, Inc.
P.O. Box 2180
Toluca Lake Station
North Hollywood, California 91602
213-985-5282
Bam Price

Anthropos Foundation °
P.O. Box 445
Hayward, California
415-538-5023
Frederick E. Heslet

ARC Seminars
1625 Interlaken Place, East
Seattle, Washington 98112

Arica Institute in America
580 Market Street
San Francisco, California 94104
415-986-8800
Receptionist

Arizona Training Laboratories for
Applied Behavioral Science °
P.O. Box 26660
Tempe, Arizona 85282
602-838-0837
Gerald L. Moulton

Art Therapy Workshop
2955 22nd Street
San Francisco, California 94110
415-824-1602
Robert Liikala

Berkeley Center for
Human Interaction
1816 Scenic Avenue
Berkeley, California 94709
415-845-4765
Trevor Hoy

Bindrim, Paul & Associates
2000 Cantata Drive
Los Angeles, California 90068
213-851-0619
Paul Bindeim

Bioenergetics Northwest
3938 1st NE
Seattle, Washington 98105
206-632-9210
Dan Barr

California Institute
of Asian Studies
3494 21st Street
San Francisco, California 94114
415-648-1489
Haridas Chaudhuri

The Center for Creativity
and Growth °
599 College Avenue
Palo Alto, California 94306
415-321-4200
Frieda Porat

Center for Feeling Therapy
1017 South La Brea
Los Angeles, California 90019
213-938-2729
Joseph Hart

Center for Human Communication °
120 Oak Meadow Drive
Los Gatos, California 95030
408-354-6466
John P. Krop

Center for Interpersonal
Development°
P.O. Box 214381
Sacramento, California 95821
916-371-0430
Martin Rogers

Center for Intimacy
and Sexuality
6169 Harwood Avenue
Oakland, California 94618
415-653-8901
Wilbur Hoff

The Center for New Beginnings
2401 S. Fillmore
Denver, Colorado 80210
313-756-5228
Clyde H. Reid

Center for Organization &
Manpower Development
School of Business
California State University
San Jose, California 95192
408-277-2139
Patrick Williams

Center for Spiritual
& Human Growth
P.O. Box 692
San Anselmo, California 94960
415-453-8088
Francis Geddes

Center for the Study
of Individuation
Box 1183
Sugarloaf, California 42386
714-585-2917 or 866-3471
P. C. Twichel

Center for Studies
of the Person°
1125 Torrey Pines Road
La Jolla, California 92037
714-459-3861
David Meador

Center for the Study of Power
P.O. Box 9096
Berkeley, California 94709
415-549-0839
James H. Craig

Communiversity
P.O. Box 1318
Bellingham, Washington 98225
Bill Chaloner

The Counseling and
Growth Center
3082 Driftwood Drive
San Jose, California 95128
408-379-1004

Deer Creek Center
P.O. Box 333
Boulder, Utah 84716
801-335-2228
Darcy Livingston or
Jude Paulbick

Dialogue House Associates°
1440 Harvard Street
Santa Monica, California
Sid Stave

Discovery°
913 Hornblend Street
San Diego, California 92109
714-272-4984
Shirley Kashoff

Duckabush River Center°
4668 Sunnside North
Seattle, Washington 98103
Tom Toomey

Edmucko Formless°
P.O. Box 216
Ben Lomond, California 95005
408-336-8256
Ed Dalton

Elysium Institute in Town
Centre (Admin. Office)
5436 Fernwood Avenue
Los Angeles, California 90027
213-465-7121
Ed Lange

Elysium Institute
Elysium Field
814 Robinson Road
Topanga, California 90290
213-465-7121
Ed Lange

Emotional Educational Services
1857 University Street
Eugene, Oregon 97403
503-686-9934
Michael B. Sun

EPIC (Educational Programs
in Communication)
P.O. Box 5178
Santa Cruz, California 95063
408-423-1149

Esalen Institute
Big Sur, California 93920
408-667-2335
Julian Silverman

Esalen Institute
1793 Union Street
San Francisco, California 94123
415-771-1710
Richard Farson

Eureka Center for
Communication & Encounter
2124 E. Street
Eureka, California 95501
707-443-4193
Judy Bradford

Explorations Institute°
P.O. Box 1254
Berkeley, California 94701
415-548-1004
Jim Elliott

Gestalt Institute for Growth
752 Bryant Street
Palo Alto, California 94301
415-326-4270
Peter D. Rogers

Gestalt Institute of Denver°
5401 South Franklin Street
Littleton, Colorado 80121
303-761-5631
Beth Prothro,
George Dovenmuehle

Gestalt Institute of Hawaii
P.O. Box 1145
Kaneohi, Hawaii 96744
808-537-1684
Tom Glass

Gestalt Therapy Institute
of Los Angeles°
337 South Beverly Drive,
Suite 206
Beverly Hills, California 90212
213-277-2918
Priscilla B. Jones

Gestalt Institute of Sacramento
3181 Mountain View
Sacramento, California 95021
916-442-9221
Lori Burns, Barbara Goldberg

Gestalt Therapy Institute of
San Diego
7255 Girard Avenue, Suite 27
La Jolla, California 92037
714-459-2693
Thomas A. Munson

Gestalt Institute of
San Francisco°
1719 Union Street
San Francisco, California 94123
415-776-4500
Art Damond

Gestalt Institute of Washington
Gestalt House
14909 SE 44 Place
Bellevue, Washington 98006
216-747-8278 or 641-2331
Charles R. Walsmith

Getting in Touch
P.O. Box 1225
Los Gatos, California 95030
408-867-4562
Rita or Lorne Bay

Good Neighbor Project
P.O. Box 585
Corte Madera, California 94925
415-841-5651
George Pransky

Group Process Institute °
P.O. Box 123, University Station
Seattle, Washington 98105
206-322-1344
Marvin Thomas

High Point Foundation °
2509 North Lake Avenue
Altadena, California 91001
213-797-3020 or 681-1033
Edith R. Stauffer

High Point Foundation °
5556 North 6th Street
Fresno, California 93710
209-439-6403
Viola A. Davis

High Point Foundation Northwest
916 9th South
Edmonds, Washington 98020
206-778-4826 or 778-2119
A. Edward Turner

High Point Foundation °
1085 Longridge Road
Oakland, California 94610
415-832-0567
John Fugitt

The Howard Institute
(Alternative Counseling
and Education for
Non-Ethnic Minorities)
765 Rand Avenue
Oakland, California 94610
415-839-9825
Don H. Noyes

Humanist Growth Institute °
P.O. Box 10626
Honolulu, Hawaii 96816
Peter Beemer

Humanist Institute
1430 Masonic Avenue
San Francisco, California 94117
415-626-0544
Sister Mary Martha

Human Potential Institute
2550 Via Tejon, Suite 2E, 2F
Palos Verdes Estates,
California 90274
213-375-0161
Henry L. Levy

Human Sexuality Foundation
1114 Irwin Street
San Rafael, California 94901
415-453-6162
Richard E. Levy

Inner Light Foundation °
P.O. Box 761
Novato, California 94947
415-897-5581

Institute for Creative and
Artistic Development °
5935 Manchester Drive
Oakland, California 94618
415-653-9133
Juanita B. Sagan

Institute of Human
Potential Psychology °
2251 Yale Street
Palo Alto, California 94306
Charanjit Singh Wallia

J'Ananda
Star Route Box 1085
Elk, California 95432
John L. Koehne, Jr.

Kairos—Los Angeles °
P.O. Box 75426
Los Angeles, California 90005
213-931-1895
Katie Wedderien, Joseph Heller

The Kemery Institute °
304 Park Way
Chula Vista, California 92010
714-427-6225
W. E. Kemery, Mary Hoffmann

Kundalini Research Institute °
Gobind Singh Shakti Sadan
575 North Hamilton Boulevard
Pomona, California 91768
714-622-9575
Michael Singh Fowlis

Lifestyle Exploration Center
1510 Grant Avenue, #204
Novato, California 94947
415-897-4116
Bruno Geba

Living Love Center
1730 LaLoma Avenue
Berkeley, California 94709
415-848-9341
Ken Keyes

Logos West °
P.O. Box 362
Lafayette, California 94549
415-284-5950
Frank E. Humberger

Primal Feeling Center
P.O. Box 112
Santa Barbara, California 93108
805-969-3710
Jonathan Young

Prism °
Box 1242
Santa Cruz, California 95060
408-336-5709
David Mills, Meg Herz

Programs in Communications
P.O. Box 2216
Boulder, Colorado 80302
303-442-2741
Hugh Pates

Prometheus
401 Florence Avenue
Palo Alto, California 94301
415-328-6137
Victor Lovell

Psychosynthesis Institute °
150 Doherty Way
Redwood City, California 94062
415-365-7941
Jim Vargiu, Susan Vargiu

Renaissance Integrated Workshop °
P.O. Box 3094
San Diego, California 92103
714-234-3934
Philip G. Stephan,
Armenak Hermez

San Francisco Psychotherapy
and Psychodrama Institute °
365 14th Avenue
San Francisco, California 94118
415-752-6249
Adele Deeths McCormick

Self-Explorations & Growth
290 7th Avenue
San Francisco, California 94118
415-668-9931
Rick Gilbert

Self-Institute °
40 Hawthorne Avenue
Los Altos, California 94022
415-948-9318
John J. Latini

Self Therapy Workshops °
340 Santa Monica Avenue
Menlo Park, California 94025
Muriel Schiffman

Seminars in Group Processes °
7433 SW Garden Home Road
Portland, Oregon 97223
503-244-8806
Leon Fine

Tahoe Institute °
P.O. Box DD
South Lake Tahoe,
California 95705
916-544-5003
Jerry P. Nims

Mann Ranch Seminars °
P.O. Box 570
Ukiah, California 95482
707-462-3514
Larry T. Thomas

National Center for the
Exploration of
Human Potential °
976 Chalcedony Street
San Diego, California 92109
A. J. Lewis, Martin Seldman

Odysseus
P.O. Box 394
Los Gatos, California 95030
408-354-7762 or 356-3232
Telemachos A. Greanias

Open End
Box 70
San Anselmo, California 94960
415-461-2373
Larry Honby

Personal Exploration Groups
2400 Bancroft Way
Berkeley, California 94704
415-841-6013
Mimi Silbert

Personescence
P.O. Box 3392
Beverly Hills, California 90212
213-652-8328
Lee Christie, Theodora Wells

Port Angeles Washington
Growth Center
c/o Vogel
Route #1, Box 429
Lake Sutherland
Port Angeles, Washington 98362

Thomas Jefferson Research Center °
1143 North Lake Avenue
Pasadena, California 91104
213-798-0791
Frank Goble

Topanga Center for
Human Development
2247 North Topanga Canyon Blvd.
Topanga, California 90290
213-455-1342
Mary Miller

Unfolding Path
1578 Willowmont Avenue
San Jose, California 95118
408-266-7051
Lew and Virginia Howard

University Associates
Publishers, Inc.
P.O. Box 80637
San Diego, California 92138
715-224-3444
J. William Pfeiffer, John E. Jones

Vantage Point
5630 Sardine Creek Road
Gold Hill, Oregon 97525
503-855-1472
Richard Cote

Viewpoints Institute °
8970 Norma Place
Los Angeles, California 90069
213-274-3252 or 274-4233
Ethel Longstreet

Venture
P.O. Box 11802
Palo Alto, California 94306
415-326-6614
Charlene Harman, Connie Houle

We Care (for Divorced,
Separated and Widowed)
121 Broadway #517
San Diego, California 92101
714-233-6866

Well-Springs °
11667 Alba Road
Ben Lomond, California 95005
408-336-8177 or 336-8594
Kay Ortmans

Western Career Development Center
109 Seminary Road
San Anselmo, California 94960
415-453-7000
Elizabeth Blickman

GOOD THINGS *DO* COME IN SMALL PACKAGES

A Review of *Face to Face: The Small-Group Experience and Interpersonal Growth*
by Gerard Egan.
Monterey, Ca.: Brooks/Cole, 1973. 162 pp., $3.50.

Richard Heslin

Some people are willing to grapple with the complexities of life and resist the temptation to oversimplify them. Gerard Egan is such a person.

He considers the human potential movement too important to leave in the hands of insensitive and slavish followers of people like Carl Rogers, William Schutz, and Fritz Perls. These are the people who, for the sake of "an angle" or a clever, eye-catching approach, will risk group experiences that range from useless and dull on the one hand to dangerous and frightening on the other.

Egan's firm philosophy that members should "own" what happens in the group clearly supports the rationale of this book. Egan is "the contract man," and with the publication of *Face to Face* he brings the theory of the contract and its implementation directly to the individual group participant.

Face to Face and *Encounter*

Face to Face is a distillation of Egan's earlier book *Encounter* (Brooks/Cole, 1970), and I expected it to be the same book except for the removal of the theoretical discussions. The book *is*, indeed, significantly shorter than *Encounter* (162 pages instead of 424—and it would really be 150 pages if the pages were the same size as in the earlier book).

I have used *Encounter* in my classes, but even though I was delighted with it and found the theoretical discussions fascinating, my students were unenthusiastic. They could understand the contract and considered it very valuable, but

they thought that Egan's scholarly comments on theories of psychological growth and group experiences were expendable.

Additions, Improvements

The theoretical discussions are gone from *Face to Face* (thereby making it more interesting), but the new book has far more to recommend it than that deletion.

Hardly a sentence has not been changed, tightened, and improved in the new version. Major new insights and aids have been added.

For example, at the beginning of Chapter 3 there is a short inventory for the reader to rate himself on a number of behaviors relevant to the goals of interpersonal growth, *e.g.*:

Genuineness—
"I do not hide behind roles or facades; others know where I stand."
Concreteness—
"I am not vague when I speak to others; I do not speak in generalities nor do I beat around the bush."
Confrontation—
"I challenge others responsibly and with care: I use confrontation as a way of getting involved with others [pp. 19-20]."

Another addition at the end of the book is an instrument that measures group climate: the Encounter Group Checklist. Its purpose is to force the group participants to admit that the group may not be meeting the contract in some specific way, thereby heightening the likelihood that they will deal with the problem. The Check-list contains a number of questions about the group. For example, under the heading of "A climate of immediacy":

> "Are there a large number of one-to-one conversations as opposed to speeches to the group?"

> "Do members avoid speaking for the group, and using the pronoun 'we'?"

Under the heading of "Cooperation":

> "Is there a climate of cooperation rather than one of antagonism, passivity or competition?"

> "Do members, when they confront one another, check out their feelings and evaluations with other members? [pp. 154-155]"

The Contract vs. Creative Ambiguity

Although there are very few weaknesses to this book's approach to group leadership, one that could be mentioned (depending on the reader's orientation) is that the contract reduces useful ambiguity.

Ambiguity about group structure and goals allows members to experience the creation of a society from the beginning, to grapple with leadership, to struggle to organize themselves toward accomplishing goals both for themselves and other members in the time available.

In a low-structure group, members learn a number of diverse things. For example, they learn (1) about themselves (their passivity, their fear of being alone with their own thoughts, their fear of taking initiative and leadership), and (2) about groups (how difficult it is to get people to agree on courses of action and how people react to being led).

However, the kind of low leader-visibility and high ambiguity that was found in early training groups is considered dysfunctional by Egan. But it should be possible to resolve these two different views of high ambiguity brought about by low structure.

The ambiguity and the extremely low profile of the traditional T-group trainers are understandable if we remember that these groups were composed of businessmen whose primary goal was to understand groups and organizational behavior.

This is an undertaking carrying a low degree of threat. For impactful change to occur, a person has to be psychologically and emotionally aroused. We can also assume that there is an optimum level of arousal necessary for learning—not too much nor too little.

It follows then that in a low-threat situation, the arousal level must be increased for learning and change, and introducing ambiguity is one way of creating that effect. But in an encounter-group setting, arousal is already high because of the nature of the group. Therefore, increasing arousal further through ambiguity would be dysfunctional to growth and change: Superoptimal arousal can, indeed, be paralyzing.

Thus ambiguity is useful in the former type of groups concerned with organizational behavior and interpersonal relations. But groups that deal with growth (either personal or interpersonal) have anxiety built into them. They do not need to use ambiguity to arouse their members.

Contracted Responsibility

The primary strength of the contract is that it encourages the sharing of responsibility. And this is not mere lip service to a concept accepted in almost all discussions about groups. Encouraging shared responsibility without giving members the means of accomplishing such a laudatory goal is irresponsible. With the contract approach, not only is the fact that leadership is to be shared spelled out clearly, but the kinds of goals the group is to strive for are indicated, thus insuring that the members know what they are aiming at, both individually and as a group.

Once they possess a shared knowledge of the group's goals, they also share responsibility for the accomplishment of those goals. Without such knowledge, the concept of shared responsibility is a sham.

The contract reduces game-playing and dependency by participants. The cry of "What are we supposed to do?" becomes almost ludicrous in a contract group. Many of us have heard this disclaimer following a vicious attack on a fellow member: "Well, isn't that what we are here for? To be *honest* with each other?"

Such a distortion of the purpose of a group and of the meanings of openness, honesty, and confrontation is far more likely to be challenged in a contract group than in a noncontract group—and not by the leader, but by a fellow participant.

In general, the contract is a constant prod to the slothful and timid to exert themselves, to stretch, to take moderate risks, to grow. It reminds them that they may not really be pushing themselves enough to produce group and individual growth.

Egan has done it again. *Encounter* is excellent reading for the professional. But *Face to Face* brings the contract right to the participants, where, in the last analysis, it should be anyway. Well done!

HOW TAVISTOCK RESOLVED THE "JOY CRISIS" AT SHELL UK LIMITED

A Review of *Toward a New Philosophy of Management* by Paul Hill.
New York: Barnes & Noble, 1972. 250 pp., $14.50.

Anthony G. Banet, Jr.

Organizations hire human beings to perform tasks. Task activities seldom exhaust the total capacities of human beings, and individuals can seldom give an organization only the capacities it requires. If an organization fails to provide outlets for the unused capacities, interference with task performance results (a "joy crisis"). To provide outlets, however, means using resources that could otherwise be directed toward the task.

This dilemma, paraphrased from Tavistock theoretician A. K. Rice, confronts many OD consultants: What can be done to meet the needs of both the individual and the organization which employs him? In *Toward a New Philosophy of Management*, Paul Hill describes how that dilemma was faced and resolved in an extensive OD collaboration between Shell UK Limited and the Human Resources Center of the Tavistock Institute in London. Hill is an internal consultant for Shell, and his chronicle is told from that viewpoint; thus, while it is a fascinating, crisply written account, his book tells you more about Shell UK Limited than you may need to know, and less about Tavistock than you might desire. Eric Trist, initial leader of the Tavistock consultant group, does provide an epilogue, but a clear description of how the consultants consulted is lacking.

Shell asked Hill and his colleagues in the employee relations planning unit (unfortunately acronymmed as ERP) to devise a program which would heighten production and job performance, while, at the same time, raising the level of employee motivation, satisfaction, and commitment. After a preliminary diagnosis, Hill concluded that the trust level among shop workers

was so low that something beyond conventional bargaining tactics was required. An action plan involving attitude change and productivity bargaining was accepted by the Shell managers. After that, Hill invited Tavistock consultants to help design, refine, and implement the particulars of the action plan.

The major intervention was nothing less than inviting the organization to redefine its task and its organizational concept in terms of two basic commitments—to make money for Shell and to protect and develop human resources within the company. Hill's text describes how that intervention was accomplished with managers, shop stewards, trade-union representatives, and line workers. In all, more than 6,000 persons were involved in a rapid value-change process, accomplished in eighteen months.

As an approach in OD, Tavistock can be described as a task-oriented, group-focused model which emphasizes (a) the organization as a sociotechnical system; (b) the importance of covert processes operating in all groups; and (c) leadership and followership roles.

The organization is the space where the interrelationship between making money and satisfying human needs occurs. The organization is always tempted to regard itself as a closed system, but in fact it must be open (that is, engage in transactions with its environment) in order to survive. The organization does not own its employees; they are "on loan" from a society which has its own objectives. For Shell, the Tavistock consultants provided the conceptual clarity that the organization needed to build a new self-concept.

The scope of that intervention reflects the range of theory and practice which has come to be known as the "Tavistock approach." The Tavistock Institute, composed of five centers variously involved in group psychotherapy, professional training, and OD, was established in 1946 in response to the multiple mental health and social problems in postwar Britain. Guided by the seminal thinking of Wilfred Bion and A. K. Rice, the Institute staff built theories and a practice to illuminate the murky world of group life, intergroup phenomena, and transactions between groups and their social environment. Through the efforts of Margaret Rioch, the Tavistock tradition was introduced in the United States in 1965. At present, the A. K. Rice Institute of the Washington School of Psychiatry is the agency in this country furthering the work of the original Tavistock group.

Bion's contribution to the Tavistock approach is the focus on covert processes, the "basic assumptions" operative in all groups. Groups frequently behave irrationally; for Bion, schooled in Kleinian psychoanalysis, that observation led to the percept of the small task group as a system, complete with wishes and fears that transcend the wishes and fears of individual members. Groups operating on a basic-assumption level become preoccupied with distortions about survival and the integrity of their boundaries, and attempt to close down their transactions with their environment.

The function of leadership in a system so conceived is to define clearly the task of the system, and to regulate and control transactions across system boundaries. Because the system has many myths about authority, it has difficulty dealing with leadership so defined, and it attempts to pressure the leader to accept instead a variety of magical, priestly, or prophetic functions.

These theoretical constructs can be discerned in Hill's account, and can be experienced in a Tavistock group-relations conference. Using a simple, highly visible structure, the group-relations conference provides a miniature society where group and intergroup processes are scrutinized and conference members are invited to explore their responses to authority and boundary regulation. If the group-relations conference usually exposes the dynamics of corruption, power, rebellion, and assassination, it does not create them: It is a lens which permits the group to be seen as a total system.

Although born in that magic half-decade of the late '40s, when Perls, Rogers, Lewin, and Moreno were blooming, the Tavistock group has maintained a low profile, weaving insights from psychoanalysis, social psychology, and anthropology into a synthesis describing the phenomena of group relations. It is the least-known wing of the contemporary group movement, perhaps because it deals with such unpopular realities as power, authority, conflict, and—sometimes—violence and death.

A word here about the sobriety and grimness associated with the Tavistock approach. At times, the heavy emphasis on work, responsibility, and role has an early-industrial-revolution flavor. Yet it is clear that the organization and its environment must transact and impact each other. Interdependence is frequently frightening, and focusing on it raises philosophical issues of freedom and control. There is abundant evidence of the tragic in this world; Tavistock's view is that it didn't create the joy crisis, it simply reports the phenomenon.

What does this book offer for the OD consultant? Conceptual clarity, for one thing. A style which respects the reality of role and boundary. An appreciation of system dynamics. And some evidence of success: *Toward a New Philosophy of Management* reports a considerable OD achievement of which a practitioner of any persuasion could be proud.

REFERENCES

For more about Tavistock and group relations, Rioch (1970a, 1970b) and Rice (1969) provide lucid introductions. Bion (1959) and Rice (1965) are more complicated, but worth the effort. Information about group-relations conferences can be obtained from the A. K. Rice Institute, Washington School of Psychiatry, 1610 New Hampshire Avenue, N.W., Washington D.C. 20009.

Bion, W. R. *Experiences in groups*, New York: Basic Books, 1959.

Rice, A. K. *Learning for leadership*. London: Tavistock Publications, 1965.

Rice, A. K. Individual, group and intergroup processes. *Human Relations*, 1969, **22**, 565-584.

Rioch, M. J. The work of Wilfred Bion on groups. *Psychiatry*, 1970, **33**, 56-66. (a)

Rioch, M. J. Group relations: Rationale and technique. *International Journal of Group Psychotherapy*, 1970, **20**, 340-355. (b)

APPLYING OD TO SCHOOL SYSTEMS

A Review of *Organization Development in Schools*
by **Richard A. Schmuck and Matthew B. Miles (Eds.).**
Palo Alto, Ca.: National Press Books, 1971. 264 pp., $8.95.

and of

Handbook of Organization Development in Schools
by **Richard A. Schmuck, Philip J. Runkel, Steven L. Saturen,**
Ronald T. Martell, and C. Brooklyn Derr.
Palo Alto, Ca.: National Press Books, 1972. 436 pp., $12.50.

Gerry E. Wiley

At last, a matched set of tools for OD in schools! Much of this reviewer's effort as an education consultant during the past four years has been spent in adapting business or industrial OD techniques and training programs for school use. The arrival of these two books will make the job easier.

Although they are written primarily for OD specialists who are involved with school systems, they would also be helpful to school administrators, curriculum specialists, school counselors, psychologists, consultants, and classroom teachers. Indeed, the theory and technology presented in these two volumes is likely to appeal to anyone who is interested in improving organizations.

Both *Organization Development in Schools* and the *Handbook* contain explicit description with sufficient detail and careful evaluation of training events. The former volume concentrates on cases of OD in practice, describing nine studies of OD interventions in school systems and giving the reader a vivid picture of these different projects. The *Handbook*, on the other hand, is concerned with tools: techniques, exercises, instruments, and designs which have proven effective in such interventions. Together, the two books complement each other perfectly.

The prime purpose of *Organization Development in Schools* is to encourage the diffusion of the OD approach in school systems. The editors assume that improvement is vitally necessary in

schools and that to achieve this improvement, the "organizational conservatism" of schools must be overcome.

The nine projects studied illustrate diverse efforts to turn school systems into adaptive organizations. The effects are carefully described and documented with evaluation results. Although at times the effort expended to produce objective evidence of results strikes me as out of proportion with the findings, such evidence does have two benefits. First it illustrates what can be measured and how such measures may be made. More importantly, it provides some tangible proof of the utility of OD which may be used to "sell" senior administrators.

Miles and Schmuck provide a very interesting and useful introductory chapter which traces the historical sources of OD and describes its main features and its application to school systems. They provide a striking conceptual model of typical interventions in the form of an "OD cube" whose three dimensions are (1) *modes of intervention*, (2) *foci of attention*, and (3) *diagnosed problems*.

School personnel will be attracted to the examples of improving classroom group processes, using group problem-solving procedures, and changing classroom interaction. They should also be interested in the list of experienced school OD practitioners. This resource list is arranged helpfully by region.

Practitioners of OD will very likely be interested in the thorough exploration of "Entering and Intervening in Schools" (Chapter 7).

But even more exciting to this reviewer than *Organization Development in Schools* is the *Handbook*. As its title suggests, it is a "tool kit" and an "assembly manual" for OD. Besides describing exercises and programs, this volume has an excellent annotated bibliography which points to sources of other approaches and techniques. Each chapter is a separate unit, and adequate cross-references allow the reader to use the chapters in any sequence he wishes.

The opening chapters deal with the OD theory developed by the authors and with their shared technology. Chapters 3 through 8 focus on six functions which must be improved to make an organization adaptive: clarifying communication, establishing goals, managing conflict, improving group meetings, solving problems, and making decisions. Each of these chapters includes a rationale for the function and the training to be done, instruments for gathering data, exercises for simulating the function concerned, procedures for use back on the job, and suggested designs for training sessions. It concludes with excerpts from readings which enlarge on the concepts presented. These are useful as lecturettes or handouts.

Chapter 9 discusses how to put components together into a coherent design. To a large extent it summarizes the preceding chapters and explains the sequence of training found to be effective by the authors. They advocate starting with exercises and skill practice before moving to application and the solving of real organizational problems, a sequence emphasized in each of the core chapters.

The final chapter, "Evaluation at Beginning, Middle and End," is one of the most important. It thoroughly outlines a component very often neglected in the human relations field: evaluation and interpretation. The chapter describes the different purposes of evaluation and the tools and techniques appropriate to each purpose. It also offers suggestions for analyzing and presenting the interpretation of data. Frankly admitting the difficulties and limitations of evaluating the complex outcomes of training, the authors do suggest some ways of overcoming them.

To me the *Handbook* is a very stimulating book. In trying to read it quickly the first time, I found myself continually stopping to consider how the ideas could be applied. I kept recalling projects and wondering how they could have been improved with the information this book offers. Or I would begin applying insights to inservice workshops I had on the drawing board.

My main disappointment with the *Handbook* is the copyright notice. All the material is protected until September 29, 1977, but I am eager to begin using it right away. Perhaps the prohibition will be a disguised blessing in that alternate exercises and activities will be devised by impatient practitioners.

Together, these two books are a treasure-trove for school personnel and for those consultants who work with them. The observations about school organizations and methods of bringing effective improvements are, in my experience, "right on."

INSTRUMENTATION IN SMALL GROUPS: EVERYTHING YOU'VE ALWAYS WANTED TO KNOW...

A Review of *Instrumentation in Human Relations Training*
by J. William Pfeiffer and Richard Heslin.
San Diego: University Associates, 1973. 306 pp.

and of

Measuring Human Behavior
by Dale G. Lake, Matthew B. Miles, and Ralph B. Earle, Jr. (Eds.).
New York: Columbia University Teachers College Press, 1973. 422 pp., $6.95.

Morris S. Spier

Consider the following intervention using instrumentation: Daw and Gage (1967) asked high school teachers to complete a leadership-style inventory to (1) describe their present principal's leadership behavior and (2) describe their (the teachers') conceptions of the behaviors of an "ideal leader." The principals to whom the teachers reported also filled out the instrument (1) as a self-description of their own leadership styles and (2) to predict their teachers' perceptions of "ideal" leadership behavior.

In individual sessions with the consultants, the principals were confronted with and counseled on the differences between their views of themselves as leaders, their teachers' perceptions of them as leaders, their teachers' desired leadership behaviors, and what the principals thought their teachers wanted in a leader. In a post-test administration of the instrument, the teachers again described their principal's leadership. Result: The teachers felt that *the principals had changed their behaviors in the direction of the "ideal" leadership which the teachers had originally desired.*

As in the example preceding, most group experiences (whether labeled counseling, therapy, growth, marriage encounter, organization-management development) aim to improve individual and/or group effectiveness. Generally, the

actual group process involves the exploration of intra- and interpersonal space. This is accomplished through the generation and working-through of data concerning personal and group functioning. My experience in leading small groups suggests that appropriately used instruments have great potential usefulness in facilitating this process and in promoting meaningful learning experiences. They may be useful in these ways:

1. Instruments can make individual learning self-involving by focusing a participant on his own behaviors that are relevant to interpersonal relations.

2. As a diagnostic tool, instruments may aid in focusing on elements of group life that are most important in the group's development, either at the outset or at any appropriate point in the group's life.

3. Instruments may be especially helpful in facilitating the giving and receiving of feedback, in designing confrontive interventions, or in simply illustrating that differences between group members may be due to differences in personal styles, needs, values, and such.

4. Instruments may be particularly useful as supplements to or illustrations of lecturettes on

group theory or on aspects of personal group functioning.

5. Instruments can help in determining group composition, *i.e.*, in designs calling for either heterogeneity or homogeneity of group membership.

6. Instruments also may be used in many formal and informal research ways, to measure both actual and perceived change as a result of group participation and to provide feedback to the facilitator on the effectiveness of his style and intervention skills.

Two books dealing with instrumentation have appeared relatively recently. Both books aim to increase awareness of, sophistication in the use of, and research into measures of social interaction in a variety of applied, research, and academic settings. Since they have different purposes, audiences, and frames of reference, they will be reviewed separately. In keeping with the spirit of *The Annual Handbook for Group Facilitators*, however, I have reviewed both books for content and presentation in terms of what they may offer persons involved in human relations training.

INSTRUMENTATION IN HUMAN RELATIONS TRAINING

This is a handbook for practitioners involved in groups and group-related activities. The authors' goal is to enlarge the facilitator's instrument repertoire and to make instruments more accessible, both in terms of awareness and knowledge of how to use. The book may be used by trainers with a wide variety of backgrounds, including those with little or no formal training in research design, tests, and measurement. One of the most appealing aspects of this book lies in the fact that the authors have drawn on their experience with the use of instruments in actual training settings to develop both a collection of instruments applicable to group work and suggestions for using them effectively.

The book is divided into three parts. Part I (five chapters) offers a broad overview of instrument theory, development, and application in a way that makes this a useful handbook. Chapter 1 provides a rationale for instrumentation, alerts the user to generally encountered

participant reactions, discusses general and specific (in small groups) advantages and disadvantages of instruments, offers suggestions for avoiding the disadvantages, and briefly looks at some ethical considerations involved in instrument development and application.

Chapter 2 illustrates a seven-step model which facilitators may use in presenting an instrument. Using the *FIRO-B* as a prototype, the authors walk the reader through phases of *administration, theory input, prediction* (in which participants predict their own scores), *scoring, interpretation, posting* of scores, and *processing.* Included also are some thoughtful notes on facilitator style and a practical list of "Do's and Don't's of Instrumentation." The chapter concludes with an overview of issues (matching choice of instrument to participant background and expectations, choosing complementary instruments, etc.) involved in designing an instrumented workshop.

The remaining three chapters of Part I examine technical considerations, development, and possible research uses of instruments. Validity, reliability, meanings of numbers, and norms are each covered under separate headings in Chapter 3. The many practical examples used to illustrate and define these concepts make them readily understandable. This chapter is certainly "must" reading for facilitators with limited backgrounds in measurement. But practitioners with more extensive backgrounds may also get some thoughts for putting instrumentation into focus for participants without the mystique of highly technical language or excessive theory. Chapter 4 provides the reader with some ideas and scaling guidelines for constructing instruments of his own. Chapter 5 discusses problems with research uses of instruments in human relations training and briefly outlines a research design.

Part II, the Instruments section, is the core of the book. In it are annotations of 75 instruments organized into three major categories with several subheadings. The first category reviews 34 instruments which have a personal focus (further classified into short, uni-scaled instruments and long, multiple-scaled instruments). The second group of 22 contains an interpersonal focus (general; pre-marriage, marriage, and family; group

274

dynamics). Then, 19 instruments have an organizational focus (organizational climate, management/leadership style, supervisor-subordinate relations).

For each instrument, the authors provide a general description covering length and format, time needed to administer and score, what the instrument claims to be measuring, possible uses, positive features, concerns, administration, scoring, and interpretation.

The objective information included is drawn from the test manual or other original sources. But Pfeiffer and Heslin also include many useful observations and pointers based on actual experience with the instruments. Information about where to order the instrument and its cost are also provided, as are references needed to locate an instrument for which there is no manual.

Users do need to be discriminating about the instruments included, not only in evaluating their technical aspects, but also in evaluating their appropriateness in group-related activities. The authors have built in their own informal judgments of instrument applicability in the quite uneven treatment provided specific measures. The authors do acknowledge their selective approach by saying that "the instruments are handled with non-uniform attention.... [because] some instruments are more useful in human relations training than others [p. 1]."

In fact, the instruments are presented with three levels of thoroughness. Those instruments which the authors feel have extremely high *general* utility in groups are given full-blown treatment. Instruments that Pfeiffer and Heslin feel have less general utility in groups (but might be useful depending on the special focus of the group) are less fully described. Finally, instruments useful only in groups with a highly specific focus are given cursory treatment; at best, the write-ups for these indicate only their existence and availability.

I was disappointed to find that only the most generally applicable instrument received the fullest treatment. The annotation of the *FIRO-B* (even excluding the valuable information the practitioner can gain from the instrument's use as a prototype for workshop design in an earlier

chapter) is the finest guide to the use of the *FIRO-B* you will find anywhere. Given the usability of the *FIRO-B* in small groups, this presentation alone could be worth the price of the book. However, both valuable time and space are taken up by the inclusion of instruments with marginal applicability (for example, the *Minnesota Multiphasic Personality Inventory* and the *California Psychological Inventory*).

At the same time, some potentially useful instruments with a more specific focus, *but with a group focus and utility nonetheless*, could have benefited from a fuller description. Also surprising, in light of the intended readership of this book, was the omission of any mention that potential users may have to present specific credentials and/or proof of adequate supervision to meet publishers' standards for purchasing some of the instruments listed, particularly those falling into the personal-focus category.

The table of contents lists the instruments according to personal, interpersonal, and organizational focus with appropriate subheadings for each. Part III acts as sort of an index by listing authors alphabetically, instruments, and desired scale or trait words (for example, "affection," "dominance," "group interaction style," "self-actualization"). A Resources section contains an annotated bibliography of additional instrument sources and books on test and measurement theory, research, and statistical methods. Also included is a listing of organizations that run seminars on instrumentation.

Overall, I found *Instrumentation in Human Relations Training* to be a practical handbook. The information it contains is a useful introduction to applied instrumentation. The test descriptions identify a wide variety of measures which practitioners have used in group-related activities. Furthermore, the initial chapters and the instrument annotations provide useful pointers for instrument choice and presentation. It is important to note, however, that any judgment of the utility of a particular instrument must depend on the user's obtaining substantial further information from the instrument's publisher, from original sources, or from some other review source or compendium.

MEASURING HUMAN BEHAVIOR

In Pfeiffer and Heslin's book, instruments are treated primarily as a *vehicle* for facilitating change. In *Measuring Human Behavior*, instrumentation is viewed more as a *monitor* of the change process. These differing frames of reference dictate different emphases on practical applicability vs. technical considerations. Thus, Pfeiffer and Heslin emphasize an instrument's applied utility. Little or no technical data are presented. They note instead that "it is incumbent on the facilitator to explore the technical characteristics of an instrument he is considering."

In contrast, Lake, Miles, and Earle focus primarily on the adequacy of instruments as reflected in evaluations of their format and technical characteristics. They note the sad state-of-the-art that exists in measuring human variability: Few efforts are made to standardize instruments thoroughly. Many instruments are used simply because they are easily available or currently popular, without regard for validity or reliability. And much valuable information is widely scattered throughout the literature with few researchers willing to systematically compile and evaluate it.

The book's dedication is to "remedying the less-than-satisfactory state-of-affairs in relation to tools for measuring social functioning."

But this is not a "text" on tests and measurements as the popularized title of this book might imply. Instead, it is an edited collection of descriptive, evaluative reviews of instruments specifically suited to the measurement of social functioning. The book is aimed at "the social science researcher . . . who wants to study some aspect of social functioning; the applied behavioral scientist who wishes to diagnose a system, evaluate a program, or explain planned change processes; and the program-based manager, practitioner, or researcher . . . [in a variety of applied settings] who needs tools to monitor the progress and effectiveness in his organization."

The book is divided into two sections. Section I consists of reviews of 84 instruments: 38 instruments with a personal focus, 34 with an interpersonal or group focus, and· 12 with an organizational focus. (Fourteen instruments are covered by both Pfeiffer & Heslin and Lake, *et al.*) Section II reviews 20 published collections of instruments.

Measures reviewed in this volume are in the general domain of research instruments developed for studying organizations, groups, and interpersonal relationships, and for studying normal individuals' functioning in them. To be included, instruments had to be available to potential users, based on some underlying theory and considerable development work, potentially useful although not necessarily well known, supported by some reasonably current statistical data, and generally not reviewed in the recent literature. The instruments included range from those familiar to practitioners (*FIRO-B, Hill Interaction Matrix*) to some that even the most sophisticated reader may find "new." As in Pfeiffer and Heslin, instruments measuring primarily "pathology" were excluded.

A typical write-up presents an instrument's title, authors, availability (source, but not cost), variables measured, format, administration, and scoring. A "Development" subheading covers the history of the instrument. A "Critique" section evaluates each instrument's technical characteristics: validity, reliability, adequacy of statistics and norms, and possible difficulties such as item wording, fakeability, etc. A "General Comment" section (usually about seventy-five to 150 words in length) covers the author's overall statement about the usefulness of the instrument. Frequently these comments summarize the statistical data presented in the critique in less technical language. Sometimes the general comments offer useful information for application, as when an instrument's ease of administration is contrasted with its complicated scoring or when potential uses are suggested (research, the determination of group composition, a measure of change).

276

The information given in the body of the review is a distillation of material appearing in test manuals, original sources, and other published and unpublished writings. Each review lists the relevant references.

The second part of the book is a review of twenty relatively recent compendia. The content closely parallels that of the instrument reviews. Title, authors, availability, testing areas covered, and a description (including criteria for instrument inclusion and the kind of information presented) are covered under separate headings. The compendia reviews also contain critique and general-comment sections with structure and content similar to those of the instrument reviews.

To aid in instrument retrieval, the authors include a "uniterm index" for each instrument (the compendia reviewed are also indexed). The system is similar to Pfeiffer and Heslin's index of scale and trait words. Readers interested in a measure related to a particular variable will find a cross-reference to instruments measuring that variable in the index. The authors' liberal use of synonyms and related terms is especially helpful. An alphabetical author index is also provided. The user will, however, need to refer to each specific review to determine the focus (personal, group, organization) of the instrument since the table of contents lists instruments alphabetically with no further breakdown.

The overall quality of the reviews is uniformly high. The information presented is precisely the kind needed to evaluate effectively an instrument's technical characteristics under accepted criteria for a "good measuring tool." Moreover, the authors have done an excellent job of assuring similar thoroughness in each of the write-ups.

Practitioners should be aware that not every instrument appearing in this book is applicable in human relations training. That was not, in fact, the authors' intent. Some of the instruments lack (at this time) adequate statistical data. Others are extremely complicated and require specialized training (for example, the projective measures included). Still others seem to have been included only because the authors found

them more interesting than useful. Many have had considerable statistical investigation or merit additional attention. As such, the practitioner may find *Measuring Human Behavior* an excellent source for identifying potentially useful instruments and compendia and for evaluating their potential usefulness (including the 14 instruments which also are reviewed in Pfeiffer and Heslin's book).

Finally, I feel the need to comment on some practical vs. scientific trade-offs that occur in my mind as a result of recommending these books to practitioners with a wide variety of backgrounds and competencies. Let me say first that I do share the excitement of the dissemination of knowledge and techniques related to human relations training. But an issue of instrument validity that deserves attention against a background of growing concern for personal privacy and test abuse, is the "validity" that arises from an instrument being in the hands of a competent user. I am concerned that untrained practitioners will become overnight "experts." I am concerned that practitioners with little or no background in instrumentation will think that they really do have *everything they've always wanted to know* without doing the additional work or acquiring the additional training necessary to select and use instruments intelligently and appropriately.

Moreover, I am concerned that while both of the books reviewed in this paper focus on applied and research uses of instruments, neither places significant emphasis on ethical considerations. Pfeiffer and Heslin cover the issue in one paragraph of about 150 words. The only mention of ethics I found in Lake, *et al.* appears as a footnote to the very last item appearing in the book.

Perhaps future volumes of this kind will include in their resources sections some references to accepted ethical guidelines such as the "Surgeon General's Directives on Human Experimentation" (1967) and the American Psychological Association's *Ethical Principles in the Conduct of Research with Human Participants* (1973). I offer these concerns and hopes here because I share with the authors the belief that more such reference books are needed.

REFERENCES

Ad hoc Committee on Ethical Standards in Psychological Research. *Ethical principles in the conduct of research with human participants.* Washington, D.C.: American Psychological Association, 1973.

Daw, R. W., & Gage, N. L. Effect of feedback from teachers to principals, *Journal of Educational Psychology,* 1967, **58** (3), 181-188.

United States Public Health Service. Surgeon General's directives on human experimentation. *American Psychologist,* 1967, **22,** 350-355.

NOT ENCOUNTER AND CERTAINLY NOT FACTS

A Review of *Encounter Groups: First Facts*
by Morton A. Lieberman, Irvin D. Yalom, and Matthew B. Miles.
New York: Basic Books, 1973. 495 pp., $15.00.

William C. Schutz

This is one of the largest studies ever done on encounter groups and, unfortunately, one of the worst. The study is a methodological morass, is theoretically obsolescent, and presents conclusions that are almost totally unjustified.

Results of the study were published in many forums long before the book was published, emerging as short articles, progress reports, partial results, and the like. The results, especially on "casualties," have been seized upon by the media and used widely as a "scientific" justification for criticizing encounter groups.

The authors set out to assess the outcomes of encounter groups, the characteristics of leaders and of groups, and the relations among leaders, groups, and outcomes. To do this, they recruited 206 Stanford students and divided them into seventeen groups, all called encounter, though they varied widely in approach. These seventeen groups comprised the study's experimental group. The control group consisted of sixty-nine Stanford students who did not undergo the group experience. Each "encounter" group was run for approximately thirty hours in whatever style the group leader chose. Observations and questionnaires were used at each session. A few months after the conclusion of the encounter sessions, approximately half of the experimental participants were interviewed. From an analysis of these data a number of conclusions were drawn. Among the major ones were these: (1) Of the 206 participants starting the groups, 7.8 percent of the total (9.1 percent of those who completed 50 percent of the group meetings) suffered significant psychological injury (p. 174). (2) In general,

supportive leaders were more helpful to group members than "charismatic" or more challenging leaders. ("High challenge or high confrontation by the leader is . . . negatively correlated with outcome [p. 435].")

This Study Is Not About Encounter Groups

Even by the authors' own definition of encounter, ten of the seventeen groups used in the experiment do not qualify as encounter groups.

> . . . encounter groups do share common features. They attempt to provide an intensive, high contact, group experience; they are generally small . . . focus on the here-and-now . . . encourage openness, honesty, interpersonal confrontation, self-disclosure, and strong emotional expression [p. 4].

This present study includes, under the rubric of encounter groups, the following types of groups: Gestalt (two groups), transactional analysis (two), Synanon (one), psychodrama (two), tapeled (two), and psychoanalytic (one). Psychoanalytic groups do not "focus on the here-and-now," Gestalt groups do not "encourage . . . interpersonal confrontation," Synanon groups do not require "honesty" in their attacks, and so on.

Many of these approaches have influenced encounter but they are not identical with it. To investigate encounter in this way is like studying Freudian analysis by observing some Freudians and some other types of Freudians like Jungians, Adlerians, Dale Carnegie groups, Holy Rollers.

Comparisons Made Between the Experimental Group and the Control Group Are Not Justified[1]

A total of 251 registered for the encounter group course. In addition, "A control group was composed of thirty-eight students who had registered for the Race and Prejudice course but could not be accommodated in the encounter groups because of size limitations or schedule conflicts, and thirty-one demographically matched students . . . [p. 10]."

Thus, almost half of the members of the control group (45 percent) differed from the members of the experimental group in that they chose not to accept the general invitation to volunteer for the groups. They accepted a personal request to take the tests administered to participants in the study in return for payment. Since self-selection is probably the largest single selection factor for normal encounter groups, the difference in willingness to volunteer between experimental and control subjects is highly significant. People who volunteer tend to be more willing to acknowledge personal difficulties. Any differences between the groups in reported psychological stress on before-after questionnaires could easily be accounted for by the nonequivalent nature of the groups prior to the study.

Further, prior to the study, more members of the control group had been in psychotherapy than had members of the experimental group (21 percent to 16 percent). Since the authors subsequently emphasize the point that the groups differed during the experimental period in that control subjects entered psychotherapy less (4 percent to 13 percent . . . "Over *three times* as many . . . [p. 201]"), the initial differences assume more importance. The totals of both groups in psychotherapy, 25 percent to 29 percent, do not appear to be dramatically, or even significantly, different.

Having started with crucially incomparable groups, the authors proceeded to increase their incomparability. Prior to the start of the groups, the experimental subjects were strongly oriented toward an expectation of emotional stress while the controls were not. "The staff emphasized in these orientation meetings that the experience might be emotionally taxing and occasionally upsetting, and described the arrangements that had been made to make University mental health facilities available to participants if the groups became emotionally stressful [p. 10]." These facilities included "the student health service, the Department of Psychiatry and . . . one of the principal investigators [p. 169]."

This startling orientation, given only to the experimental group, has long been abandoned by most of the group leaders I know. The self-fulfilling-prophecy aspect of these warnings is so blatantly obvious that to present them to the experimental subjects and not to the control subjects is in itself sufficient to dismiss any subsequent findings about differences in emotional stress ("casualties" in the authors' term) between experimentals and controls. The prospective encounter group members, entering a new and largely unknown situation, are told by psychiatric and psychological experts that encounter groups are potentially "taxing," "upsetting" and "stressful"; so much so that special arrangements have been made for them with the official mental health facilities of the University, and the Department of Psychiatry and one of the principal investigators are standing by just in case.

If that was not enough to convey the frightening aspect of encounter groups, the authors capitalized on an untoward event early in the group's life to emphasize the danger. One person committed suicide after two meetings (the authors acknowledge that the suicide could not reasonably be attributed to the few hours the person spent in the group). Following that upsetting event, ". . . the leaders were informed and urged again to refer troubled students to appropriate sources of help. Most leaders read the letter aloud to their groups [p. 169]."

If group members had not gotten the message before, this certainly brought it home. The participants were again being urged to interpret their experience as very dangerous, with a high probability of leading to emotional stress, perhaps even suicide, and were advised to seek professional help before it was too late.

[1]I wish to thank Dr. Eugene Cogan, Director of Research Design and Reporting, Human Resources Research Office (HumRRO), for his assistance in analyzing the statistical and design aspects of the study.

Thus the experimental-control comparisons were made between (a) a group of people who volunteered for encounter and who were told that the encounter groups would be an emotionally stressful experience for which psychiatric facilities were available; and (b) a group of people, half of whom chose not to volunteer for encounter, and who were told nothing about any emotional stress. The authors found that the first group reported more emotional stress, saw each other as more disturbed, and sought more psychotherapy. Astonishing!

Comparisons Among Encounter Groups Are Unjustified

Even if the experimental-control comparisons are not legitimate, there remains the possibility that significant differences exist among the various types of encounter groups. The authors seemed to have an initial interest in contrasting the various types of encounter.

> Part of the reason for insuring this divergence was to discover whether the conventional labels they represented, labels such as Gestalt, sensory awareness, T-group, and so on, had any real meaning in describing what they actually did as encounter leaders [p. 226].

They didn't. There was no consistency between two groups representing the same approach (e.g., psychodrama, Gestalt).

The authors then set out to find out if there were meaningful differences due to leader styles regardless of their original orientation. Since this investigation was exploratory in that they had not set up any categories of leader styles beforehand, research problems arise.

This approach was precarious because there were so few groups compared to the large number of uncontrolled and possibly important factors other than leader style. The problem is this: The following groups (among others) differed in outcome: (1) A twenty-three-member Synanon group, meeting at Synanon House in Oakland for eight weeks for three-hour sessions; ten dropouts; no appointed leaders. (2) A psychoanalytic group of eleven members which met in a dormitory lounge at Stanford for ten three-hour meetings; four dropouts; led by a psychoanalyst of twenty years experience. (3) A personal-growth, black-white group of nine members meeting for two

two-hour meetings followed by five hour meetings two weeks apart; two dropouts; led by a black psychologist who cancelled the last meeting because he felt the group was not getting anywhere.

Are the differences among these three groups attributable to leader style, or to the theoretical orientation of the leaders, personality of the leaders, interaction of leader and members, group size, racial composition, race of leader, pattern and length of meetings, location of meetings, number of leaders, or some combination of all or some of these?

A sound test of the effect of leader style on the outcome of the group requires controlling or counterbalancing other factors relevant to group outcome. In this study there are several significant variables that varied widely among groups. Two obvious examples are group size and the pattern of meetings, two factors that are pertinent to group functioning.

These groups varied in beginning size from nine to twenty-three members, in ending size from five to fourteen members. Clearly, matters of intimacy, amount of attention, subgrouping, morale due to missing members, and other significant factors could be very different in a five-person group from one almost three times as large.

One group met twice for twelve hours each, one met ten times for three hours each. The others varied within that range. Fritz Perls and Carl Rogers, among others, have commented on the advantages of the longer, more intense meeting pattern, while many psychoanalysts feel that the interval pattern is best.

Additionally, if leader style is to be examined, the representativeness of the leaders in the study of leaders to whom the results are to be generalized is crucial. In this study, there seems to have been a curious selection of leaders. The authors claim, "All were highly experienced group leaders, and were uniformly esteemed by their colleagues as representing the best of their approach [p. 11]."

Although it is difficult to find out who the fifteen group leaders were ("research confidentiality"), it is known that those who were chosen included the only leader ever banned from giving groups at Esalen and one leader who was excluded for a period of several months due to some questionable occurrences in his groups. (These leaders accounted for five of the sixteen "casualties" in all the groups. The Synanon group, which had no designated leaders, accounted for two more. These leaders also accounted for four-fifths of the leaders who defined the "charismatic leader" category.) The leader chosen to represent "Esalen eclectic" at the time of the study had virtually no training as an encounter leader. The question of whether the group leaders are representative of any particular group of group leaders was not dealt with by the authors; a first examination suggests that they may be quite a unique group of leaders.

To make some order out of this melange of leaders, philosophies, races, sizes, and meeting times, the authors used a time-honored statistical device for extracting order from chaos—factor analysis. This yielded four factors which were interpreted as "leader types." However, as might be expected from the heterogeneity of the data, even the device of factor analysis was not equal to the task of making the data meaningful.

Ratings of leaders on twenty-eight items were made for each meeting. These ratings were then factor-analyzed to derive "leader types" which were correlated with the "casualties." Even if the casualty measure were sound (see below), the leader types derived in this way are illegitimate. Following are Dr. Cogan's comments on the factor analysis:

A series of factor analyses is applied to a set of leader-by-session observations. In the nomenclature defined by Cattell, the data elements of "r" (regular) factor analysis are thereby mingled with the elements of "p" (ipsative) factor analysis and computations are made as if the data elements were uniform.

This procedure has a serious statistical flaw: observations are not independent; session observations are intermixed with leader observations and leader observations are intermixed with session observations.

Aside from the purely technical statistical point above, there appears to be no sensible basis for interpreting how factors relate to person (leader) or group session (stage of group interaction). To interpret the results as leader-pertinent, requires the assumption that a leader is "independent" of himself in succeeding sessions. This

does not appear to be reasonable. This reviewer has never seen an analysis of this sort nor a discussion of such analysis, and sees no way to interpret the results sensibly . . . (Cogan, 1974).

Thus, in order to interpret the results as they do, the authors must assume that whatever the leader does at one group session is in no way influenced by what he has done at any previous session, a rather preposterous assertion. Attempts to compare groups or leaders are just not possible with these data.

Conclusions About Casualties Are Unjustified

Probably the most horrendous deficiency of the study is the concept of an encounter-group casualty. The "data" on casualties from this study have been quoted 'round the world (including *Reader's Digest*), although they are derived through the most unscientific of methods, and although they are based on a very questionable theoretical conception.

Methodology. I was informed by one of the authors that all of the ratings of casualties were done primarily by one author with help from his assistants. (The chapter on casualties was written by Yalom, the psychiatrist.) There is no report of any independent evaluation of casualties by someone unrelated to the study, or even independent judgments systematically done by two or more staff members. The decisions about casualties were made with the knowledge that the participant had been in the experimental group, not the control group. In fact, no control-group member was even interviewed following the study. This difference is dismissed with the statement, "We do know, however, that very few controls requested psychotherapy in the eight-month follow-up period [p. 193]." There was also no systematic work done on assessing the psychological state of the group members prior to the study.

In short, almost all elementary research considerations were ignored in defining casualties. In contrast, a good example of a competent design was described recently in a study of the effects of groups.

Criterion measures for the experimental group and the two control groups included the following measures . . . They were administered in a modified Solomon four-group design. In this design half of the experimental group and half of the control group are given pre- and post-measures; the remaining halves are given post-only measures. This permits the assessment of changes caused . . . by the acts of filling out the instruments as such and separating of these from the actual effects of the treatment (Miles, 1965).

If "casualty assessment" is used as the criterion measure, this design would have taken care of many of the problems with the study of casualties. The puzzling aspect of this situation is that this elegant method was used in a 1965 publication by one of the authors of the present study.

In summary, the designation of someone as a casualty is a nonobjective, uncorroborated opinion of one staff person.

Let us examine the nature of his concept of a "casualty." From the extensive descriptions given of each of the casualties, several properties of the definition are discernible.

Because of the failure to have a measure of the emotional state of subjects prior to the study, it is highly questionable whether five of the sixteen casualties could be attributed to the effects of the group. The author often acknowledges this (". . . it is very difficult to know whether or not this is directly related to her group experience [p. 191].") Several people seem to have simply continued the development with which they entered the group. Collateral events also call into question the causal relation between group and "casualty." One casualty started taking LSD and marijuana at the same time he started the group. How then can we assign causality to the group?

The author's view of the meaning given to entering into psychotherapy is somewhat unusual. He sometimes views it as a sign of a possible casualty, though he later acknowledges other possible interpretations.

The group experience is apparently considered a bad one if the participant was in a negative state at the time of the interview, regardless of subsequent development. Five of the casualties were reported to be making moderate to excellent progress in psychotherapy (and one is considering therapy for the first time) subsequent to the study. It would seem to me quite reasonable to interpret seeking therapy as a positive outcome of the groups, especially since the author reports several positive outcomes of psychotherapy.

For example, "one of our most obvious casualties" was a fat girl. On two occasions in the year prior to entering a group she had sought psychotherapeutic aid because of her low self-concept and her obesity. She entered the encounter group for similar reasons. Following the group she was seen for five months in therapy, during which time she made "moderate strides by losing weight, and gradually increasing her self-confidence [p. 189]."

"Nevertheless," the author states, "there is little doubt that her experience in the group was destructive." The reason: "She sought psychotherapy not electively but as an emergency measure to undo the injury to her already deficient self-image [p. 189]."

I would guess that most therapists would be delighted if every obese, low-self-esteem patient who came to them after unsuccessful therapy was losing weight and growing in self-esteem after several months in therapy.

In summary, casualties in this study are persons who (1) were told that they were about to undergo an emotionally stressful situation, (2) observed a suicide and were urged again to be careful and not to hesitate to go to therapists who were waiting for them, and (3) were then judged by the very experts who had thus oriented them to be people who had undergone great stress.

What Is To Be Learned From This Study?

Surely, with all these data something of value must emerge. Even if all the conclusions are unsupportable they may still be true. Let us look.

The figure of 7.8 percent (or 9.1 percent) casualties is appalling. It is far above any other figure reported. The recent study of Bebout (1971), the survey done by NTL (Maliver, 1973), and a study of a two-week group laboratory (Schutz & Allen, 1966), all report considerably less than 2 percent negative outcomes. Bebout, for example, reporting on his recent study of 1500 people participating in 150 encounter groups over a three-year period, was quoted as saying that "only two could be considered casualties: an obese woman who was rejected by the rest of the group, and a young man who fell in love with the leader, who rejected him" (Reinhold, 1974).

Theoretically, the present study applies a conservative, medical model to the encounter movement which is revising that model. Encounter has emphasized self-responsibility, as have Gestalt, EST, Arica, and many other related developments. The orientation of this study is based on a doctor-oriented, "we-know-what's-best-for-you" philosophy. Describing the encounter experience in frightening terms not only orients the participants in a biased fashion, but immediately places them in the patient role. They must be prepared for their stressful experience by the experts, then be put in the care of the doctors when they arrive at their anticipated moment of helplessness.

Further, each participant is provided with a built-in defense. If things don't go well it is the fault of the group or the leader. Such statements occur frequently from both participants and authors in describing casualties. ("Her negative experience was a result of an aggressive, intrusive leadership style [p. 182].")

All this is anti-encounter. The aim of encounter is to help the participant find his own strength, not to tell him immediately that he is entering into a situation that may be too much for him. Encounter will help him learn that he chooses his own reactions, not to encourage him to blame others for his own difficulties.

The recent work of Laing (1967) and the sense of the evolution of a human being seems not to be appreciated in this study. It is virtually impossible to assess the significance of where a person is after a group experience unless it is known where he was before he started the group and where he goes in the future. Different people need different experiences at different times. They do not all need a sensible, supportive, loving atmosphere all the time. People are much more complex. Our obese girl may have arrived at higher self-esteem and weight reduction some

other way, but she *did* arrive there after her group experience. Apparently that's what *she* needed, *at that time*, to make progress.

The key issue for me in considering leadership and encounter outcome is self-deception. Are the leaders aware of themselves, and do they know how to help others get there? This study is a case in point. How could three professionals, men of some substance in their fields, execute and publish a study that would not pass a freshman research design course? I can only speculate, but their own leanings peek through at times. They describe encounter as "the interpersonal equivalent of skydiving [p. 3]"; Gestalt therapy "has been a militant, proselytizing movement [p. 11]"; and "in the hyperbolic togetherness" of the marathon, if defenses are not dropped the group "vigorously sands them away [p. 13]."

In at least two instances the authors minimize what appear to be positive findings. In reporting group members' peak experiences of the past six months, the authors state that "only seventeen (16 percent) indicate that the experience had taken place in an encounter group [p. 117]." Since the encounter group only occupied thirty hours of the past six months, or about 0.7 of one percent, the fact that 16 percent of peak experiences took place during that period (twenty-three times chance) could be interpreted as quite remarkable.

In their first report of change, the authors report that in the short post-study, 34 percent of the participants are moderate or high changer/learners, compared to 16 percent negative changers (omitting unchanged and drop-outs). The controls had 17 percent positive and 23 percent negative [p. 108]. Thus the controls have a net of minus 6 percent positive changes and the experimentals plus 18 percent, again a difference (24 percent) that could be interpreted quite favorably to the groups. ("Suffice it to say that fewer controls showed positive gain . . . [p. 108].")

In another instance, the authors use an extraordinary interpretation to make another point against encounter. Commenting on the difference between the number of control and experimental subjects who had dropped out of college subsequent to the study, they say, "This

284

difference approaches significance (p equals .18) [p. 215]." A p value of .18 is quite a distance from the conventionally accepted p values of .05 or .01.

Many of the authors' findings seem remarkably similar to their earlier written pronouncements. For example:

> . . . mere catharsis is not in itself a corrective experience. Some cognitive learning or restructuring seems necessary for the patient to be able to generalize his group experience to his outside life; without this transfer or carryover, we have succeeded only in creating better therapy group members (Yalom, 1970).

> Much encounter group practice attacks cognitive functioning as sheer rationalization and defensiveness and stresses the importance of "gut" feelings as the basic coin of exchange. Yet the study repeatedly demonstrates that thought is an essential part of the learning process [present study, p. 422].

Certainly encounter groups have faults. No activity so widespread with such a rapid growth rate could develop without drawbacks, misunderstandings, misuses and distortions. I hope we will always be aware of these and do what is feasible to minimize them. Let us also keep them in perspective relative to the values of groups for the thousands of people that have passed through them. The profundity of the encounter group experience deserves more sophisticated research.

In summary, this book is an unfortunate event. Virtually all of its conclusions are without a shred of support. The authors make sweeping generalizations about encounter that are quite unjustified and, due to their widespread publicity, have been very damaging to the growth of the field. My hope is that the "results" are quietly interred and that the failure of this study serves as an inspiration to others to do sound, self-aware research that matches in competence and sensitivity this area that has proven to be so valuable, therapeutically and theoretically.

REFERENCES

Bebout, J. The use of intensive small groups for personal growth: Progress report of a four-year study of encounter groups. Paper presented at American Association for Advancement of Science Convention, Philadelphia, 1971.

Cogan, E. A. Personal communication, 1974.

Laing, R. The politics of experience. New York: Ballantine, 1967.

Maliver, B. The encounter game. New York: Stein and Day, 1973.

Miles, M. Changes during and following laboratory training: A clinical experimental study. Journal of Applied Behavioral Science, 1 (3), 1965.

Reinhold, R. Encounter movement, a fad last decade, finds new shape. New York Times, Jan. 13, 1974.

Schutz, W., & Allen, V. The effects of a T-group laboratory and interpersonal behavior. Journal of Applied Behavioral Science, 2, 1966.

Yalom, I. The theory and practice of group psychotherapy. New York: Basic Books, 1970.

CONTRIBUTORS

Anthony G. Banet, Jr., Ph.D.
Midtown Community Mental Health Center
Marion County General Hospital
960 Locke Street
Indianapolis, Indiana 46202
(317) 630-7791

James Barott
University of Idaho
Moscow, Idaho 83843
(208) 885-6111

Millard J. Bienvenu, Sr., Ph.D.
Professor and Head
Department of Sociology and Social Work
Northwestern State University
Natchitoches, Louisiana 71457
(318) 357-5902

David G. Bowers, Ph.D.
Center for Research on Utilization of
    Scientific Knowledge
Institute for Social Research
University of Michigan
Ann Arbor, Michigan 48106
(313) 764-6108

Clarke Carney, Ph.D.
Counseling and Consultation Services
Ohio State University
Student Services Building
154 West 12th Avenue
Columbus, Ohio 43210
(614) 422-5766

George O. Charrier
President, Development Systems, Inc.
5710 Winton Road, Box 102
Cincinnati, Ohio 45232
(513) 541-1635

Myron R. Chartier, Ph.D.
Assistant Professor of Speech-Communication
American Baptist Seminary of the West
1300 E. Covina Hills Road
Covina, California 91724
(213) 332-4034

Cary L. Cooper, Ph.D.
The University of Manchester Institute
    of Science and Technology
Department of Management Sciences
P.O. Box 88
Manchester, England M60 1QD
061-236 3311

Robert P. Crosby
Leadership Institute of Spokane (LIOS)
(Staff, Whitworth-LIOS MA in
    Applied Behavioral Science Program)
P.O. Box 8202
Spokane, Washington 99203
(509) 624-8437

A. Steven Crown
c/o Stephen C. Iman
Pitzer Hall
Claremont Men's College
Claremont, California 91711
(714) 626-8511

Roger A. Dixon
Chief, Office of Management Systems
National Bureau of Standards
U.S. Department of Commerce
Boulder, Colorado 80302
(303) 499-1000

A. Donald Duncan
Administrative Assistant for Human Relations
Yonkers Public Schools
145 Palmer Road
Yonkers, New York 10701
(914) 963-4567

Ord Elliott
Procter & Gamble
2200 Lower Muscatine Road
Iowa City, Iowa 52240
(319) 351-2310

Dave Ford, Ph.D.
Krannert Graduate School of Industrial
    Administration
Purdue University
Lafayette, Indiana 47909
(317) 494-5027

Jerome L. Franklin, Ph.D.
Center for Research on Utilization of
Scientific Knowledge
Institute for Social Research
University of Michigan
Ann Arbor, Michigan 48106
(313) 764-6108

Jack R. Gibb, Ph.D.
8475 La Jolla Scenic Drive
La Jolla, California 92037
(714) 453-0133

John T. Hall
Chief, Management and Organization
Division
A-902 Administration Building
National Bureau of Standards
U.S. Department of Commerce
Washington, D.C. 20234
(301) 921-3567

Stanley M. Herman, Ph.D.
TRW Systems Group
Building E-2, Room 7043
One Space Park
Redondo Beach, California 90278
(213) 535-4321

Richard Heslin, Ph.D.
Associate Professor, Department of
Psychological Sciences
Purdue University
Lafayette, Indiana 47907
(317) 494-8551

John L. Hipple, Ph.D.
Counselor, Student Counseling Center
University of Idaho
Moscow, Idaho 83843
(208) 885-6716

Michael Hutchins
Counselor, Education Department
University of Idaho
Moscow, Idaho 83843
(208) 885-7079

Stephen C. Iman, Ph.D.
Assistant Professor of Psychology
Pitzer Hall
Claremont Men's College
Claremont, California 91711
(714) 626-8511

Blake D. Jones
c/o Stephen C. Iman
Pitzer Hall
Claremont Men's College
Claremont, California 91711
(714) 626-8511

John E. Jones, Ph.D.
Director of Consulting Services
University Associates
P.O. Box 80637
San Diego, California 92138
(714) 224-3444

Sidney M. Jourard, Ph.D.
Professor of Psychology
University of Florida
Gainesville, Florida
(904) 392-2289

Jon L. Joyce
824 Shrine Road
Springfield, Ohio 45504
(513) 322-4454

Hank Karp, Ph.D.
Department of Management
Old Dominion University
P.O. Box 6173
Norfolk, Virginia 23508
(804) 489-8000 Ext. 347

Arthur G. Kirn
Arthur G. Kirn and Associates
106 North Beacon
Hartford, Connecticut 06105
(203) 523-9365

Marie Kirn
Arthur G. Kirn and Associates
106 North Beacon
Hartford, Connecticut 06105
(203) 523-9365

Charles L. Kormanski
Counseling Center
Altoona Campus
Pennsylvania State University
Altoona, Pennsylvania 16603
(814) 944-4547

S. Lynne McMahon
4604 Springfield Avenue
Philadelphia, Pennsylvania 19143
(215) 349-8410

J. William Pfeiffer, Ph.D.
Executive Director
University Associates
P.O. Box 80637
San Diego, California 92138
(714) 224-3444

Judith James Pfeiffer
1295A Prospect Street
La Jolla, California 92037
(714) 459-6154

Gerald M. Phillips, Ph.D.
Department of Speech
305 Sparks Building
Pennsylvania State University
University Park, Pennsylvania 16802
(814) 865-4072

Anthony J. Reilly, Ph.D.
Director of Human Resources Development
University Associates
P.O. Box 80637
San Diego, California 92138
(714) 224-3444

Charles M. Rossiter, Jr., Ph.D.
Assistant Professor
Department of Communication
Merrill Hall
University of Wisconsin
Milwaukee, Wisconsin 53201
(414) 963-4261

Philip J. Runkel, Ph.D.
Center for Educational Policy
and Management
University of Oregon
1472 Kincaid Street
Eugene, Oregon 97401
(503) 686-5067

Marshall Sashkin, Ph.D.
Assistant Professor of Management and
Organization Sciences
School of Business Administration
Wayne State University
Detroit, Michigan 48202
(313) 577-4515

William Schutz, Ph.D.
Big Sur, California 93920
(408) 667-2200

John J. Sherwood, Ph.D.
Professor of Social Psychology and
Administrative Sciences
Krannert Graduate School of Industrial
Administration
Purdue University
Lafayette, Indiana 47907
(317) 493-1883

Morris S. Spier, Ph.D.
Manager, Personnel (Marketing)
Pharmaceutical Division
Eli Lilly & Company
307 McCarty Street
Indianapolis, Indiana 46202
(317) 261-2638

Joan A. Stepsis, Ph.D.
2783 Caminito Cedros
Del Mar, California 92014
(714) 755-6264

Herbert A. Thelen, Ph.D.
Department of Education
University of Chicago
Chicago, Illinois 60637
(312) 753-3828

Harvey Thomson
Robert H. Schaffer & Associates, Ltd.
4601 Montclair Avenue
Montreal, Quebec, Canada H4B2J8
(514) 487-4850

Gerry E. Wiley
356 Clarendon Drive
Ancaster, Ontario, Canada
(416) 648-2214